Rookie Teaching For Dummies®

D0131927

Planning for a Substitute Teacher

Don't leave your substitute teacher in the lurch! You shouldn't just leave lesson plans — make sure you also include the following:

- A copy of your class schedule (and the bell schedule if your school has one)
- A seating chart for every class (if you don't assign seats, make sure you indicate that)
- A map of the school, including directions to each of your rooms if you teach in more than one or if students receive instruction in other rooms (like the music room or gymnasium)
- Emergency instructions, including the evacuation route assigned to your room (if you have multiple rooms, include the evacuation routes for all of them)
- Important information about students, including medical conditions
- A copy of all your policies, including bathroom and hall-pass policies
- A complete student roster, on which the substitute can record attendance
- An explanation of all your duty assignments (substitutes usually have to fulfill duties as well as cover classes)
- The name and room number of a nearby teacher who can help out if things go wrong or add to the assignment if the kids are finishing too early
- A list of trustworthy kids in each class (and perhaps a list of kids the substitute should keep her eye on)
- Your home phone number, so that the substitute can contact you if all else fails

Note: Do *not* leave your grade book behind, even if you trust the substitute, because you cannot guarantee its safety or security.

Keys to a Successful Observation

If a supervisor or administrator is rating your class, here are a few tips to keep in mind:

- Include lesson plan elements required by your school district (such as the anticipatory set, learning objectives, review and wrap-up at the end, and so on).
- Showcase your best material.
- Move about the room during class.
- Don't make any big changes to the way you do things in class.
- Show that you and your students get along.
- Don't worry if your kids aren't absolutely silent, unless your supervisor is grimacing.
- Involve lots of kids in the lesson, making sure to speak to different areas of the room, to both sexes, and to students who don't raise their hand as well as those who do.

Rookie Teaching For Dummies®

Cheat Sheet

Things to Accomplish on the First Day of School

Trying to decide what to do on the first day of school? Try to get as many of these things out of the way as possible:

- ✔ Explain the important rules of your classroom; pass out a printed copy of these rules for your students and their parents to sign and return to you.
- ✔ Discuss emergency and safety procedures.
- ✔ Introduce yourself to your kids.
- ✔ Explain your grading system.
- ✔ Pass out textbooks.
- ✔ Collect a card including parental information, phone number, and home address.
- ✔ Discuss major projects and milestones for the year.
- ✔ Explain how to get extra help or tutoring.

Ways to Handle Minor Behavior Problems without Involving the Main Office

Here are a few things you can do to squelch bad behavior without resorting to administrators:

- ✔ Walk toward the offending student's desk and stand beside it, but don't interrupt what you're saying or doing.
- ✔ Shoot the icy stare of death.
- ✔ Use humor to defuse explosive situations.
- ✔ Rearrange your seating chart.
- ✔ Threaten the loss of privileges or additional homework.
- ✔ Give a pop quiz.
- ✔ Give detentions generously.
- ✔ Call a parent or coach.
- ✔ Send the student to another teacher's room.

For Dummies: Bestselling Book Series for Beginners

Rookie Teaching

FOR

DUMMIES®

by W. Michael Kelley

WILEY

Wiley Publishing, Inc.

Rookie Teaching For Dummies®
Published by
Wiley Publishing, Inc.
909 Third Avenue
New York, NY 10022
www.wiley.com

 is a trademark of Wiley Publishing, Inc.

About the Author

W. Michael Kelley taught high-school mathematics for seven years and loved every minute of it. Along the way, he managed to scrape up a few awards, including recognition from the Maryland Council of Teachers of Mathematics as an Outstanding High School Mathematics Teacher. Even more important to him, however, was that his students voted him their favorite teacher a whole bunch of times.

He now works at the University of Maryland at College Park as an Academic Technology Coordinator for the College of Education and writes books in his spare time, including *The Complete Idiot's Guide to Calculus* and *Master the AP Calculus AB and BC Tests*. Even though he's not officially a teacher anymore, he does maintain a Web site, www.calculus-help.com, which provides free help for thousands of bewildered calculus students every year.

Mike lives in southern Maryland with his wife, Lisa, his new son, Nicholas, and his cat, Peanut. Although he still hopes to one day rule Spain as a kind and just dictator, he's beginning to think that just may not happen.

Dedication

For my new son, Nicholas. As I write this, you are still but a big bulge in your mom's belly, but we're expecting you any day now, and I can't wait to meet you. I have waited all my life for your arrival, and any day, I will get to see you face to face. I pray that I will be a good dad, and that you'll be a much better baby for me than I was for my parents.

As always, for Lisa. You've brought joy to my life, order to my house, and a son into my heart. You are the girl of my dreams, and I love you more every day. Thanks for all your help, advice, and proofreading skills, and for making this book better than it ever could have been without you.

Author's Acknowledgments

This book would not exist if it weren't for all the people who allowed me to spend time with them and ask them all sorts of embarrassing questions. I did my best to credit people where it was appropriate and to omit people's names if they were too embarrassed to have them attached to the fantastic stories they told me. In some cases, things got lost to editing and space restraints, and for that I apologize, but to these people I still offer my greatest thanks.

Some of the people who helped me the most, and who were generous enough to share their experience, advice, ideas, and time, include the following: Katie Booth, Chris Borkowski, Gloria Brown, Summer Cox, Terumi Cox, Malinda Ellerman, Fran Favretto (and her EDHD419B class), Sharon Feather, Mary Freeland, Brock Fulton, Christy Gallihugh, Rob Halstead, Susan Hammond, Jackie Herath, Debbie Horstkamp, Katherine Hudson, Jackie Johnson, Stacy Karcesky, Vicky Karol (and her class of Calvert County rookie teachers), Beth Kawecki, Maureen Lawson, Marie Limburg, Tim McHugh, Kevin Michael, George Miller, Lindsay Miller, Glen Moulton, Sue O'Connell, Becky Reyno, Walter Sampson, Julie Schenk, Lori Stevenson, Eric Stroh, and Will Van Nort.

To the best friends a rookie teacher could ever have, Rob Halstead and Lori Daugherty. You guys were my support system when I needed it most, and I could never thank you enough. Lori, if it hadn't been for our shared planning period, I wouldn't have made it through the school year. Rob, you're a great friend, but you already know that. Who else could endure me but a pal with reserves of patience as vast as yours?

To the kids who touched my life. You guys were the reason I taught, and you always made it worth my while. Because of you, I never regretted a day I spent in the classroom.

To all the experienced teachers at Northern High School who guided me when I was new, especially the folks in my department whom I considered mentors as well as good friends. Special thanks to Heather Bogstead, Lloyd Donaldson, Beth Guerra, Jim Hall, Bill Halstead, Mark Hammersla, Mike Johnson, Duke Jones, Karen Neal, Kathleen Parlett, Debbie Pulley, Bob Riccardo, Jill Rodriguez, Candy Spain, Sherry Spickes, Tommy Tucker, Kitty Vogel, Rick Weber, and Debbie Wilson.

To all my public-school teachers, especially Daniel Brown, Ron Gibson, Jack Keosseian, Sherry Momberger, and Regina Supanick.

To my family, without whom I'd be a raving lunatic — Lisa, I can't imagine living with me, and I don't know how you do it; Dave, a great brother and the reluctant King of Drywall; Mom, the nicest lady I know, and the world's greatest purveyor of baby clothes; Dad, the first guy who taught me how to be funny, and who is always very proud.

To my friends Matt Halnon, Chris Sarampote, and Donna Marschall, who laugh at my jokes, even when we all know they're not funny.

Finally, to all the folks at Wiley who made this book a reality. I have always dreamed of writing this book, and had it not been for the support of Roxane Cerda, it wouldn't have happened. She pitched it to the folks in charge and convinced them I was the guy for the job; for that I am forever grateful. Thanks also to Pam Mourouzis, Norm Crampton, and Elizabeth Kuball (who loved the Winnie Story), three of the most supportive and accommodating people in the publishing world. If I had to describe myself as an author in one word, it would be *needy,* and these guys never minded at all (or at least didn't act like they minded).

Publisher's Acknowledgments

We're proud of this book; please send us your comments through our Dummies online registration form located at www.dummies.com/register/.

Some of the people who helped bring this book to market include the following:

Acquisitions, Editorial, and Media Development

Project Editor: Elizabeth Kuball

Acquisitions Editors: Pamela Mourouzis and Norm Crampton

Acquisitions Coordinator: Holly Grimes

Technical Editors: James Benton and Margaret Taylor

Editorial Manager: Michelle Hacker

Editorial Assistant: Elizabeth Rea

Cartoons: Rich Tennant, www.the5thwave.com

Cover Photo: © Royalty-Free/CORBIS

Production

Project Coordinator: Maridee Ennis

Layout and Graphics: Amanda Carter, Seth Conley, LeAndra Johnson, Stephanie D. Jumper, Tiffany Muth, Jackie Nicholas, Jeremey Unger

Proofreaders: John Tyler Connoley, John Greenough, Andy Hollandbeck, Carl W. Pierce, TECHBOOKS Production Services

Indexer: TECHBOOKS Production Services

Publishing and Editorial for Consumer Dummies

Diane Graves Steele, Vice President and Publisher, Consumer Dummies

Joyce Pepple, Acquisitions Director, Consumer Dummies

Kristin A. Cocks, Product Development Director, Consumer Dummies

Michael Spring, Vice President and Publisher, Travel

Brice Gosnell, Publishing Director, Travel

Suzanne Jannetta, Editorial Director, Travel

Publishing for Technology Dummies

Andy Cummings, Vice President and Publisher, Dummies Technology/General User

Composition Services

Gerry Fahey, Vice President of Production Services

Debbie Stailey, Director of Composition Services

Contents at a Glance

Table of Contents

Introduction

*1*t took me a long time to learn how to drive a car with a manual transmission. When I was 15, I was a pretty good driver (at least compared to other 15-year-olds). I drove my mother around on weekends while she ran errands and, after a few months of this, she was even able to breathe in the car when I was behind the wheel. After all, I had taken months and months of driver-education classes and learned about all sorts of things, like why you should push on the brake pedal *before* you get to the stop sign and what a blind spot is. Driving was a whole lot like the books said it was going to be, so when I finally climbed behind the wheel, I felt prepared.

Figuring out how to operate a stick shift was an entirely different story. The car instruction manuals made the process seem very easy. "To begin driving, fully depress the clutch and put the car into first gear, then ease up on the clutch and, as you do so, slowly depress the gas pedal." How hard could that be? It's only one sentence! Well, I found out exactly how hard it was to execute that one sentence as I tried to pull out of my driveway the first time in a car with a manual transmission.

The car lurched and jumped like a bucking bronco trying to throw me from the saddle. I think I could actually feel my brain slamming against the inside of my skull. "This is impossible!" I thought, as I fought to gain control of the car, to no avail. After numerous attempts, I was making no headway at all, so I decided to enlist the help of a family friend, who was able to master the mystical art of the five-speed engine.

My lesson lasted for about 15 minutes, and I could tell it was truly over when my friend ran from the car screaming in terror. How could it be that something people do every day, with no trouble at all, could be so hard to figure out?

Beginning a teaching career is like learning how to drive a manual transmission. In fact, it's like learning to drive about 50 stick shifts all at once!

About This Book

Just like learning to drive a stick shift, the best way to learn is by doing. However, that's definitely not the fastest way. Older teachers always told me,

"Don't worry, these little things work themselves out in time, and you'll turn out to be a fine teacher."

"That's great," I thought, "but what am I supposed to do in the meantime?"

What every rookie teacher needs is an experienced teacher to sit down with him and provide practical advice. However, the more advice you get, the more advice you realize you need. Like most rookies, I discovered how to succeed as a teacher the hard way. Over my years of teaching, I figured out a lot of stuff on my own, but I also picked up lots of tips and tricks from my colleagues. I often found myself saying, "If only I'd known that when I was new — it would have saved me so much trouble!"

And that's exactly why I wrote this book. I wanted to take all that advice and experience and distill it into one volume, so that you can start driving in no time at all. I wanted this book to be more than just my experiences, though, so I decided to broaden its scope. To do so, I talked to numerous people, including the following:

- ✔ Prospective teaching candidates, to find out what they were the most nervous about

- ✔ Student teachers, to find out what skills they felt they needed the most help with

- ✔ Rookie teachers, who shared stories both inspirational and tragic, so that others could benefit from their example

- ✔ Experienced teachers, who are battle-worn and can solve in a snap most problems that seem insurmountable to rookies.

- ✔ Principals, who told me what they look for in a rookie teacher and what expectations they have

- ✔ District administrators, who told me how they evaluate rookies

- ✔ School nurses, who provided a heads-up about what sorts of medical conditions rookies should be familiar with

- ✔ Former students, to find out what it is about a teacher that earns their respect, and what they don't like at all

The result is a set of tried-and-true methods that make a good teacher into a great teacher. Some of the information in this book you'll already have figured out, but a great deal of it may surprise you!

Unfortunately, some teacher-preparation programs try to shield their students from the often harsh reality of being a teacher. I don't think they do it to be mean or to handicap their students — it's just that education classes are often warm, supportive environments, but classrooms rarely are, at least at first.

Many new teachers quit every year because, even with years of education courses under their belts, they had no idea what teaching was really going to be like — and I think that's a crime. In my opinion, the best way to be prepared is to know what to expect ahead of time, so that you know how to respond. So, in addition to giving you the tried-and-true advice of the pros I list earlier, I've made it my job to try to warn you about almost any situation that can pop up in your rookie year. You'll find tons of real-life examples and plenty of those "Here's what you shouldn't do" stories (most of them, unfortunately, starring me). This is my way of helping you measure how deep the water is before you dive in.

You may find yourself getting a little nervous, because in many cases, I outline the worst-case scenario and what to do if bad things happen in class. Don't misunderstand me. That doesn't mean I don't think you can handle it or that you should reconsider your decision to become a teacher. Nothing could be farther from the truth! I just want you to be prepared.

If you were about to try skydiving (another risky proposition), I'm sure you'd want someone to explain ahead of time how you'd feel when you leapt from the door of the plane and who told you what to do if your parachute became entangled or didn't open. Even though you may feel better if that person simply said, "When you jump, you may feel a slight breeze, and then you'll be safely on the ground before you even know what's happened," you're much more likely to survive with the more honest advice.

Conventions Used in This Book

This book is fairly straightforward, but I do use a few conventions that you may want to be aware of:

- ✔ **Terminology:** I use language that was commonplace in my school district, but it may differ slightly where you teach. I use the term *elementary school* to describe kindergarten through fifth grade, *middle school* to describe sixth through eighth grade, and *high school* to describe ninth through twelfth grade. Some districts have grammar schools, junior high schools, senior high schools, preparatory schools, and schools of hard knocks, so if that applies to where you are, you'll just need to make the translation in your mind.

- ✔ **Gender-bending pronouns:** When I'm speaking about a generic student, I won't always use the standard masculine *he*. For example, I may say, "If a kid is becoming a troublemaker, speak to *her* parents at your earliest convenience." Call it a weird hang-up of mine, but I think always assuming that whatever random person you're talking about is male is odd, even though that's been the standard followed by linguists for a long, long time. I do try, however, to use *he* and *she* fairly equally throughout the book, just to be fair.

Foolish Assumptions

For the most part, I make very few assumptions in this book. But it's safe to say I do assume a few things about you. You're probably acquiring the basic teaching skills in a college or postgraduate program, or you just graduated from college, so you know all the theory. You know how to construct a lesson plan or two, know more than you ever wanted to about educational psychology, and are filled to the gills with knowledge about school law. If you haven't already done so, you're about to climb into the driver's seat of your classroom, jolt and shimmy down the street a few times, and begin to wonder, "What am I not doing right?"

You're tired of people telling you what the clutch does, or the theory behind transmissions in general. You just want to drive! "Tell me how to work my feet so I can get this beast moving!" is your common refrain. You recognize, however, that the only way to actually figure out how to use that car (or manage that classroom) is to ask for some practical advice from someone who's already done it.

One assumption I *don't* make is what grade level you're teaching or planning to teach. When I was writing, a lot of people asked me, "Is this going to be a book for elementary teachers or secondary teachers?" and they were surprised when I responded, "Both." For some reason, most teachers think that what's applicable to one group is not useful for the other. However, I found that all the teachers I interviewed, no matter what the age of their students, gave me the same basic advice. Of course, there are some differences, but those are covered in your training courses in college or graduate school. The result: I was able to write a book that applies to everyone, and I give examples for all age groups as often as possible to demonstrate that these ideas are not age-specific.

What You Won't Find in This Book

Now that you have some idea of what this book contains, I want to fill you in on exactly what it doesn't:

- ✔ **Inspirational, tear-jerking stories:** You can find all kinds of books out there that try to convince you to teach by relating emotional tales of how teachers shape the future. There's no doubt in anyone's mind that teachers do inspire the leaders of tomorrow, but those stories don't tell you what to do if a students openly defies you in class (which definitely will happen to you, no matter how much you may hope it won't). This book gives you all sorts of strategies for getting and maintaining classroom control, but it won't ever be made into a dramatic and heart-gripping, made-for-television movie.

✔ **Standard educational theory:** You already have lots of basic knowledge when you exit a teacher-education program, so I don't spend any time rehashing any of that in the pages that follow. I don't tell you what the basic parts of a lesson plan are, but I do help you spruce yours up. I don't debate the merits of a standard grading system versus a normalized grading system, but I do help you figure out which system to use and then show you how to calculate your grades.

✔ **Salsa recipes:** If it's help with Mexican food you're after, you not only have the wrong book, you're standing in the wrong section of the bookstore, for Pete's sake.

What you will find in this book is solid advice, practical tips, and some smiles along the way.

How This Book Is Organized

Even though this book consists of 23 chapters divided into 6 major parts, you don't have to read them in numerical order. Each chapter is completely self-contained and modular, so that you can start reading at any point and not have to worry about missing important concepts from other chapters. That way, you can read the chapters as you need them, or just sit back and digest the book from front cover to back cover (not literally of course, unless you're craving a high-fiber diet). Here are the parts in this book, to help you get the lay of the land.

Part 1: What They Didn't Teach You in College

You can't help but look back after you've started teaching and realize how useless a lot of that junk you learned in your education classes was. You start to wonder why the professors stressed the things they did (the five indicators of a properly constructed behavioral objective, for example) and didn't talk about the things you're most curious about (like what to do if a kid throws up). These chapters serve as a cold-water-in-the-face introduction to the world of education, and fill you in on how it's not exactly what you may have anticipated.

Part II: Managing Your Classroom

Establishing discipline is the chief concern of rookie teachers — and it should be. If you have an orderly classroom, rhythm, music, then, my man, who could ask for anything more? Besides showing you how to metaphorically "crack the whip," I'll also show you how to set up your room and get used to your new home away from home.

Part III: Delivering Instruction

Teaching isn't just about imparting knowledge, it's also about pizzazz! The best educators are also entertainers, so these chapters show you how to become a legend in your students' minds. I also help you hammer all the kinks out of your grading system before your first set of report-card grades are due.

Part IV: Meet the Supporting Cast

In this part, you get to know administrators, co-workers, parents, and students intimately. I introduce you to the kinds of people you meet and help you cope with all the people you're supposed to please.

Part V: Duties Other than Teaching

In these chapters, I give you a leg up on all the paperwork that awaits you as a rookie, help you handle all your extracurricular activities, and even provide a basic primer about childhood illnesses and medical conditions you should be aware of. Even though your primary job is to teach, you have all kinds of other responsibilities as well, both in your classroom and outside it.

Part VI: The Part of Tens

It's a Dummies trademark — the chunk of chapters in the form of top-ten lists. Here you find out ten things that always happen to rookie teachers (so you know what to expect). I also help you look out for common rookie errors and offer some tips about how to use technology in your classroom. Finally, I give you a list of ten great Internet resources that can make your life as a rookie teacher a bit easier.

Icons Used in This Book

Here and there, sprinkled in the margins of the book, you'll find little pictures that point to important parts of the text. Here are the icons I use and what they mean.

These little nuggets of advice will save you valuable time or prevent headaches in the future. It's sage advice from teachers who already have suffered the slings and arrows of bad decisions.

When I was a rookie, I sometimes felt like I was creeping through a minefield of potential problems. One wrong turn and . . . ka-blammo! Think of these warnings as little flags a minesweeper has placed in the field before you, so you know where you can safely step and where you definitely can't.

File these things away in your mind because, somewhere down the road, you'll be glad you did.

Every now and again, I offer advice specific to teachers of the little ones, my dear Watson.

Older kids sometimes require some strategies of their own, and this symbol will help you spot that advice.

Where to Go from Here

I've done my best to base all the advice in this book not just on my own crackpot ideas, but also on the bevy of interviews I conducted. However, you're still bound to find things here and there that you may not agree with. I do contend that all the tips I include in these pages worked flawlessly for me as a teacher, and helped me to form a strong and lasting bond with my kids that lasts to this day. Even so, you'll probably find yourself saying, "No, I couldn't do that" every now and again.

Just keep in mind that no two teachers are exactly alike, and even though you'll probably find 95 percent of this book useful, you may throw a few of my ideas out in favor of your own opinions and style. That's fine! I'm not trying to turn you into a disciple of mine — I just want to let you know what issues you'll need to think about ahead of time. Even if you end up disagreeing with me occasionally, you'll still be forming your own strategies and policies, and that's what's most important, after all.

With all that said, I hope you enjoy reading this book as much as I enjoyed writing it. Teaching is the most rewarding job out there, despite all the challenges facing modern-day education, and I hope this book will provide guidance and give you the help you need to succeed. I want you to walk into your building every day with a smile on your face and a skip in your step, knowing that you and your kids are not only going to gain knowledge but are also going to enjoy your time together.

If you like what you read (or even if you don't), the folks who publish this book would love to hear from you. Drop them a line via their Web site at `www.dummies.com`, or contact me directly through my Web site at `www.calculus-help.com`.

By the way, I eventually learned how to drive a stick shift, and I actually got quite good at it. I know you can do it as well!

Part I
What They Didn't Teach You in College

The 5th Wave   By Rich Tennant

"It looks like you've been playing cards instead of practicing your counting again."

In this part . . .

It's time to draw back the curtains and march proudly out of college and into (gasp!) the real world! No matter how much preparation you have in college, nothing can quite prepare you for what you're going to face when you're all alone in front of your first class. Things have changed since you were in school, and you'll notice it right away. However, it's not just the classroom that will bring surprises and shocks during your rookie year. You'll also have to deal with society's preconceived notions about what a teacher is.

In this part, I help you figure out just where you fit in the grand scheme of things, both at your school and in your chosen occupation. I also bring you face to face with a universal truth: Most of the stuff you learned in your teacher training is utterly useless in the classroom! But don't worry — I give you all kinds of information that you *do* need, and nothing you don't.

Chapter 1

What Have You Gotten Yourself Into?

· ·

In This Chapter

▶ Exploring how teaching compares to other occupations

▶ Understanding the unique demands teachers face

▶ Anticipating the challenges you'll face before your first day of work

▶ Coping with the chaos of your day-to-day life

· ·

Most new teachers are shocked by how different their perception of the teaching profession and teaching itself tend to be. In order to reduce the transitional shock from perception to reality, this chapter focuses on some of the biggest unexpected adjustments that you'll need to make as you earn your stripes as a teacher. As you read this book, you may find that not every single thing applies to you directly, but you can still find underlying commonalities that affect all teachers. In addition, remember that even though teaching probably won't be exactly the way you pictured it, by no means should you fear those differences. The little unanticipated variations from the expected are often what make teaching the job that so enticed you in the first place.

Real World versus School World

The world inside the school walls is vastly different from the world outside those walls; however, a haunting, underlying similarity exists between the teaching profession and every other job that you could have taken. These differences make people refer to the "real world" in class, as in the common apologies, "You'll need to know how to divide decimals in the real world," and, "In the real world, people use these spelling words, so unless you want to look like a dolt, you need to memorize their definitions." In this section, I show you how both worlds you'll be living in compare and contrast.

The similarities

Even though teaching has more dissimilarities than parallels with the so-called real world, you'll find universal laws that hold true in both. Understanding how your new world stacks up to the one you're used to is a necessary first step in preparing for the teacher's life.

- ✔ **Your performance will be evaluated based largely on numbers.** Even though *tons* of books are written about the little emotional things that make an entire career "worth it" (*Chicken Soup for the Retiring Biology and Life Sciences Teacher's Soul*–type books), suggesting that a teacher is a good one if she makes a difference in *just one kid's life,* the reality is that your proficiency in the classroom will be judged according to numbers, just like in most professions. Ultimately, test scores, grade distributions, and standardized assessment scores speak more loudly than anything else when it comes to administrators, especially early in your career. However, if your numbers aren't quite up to the par they set for you, especially at first, never let that blind you to the good, albeit immeasurable, things that you're accomplishing in the classroom. Just because you can't quantify something doesn't make it any less worthwhile of an objective.

- ✔ **You will get both praise and blame that you don't deserve.** Take it all in stride. The good days and the bad days will eventually offset each other. So, if things look bleak, give it a week or so, and the clouds will begin to clear. However, this works both ways. If you're feeling on top of the world, don't get too big for your britches. Even the most experienced teacher is bound to wind up in extremely sticky situations, and they always come out of the blue. Always be on the lookout for problems, and try to head them off before things get ugly.

- ✔ **Most people don't want to hear about what you do at work.** Even though everyone's been in school and can relate to your job, don't assume that people want to hear about your great lesson plan on teaching condensation to elementary-school science students. As much as you may be changing the future and exciting kids about learning, realize that other people's apathy is nothing personal. In fact, keeping most educational opinions to yourself is usually to your benefit. If prodded, many people will launch into a diatribe about "what's wrong with education."

Teaching is an admirable career, full of sacrifice and too often bereft of the reward and recognition it deserves. But be sure you don't slip into the mindset that you're doing society a favor by teaching, and that society should, in turn, pay you back in spades. You and I both know that teaching is one of the few truly humanitarian professions left, but trust me when I say that the rest of the world would rather us not belabor the point.

The differences

Teaching is undeniably as unique a career as they come, and in many ways, it's completely, utterly, and shockingly different from other jobs. Most of these differences are practical rather than philosophical, and if I sound like I'm starting to get a little bit too deep into academic speak here, let me dispel that perception with the first stark contrast I make between the real world and the school world:

✔ **You don't get to eat or go to the bathroom when you want.** You haven't lived until you're forced to eat lunch at 10:05 a.m. or until you've sweated out the last ten minutes of a class period, with a dire urge to (I'll try to put this politely) relieve yourself. Biological needs play a bizarre starring role as you get used to teaching. Veteran teachers are so used to this schedule and are so well adapted to it that you can set your clock to the time that they use the restroom (not that you'd ever want to do that, but you get my point). Do yourself a favor: If at all possible, find out what your schedule will be the summer before you start teaching, and govern your life by it. Eat lunch at home when you'll eat it at school. Practice a little self-control in the bathroom department, and only go at the times allotted by your upcoming schedule. You may consider this preparation to be a little ridiculous, but if you're not used to such rigidity in your schedule, it may be an unwelcome surprise later.

✔ **You'll be expected to do a lot that has nothing to do with your training.** Even though you've spent years preparing for a life of teaching, you're also going to have to serve as the police. Some schools have a police and security presence these days, but, in most cases, the system is miniscule at best. You'll be expected to police kids as they eat, play, walk in the halls, use the restroom, attend sporting events, attend school-wide assemblies, and so on. In addition, you'll most likely be asked to participate in a school-based activity, sponsor a club, or coach a sport *even if you have no experience in that club or sport whatsoever.* Flip to Chapters 17 and 20 for more discussion of extracurricular activities.

✔ **Your free time is going to take a huge hit.** Most teachers use the term *9-to-5 job* very contemptuously. They curl their lips and produce spittle when they talk about people who can just leave work at 5 p.m. and not have to grade, plan, and wonder what to do about that weird kid in social studies who keeps spitting on other kids. You should expect to give up lots of your own time (and spend lots of your own money), especially if you're going to make fun and engaging lesson plans. You can find tons of lesson plans in books and online, but you'll find that none are ever *quite* right for you. You'll spend a lot of time tweaking these plans, so they work better for your kids. Plus, don't forget that you have to master the material before you can hope to teach it — you're about to find out just how much you really forgot from your own schooling!

✔ **Your summers are "work free."** This difference is no longer true universally, as it once was. I never experienced "year-round school," and I'm thankful for it. All that time you spent at school and at home, grading and working yourself to the bone, is rewarded with a little more than two months of vacation. Don't be surprised, however, that your summers are rarely, if ever, actually vacations at all. Don't forget that you have to stay certified, and that takes a lot of classes and workshops. Furthermore, you're not earning a king's ransom, so most people take extra jobs during the summer.

You actually earn all your pay only during the academic year, so summer is technically an unpaid vacation. Many school systems will take your annual pay and divide it up so that you receive the same pay during the summertime as you did during the school year. However, some systems will offer you a choice. If money management isn't exactly your strong suit, don't elect to take larger paychecks that end when the school year does. If you're given more money, you may end up spending it. On the other hand, if you know yourself well and you're confident you can set enough aside to make it through the summer without having to bum meals off your friends, you'd be wise to take the larger paychecks that end when the school year does. That way, you can be earning interest on your income that much sooner.

Practical potty talk

If you're someone of weak composure, bear with me for a moment or two. I'm almost willing to bet that most teaching books don't address this issue, but it's one that most rookie teachers wonder about and are hesitant to address. What if they *really* need to go to the bathroom, and they can't wait until the end of class? This topic is actually a very important legal issue. The key point is *supervision*. You can't leave your class unsupervised, even for a moment. Therefore, making friends with one of the teachers in a classroom adjacent to yours is essential. If you're a *floating teacher* (you change classrooms some or every period of the day), you have more work cut out for you; you'll have to find a buddy teacher for every classroom you're in.

If things get (ahem) dire, give your class a good excuse for why you have to leave the room (the principal asked to meet with you quickly after the period got underway, or you have to deliver a note to another teacher), and ask your buddy teacher to keep an eye on your class while you're gone. (By the way, make sure that the excuse matches the length of time you expect to be gone.) This practice is applicable for all reasons that you may need to leave the room, even if you're just going into the hallway to speak with a student you've sent out for disciplinary reasons. Don't shut your door behind you as you leave! This cuts you off from the rest of your students, and anything can happen in your absence. Leave the door open and make it a point to keep looking in on them. Keep this question in mind: "If this were ever brought into a court of law, could I prove that the students were in some way supervised?" If so, you'll be fine. You're allowed to go the bathroom if you have to.

Bearing the Instructor's Burden

Teaching is a unique profession in that you're basically isolated from your colleagues from the first minute of the first school day and are expected to learn as you go with little or no help during the day. It's a difficult chore and a heavy burden to carry, especially when things aren't going well. You'd think that you could lean on your experience as a student teacher in these times, but you'd be surprised how different your actual teaching experience will be from your time as a student teacher.

Sink or swim!

Have you seen those TV shows where they demonstrate that babies can swim without instruction as soon as they're born? They toss infants into a swimming pool, and the little guys just swim like tadpoles without a care in the world! That's what it's like to teach. You get tossed right into the water, and everybody stands back and watches. "Is he going to make it? He may be in trouble, but let's just watch what happens. He may pull through after all, and if he doesn't, we'll drag him out and throw somebody else in instead."

Stop and think about that for a second — it's actually pretty scary! School systems aren't interested in making you a good teacher. They expect you to be good based on your college training, and without a whole lot of experience under your belt. Even worse, you're not going to swim very well when you first get tossed in. Teaching your first class based on what you learned in college is like being asked to swim across the Atlantic Ocean with nothing more than those little inflatable armbands. You'll stay afloat, but you'll swallow a *lot* of water along the way.

One of the new teachers I interviewed relayed this story to me. He was taking a class down to the media center for the first time. The class he was taking there was deemed a "behavior problem" (or more appropriately, a powder keg ready to explode), so the thought of simply walking the group as a whole to the library was a daunting exercise in itself. After they arrived with no calamity to speak of, he sat his students down at the available computers and had, what he deemed, a rather successful lesson explaining how to use the school's electronic and online resources. However, the librarian contacted him the next day, enraged. Evidently, his class was so quiet and focused because they were in the process of stealing pieces of the computer. Of the 30 computers in the lab, 23 were no longer functional, and the librarian held him flatly responsible for not keeping an eye on his kids.

That sort of thing is quite a wake-up call, and it's the result of a common practice among principals. (By the way, that teacher-principal relationship is a tricky one, so I discuss it more in Chapter 13.) You'd think that, as a new teacher with little experience and a lot of learning to do, your administration would remove as many obstacles as they possibly could to ensure that you'll be as successful as possible. Unfortunately, this probably isn't going to happen, and it all falls under that sink-or-swim mentality. In their view, putting you in a rough situation is the best thing that they can possibly do. That way, you have "ample opportunity to gain experience." How generous! Here are the most common adversities you'll face as a newbie:

✔ **You'll probably have the "bad kids."** If veteran teachers have any input in the scheduling process, they'll do everything they can to make sure that they get a good group of students or classes for the following year. Think about it — you'd probably do the same thing in their shoes. Before you get too bitter, just remember one thing: They were in your shoes once, and they had to go through the same thing you're going through. So they're more than content to let you experience the joy and fun of tough classes. Remember that even the bad classes can be transformed using effective discipline tactics, which I describe in Part II.

✔ **You won't have the greatest classroom if you have a classroom at all.** When it comes time to choosing classroom space, veteran teachers will leave you slim pickings. If there are more teachers than available rooms, the new teachers usually draw the short straw and become *floaters,* the stoic nomads armed with only an audiovisual cart (the one that's so hard to drive because it always swerves to the right when you push it) to hold their meager possessions and stacks of papers to grade.

✔ **You won't get to teach the cool classes.** Don't forget that you're not coming into a fresh ecosystem when you start teaching. Most likely, that school has been around for a while, and so have most of the teachers — and they've all carved out their little niches. The upper-level courses and electives already have teachers whose names are synonymous with them, so don't expect to march in and assume leadership of the classes and coursework that you've always dreamed of. Even if you have terrific qualifications in a given subject area and are actually more qualified than the current instructor, that doesn't amount to a hill of beans, so eat your humble pie and wait your turn. Something will eventually open up, even though you may have to wait a couple of years (or more).

Don't let any of this discourage you. Most of the negatives I've laid out here are true, in one form or another, in any job that you take. Having to pay your dues is simply the way of the world. Although all these things are frustrating and sometimes overwhelming, most people survive and even have great success in the face of such obstacles. In fact, it's through the struggle that you gain the respect of your co-workers and students alike. Only through the refining fire of the sink-or-swim trial do you gain professional stature and experience.

Jack or Jill of all trades

Pretend for a second that you're an accountant ready to begin work in a prestigious office. On the morning of your first day, the CEO of the company comes into your office and greets you. "We're glad to have you on board," he says. "It's tough to find a good CPA these days, and we feel pretty lucky to have you on the team." You grin inwardly, knowing that you excelled in all your classes for just such a moment as this. You're wanted; you're *needed,* in fact. And then, he says something baffling. "I know you're an expert in foreign currencies, exchange rates, and that sort of thing, which is exactly the reason we hired you. No one else can chug those numbers with quite the proficiency you can." So far so good, but his look is somber. "Here's the problem. Between the hours of 12 and 2 p.m. each day, we really don't require your skills, so we'll need you to so some electrical wiring work around the office. We saw that you took some physics in college, and we've got an electrician's hat for you and everything. Welcome to the office — and can you fix my lamp when you get a chance?"

As ridiculous as that scenario may sound, it happens all the time to teachers. For example, the choir teacher at my former school had to teach a few Spanish classes, even though she had just taken a few Spanish classes in college. Even if you have no formal training in a subject, you just may find yourself teaching it! This isn't such a big deal to elementary-school teachers, who teach just about every subject there is, but if you're a middle-school science teacher, don't be surprised if you're asked to teach a class or two of language arts! Most state certifications allow a teacher of one subject to teach "out of content area" for a couple of class periods each instructional day.

Facing adverse conditions

Even though rookie teachers have it tough, they're not the only ones. You're bound to carry burdens that aren't unique to those green behind the ears. These common frustrations aren't only a little annoying — they are, in fact, extremely detrimental to learning. Among all the teachers I spoke to, two completely different complaints arose time and time again: the lack of supplies and resources available to teachers and the temperature in the school building.

You probably already know that you're going to have to buy most of the things you'll need in the classroom. I'm not talking about paper clips and staples or overhead projectors — those items are usually provided by the school system. Supplies for in-class experiments and projects, stickers or awards, and even the constant and pressing need for boxes of tissues will have you constantly reaching into your wallet or purse. Furthermore, your classroom is going to be as boring as a sensory-deprivation tank if you don't have some colorful, fun, and engaging decorations on the walls. Although your school may have some posters that you're required to display, the bulk of the decorating will fall to you.

You can offset some of the costs you face. Many elementary schools publish a list of materials that students are required to bring with them on the first day of school. Anything the kids bring from home is one less thing you have to provide. One teacher I spoke to added "Bring a box of tissues with you" to the list, thereby creating a small stockpile of tissues in the classroom. By collecting all the boxes and only putting out one box at a time, she was able to keep her kids swaddled in tissues until the end of the year. Furthermore, the tissues in her room were much softer than the industrial 120-grit sandpaper tissues schools buy. Why am I focusing so much on facial tissue? You'll understand in February when all the students in your class are oozing out of all their facial orifices, and the office is out of tissues for the rest of the year. High-school parents were much less keen on the idea of sending tissues, but I motivated my students to bring in boxes by offering small bits of extra credit. (High-school students would kill their cousins for extra credit.) You may want to try this tactic yourself if you have trouble getting people to pitch in to the tissue stash.

The second biggest complaint about school conditions is the temperature of the classrooms. Let me set the stage for you. It's October, and temperatures are finally beginning to fall. As I enter my classroom, I feel my door stick a little bit in its frame. "Hmmm," I think to myself. "That's odd." The little mystery is soon explained by an agonizingly hot gust of wind that hits me in the face as the door swings open. My room is so hot that my extensive duct taping has given up the ghost, and all my posters (about 75 of them) are lying on the floor, curled and bent beyond recognition.

I knew that learning would be difficult in such an atmosphere. In fact, staying awake would prove just as tricky. In essence, I was going to have to teach that day in a volcanic cave full of desks. I immediately reported the situation to the office, hoping that (at the worst) it would be rectified by the end of the school day. It was rectified — but not until April! I bought fans, opened the outside door, and did whatever I could, but it was truly a nightmare. Evidently, some part was on order and then this and that happened to delay the shipment. All I knew was that I spent most of the class period sweating through my shirts, and the kids were miserable.

In fact, I think that they had it worse. As they went to their next class, the temperature changed dramatically. Down the hall, my friend Tim McHugh taught in a room that was so incredibly cold that (and I am not exaggerating here) *it hurt to breathe.* He taught in a ski parka and gloves and confessed that he still shivered so badly that he ached. The situation gets even dicier if students have classes in a trailer outside the school building, the new necessary evil of overcrowded schools. My wife taught in a trailer whose air-conditioning couldn't battle the heat during the late spring and, conversely, whose heat couldn't battle the winter temperatures, either.

Whether they be from an oppressive classroom temperature or a debilitating lack of supplies, you'll have plenty of woes. Is there an upside to all this? Believe it or not, yes. These issues are undeniable, affecting everyone, and, therefore, offer you a chance to speak frankly and honestly to your students about something other than, for example, mitosis. Dealing with these issues and your feelings about them help you to form a bond between you and your students in the same way that you can walk up to anyone on the street and start a conversation about the weather. Allowing them to voice their opinions, to vent frustration, and to cope as a group is an invaluable experience, so don't miss an opportunity to bond with your students, even about so mundane a topic.

If talking to toddlers and teens about your occupational frustrations doesn't appeal to you, don't worry — it's not the only relief you'll get from the doldrums of your working conditions. There are other adults in the school whom you may even see occasionally. However, there are very specific politics wrapped around the relationships you'll have with your colleagues and administrators. Knowing where to complain, how to voice your concerns, and whom to trust in the faculty lounge are just a few of the skills you'll need to develop. I focus on how to get along with everyone else in your building in Part IV.

You're the Adult Now!

When you exit college (or graduate school) with all your training complete, to say that you're familiar with how the educational system works is an enormous understatement. If teaching is your first career, you've been hip-deep in the educational system for your entire cognizant life. If you're entering teaching as a second career, surely the coursework and training you had to undergo for certification purposes was enough to remind you of the joy of taking classes. There's one big difference now, however: You're in charge, and things look a lot difference from this side of the big desk.

Performing six shows a day

First and foremost, you need to understand your role as the grown-up. Your bosses think that you're there primarily to teach content and secondarily to provide a classroom atmosphere fertile for learning. Your students, however, know that you're really there to entertain them and (if you have to) teach them something. You're the Wayne Newton of Language Arts now.

The bell rings. Boom! You're on. Go out there and have a great show. Try the joke with the funny voice and manage to squeeze in how, exactly, to diagram a sentence while you're at it. A little while later, the bell rings again, and you have two or three minutes to compose yourself before the next show time. The only differences between you and a Vegas entertainer is that you have to perform more often, to a captive audience (instead of people who *pay* to be there), and you actually have to teach while you're at it.

The elementary-school teachers I interviewed accepted their role of entertainer far more easily than did the secondary teachers. Younger kids need constant pizzazz to keep them alert and on track. Things have to be quick, constantly shifting, vibrantly attention grabbing, and always exciting. But even as a secondary teacher, you're the center of the students' attention for the entire time they're in your classroom, and your mood and actions hold sway over everything that happens. Many teachers feel that they're not paid enough to entertain the kids — and that's unfortunate. These faculty always seem to be the exact same group that complains when in-service meetings are boring, or if they feel that they're being "talked at" rather than actively engaged when they're not the one in charge. Try to teach your class in a way that would keep you both interested and entertained if you, yourself, were a student.

Does this mean that you need to begin every lesson by jumping through fiery hoops while juggling on a unicycle? No, but I'd pay to see it, especially if you could teach the finer points of the French and Indian War while you did it. You can do all sorts of little things to spice up your lessons, which I discuss in Chapters 11 and 16, but you need to remember that holding your students' interest is just as much your job as making sure that they pass their quizzes and tests. In fact, you'll grow to see that entertained students and successful students are often one and the same.

Make no mistake about it. Whether you're a secondary teacher and you have a bunch of distinct shows every day, or you're an elementary teacher and all those shows blend into one long performance, it's exhausting and often thankless work. The more involved your lesson plans and the more interactive your activities, the more draining it is. But as your kids figure out that you design your classes first and foremost with them in mind, they'll grow to trust you, and your relationship will begin to turn from teacher-student into mentor-student, with the ultimate goal of becoming allies in the educational process. Although mentally, physically, and emotionally taxing, developing a strong trust relationship with your students provides benefits that far outweigh the inherent drawbacks.

Working in Neverland

Remember Neverland, the home of Peter Pan and the Lost Boys? The land where no one grew up and everyone could fly? Well, school will be your own personal Neverland, where only you get older, but each generation of kids stays exactly the same age. (And you'll swear that they can fly based on their limitless well of energy and enthusiasm.) It's a land with rules unto itself that don't apply anywhere else in the world. For example, chewing gum is rarely allowed in Neverland, and in Neverland you have to ask permission before you use the restroom.

One thing you must always keep in mind is that the rules of Neverland and the rules in the adult world are not at all the same. For instance, regardless of how old the students are, most of Neverland's residents suffer from a severe lack of perspective. Tears flow freely and often within the bounds of this magical land, no matter how old the resident. Each test is the *end of the world* and causes severe stress and panic. Every emotional or interpersonal crisis can actually make time stand still for those involved. I defy anyone to try to teach the quadratic equation to a girl who was dumped by her boyfriend of *six whole months* right before your algebra class began. You may as well try to train a dog to weave with a loom, because you'll have the same amount of success.

You need to remember one key rule during your visit to this exotic and strange country: You are only a visitor to Neverland and are not a resident yourself. You are, in fact, an ambassador from the adult world and are there to (in some fashion) help these children transition into a world where people get older, time gets faster, and trapping lightning bugs in jars slowly loses its allure. In plain and bold terms, always act your age because Neverland residents don't respect people who are constantly applying for citizenship after they're adults and, thus, far too old to qualify.

The spotlight's on you!

If you piled up everything that you've discovered, accumulated, and experienced during your student-teaching term, the heap would be considerable. However, the one thing that student teaching doesn't offer you is a chance to do things from scratch. You were always working within your sponsor teacher's guidelines, in a room that was already prepared for you, with a plan of action that was already in place.

You'll feel overwhelmed when you walk into your new job, and everything depends on *you*. I talked to a teacher who arranges student-teaching placements and then follows up after those student teachers find jobs. She happened to walk in on one of her students who'd just been hired as he stood alone, in the dark, in his future classroom. He evidently didn't hear her enter the room because nothing broke his unblinking gaze as it swept back and forth across the desks piled along the walls and the vast, open floor. As he turned, he looked at her with wide, unblinking eyes and said, "There's nothing here . . . *nothing*. Where do I start?" She had no response other than to comment to herself that perhaps she hadn't expressed to the teachers the enormity of the task before them.

When you arrive on your first day, there are no rules, lesson plans, seating arrangements, or decorations. The task of putting together a successful school year is truly daunting because it is made up of so many individual composite parts. You may get a feeling of abandonment as you pass from the nurturing embrace of student teaching to the full immersion of professional teaching. Therefore, your best bet is to find allies among your new colleagues as soon as possible, so that you feel you still have a support structure in place.

Facing the Daily Grind

Each and every day, you'll be faced with quite an impressive, if not intimidating, list of things that need to be accomplished. First and foremost, you have to provide competent, meaningful, and (if you have time and energy left) engaging lessons for each of the classes that you're teaching. On top of that, you have to grade the results of those lessons, tutor after school, make parent phone calls, hold administrative and parent conferences, and participate in whatever extracurricular events you're tied to. Throw in any detentions or punishment assignments that you have to supervise, your duty assignments, and the chin-high stack of paperwork that needs filling out nearly every period, and it's enough to make you want to quit your job and become a Domino's pizza delivery person (unless you already are one during the evening to help pay the bills, that is). Just making it through every school day is a chore in and of itself.

Managing the school day

What one word would best describe the typical school day? How about *hectic?* No, that's as giant an understatement as describing the pain you experience when being impaled as "a brief, tingling sensation." The best word I have ever heard used to describe the school day is *triage.* If you aren't familiar with that word, picture in your mind's eye a war-torn battlefield, cluttered with wounded soldiers. The injured fighters suffer from a variety of different wounds, and they are each in a unique state of emergency. Some require immediate care, and some can be stabilized and receive medical attention later.

The triage doctors attend to each of the wounded and decide, on the spot, the order in which everyone will be helped. The most seriously injured are taken first, but only if there's a good chance of saving them (some are too far gone to be worth the effort, as callous as that sounds). However, the triage doctors do more than just order the casualties. They also must tend to those waiting, to keep them alive until more specific attention can be given them. In other words, the triage doctors and nurses are jugglers of lives, keeping hundreds of balls in the air at the same time until each can be attended to.

I know, I know — leave it to a guy to come up with such a gory metaphor, but it describes exactly how I felt every day during instructional hours. You will be asked to do *numerous* things, and you probably won't be able to accomplish them all. You're going to have to prioritize, organize, and reorganize every moment of the school day. The hardest thing is deciding what has to go because your time is limited. Usually, your coolest and most innovative lesson plans are the victims of triage, and that's natural, so don't sweat it. Not all your lessons are going to be powerhouses.

Lesson plans and grading

Week to week, all kinds of different paperwork is going to pop up that will need your attention. However, as unavoidable as death and taxes, lesson planning and grading are two kinds of paperwork that will become part of the daily routine. In fact, they're the bookend activities to your time in the class-room. You must plan before lessons to both ensure your understanding of the material to be covered and to consider the most effective method of present-ing it. Grading is the by-product of assessment, to see just how effective that lesson was in retrospect. In order for your time in the classroom to be most productive, you must be fully immersed in both planning and grading.

One thing I don't talk much about in this book is how to write a lesson plan. If you've been through a teacher-training course, you know the important elements of a lesson plan and what your professor or cooperating teacher required. After you've taught for a year or so, you'll probably also discover that making up lesson plans like you did in college is absolutely ludicrous. They are way too time consuming, and you'll find a style that better suits your individual needs as you gain experience.

You do need to find out if your school requires you to turn in your lesson plans. Some schools absolutely require lesson plans on file, and some simply require you to file lesson plans on the days you're being observed by an administrator. Others, thankfully, are more relaxed, and only want you to have "evidence of planning" if a superior ever requests it (and you'd better hope it's not requested, because that usually means that somebody thinks you're slacking).

The style of lesson plan that you use doesn't really matter. I was a math teacher, so my lesson plans were usually lists of important topics to cover with illustrative examples of each. I felt that an unstructured plan gave me some working room and, at the same time, established my goals.

My good friend Rob wasn't comfortable with such a vague plan, and his plans were nearly word-for-word what he'd say in class. "Today we're going to define and talk about circles. First let's talk about what a circle is . . ." — that sort of thing. This helped him work out exactly how class would flow and made him feel more confident as soon as class began. Neither of these styles is better than the other; it's just a question of what you need to do in order to be prepared.

The further into your first school year you get, the more you're going to hate writing lesson plans, and the more tempted you'll be to fly by the seat of your pants. *This is a very bad idea,* no matter how comfortable you feel with the material. There's no feeling quite like the cold chill of panic running down your spine when you realize that you've been teaching the wrong thing for the entire class period, and that class period is about to end. Furthermore, anticipating and preparing for student questions makes you look a lot smarter in front of your class, which is a key element to gaining their respect. They need to know that you know exactly what you're talking about.

After you've set up your plan and delivered the lesson, you eventually have to assess the students' understanding. It's hard to quiz or test too much; in fact, most new teachers assess too little because they feel that it breaks up the flow they have going in class. One new teacher I knew looked back at the end of the nine-week marking period and realized that he'd only given one quiz, and he'd even forgotten to grade it!

Don't let assessment be an afterthought, because it's the one thing parents and administrators can see and use to judge your performance. If you end up fudging with the grades a little because you didn't have enough real numbers to base grades upon, you're heading for trouble. However, you have to keep one thing in mind, and that's the volume of papers you'll be grading. One assignment in each class each day translates into between 500 and 900 papers to grade by the weekend! Just like everything else that I've discussed in this chapter, the name of the game is anticipation, preparation, and finally, commitment, after you've formulated a plan of action.

The school-day marathon

I don't think that many people remember just how tiring the school day is. During my tenure at the high school where I taught, the school district switched from an appointed to an elected school board. The result? A ton of "innovative" ideas to improve education. One older gentleman insisted that kids should be in schools longer. Even though, for example, my school dismissed at 2:20, he insisted that students should be held at school, kept active in one way or another, until 6:00 p.m., so that parents could get home from work before their kids. I understand the benevolent motivation — reducing the number of "latch-key" kids. However, I think he forgot how long school really is and how exhausting being a student can be.

He, with all the other candidates for the school board, was permitted to "shadow" a student for one day. That is, they followed a student to all her classes and even had lunch with her in the cafeteria. The gentleman with the (in essence) day-care plan shadowed a student who attended my class at the end of the day. When he came in, he looked a little rumpled — I think the day had been rough — but I looked forward to speaking with him after I got the students started on their assignment.

Unfortunately, I never got my chance because he slept soundly (and loudly) for my entire class. I didn't have the heart to point out to him the irony of the situation, because a school day of regular length was even too much for him. However, I was pleased to see that he was defeated soundly during the election.

Chapter 2

Dealing with Society's Nutty Notions about Teaching

In This Chapter

▶ Understanding how others view the teaching profession

▶ Placing your educational training in perspective

▶ Responding to pervasive teacher myths

▶ Overcoming prejudices and biases the public has against educators

Some people (including, surprisingly, a few of your education professors) have no idea what teaching is all about. A few will go so far as to question your competence and even your intelligence as soon as they find out what you do for a living. In this chapter, I discuss this small but vocal portion of the populace that took me completely by surprise when I taught. When I entered the profession, I inherently believed that all people held teachers in the same high regard that I did. In actuality, though, many people are at least suspicious (if not overtly contemptuous) of educators. This suspicion (or downright hatred) stems from certain prejudices and misconceptions about teaching.

"Those Who Can, Do; Those Who Can't, Teach"

How many times have you heard that ludicrous statement? As if that's not bad enough, here's the amended version: "If you can't do, teach, and if you can't teach, teach gym." Nasty, just nasty. However, you'll encounter this prejudice more than any other as you progress in your career.

Teachers aren't always viewed as academicians and mentors anymore. In fact, they're usually viewed somewhere along the spectrum between these two extremes:

- ✔ **The brainy, book-smart professor who has no practical knowledge:** In this view, sure you've been at the business of education for years and years to finely tune your mind, but somewhere in the midst of it, you've lost sight of what's really important. Final result: Yeah, you're smart, but who needs anybody that smart? You've lost touch with reality. If you had to cope in the real world, you'd shrivel up and die because all your book learnin' isn't going to get you anywhere.

- ✔ **The marginally intelligent teacher who's only teaching because he or she couldn't get a *real* job:** People will be suspicious of why you chose to teach at all. Didn't you know that teachers don't make a lot of money? Weren't you aware that most kids hate school? Why would you knowingly walk into a job like that? Furthermore, these days, the importance of your job is measured by the paycheck that comes along with it. Clearly, then, if you were competent in any *real* skill, you could've found a better paying job. Therefore, you obviously picked teaching because you lacked any marketable skills.

After all the time you've spent in preparing for this job, being categorized, labeled, and discounted so easily is likely quite frustrating for you. Despite the fact that, in America, the law (at least in theory) is "innocent until proven guilty," in educational circles, the rule is "incompetent until proven competent." However, in time, a good teacher is able to dispel the cloud of suspicion hanging over his or her head and reputation. Before you look at how, exactly, to go about doing that, take a closer view at commonly held beliefs about teachers' inherent incompetence.

People are going to be watching you, especially because you're a new teacher, hoping to catch you when you screw up. Elementary students generally aren't quite as excited about catching their teachers in an error, but elementary students also have additional expectations. They not only expect you to know what you're doing, but they also expect you to know how they feel and to act accordingly. Teenagers are consistently under the assumption that everything an adult does is designed, specifically, as a personal affront to them, so they don't expect the same nurturing atmosphere that a younger child requires.

By the way, even if you have a lot of real-world experience and enter teaching as a second career to share the knowledge that you've gained, you still can't win. Although your credentials won't be drawn into question, the issue will instead be "She's too old," or "He's of too technical or vocational a mindset," and as a result, you can't *connect* with today's students. So, whether you're viewed as a rookie who's too inexperienced or as a veteran who's too grizzled, you'll wind up pushing against stereotypes. You have to come to terms with this. When you can live with the fact that you'll have to establish competence in the face of some degree of doubt, you're already one step ahead of the game.

Who wants to be a dunderhead?

Like the majority of people in the United States, when the game show *Who Wants to Be a Millionaire?* made its TV debut, I was riveted. I watched so many episodes that they all blur together in my memory — except for one particular episode that I'll never forget. Regis Philbin, dressed in his usual dapper shiny tie/shirt combination, asked this question to the contestant in the hot seat: What element is most commonly found in the atmosphere? The choices were oxygen, carbon, hydrogen, and nitrogen.

That poor contestant thought that he had a ringer to answer this question for him. He used one of his lifelines and phoned a friend who just happened to be none other than a high-school science teacher! Easy money, right? Not exactly.

Given the choices, the teacher friend responded that he was sure the answer was either carbon or hydrogen. He wasn't sure exactly which one, but it was one of those. Because the contestant couldn't decide between the two, he elected to take his 50-50 hint. (This means that two incorrect answers are removed, leaving one correct and one incorrect answer behind.) Guess which two elements were immediately removed as wrong answers? That's right — carbon and hydrogen. So not only was the high-school science teacher wrong, he wasn't even close. The correct answer was nitrogen, much to the surprise and chagrin of the science teacher.

Unfortunately, this incident did more than hurt the contestant's chances of being a millionaire: It damaged the perception of the American public school system more than 100 studies by independent researchers could ever have done. It was an undeniable gaffe. Education has clearly gone down the tubes, and the ruin of mankind is imminent, if a science teacher can't answer a question about the relative composition of the atmosphere!

For one second, though, let's give the guy a break. He was nervous and on TV, and he probably felt the pressure of being a so-called expert on the subject, knowing that everyone was expecting him to get it right. It was win or lose with one swing. Perhaps he didn't hear the word *atmosphere* in the question. If we're talking about the human body, carbon is a much more reasonable answer. Maybe he was just completely wrong. What does it matter? This teacher is one guy out of hundreds of thousands of educators, but for one day, he was the spokesperson for competency in education and he said "maybe hydrogen."

People were jumping on the bandwagon to criticize this teacher faster than you could say, "That's my final answer." Unbelievably, among the more vocal critics was Princeton University. In their November 16, 1999, edition of *The Princeton Spectator,* they explained that the teacher's inability to answer correctly "doesn't say much for education in America." Not even an educational institution was above taking a cheap shot at schools in America, based on some unknown schmo who screwed up a game-show question. Is that fair? No. Is it common for things like that to happen to educators? Yes.

Establishing Your Competence

When I was in college, I heard one piece of advice over and over from my education professors: "If you don't know the answer to a question, don't be afraid to tell a student that you're not sure, but you'll find out and get back to him or her the next day." Technically, this is good advice, but — and this is important — only if used in moderation. It's roughly the equivalent of a girl telling a guy, "Don't be afraid to cry in front of me." Sure, she wants the guy to be able to express emotions, but if he ends up crying all the time, even during commercials for long-distance phone service, she's going to get uncomfortable.

Winning over students

The unwritten rule is that guys don't cry very often. If they do, the natural order seems a bit out of whack. Similarly, if the teacher is constantly remarking that he or she doesn't know the answer to something, kids start to get antsy about whether, in fact, that teacher knows anything at all. If you don't know the answer to something, it may very well be because that issue is irrelevant to the topic at hand or that the answer is more of a tangential distraction to what you're trying to accomplish.

Instead of always replying that you don't know the answer to something, if the question raised is not key to his understanding, tell the student why you'd rather not discuss the issue. A reply of, "That's a complicated issue, and the answer to it would cloud what I'm trying to explain here," is a valid response. Most of the time, not knowing the answer to a question isn't a reflection of your competence at all, and this is a good way to defuse the question without losing stature in students' eyes. You can also try the "That's a great question! The first person to find the answer and bring it to me tomorrow morning gets a few extra credit points" trick, so that the kids can get involved in finding the answer, as well.

On the other hand, if you're constantly dodging questions like dodgeballs, you'd better spend some more time planning your lessons. Otherwise, the students will assume the role of the cowboy outlaw, shooting at your feet and drawling, "Dance fer me, pardner." It's up to you to find that fine line that determines when you admit that you don't know and when you press on in the face of it.

Winning over parents

Students will usually decide whether you know what you're doing based on an overall impression of you, day in and day out, rather than on isolated things you do or say. However, the same isn't true for parents. Although it takes weeks of you screwing up in front of a class to lose its respect, it may take only one botched first impression for a parent to think ill of you. Therefore, your best chance to establish that you're competent lies in Parent

Night. All schools have different names for this activity — my school called it Back to School Night. However, the general gist of the activity is the same: After school has been back in session for a few days or weeks, the parents are invited one evening to come to school and visit their children's teachers.

The following list gives a few things you can do before and during Parent Night to establish your professional ability (some tactics are obvious, and others are subliminal):

- **Proudly display your certificates and awards on the walls of your classroom.** Teachers are usually very modest about their achievements, but they shouldn't be. Doctors, dentists, psychologists, and business-people hang nicely framed diplomas and certificates on their office walls, and you should do the same. If you've received recognition in your teacher training, hang those certificates up as well. This action speaks of your professional skill in a relatively humble but tangible way.

- **Discuss your background and training.** Sure, you got into teaching because you love kids, but that shouldn't be your lead-off statement in your presentation to parents. You should begin with a brief verbal rundown of your résumé and a summary of the schools and programs in which you've been trained. Stick with the major ones, though. Don't draw attention to your five summers as a Girl Scout camp counselor, unless that skill is particularly relevant to your job.

- **If at all possible, use technology in your presentation.** In this day and age, your comfort with and adept use of information technology is inexorably linked to your ability to perform successfully in the class-room. You may not completely agree with that statement, but that's what your audience will be thinking. If you show them that you know your way around a computer, they'll begin with the assumption that you're a pretty smart cookie because the average person is still nervous around computers and new technology.

- **Dress the part.** Don't even think about wearing sneakers or jeans on this night. Dress up. I'm not talking ball gown or tuxedo, but you should be wearing your finest professional attire. Your dress needs to reflect your personality and your goals for your class, and it also needs to reflect your status as head of that classroom. Guys, if you have a suit, this is the night to wear it. At the very least, you should wear a tie and dress slacks (a shirt wouldn't hurt, either). Ladies, wear a "power outfit" that says, "I am professionally trained." In other words, a suit is the best option, but lacking that, a nice dress or blouse and slacks/skirt combination is the way to go. Don't wear whimsical clothes that you may wear to put your students at ease. You want parents to think, "She looks like a business-woman" not, "Where can you buy a smock covered in cartoon characters?"

Of course, although first impressions are important, you'll need to back that up with a teaching style that engages students, promotes you as a teaching professional, and makes everybody, including parents and administrators, happy. You need to conduct yourself with such professionalism that any mistakes you make (and you will make them, trust me) will be viewed as exceptions to the rule rather than indicators of incompetence.

Looking Inside Those "Educational Studies"

You can find more educational studies out there than marshmallow chicks during Easter time, and they reach all kinds of wacky, puzzling, and often contradictory conclusions. I've had more obscure and wholly unjustifiable study results reported to me by administrators than I care to count. Unfortunately, most people didn't major in math in college, so they don't possess a sophisticated enough mathematical sense to sort through and dispel the more outrageous and misinterpreted numbers. Therefore, the general public maintains a decidedly negative opinion about the educational system and its achievements as a whole.

Most news reports these days concerning education are always drawing worrying conclusions that the United States is ranked number 1,512,316 among industrialized nations in the areas of science and math, or something along those lines. Even if you can't, yourself, distinguish between valid and invalid studies, you should keep in mind that there's always something lurking beneath the surface of these reports, and hidden agendas have a way of contorting the way that numbers are presented.

Interpreting statistics

Benjamin Disraeli, a British prime minister of the nineteenth century, said it best: "There are three kinds of lies: lies, damned lies, and statistics." There's even a book, written by Darrell Huff in the 1950s, but still in print today, called *How to Lie with Statistics.* So much of educational practice is driven by "objective" data that it's important for you to take all these results with a grain of salt.

When I started teaching, some system-wide exams were being revamped. They decided that multiple-choice exams were no longer useful for measuring student achievement because, even if test-takers guessed on all the questions, the students would still get approximately 25 percent of them right. Therefore, they proposed moving to an essay- and rubric-based system instead, where the responses would be graded, according to content, on a scale from 1 to 4. A score of 1 would represent an attempt at the question, and a 4 would reward mastery of the question.

This plan satisfied the testing coordinator until a faculty member at my school realized something during our training: "If a student writes anything, he or she gets a score of 1, correct? The student doesn't actually have to have any knowledge at all. So, if the student guesses at every question, he or she will consistently get 1 out of 4 points and receive 25 percent overall. Isn't this exactly what you were trying to avoid?" Under the guide of numbers, an agenda was being promoted, and the only appropriate response to the criticism was "oopsie daisy."

I want you to remember this basic principle of research: *Correlation does not imply causation.* In other words, the fact that two events seem to occur together doesn't mean that one event causes the other. For example, one study a few decades ago made the shocking discovery that the more frying pans a family owned, the better the children of that family did in school! Can it be that easy to have smarter kids? Was it the iron in the frying pans building intellectual muscle as it was inadvertently consumed, stuck to eggs and bacon?

Whenever you're handed a hot fact right out of the frying pan, take time to look for underlying, contributing factors.

Of course, frying pans have nothing to do with test scores. The underlying factor is that people who own more than one frying pan are most often richer than those who own only one. In fact, how many frying pans does one family really need? One is usually enough to get by, so those who buy more have money to spend on things other than the bare necessities. Thus, the study was actually showing that students who come from wealthier backgrounds did better than kids whose parents had significantly less money. The presence of multiple pans may have correlated with higher scores, but the pans certainly didn't cause the scores.

Don't be too quick to change the way that you do things in the classroom based on individual research. Give any findings time to pan out as both legitimate and practical before you revolutionize everything you do.

Considering grade inflation

No matter where you drive or how long the trip takes, you're likely to see 500 bumper stickers that say, "My child is an honor student at James Earl Jones Elementary School." Well, maybe it doesn't say that exactly. I don't think that

James Earl Jones actually has an elementary school named after him, but you get the picture. (I don't think the fact that he was the voice of Darth Vader should count against him.)

Some people actually view these bumper stickers as evidence of grade inflation in America. "When I was young," these people say, "it was *hard* to get an A, and we liked it like that! We walked to school in the snow, surrounded by diseased howler monkeys, and no one complained! These days, anybody can get good grades because all schools want to do is look good, so they doctor the marks."

Schools do want to put the best light on things. For instance, a school never advertises that it got the lowest standardized test scores in the state. However, to assume that crowing about your accomplishments results in grade inflation is far fetched. I tend to believe that increased attention on anything, educationally related or not, merely raises suspicions. Furthermore, I believe that a lot of people are eager to compare the current educational system to the glorified system of their faulty memories without having set foot in a school in two decades.

No evidence exists of a widespread epidemic of grade inflation. In fact, most studies show that grades are about the same as in previous decades. If you want to read one such report, check out *Changes in High School Grading Standards in Mathematics, 1982–1992* by Dan Koretz and Mark Berends. You may hear the argument, "But I saw a school that had seven valedictorians with straight-A averages!" Although more students are trying harder to get good grades to get into college, that doesn't mean that schools are easier.

You've been through teacher training. You know how steep expectations have gotten. One first-grade teacher told me, "They're expecting these kids to write in complete sentences that are spelled correctly by February! I remember when we focused more on having to teach the kids to read!" When people say that schools are slacking, you're likely to take it personally, so I advise you to arm yourself with studies of your own. Most people's opinions about grade inflation are based either on fallacy or completely unfounded opinions, so introducing a truthful study usually disarms such arguments.

Forgetting Those Education Classes

I make reference to your teacher training quite a few times throughout this chapter and this book, and it's about time you find out the cold, hard reality about most teacher-preparation coursework: It's just as practical as a fly-swatter would've been during the Egyptian plague of locusts. You've spent years and years and taken credit upon credit learning to differentiate between behavioral, Freudian, and humanistic psychologists. You know about multiple intelligences, token economies, and mnemonic devices. Do yourself a favor and forget all of it as soon as you possibly can!

Why am I regaling you with warnings? Because most of your education professors are also the purveyors of a massive misconception in the field of teaching. In the words of one of the supervisors I interviewed, "Teaching textbooks are extremely useful everywhere but inside the classroom." In his mind, and I agree completely, tips on teaching content and studies of educational philosophy aren't that important. Most people figure out how to teach as they go. Instead, more practical instruction is needed, such as how to keep your rear end from jiggling too much when you erase the chalkboard, because that's one of the first things your students will notice.

I'm not saying that these theories are unimportant or invalid. (That would be a little presumptuous of me, now wouldn't it?) What I mean is that schools would be better served by giving teachers more practical advice during their training. Far be it from me to criticize the system in place, but this is what I heard over and over again during my interviews. Most teaching candidates want to figure out one thing far more than anything else: how to keep a class under control, especially right after lunch when the cafeteria served Mexican food. Unfortunately, this type of experience can only be gained in a real classroom, and you'll have to figure it out like the rest of us did — on the fly.

When I left college, I was chock full of educational theory. In fact, if you poked me in the stomach (like they do that little Pillsbury Doughboy), I would giggle and inadvertently name the five characteristics of a behavioral objective. Of all the things that were forced into me like commuters onto a subway, two things still lurk about in my memory: Maslow's hierarchy of needs and Piaget's cognitive stages. I thought that those theories were pretty neat, and I strove to involve them in some way or another in my curriculum.

For a moment, let me remind you about Maslow's pyramid of needs (if you're keeping score at home, this is the second Egyptian reference in this section). Think back on your Educational Psychology course for a moment. According to Maslow, there were five stages of needs, beginning with survival needs and progressing to self-actualization. In order to progress from one level to the next, all your needs from the previous levels had to be completely met. In case you're a little hazy on those needs, Figure 2-1 shows a typical Maslow chart to refresh your memory.

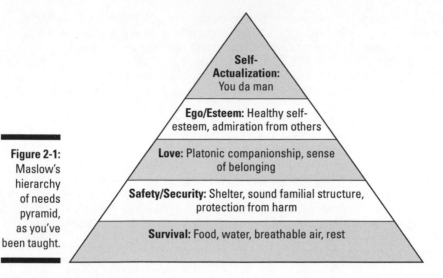

Figure 2-1:
Maslow's
hierarchy
of needs
pyramid,
as you've
been taught.

Here's the thing. How in the world are you supposed to apply that to every-day teaching? In your warm-up activity, do you provide food, progress to shelter construction as a group activity, and then group hug? At what time can you squeeze in your lesson about the difference between gerunds and infinitives? In practical terms, learning falls somewhere between the love and ego/esteem layers (like a delicious cake filling), and students whose previous layers are not iced can't learn as successfully. Can you see the problem with that? You have little control over the basics. You can't really watch their diet at home or make sure that their innate sense of security is intact. All you can do is provide for them while they're in your classroom.

As you gain more and more experience, you'll find out what students really need to feel comfortable and thrive at school. Based on my experience as a high-school teacher, Figure 2-2 shows a more appropriate, albeit a little tongue-in-cheek, hierarchy of the needs of adolescents. As you can see, the most basic need of the average student is to have the coolest possible ride to school, and the ultimate goal of every student is to have a boyfriend or girlfriend, preferably a member of the same school, so everybody knows he or she actually exists, and you're not just making him or her up in a desper-ate attempt to vault over stages of the hierarchy.

Look at that pyramid closely for a moment and notice its most important fea-ture. At no level does learning actually appear in the hierarchy. That's right! Students believe they can reach educational utopia without actually learning anything. I think that would have been useful to know when I was a rookie.

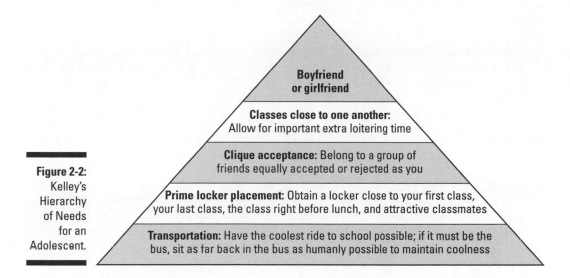

Figure 2-2:
Kelley's
Hierarchy
of Needs
for an
Adolescent.

By the way, while I'm on the topic, here's my favorite quote of Maslow's: "People are not evil; they are schlemiels." This statement truly embodies his humanistic tendencies, saying in essence that mankind is not inherently evil but is just boneheaded sometimes. (He also gets points for using Yiddish.) This philosophy should govern the way you view a class. After all, they're just kids, and they're not purposefully evil (at least not usually). However, some days, you may have to repeat that like a mantra, just to stay sane.

As rigorous as a teacher's educational preparation is, you'll find that most of it has very little worth to you in practical matters. Furthermore, you'll be viewed as pretentious if you actually try to use what you've learned. You may revisit these old topics and theories again as you take courses to either advance in your teaching career or merely keep your certification current. However, you'll rarely find them applied or even remembered in most class-rooms. Your education professors would be appalled!

Piaget gets panned

Okay, so my dream of involving Maslow's pyra-mid wasn't completely dead; I just had to revamp it a bit to make it more applicable. Still, my dream of one day invoking the name of Piaget, and thereby somehow justifying all those philosophy and psychology classes I had to take, was yet unfulfilled. My chance finally came when a representative from the Maryland State Department of Education spoke to the secondary math teachers at an in-service meeting.

We were reviewing prototype items of an upcoming, state-mandated assessment test.

(continued)

(continued)

Somewhere along the line, state administrators had gotten the fantastic idea that testing students out the wazoo was going to improve instruction, elevate test scores, and make the world a happier place in general. However, the questions they planned on asking the kids were extremely advanced. Not only did students have to show mastery of basic math techniques, they had to confront a completely abstract situation and write a brief essay about the underlying mathematical elements that would allow them to solve the problem at hand.

In case you didn't know this, most people fear and hate math in the same way they hate and fear bear maulings, and this test seemed not only scary but way too advanced for the average high-school student. Keep in mind that *every* kid had to pass this test, including low-level and even developmentally challenged students, in order to graduate from high school. The State's position was that a harder test meant a better quality of graduating student. My colleagues' stance: If only 10 percent of students are graduating, isn't that a bad thing?

I had my chance. "Let's remember Piaget for a moment," I chimed in as intellectually as possible. (I wished I had a pipe or something intellectual to puff on.) "According to his study on cognitive stages, adolescents pass into the Formal Operational Stage at varying times in their adolescent years. It is this stage in which students are finally capable of approaching a problem from an abstract perspective and forming deductive arguments and answers. Aren't we penalizing, and in fact *failing,* students for not progressing through Piaget's stages according to our own agenda?"

The room was quiet. People were either considering my proposal or wondering who the blazes Piaget was. Finally, after a few beats of silent introspection, the answer came from the State Department of Education representative. "Regardless, this is the way we're going to go." She delivered her retort with a face that said, "Most educational theories are just treacle anyway, don't you agree?" That's when I knew. Educational theory is all well and good, but no one, even at the highest levels of education, sees any need to actually apply it.

Chapter 3

How Things Have Changed in the Classroom

- -

In This Chapter

▶ Examining recent positive and negative changes in the teaching profession

▶ Understanding and relating to students of the twenty-first century

▶ Adjusting your teaching methods to the needs of modern students

▶ Avoiding conflict by anticipating areas of contention with parents and students

- -

*Y*ou may be young, eager, and willing to bend over backwards to identify with your kids' needs, but you're going to find that the kids you're teaching will little resemble the kid you were at their age (even though, in some cases, you're not *that* much older than they are).

In this chapter, I highlight some of the ways in which contemporary education may differ from the way it has been in the not-too-distant past. Some things have improved (and others have not). You'll need to recognize these changes and adapt in order to keep your instruction meaningful.

Changes for the Better

Most people tend to look back on the past as a simpler, more peaceful, and more idealistic time. They hearken back to the "good old days" and view modern educational theories and advancements as unnatural and unnecessary. However, I want to defy that natural tendency of human nature and first focus on the way that education has *improved* in the last 50 years or so:

✔ **Schools afford the same rights to students of different races.** It wasn't very long ago that schools were segregated. In fact, it wasn't until the 1954 *Brown v. Board of Education* Supreme Court decision (which overturned an 1896 ruling that "separate but equal" facilities were acceptable) that the process of desegregation began. The process did not happen quickly. In fact, some school systems took decades to comply with the ruling. This isn't to say that there is still no racial divide when it comes to achievement and test scores, but these issues could never have been addressed without the Supreme Court ruling that segregation had no place in public education.

✔ **Sexual stereotypes restricting female students are not as common or pervasive as in the past.** Girls took home economics and boys took industrial arts — that's the way it was. When it came to advanced math or science courses, girls were actively discouraged from enrolling. To add salt to the wound, girls were told that their brains weren't capable of handling the abstract thought that went into such courses and were steered away from such classes "for their own good." This is, of course, a ridiculous line of thought, and young girls are finally receiving the encouragement they need to pursue such coursework.

✔ **Teachers are adapting their coursework for students with different types of learning styles.** I would trade in everything I learned in college just for a better understanding of Howard Gardner's *Theory of Multiple Intelligences.* It broke the mold in teaching, finally acknowledging that different students learn in different ways, rather than through lecture, recitation, lather, rinse, repeat. Most likely, you heard about this a lot in college; in fact, you probably made up a drinking game with all your pals in the education program based on the theory ("Every time the instructor says *kinesthetic,* you have to take a drink!").

It is absolutely essential that you understand this theory and apply it in the classroom, for a number of reasons (check out the nearby sidebar for a summary of the theory in case you're a little rusty). First, the theory has tangible and obvious relevance to lesson planning. Second, the general public knows about this theory. It's not uncommon for students to say, "I'm a visual/spatial learner — can you draw a picture for me?" The response, "Well, I'm a bodily/kinesthetic teacher. Would you like a punch in the mouth?" is, at best, counterproductive.

✔ **Schools are addressing student needs other than merely curricular needs.** This is both a positive and a negative, but the rewards slightly outweigh the drawbacks. Your role as an educator is more than simply an imparter of knowledge. You must also demonstrate and model acceptable social behavior, especially in this increasingly depersonalized age. Unfortunately, much of society expects teachers to act as surrogate parents, and at times you'll feel overwhelmed by all the different roles you have to play in your students' lives. However, if not you, then who else?

✔ **Teacher salaries are beginning to rise.** No longer does teaching mean a life of poverty. However, the pay is still nowhere near proportional to the skills you possess and the training you endured. Be careful, though. Some school systems are cooking the books when it comes to salaries. Make sure to look carefully at the salary scale for your school system. Some schemes draw you in with high initial salaries but will only offer you modest increases for the rest of your career and max out fast. If there isn't a lot of disparity between the starting and ending salaries in your district, ask yourself if the money you're making now will still be attractive to you when you're retiring.

All in all, the profession of teaching has made some terrific strides in a very short time. Make sure to keep these in mind as you enumerate the ways in which things have, instead, worsened.

A quick review of Gardner's Theory of Multiple Intelligences

In case you're hazy on the whole multiple intelligences idea, here's a quick review of Howard Gardner's Theory of Multiple Intelligences. As you prepare your daily lessons, you need to consider how to involve each of these groups in your teaching. Understanding individual intelligences helps you understand how to deal with each student on a personal level, so that you can gain the trust and respect of each.

✔ **Logical/Mathematical Intelligence:** Students learn best when posed with complex reasoning exercises. They enjoy peeling apart layer upon layer of a situation to find patterns and typically approach things from an abstract viewpoint. These students want to figure things out on their own.

✔ **Musical/Rhythmic Intelligence:** Learners are especially sensitive to rhythm, sound, tone, and cadence of language. Rhymes and songs that accompany your lessons are especially helpful for this group.

✔ **Bodily/Kinesthetic Intelligence:** Don't fence in these folks. They need to be active and moving around to learn best. They tire of constant notes and pine for activities that get them off their seats and into the action.

✔ **Verbal/Linguistic Intelligence:** It's all about your delivery for these guys. Your speech rather than your gestures and notes, burns your lessons directly onto their brains. They're typically good at word manipulation and debating as well.

✔ **Visual/Spatial Intelligence:** Don't be surprised if this group doesn't take notes. (Neither do lazy or unmotivated students, and you'll have to figure out how to tell the difference.) It's all in the eyes. If a student cranes her eyes upward when she tries to remember something, she's accessing her visual memory database and is most likely a visual/spatial learner.

✔ **Intrapersonal Intelligence:** This student is extremely self-controlled, humble, and very introspective. Of all my students, my favorites fell under this category, because they were bright, kind, focused, and rarely a behavior problem. Self-motivated and intent upon succeeding, these pearls are

(continued)

(continued)

often overlooked in class because they're not usually very outgoing. Show these students how the material you teach impacts them, or use class time to challenge the way they view the world, and you'll snare an intrapersonal student instantly. They're quick to thought and slow to speech, because thinking is just as important as actually reaching an answer (if not more so).

✔ **Interpersonal Intelligence:** These are the great negotiators of your class. Be careful with these guys — they're slick and can instantly derail your train of thought, often to negotiate you out of deadlines and homework. However, if you can help them harness their powers for good rather than evil, they're your ambassadors to the class. They need your lessons presented in a way that's meaningful to their life.

✔ **Naturalistic Intelligence:** These learners feel a connection to nature and the world. It's important that you don't conduct yourself in a way that's offensive to these folks. Do you recycle? You should, and these guys are more than willing to help you plan a program if you don't have one in place. Be sensitive to the naturalists in your class, because what they believe is an integral part of their personality, and they can't learn from you if they find your actions offensive.

In Chapter 2, I give educational theory a hard time. Most people throw theory out the window in the face of a live, writhing group of third-graders. However, I'll go on record as saying that I think Gardner's theories are important enough to warrant review and reflection before every school year begins, as you decide how to tweak your instructional style.

Changes for the Worse

People love to criticize things. One of the defining aspects of the human race is that people need to feel like they have an important opinion on just about everything. Unfortunately, one of the topics about which people like to contribute their two cents is the world of education. In fact, for most people, two cents is just the cover charge — they're more than willing to open up a line of credit if the topic of conversation is the state of America's school system.

Any criticism of education is typically a criticism of society in general. Kids are changing, parents are changing, and rules are changing, but most of these changes are simply repercussions of other, more sweeping societal changes occurring outside school walls. You can do your best to mold the minds of your students, but remember that you only see them for so many hours in the day. There are a lot of other influences at work in them as well.

✔ **Teachers, as authority figures, are not automatically deemed worthy of respect.** When, exactly, did school become the establishment and students become the oppressed minions? Was it the day teachers started wearing Viking hats and reinstated the whipping post as punishment for sloppy handwriting? No one knows for sure, but the type of respect that Beaver Cleaver had for his teachers on television isn't the norm anymore. Authority figures don't have the same inherent influence they used to.

In fact, some students even liken school to prison. If you stop to think about it, the systems are not altogether different. Regulated schedules, designated break periods in the "yard," and strict rules governing every aspect of day-to-day life are the norm in both cases. Because most adults don't like being supervised too closely, and even view a little law breaking, like excessive speed or careless driving, justifiable and even necessary, kids reflect that behavior. Therefore, those who are there to control and enforce the rules are the party poopers and the bad guys. Again, children respect teachers less because most adults treat their authority figures (the President, their bosses, the police) with contempt as well.

✔ **Parents are more willing to side with their child in a student-teacher conflict.** If my teacher called home to tell my parents I was misbehaving in school, man oh man, there was going to be trouble when I got home. Not so anymore. I've already discussed the societal tendency to distrust those in authority, and parents are more than willing to believe their child over you for all kinds of reasons.

First, believing their child means that *you're* the one who has the problem by overreacting, whereas their precious angel (whom they're responsible for) remains without blemish or sin. Second, what does a new teacher know? I mean, if you were an experienced teacher, then *maybe* they'd consider the charges, but a rookie has to have the facts all wrong. Finally, punishing their student causes conflict in the household and is, all in all, a real downer for the whole family, especially if the kid is being punished for a reason the parent didn't even witness.

Have your facts, evidence, and witnesses straight when you approach a parent conference or phone call. I go into more specific detail in Chapter 15.

✔ **Parents are far quicker to bring legal action against you.** Again a reflection of society, parents are fully aware of both their rights and the rights of their students. If they feel you're infringing on these rights in any way, they won't hesitate to climb right to the top of the ladder to complain. They don't like your class rules or the way you disciplined their kid? They're calling the local superintendent. Your job can be lost in a fraction of a second, so always consider how your actions could be interpreted if you had to defend them in a court of law, because you just may need to do so.

If at all possible, avoid legal entanglements, even if it means occasionally compromising along the way. In other words, instead of fighting tooth and nail with parents every time you disagree, you'll have to choose your fights carefully. How do you decide when a cause is worth fighting for? Let your conscience be your guide. (I discuss the idea of "picking your fights" with students in Chapter 8, and you can apply most of the same principles to arguments with parents.)

A calculated cheating scandal

As a rule, students don't like to rat on one another; that is to say that they're hesitant to turn state's evidence on someone, even if they really have the goods on them. However, I overcame that modest reservation in my students by offering extra credit to students who tattled on one another, especially when it came to cheating.

It was through just such an informant that I learned about my first scandal. Evidently, one of my calculus classes had masterminded a plan to cheat on a test. About 75 percent of the students figured out how to store their class notes in their handheld calculators. Because calculators were allowed on the exam (and these calculators are relatively advanced), they were able to type, word for word, notes and class examples into the devices and use them without drawing any attention to themselves during the exam.

However, by the time I found out about the scandal, the school day was over, and some of those involved found out I'd been tipped off. The next day during class, I collected calculators as the students walked in and examined their computer memories. Of the 19 students in class, only 4 still had the illegal content stored. Many of the others had either ditched the notes after class or erased them upon hearing of my anonymous informant.

It was devastating to me. I had taught most of those students for three or four consecutive years, and I was very upset to think that they'd betray my trust and confidence. Of the four I caught, only one admitted any wrongdoing, and the parent of that child was very cooperative with both the principal and me. One student originally resisted any wrongdoing but eventually confessed: "That class is hard, and I'll use any means necessary to gain an advantage. You caught me this time, but I'll do it again, if not in your class, then in another one."

The other two cheaters were far less upfront about their motives or guilt in the matter, and their parents were a large part of the reason. They wouldn't believe, even for a moment, that their children had participated in a cheating scandal of unprecedented proportions at the school. In their minds, if 14 students did something, then clearly the teacher didn't make it clear that what they were doing was wrong. "Did Mr. Kelley ever *say* that you weren't allowed to use notes on the test? How can he prove it?"

Furthermore, even if they were wrong, was the school prepared to discipline 14 of its brightest students? What about the kids who cheated but were smart enough to erase the evidence? Wouldn't they get punished? Additionally, how was any of this fair to their poor, poor, child who was identified so cruelly as a cheater in front of all her peers? Some parents were even considering legal action against the school and against me personally.

The result? None of the students were suspended, and the four I caught were allowed to receive 59 percent of the grade they earned on the exam. You read that right — they didn't even get a 0 on the exam. This decision was partly my principal's and partly mine, because we knew that any other decision would probably result in hearings, legal battles, and hassles that just weren't worth the lost time and extra work that would follow.

By the way, I received a note from a colleague when I felt the most dejected. She wrote that she'd experienced a similar ordeal when she caught some honors students plagiarizing their research papers. Her advice, and it was sound advice, was to remember that these are just kids, and they don't usually stop to consider the consequences of their actions. In their minds, it's not personal. In fact, they rarely stop to contemplate their actions beforehand at all. Above all, she reminded me not to question the trust and respect my other classes and I shared. Good advice.

Don't get overwhelmed by the way some things have changed for the worse. Most of the same challenges, in one form or another, face people in every profession, so society's not picking on you personally, even though it sometimes feels that way.

What's With These Kids Today?

Today's kids are a completely different breed than they were even ten years ago. They eat different things, they sing different songs, and they watch different cartoons than you did. If you need convincing, spend one Thanksgiving really watching the Macy's Thanksgiving parade. I used to know who all those giant balloon characters were. Hey, look, it's Garfield, and there's Snoopy and Underdog! There are a lot more balloons I can't identify anymore, so I guess cartoon technology has progressed beyond the Speed Racer of my youth.

It would be more than a little naïve of me to say that changes in cartoon culture are the most far-reaching and influential changes affecting the youth of today. In fact, twenty-first-century children have a lot more on their minds than I did when I was young. Reality, usually harsh reality, has already rained on the innocence that used to radiate from young children. Here are just a few of the ways kids of today are different from kids from a couple of generations ago:

 ✔ **Kids know a lot more about sex a lot earlier than they used to.** Even very tame and family-friendly television shows talk about sex frequently, and they often depict it quite graphically. This type of programming is not scheduled with the ultimate purpose of corrupting our youth; it merely reflects the morals and standards by which the majority of society abides. Kids don't know about sex because there's a lot of sex on TV; kids know a lot about sex, because sex is everywhere.

 Throw in the fact that the kids are entering, learning about, or being faced daily with the ravages and blessings of puberty, and you end up with kids who have sex on their minds constantly. Even younger kids are more likely to notice sexual references, even if they can't yet identify with the biological urges motivating them. One thing you can be sure of: If there's any way what you say in class can *possibly* have some unintentional sexual connotation, your students will find it, and they'll uncover it with lightning speed.

 ✔ **Kids probably know more about technology than you do.** This has generally been the rule for about 25 years, but technology back then meant being able to rack up a high score in Space Invaders or knowing the score in Pac Man that caused the machine to malfunction. These days, you have to be computer literate, sometimes just to be able to turn your grades in at the end of the grading period or turn in your attendance each day. The good news is that your students are more than willing to teach you what they know and help you become more comfortable with computers if you're not already.

✔ **The gap between students who want to do well in school and those who are uninterested in school has widened.** There have always been kids who are interested in doing well in school and those who couldn't care less about what their grade is, just as long as they pass for the year. The students falling into the latter category have gotten far more scientific in their approach to meeting those minimal requirements. You'll regularly hear students say things like, "I have a 62 average in the first three grading quarters for your class, which means I only need a 54 percent this quarter to pass. So, I'm not going to waste my time studying for this test; I can manage a 54 with my eyes closed."

On the other hand, students who are intent upon always getting high scores and attaining a grade point average so high it can be actually be spotted by astronauts in space are fighting tooth and nail for every point they can manage. These "grade grubbers" will argue every deduction on a quiz and (with bottom lips quivering in mock sincerity) confide in you that "My mother is going to kill me if I get anything less than an A on this test! I'm serious! She took a large insurance policy out on me just last month!"

Stand firm in the face of grade grubbers and don't kill yourself trying to motivate the chronically unmotivated. I give you some coping strategies for both in Chapter 12.

✔ **Kids are coming to school with a lot more emotional baggage than they used to.** You may be limited in the number of carry-on bags you can bring onto an airplane, but some students have no such limit for emotional baggage. Although depressing to think about, histories of abuse, neglect, and indifference leave some students emotionally unavailable to you when you begin class. It takes time for these students to trust you, and sometimes even trust is not enough for them to overcome the issues they're dealing with at home to allow for a successful academic year.

For example, one of the teachers I spoke to had a young woman who was emotionally distant in class, who was unable to focus or keep her mind straight. After some snooping and some shrewd observations, the teacher realized that one of the boys in her class was actually "pimping" her to other students during the school day! He was, in fact, scheduling paid sexual rendezvous for her, against her will, with male students throughout the school day. The girl was humiliated, clearly intimidated, and scared out of her wits. Upon making the discovery, the teacher had him removed permanently from class, and the girl was finally able to focus again.

Stay fully upgraded

I am an insufferable computer geek. Ever since I was in the sixth grade, I've loved tinkering around with, playing video games on, and writing programs for computers. The one thing that never ceases to amaze me about these machines is their lightning-fast evolution. In college, I had one mean computing machine, the Commodore 64 computer, which most people nowadays haven't even heard of.

It was not a computing giant, but it was cheap and dang handy. In fact, you didn't even have to buy a monitor — it just hooked right up to your television set. However, in the eight years since I graduated from college, computers have changed from a cute little video abacus into a juggernaut of electronic and number-crunching fury.

The technology advances alone are staggering. The computer sitting on my desk is nearly 2,100 times faster than my little Commodore and requires approximately 4,000 times the amount of memory! Keep in mind this is only eight years of advancement in computer technology. By the time you finish unpacking a new computer from the box, it's already well on its way to being obsolete.

Kids and society evolve just as quickly as computers do. Even if you've only been in college for four or five years, you'll be surprised just how much young people have changed while you were away. Lingo has changed. Dress has changed. In many cases, even morality has begun to mutate. The societal line between right and wrong is a living, breathing entity and is constantly changing. Do your best to stay in touch with the culture of the youth you're teaching so that you can speak to them in terms they'll understand. (But don't forget to always act your age — refer to the discussion of Neverland in Chapter 1.)

One word of caution: Newer and flashier is not always better. Did you know that the computers in the Apollo spacecraft (the rockets that landed on the moon) were less powerful than most handheld calculators of today? Those computers accomplished amazing, inspiring, and wondrous things, and so can you, even if you're not the newest model on the market.

You already have a lot of roles to play in the drama of your students' lives, and those lives have become more and more complicated in this modern age. You'll have to decide early on how willing you'll be to address the issues that face them outside the classroom as well as inside. I've always found that a teacher who is aware of the reality facing today's students and isn't afraid to address tough issues when they arise is far more effective than a teacher who chooses to be blind to the adversity facing his students, erecting yet one more wall of isolation in those students' lives.

Part II
Managing Your Classroom

The 5th Wave   By Rich Tennant

"Of course graphics are important to your project, Eddy, but I think it would've been better to scan a picture of your worm collection."

In this part . . .

The school year is closing in. Before long, students are going to be streaming through your classroom doors, and you'll feel like you're Dorothy in that giant cyclone that took her to Oz. So much is happening so fast, you can hardly figure out which way is up!

First things first: You need to get acquainted with your school and get yourself ready for the dreaded start of classes. In this part, I walk you through that first day, and help you get things started on the right foot. But the first day is just the beginning! What can you do to both keep your kids under control for the rest of the school year and earn their respect in the process (without giving out money to win them over)? In this part, I give you some practical advice about classroom management, and even help you manage your reputation with a few frank words about sexual harassment.

Chapter 4

Finding Your Way Around

● ●

● ●

*E*very school is a completely unique beast unto itself. At first glance, you can see that blueprints and floor plans are different from one school to another, but the differences extend much deeper than that. Each school also has its own personality based on its inhabitants, its vision, and the number of french fries you get when you buy lunch.

In other chapters, I discuss how you fit into the world's perception of education in general, but in this chapter, I help you fit into the specific environment of your school. Before you can be a success there, you need to understand how the school is run, who the important players are, and how to make sure that you're not causing too many waves when you first set your dinghy into the water.

Topping Your To-Do List: Read the Rule Book

Depending upon the personality of your principal, your school may have very strict or very laid-back rules about day-to-day behavioral issues. However, all schools have black-and-white policies when it comes to core issues, and these policies are all set forth in your faculty handbook. You should receive one of these massive binders on or before the first day you report to work. Definitely read this massive text, even though it's probably the last thing in the world you want to do. Why? The worst thing a rookie teacher can do in a new school is to start off by breaking the big rules.

I know that you have lesson plans to create, textbooks to track down, and decorations to hang before students show up, but spend your first day carefully reading that faculty handbook. You'll be held responsible for adhering to all the rules in that binder, and claiming that you didn't know something was wrong because you didn't have time to read the handbook isn't going to endear you to your principal.

Finessing fire drills

Most schools have to follow a state-mandated plan of fire drills; for instance, my school was required to have one each month. (Some schools also have earthquake and tornado drills, but they're not very different in spirit.) When the fire alarm sounds, your school has specific expectations of you. And because these expectations may vary from school to school, you need to understand exactly what is expected of you, and the rulebook should cover this topic in detail. Watch out — the fire alarm is loud and usually catches you completely off guard. You won't be able to think clearly when it goes off, especially if the kids are startled. (The fire drill in my school was so loud that I almost swallowed my tongue every time it trumpeted.)

Most schools require you to do the following:

- ✔ **Make sure that students know the appropriate evacuation route ahead of time.** This is no big deal for secondary teachers; however, for elementary-school teachers, this requirement means explaining what a fire drill is all about and how to react to the alarm. Don't panic students with stories of raging infernos; instead, introduce the fire drill as a natural part of school, which can be expected and reacted to in a calm fashion. Teach your students more than one way of escaping your classroom, in case one exit is blocked by fire. Younger children need practice if you don't want them to panic when the alarm goes off unexpectedly.

- ✔ **Don't leave your classroom until all your students are out.** I hope that I don't have to explain why. Take a minute and try to think whether any of your students are out of your room, at the water fountain, or in the bathroom. If so, you need to round them up. Don't leave a little boy running through the hallway with his underpants down around his ankles, panicked because the fire alarm went off the first time he got his courage up to use the bathroom during school. (If you're curious, yes, that little boy was me in third grade, and I'm still traumatized because my teacher didn't wait for me.)

- ✔ **Take your attendance book with you, and check roll to make sure that all your students are with you.** At this point, you usually have to write a note signifying that all your students are present, write your name on it, and send it with a student to a designated area where an administrator will collect it. This way, the principal knows if any students aren't accounted for.

✔ **Keep your students in one place and continue to supervise them.** The fact that you're outside doesn't mean that you don't have to keep an eye on your kids. You should be on alert for anything and ready to herd your students to a safer area if need be. If your designated evacuation area is near a main road, make sure that the kids stay away from it. It would only take a second for a passing motorist to pull an unsupervised student into his or her car and leave without a trace. How's that for a terrifying thought? Not only would you be fired, you'd probably be on the news as well!

If older kids have to pass through a parking lot to get to your designated meeting spot, make sure that you watch them closely. Some students may seize the opportunity to causally drag a key across Mrs. Rodriguez's car and ruin her paint job because she failed them in Spanish last marking period.

Enforcing policy: Honor codes, dress codes, and secret codes

Even when you aren't dealing with an emergency, schools have plenty of rules and regulations to follow. Each and every day, you'll have to enforce policy, so you should once again refer to your teacher's manual, paying special attention to the following rules, if they apply to you. Make sure that you can answer all the questions I list for each policy item.

Honor code

Does your school have a policy concerning academic dishonesty, aside from saying that it's bad? Are there clear consequences if a student is caught cheating? How do you report such an incident? Is there a peer-review board? You should know all these things because accusing someone of such transgressions is very serious business, and you want to make sure that you follow procedures if you suspect it in your class.

Attendance policy

Is there a maximum number of days that a student can be absent from school, whether excused or not? How many times can a student be late to your class before the administration steps in? What happens if a parent drops his or her child off at school late? What sort of paperwork needs to be filled out if a student's tardiness or absenteeism is becoming a problem? How do you report your attendance every morning to the main office? Who accepts parents' excuse notes when a child is absent — you or an attendance official? When attendance gets ugly, the result may be that a student doesn't receive credit for the school year or doesn't advance to the next grade. Make sure that you know exactly how attendance works before the first day of school.

"Fired" drill?

When I was a rookie, I was very good about fire drills. I knew the drill, so to speak, and I was on top of every last detail. I felt confident in my role as Emergency Protector Guy. As the years rolled by, I began to get a little more lax in my fire-drill procedures. Sometimes, I'd forget my attendance book and sort of fudge my way through the head count after I got outside. "Does it look like everyone's here? No one trapped by burning rubble? Fine." Fire drills became old news, and they quickly lost both their intrigue and immediacy in my mind. I knew this was bad, because if there ever were an emergency, I'd be caught off guard, but what were the chances of that?

Well, nothing tragic ever happened, but something very sneaky did. At the apex of one particularly ordinary fire drill, I was about to do my ordinary attendance check and send it with the ordinary note that said, "All present." On a spur of motivation, I decided to actually crack open the attendance book and take roll. Guess what? One of my students was gone. I swore she'd been in my classroom with me not two minutes ago, and I saw her leave with everyone, but now she was completely AWOL. She was a nice kid, too — very responsible and polite — so I knew she wasn't darting away for an impromptu make-out session with her boyfriend in the forest surrounding the athletic field where I stood, dazed.

What should I do? I knew that she was alive and safe, or was at least relatively sure about both. Should I send down the ordinary "All present" note and hope for the best? Who would really find out I was lying, anyway? She was alive, right? What to do? What to do? At last, I

swallowed my pride and submitted a note that read, "Gail Friffindorf is missing, and I cannot account for her. Very sorry. Will clean out my desk and be gone by the morning." (By the way, I'm reasonably sure that Friffindorf was not her actual name.)

Moments later, my vice-principal approached, accompanied by the student with whom I'd sent the note. The V.P. was not a happy lady, and the kid looked stricken, sure I was at the very least in big trouble, and very possibly about to die at the hand of the administrator, right there in front of the whole class. However, when the towering administrator got up to me, she broke out into a laugh (she had a great sense of humor on top of being fantastically strong and intimidating).

Before my class began, she'd actually instructed Gail to "disappear" after the fire alarm sounded. The administration wanted to know who was actually taking roll and who was just playing along, and I passed the test. Sweet, little, innocent Gail was a double agent! I was shocked and more than a little impressed at her mild act of subterfuge. More important, though, the point had been driven home in my mind. Even though these drills were interminably boring, they were nonetheless important for the safety of my students.

Had I been a rookie teacher, that would have been a defining moment in the decision whether to rehire me. Neglecting my duty to supervise my kids (even if there was no real danger) would've been a big red mark in my personnel record. The moral of the story is twofold: Take your fire-drill responsibilities seriously, and never again trust Gail Friffindorf.

Dress code

Does your school require a uniform of any kind? What sorts of clothes are forbidden at your school? Are shorts allowed? If so, how short is too short? Are there restrictions on the lengths of skirts or the necklines of girls' tops? Can students wear hats inside the building? What sorts of T-shirts are considered inappropriate for school? How many piercings is too many? Are nose and tongue rings okay?

The dress code is a very sticky issue in secondary schools. Students really want to stand out from their peers in one way or another, and clothing is the easiest way to stand out from the crowd, aside from dying your hair colors that nature never intended, which is also all the rage. Always be on your guard, because students will constantly try to slide things by unnoticed.

You have to be consistent and relentless when it comes to dress-code enforcement. This is grueling work because it never ends. Administrators are slow to punish dress-code offenses with strict penalties because doing so brings negative publicity. Even though parents know the dress code ahead of time, they often don't agree with it and have no problem with their children employing a little civil disobedience in their clothing choices. By the way, be very careful how you handle dress-code violations when the offenders are of the opposite sex; I discuss this in more detail in Chapter 9.

Hall-pass procedures

Does your school have a standardized hall pass? How many hall passes can you issue in a class period before the administration thinks that it's too many? Can you send out more than one student at a time if there are conflicting emergencies?

I always enjoyed wacky hall passes; they were a lot more fun than the standard clipboard pass that students would sign out when they left. I had two favorite passes. One was a 6-foot-tall cardboard standup of Captain Picard from *Star Trek: The Next Generation* that students had to carry with them on their trips to the restroom. Oh, the stories that little gem generated. You can imagine how surprising it would be to see a tall man standing outside the stalls in the girls' restroom. That eventually was phased out, due to water damage (and, no, I don't want to think about how that could have happened). I eventually settled on a 4-foot-tall red plastic candle used to decorate lawns for Christmas. Eventually, one of my school's administrators tried to shame me publicly by stating that "tacky lawn ornaments" were not appropriate passes because you couldn't record students' names and the dates and times they were out of the room on such an eyesore. Instead, he mandated clipboards for all hall passes. I had no choice but to comply, so I duct taped a clipboard to my giant candle. Now *that's* an eyesore. (By the way, you may want to wait until you get tenure to do something like that.)

Dressing down on Day One

Shortly after I began teaching, our school got a new principal, and one of his first agenda items was to tighten up the enforcement of the dress code in our building. The dress code was a big deal for the school system in general; the rules were numerous and extremely specific.

Even when it came to "suggestive" or "inappropriate" clothing, the rules were very clear. No tank tops. No spaghetti strap tops. No plunging necklines. Shorts were another matter. One year, no shorts were allowed; the next, shorts were okay but only if they fell within 1 inch of the knee. Another year allowed 3 inches of thigh to be exposed. So many rule changes were made in such a short period of time that students felt they could probably wear anything to school (even if it violated the rules), plead ignorance, and be forgiven for their fashion transgressions. Strangely enough, the same population of students kept "forgetting" the rules.

To be honest, I was ready for the new crackdown on dress code. Some days, my algebra class looked like a nightclub, except with desks. Girls wore shirts with completely open backs, held on only by thin strings. Guys wore their jeans so low that the waistline occasionally chafed their knees. Why so low? So they could show off boxer shorts that they wore over their real underwear.

Enter the new principal. He decided that during freshman orientation (an event held the Friday before school started, during which only freshman would report to school and learn their way around the building), he would stand outside the auditorium as the students arrived. Any students who didn't meet the dress code would be pulled aside and led to the office by a pair of teachers who would explain why they violated the dress code (as if they didn't know). The students would then have to call their parents at work and ask them to bring a change of clothing.

My buddy Rob and I were those two teachers. We led the incoming freshmen on the walk of shame from the auditorium to the main office, during which most of them would sob loudly and heavily. It was their first day of school and they were already in trouble — and they could easily have prevented it. Because of all the weeping and drama, that little parade of fashion violators became known affectionately as the Tear Train.

The train rolled out every year from then on, but the number of passengers quickly lessened because the message spread as quickly as butter on a hot griddle: "They enforce the dress code at school, and if your parents can't get off work to bring you a change of clothes, you have to wear these giant, old, oversized gym uniforms that make you look like a disheveled hobo." The Tear Train is a great example of how to appropriately enforce school policy. Strict, by the books, and consistently enforced, that small effort went a long way toward establishing both the administration's and the faculty's authority and the need for students to follow the rules of the school they were about to enter.

I do love wacky passes, but if you use one, make sure that yours isn't inappropriate and that the school won't mind all that much if you use it.

Do keep in mind that you can go overboard. Having students carry a 60-pound Civil War cannonball to and from the potty is a little much. Be aware that if you use a wacky hall pass, you become very visible, and if students are constantly walking through the hallway with a 10-foot-long inflatable goldfish, people are going to think that you have no classroom control because your students are consistently wandering about.

One last thing about hall passes: Never, never, never write a pass for a student to miss someone else's class. Don't assume that one of your students can stay behind and miss gym class to make up a test for you. You're sending an implied and evil message when you do that. In essence, you're saying that your class is more important than the other teacher's class, and that sort of unspoken arrogance, even if unintentional or not meant malevolently, will quickly get you pegged as a "pretty boy" or a "princess" by your colleagues. Don't intrude on other teachers' class time unless you ask that teacher in advance.

Cell-phone policies

Not all schools allow their students to carry cell phones, and those that do usually have very specific policies regarding when they can be used. In my experience, schools allow their students to have them, but they must be turned off during classes. A ringing phone during class means swift and automatic punishment.

Even if there is no strict school policy, you should *never* let your students have access to cell phones or Web-enabled electronic devices during exams. Students can use these items during class to communicate test items and to receive answers from their peers outside the room. Without leaving the room, students can inform all of North America exactly what questions are on your test, and you'll never know it.

Modern phones include features like text messaging, which means kids can type words and symbols back and forth to each other instantly. Think that this is just paranoia? Think again! College kids are starting to get caught cheating with text-messaging phones and devices pretty regularly, and it's only a matter of time until younger kids figure it out as well.

Specific elementary issues

How are students dismissed at the end of the school day? Where do students store their personal items — in a desk or a storage tray? How does the administration want your class to walk through the halls? How do the kids buy lunch? Do students bring in an extra set of clothes in case of an accident? If so, where are these clothes stored? Who's allowed to pick up children from school if the parents are divorced? What do you do if one of your students injures himself at recess? Do you have to file paperwork? Are you allowed to administer first aid?

Some of these issues won't be addressed by school policy. You'll have to stop and consciously apply some common sense. Follow the advice of the Boy Scouts and always be prepared for these situations before they happen.

Reading the faculty handbook is sort of like reading a cookbook. You can only read so far before you start thinking, "Forget it — I'll never remember all this. I'll just read it if one of these things ever pops up." Don't think like that. You need to have the correct administrative policy floating around in the back of your mind so that you can spend your time dealing with the situation instead of having to orient yourself to it.

When I played Little League baseball, the coaches told me that before every play, I should ask myself, "What would happen if he hit the ball to me in the air or on the ground?" That way, if the play was mine to make, I already knew what to do, and I didn't have to spend precious seconds mulling over all the possibilities. The same goes for teaching — a little anticipation goes a long way; otherwise, the play is usually over before you get the ball out of your glove.

Establishing Your Rules

Your classroom has to be an independently functioning piece of the school surrounding you, and it will function best if you assign meaningful rules and reinforce them consistently. However, choosing your class rules is a bit over-whelming. A few rules are obvious: No fighting, no gum chewing, no jabbing your neighbor with your pencil and breaking the point off in his or her leg — that sort of thing. The rest of the rules are pretty much up in the air, and you'll have to pick out a set that best complements your personality.

Do you hate it when students talk out of turn in class or interrupt one another? One of your rules had better be that students must raise their hands to be recognized by the teacher. Do you hate it when students bolt out of their seats when the bell rings, even if you're in midsentence? You'd better stipulate that you, the teacher, and not the bell, dismiss class. In other words, identify your idiosyncrasies and form your rules with them in mind so that students won't constantly be trampling on your last nerve without even knowing it.

My favorite elementary-school teacher, Ms. Breslin, had one particularly personal rule that I still remember. On the first day of class, she ran down the three big no-nos in her class:

✔ Never say "Shut up" to anyone in my class, or you'll miss recess.

✔ Never laugh at another student's mistakes.

✔ Never, ever, say the word *snow.* "I don't care if the weatherman is calling for 3 feet of snow and school will probably be canceled the next day. Just don't say it," Ms. Breslin said.

When you've found out just how wound up kids get about the possibility of days off from school, you can understand exactly why that final rule was put in place. It perfectly illustrates a practical way to keep kids from irritating you, and I remember it as clearly as if she had told me yesterday.

Here are a few other things you should keep in mind as you create your set of class rules:

- ✔ **Your rules can be more, but not less, stringent than the rules of the school.** Think of yourself as an independent state in a larger nation. If national law says that murder is illegal, state legislature can't make a less restrictive law, for example, allowing murder in Idaho. Similarly, if your school specifically states that wearing hats indoors is against the rules, you cannot turn around and allow hats in your classroom, even if indoor hat use doesn't bother you at all.

- ✔ **Keep the rules simple, but not too simple.** My first set of class rules was approximately four single-spaced, typed pages. I had a rule for every eventuality and every circumstance. I told students when they could sharpen pencils, when and how often I would answer questions, and whom I thought they should ask out to the prom. That's a bit much. However, too few rules leave things open to interpretation, and that's always a bad thing. Students get more and more like lawyers every day, and you don't want to afford them a chance to "work the system." Generally speaking, the younger the kid, the fewer rules you should have in the room. This doesn't mean you are more lenient, it just means your rules should be more general and easier to remember, such as "Do your best," "Be kind to others," and "Don't throw the turtle."

  One of my teachers had only one rule: Do what is necessary. There's a problem with that directive, which I hope jumps right out at you. That's exactly what everyone does every minute of the day, without being told. People breathe, people blink, people cry when they fail quizzes, and people conduct themselves in a way that they think is appropriate. This rule doesn't help the students understand what you expect of them, which is the whole point of rules in the first place — you're trying to explain how to succeed in the artificial environment you've created.

- ✔ **Don't get too specific, or you'll paint yourself into a corner.** What's wrong with the rule, "You may go to the restroom only two times each marking period, so do not ask for extraneous bathroom passes"? As soon as you limit the number of passes students can get, those potty breaks are considered personal leave. In other words, students may make a point of using their two breaks each marking period, even if they just want to get up and stretch their legs. Staying current with everyone's passes is a record-keeping nightmare, and if they aren't over the limit, you've left yourself no right to deny someone the right to leave the room, even if you suspect something fishy, such as a rendezvous with a significant other at a secluded spot in the auditorium.

On the other hand, what happens when a kid has three significant emergencies during one marking period? Can you really deny him access to the bathroom if he's sweating, crying, and doing a dance that can only be described as "urgent"? Breaking the rule puts the first trickle of water through the dyke, and soon enough, just like the little Dutch boy who tried in vain to stem the tide, you're going to run out of fingers to plug up the holes.

✔ **State your rules in a positive way.** Remember, you're not writing rules as shatteringly important as the Ten Commandments, so there's no need to begin each with "Thou shalt not," such as "Thou shalt not haveth thine notes before thee during thine exams." This is especially true with younger kids, who respond much better to rules that are positively, rather than negatively, phrased. For example, "Walk in the hallways" is a much friendlier translation of "Don't run in the hallways."

✔ **Make your rules a visible part of your classroom.** Young children cannot just be told the rules and be expected to comply. You need to *teach* them appropriate behavior, just like you teach them the rest of your school-appointed curriculum. Practice walking in a line, walking quietly, and not punching one another in the eye. To keep the rules foremost on everyone's minds, and to make referencing them easy, post them on the walls of the room.

The best way to make sure that your rules are appropriate is to have a veteran teacher look over them and give you her opinions on their feasibility, appropriateness, and enforceability.

Most of this chapter is about rules, but so will the handful of days you spend at work before the students arrive. When you feel comfortable operating under the structure of your school's policies, you can move on to other things to prepare yourself for the school year.

Getting Your Bearings

Make it a point to meet as many people in the school as you can before the students arrive and teaching becomes your primary task. Start with the people housed in the rooms surrounding yours. Hopefully, these people teach either the same grade as you or the same subject area, so you always have an icebreaker for your initial conversation. For example, if you're a biology teacher, you can say something like, "So, how about that photosynthesis, huh? Pretty crazy stuff!" (Go ahead and use that line — you have my permission.)

Finding a buddy teacher

You're bound to find a veteran teacher with whom you feel comfortable and who doesn't mind helping out a rookie in need. Even though some veterans don't like rookies much at all, you'll find someone willing to take you under his or her wing. This individual, whom I will refer to as your *buddy teacher,* is the most important part of a successful first year. You'll have so many rules, so many meetings, and so many multicolored memos in your mailbox that you'll go nuts if you don't have someone who's already been through the fire and survived. Some school systems pair you up with such a person, but that doesn't preclude you from making some friends on your own.

By the way, you should have your buddy teacher take a look at your student rosters when you get them because you should find out ahead of time if any of the kids have really bad reputations. Those touchy-feely teacher books adamantly oppose such a practice, arguing that it causes you to "label" the student and automatically expect poor behavior from him or her, thus continuing the cycle of learned helplessness and not allowing to the student to blah, blah, blah. . . . Be realistic. You want to know who's most likely to stab you or steal your purse if it's left unattended for ten seconds. That doesn't mean that you should treat that student differently. It's just nice to have a heads up.

You should also find out if you have any celebrities in your classes. These kids aren't stars of the stage and screen — they're people who have a background that you should know about. They have parents on the Board of Education, are the offspring of one of your fellow teachers or administrators, or are in some way politically connected. When it comes to these students, two words apply: *kid gloves.* Don't give yourself an extra headache by making an example out of the state senator's daughter unless she really deserves it, and be ready to deal with the fallout, because it'll be quick and severe.

Pairing up with a fellow rookie

No one quite understands your pain like another rookie teacher, so the second order of business is to scope out a newbie like yourself and attach yourselves to each other at the hip. You need someone to mourn with, celebrate with, vent to, commiserate with, and spend time with outside the classroom. Teaching isn't like other jobs where you can find lots of other people your age whom you talk to every day. In most senses of the word, your students are basically your co-workers, and hanging out with them on the weekends is both weird and wildly inappropriate.

I had two rookie buddies when I started out, Lori and Rob. Lori and I had the same period for planning, and we sat together every day, planning lessons, sharing horror stories, and bleakly wondering if we'd survive the year. Rob and I became close friends, hung out on the weekends, shared lesson-plan ideas, and had a longtime competition to see who had gone the longest without a real date. Teaching always seemed to devour our time and limit our social excursions, and it was a contest neither of us particularly wanted to win. However, the loneliness and separation that plagued my professional life and personal life were eased significantly thanks to the two of them.

Meeting the administration

The final group you want to touch base with is the set of administrators presiding over your school. A good relationship with these folks is essential to a smooth academic year. Make sure to introduce yourself to every principal and vice-principal at your school. Find out where their individual responsibilities lie so that you'll know where to send troublemakers (not that you'd have any in *your* classes). For example, if a student is a chronic tardiness offender, you should find out who's in charge of attendance-related issues.

Here's a very important tip that I learned the hard way. Make sure to rotate the administrators to whom you report problems whenever possible. One week, approach Dr. Moulton with your class-related woes, but the following week, definitely go see Ms. Neal instead. If you keep working with one administrator, he or she is eventually going to get tired of looking at you or is going to think that you're way too needy. I don't mean that administrators don't want to help you; they do. However, in their minds, the number of times they see you in one school year is inversely proportional to your success for that year. In other words, if they don't see you too often, things must be going well.

Mapping Out Important Locations

My school must have been designed by bees. The building has an infinite number of teeny little passageways that wind around one another and twist and turn in ways you could never possibly anticipate. No matter how hard a new student tried to find his or her way around, that student was doomed from the start. All the hallways were mirror images of one another, and the building had no windows, so you couldn't even get the lay of the land. It took me a week of school to figure out where the gym was, and seven years later, I still couldn't navigate the English wing.

Touring the school on your own before students arrive is definitely worthwhile. That way, you can feel more comfortable in your natural habitat and assist the students when they get lost. To start with, you should find your room, the cafeteria, the main office, and all the adult restrooms near these locations. You should also look for these key places, each of which will be extremely important to you sooner or later:

✔ **Faculty lounge:** The fortress of solitude. The cone of silence. (Notice that I did *not* say "the lap of luxury.") This room usually serves as the teacher's lunchroom, coffee filling station, caffeine repository, and home of the refrigerator to house your brown-bag lunch. Oh, the things you'll see in here. Between the frustrated venting, heated debates, and naughty lunch chatter, no room is quite so interesting or dangerous. It's the one place where you'll actually be surrounded by adults, and no one calls you Mr. or Mrs. for a quick, 30-minute stint every day.

You *have* to spend some quality time in the faculty lounge. For one thing, you need to be around people your own age, no matter how committed a teacher you are. They'll become your best friends and allies, and you need their support. If you don't come to lunch and make it a priority to meet your fellow teachers, they'll view you as reclusive and antisocial, and that's how negative rumors begin.

One word of caution about the faculty lounge: Remember that the walls have ears. Don't say anything in there that you don't want to become public knowledge, even if you inherently trust every single person in the room. If you're mad at the principal or ticked off at a colleague, this room is not the place to air your frustrations. I've found that a cosmic rule governs the teachers lounge: If you ever talk negatively about a colleague in the lounge, he or she will walk in right in the middle of your tirade when you're doing an unflattering imitation of that teacher. I swear — it happens four times out of five.

✔ **Copy room:** I love the smell of photocopying toner in the morning, and so will you. It's that friendly little scent that says, "I've planned an excellent lesson with handouts to show for it," or, "I hope the kids will be quiet and leave me alone while they do this stupid word search." Find out if you need a code to operate your copier and what sorts of restrictions and limitations (if any) are placed on the number of copies you can produce each school year. Buy some brightly colored paper to use on the occasional worksheet, just for variety. (Pastel paper is a little easier on the eyes, but it's very overused in schools, so it doesn't have the same effect. The kids have seen hundreds of canary yellow handouts, but retina-scorching neon yellow is always an attention grabber. Any assignment on such paper is automatically more interesting.) The kids appreciate little gestures like that more than you'd think.

✔ **Media center:** If you don't have library time built into your schedule but you still need to take your classes there during the year, find out how to go about scheduling those visits, and sign up as soon as possible. If your students have book reports to do on a regular basis and you plan on getting them into the library, your best bet is to plan those dates at the beginning of the year and claim them on the media center schedule before things get too crowded.

The media center is usually the place to sign out equipment, such as overhead projectors, VCRs and DVD players, tape recorders, and televisions. School budgets aren't high, so these supplies are in great demand,

and it's first come, first served. I needed an overhead projector for the entire school year, so I was always one of the first people in line when the media center opened in order to secure my reservation.

✔ **Personal telephones:** Although some schools provide a telephone in every room for teachers, most aren't so equipped. Although the phones in the main office are fine for normal calls, some calls do require a bit more privacy. How many people need to hear you place a doctor's appointment for your burning rash? In addition, some calls to parents really shouldn't be overheard. If your school doesn't have phones for that purpose, ask to use the administrators' or guidance counselors' phones in private.

You can't really feel comfortable as a teacher in your school until you feel comfortable in the building. Don't be shy about asking other faculty for directions until you get your bearings.

Chapter 5

Setting Up Your Classroom

*Y*ou catch on fast and quickly understand how the puzzle piece of your classroom fits into the larger, overall jigsaw puzzle that is your school. But what about the room itself? How are you going to create an environment that suits your tastes and is both fun and inviting to students?

Elementary teachers usually undertake this responsibility with enthusiasm, exhibiting an almost Martha Stewart–like ability to create amazing decorations from simple construction paper. Secondary teachers, however, are usually much more lackadaisical in their decorating responsibilities.

Remember that your classroom reflects on you directly. A well-done room has its own personality and demands to be examined more closely by those who enter it. It swallows you up, but it makes you happy that you're there.

In this chapter, I discuss the most important parts of your classroom and how to ensure that they're effective and all work together. I even give you tips and direction in case you'll be a "floating" or "roaming" teacher, and thus have no room to call your own.

Building Blue-Ribbon Bulletin Boards

Nothing about teaching intimidated me more than having to create bulletin boards. I'm probably the least artistic person in the world. Trust me. If I tried to draw a buffalo, it would end up looking like a half-eaten bowl of coleslaw.

Therefore, the prospect of having to create a living, interactive piece of artwork in my room was extremely unnerving when I began teaching. However, the good news is that there are ways to create bulletin boards even if you, yourself, haven't a single artistic or creative bone in your body.

In my mind, classrooms have two kinds of bulletin boards: One kind entertains, and the other kind informs. There's nothing wrong with a primarily decorative bulletin board, just as long as that's not the only type you have in your room. You need at least one board, especially if you're an elementary-school teacher, that reflects something you're discussing in class. This instructive board adds unspoken content to your lessons and properly engages those students who are primarily visual.

Designing decorative bulletin boards

Each grade level has a tendency to fall into a stereotypical bulletin board, when the primary focus of that corkboard canvas is decorative. For instance, I think that it's a federal law that elementary-school teachers have a calendar-themed bulletin board. Typically located near the front of the room or near the primary chalkboard, this decorative board hosts a blown-up calendar page with cute, red, cutout apples on the days. March means a green background with leprechauns, clovers, rainbows, and pots of gold. October brings a black or orange background with comical skeletons, black cats, and 17,000 little jack-o-lanterns. Black History Month means the traditional cardboard pictures of Martin Luther King, Jr., Duke Ellington, and George Washington Carver that were around when you were little.

Secondary teachers, you do it, too. How about the ever-present announcements board? You know the one I'm talking about. It has the sports schedule from four months ago and the lunch menu from the first week of the school year stapled to it. Why do I classify these as decorative rather than instructional? You know why. You stop updating them after November passes by, as soon as the administration and your supervisor think that you're keeping it updated daily.

I'm not saying that these stereotypical bulletin boards aren't useful; I'm just saying that they're commonplace and bland. At best, they provide a nice fall-back option if you don't have a better idea. If you're required to keep this kind of bulletin board, I challenge you to do it (even if you must do it on a bulletin board) in a unique way. For example, if you must keep an announcement board, add student birthdays to the list of important school events. Whatever method you use to brighten up your boards, don't simply default to the unoriginal just because the local teacher-supply store sells ready-made calendar packets and the time investment would be minimal.

In the following sections, I give you some decorative bulletin board ideas (some more original than others) to help you break out of your creative slump.

If none of the following ideas appeals to you, you can always try a bulletin board with a positive message about teamwork or an antidrug message. My friend Rob the math teacher gets the gold in this category. His first bulletin board said, "Here's one equation we don't want to solve: students + drugs = ?" I give him points for creativity, with a positive message that even ties into his subject area.

Showcase student work

Nothing is quite so encouraging to a young student as seeing his or her work proudly displayed by the teacher as a paragon of excellence. However, don't let the exhibit get too crowded with tons and tons of outdated work. Remember that parents have refrigerators at home whose magnets are just itching for papers like that.

One word of caution, though: As students get older, they like being singled out less and less. In fact, many middle- or high-school students would be mortified if you hung up their work. You don't want everyone to think that student's a nerd, now do you (thereby subjecting him or her to a cascade of wedgies and quite probably noogies)? Your best bet is to ask a student for her permission before you hang her work up in front of the class. If you do, you get a chance to personally congratulate her and offer sincere words of praise while simultaneously avoiding any legal issues inherent in such a display. Don't forget that your students own the copyright to their work, and you can't use it without their permission, as silly as that may sound! You may not need the express written consent that Major League Baseball requires of you to rebroadcast its games, but you do need students' permission.

To be extra safe, you may want to check in with your school's administration and ask if displaying graded work is okay. Even if it is, make sure the student doesn't have an IEP that prohibits you from doing so. There's no need to get in legal trouble for trying to do something nice!

Another option that I found particularly effective for older students is the "Wall of Fame." Each marking period, one of my bulletin boards would contain the names of my top 25 students (of the approximately 140 students I taught each day). Some students even asked to post a photo of their choosing alongside their names because they were so proud to have been recognized.

Display photos of your class

Kids love pictures, and they like pictures of themselves even more. Nothing personalizes a classroom more than tons of photographs of its inhabitants. This practice fosters a true sense of community while also taking up annoying bulletin board space for which you can come up with no other plan. Talk about turning lemons into lemonade!

Bulletin board tools of the trade

I look back at my first attempts at a bulletin board fondly — and with a slight grimace on my face. Although I put more effort into those displays, they looked terrible. After a few years, however, I absorbed a few tricks from other faculty members, which made my life much easier:

✔ **Use fabric rather than construction paper as your background.** My first boards had the standard construction-paper background, and stapling all those sheets next to each other took forever. When I was done, I still had tons of little seams where the paper met, and I'd used about eight million staples. That's not the bad part, though. Construction paper fades in about ten minutes. If you move anything around, small, dark ghosts always mark the original positions of the relocated items. Fabric doesn't fade nearly as quickly and can be reused year after year. You can buy all sorts of neat and colorful fabrics, and fabric takes about one-fifth of the time to hang as the much-less-durable construction paper. Hang the cloth by stretching it tightly and liberally thumbtacking it all around the borders of the board. Cover up all those unsightly thumbtacks with premade bulletin-board borders from the local teacher-supply store. (Thanks to Jackie Johnson for the tip.)

✔ **Use precut letters or a die-cutting machine for all the words.** Unless you have fantastic handwriting, stick with these options. Whatever you do, don't use those stencils you had in elementary school, or your room will look like an army warehouse. If you've never used a die-cutting machine before (you might call them letter or shape cutters), ask your media specialist how they work. If they're not available to you at your school, they're probably housed somewhere accessible to the teachers of the entire district. Be sure to laminate the paper you use with the die cutter *before* you actually cut out the letters; they'll come out crisp and sturdy. If you cut the letters first and then laminate, you'll have a ton of careful cutting to do, and that takes forever.

✔ **Don't use corrugated paper borders or backgrounds.** Students and adults alike have a predisposed urge to flatten out the ridges in these backgrounds. It's similar to the inborn urge to pop those bubble wrappings that protect the contents of boxes. If you insist on using them, before long, you'll find all sorts of ugly dents in the bulletin board, and for mildly obsessive people like me, that's unacceptable.

Just like every other aspect of teaching, you'll eventually develop your own style of bulletin-board design. Just keep in mind that you want the things you hang up to be as sturdy, reusable, and dynamic as possible.

Find out if your school media center owns a digital camera that you can sign out to snap a stack of pictures during your next class activity. Also, if you don't already, make sure that you subscribe to the local newspaper. Every now and then, you'll find a story about or a picture of one of your kids; clip it and post it on your bulletin board. Be sensitive, however, to students who don't want their pictures taken, or who are embarrassed by any pictures of themselves that you've posted.

Create a scoreboard for student competition

The most important thing I learned as a teacher was that you should never wear a tie with a polo shirt (the kids snicker at you). The second most important thing would have to be that kids *love* competition. It doesn't matter who their quarry is; a fierce (but friendly) day-to-day contest with others can foster a healthy sense of competition and fair play. No matter how much you squawk and flap your arms, some students will never understand that they'll one day have to use the concepts from your class in the real world. However, you can easily make those concepts important in the school world by the simple practice of keeping score.

My brother tells a story of his fourth-grade teacher, who transformed a long bulletin board into a detailed racetrack. Because the movie *Star Wars* was extremely popular at the time, she designed a racetrack located in the far-off world of Dagobah. (I award you ten geek points if you knew that's where Yoda lived.) Each student began at the left side of the board, and moved back and forth based on such things as how many spelling words they got correct and incorrect. He loved it, and it provided all the motivation he needed to study.

If you don't have the same students every period, you can still run a contest. I taught six different classes each day, and in my contest, each was allowed to choose a mascot of some kind, which was posted on the board at the head of the class. At the end of each week, I'd average all the grades I'd given to each class. Say that Period 6 averaged 83 percent for that week; they would, in turn, receive 83 points in the competition. I kept a running total of the points for each class during the marking period, and the class with the most points at the end of the race won a pizza party.

Creating instructional bulletin boards

You should have at least one bulletin board with instructional or practical value in your classroom. These boards don't have to be a burden. In fact, if you play your cards right, they can actually take some of the more annoying burdens off you.

Your instructional bulletin boards are a natural focus point for your room, so make sure that they're neat, well designed, and not trivial in nature. Make it look like you designed the display because it was important to you, not because the school is making you do it, even though that's probably closer to the truth.

In the following sections, I fill you in on a few strategies that I've found make a content-based bulletin board more effective.

Tie in a contemporary theme to your subject

I only remember one bulletin board from all 12 years of grade school, even though I probably saw upwards of 120 of them during that time frame. It was Ms. Momberger's language-arts class bulletin board, when I was in seventh grade; the topic was words that sound alike but have different meanings, like *principal* and *principle.* It doesn't stick in my mind because I was so gassed up about homonyms at the time. Instead, I remember it because I loved the movie *Ghostbusters,* which was all the rage then. And Ms. Momberger's bulletin board was titled "Tricky Word Pairs Don't Scare Us" and featured a large *Ghostbusters* logo at its center, the nervous-looking ghost with the big red slash through it. She confessed to us that she chose that title because the actual *Ghostbusters* motto ("I ain't afraid of no ghosts") was so grammatically incorrect that it made her shudder with revulsion. However, that small effort she made to try to connect with my world made a huge difference.

Design a record-keeping board that reduces your administrative duties

If I had to exercise a little precognition and try to predict what one phrase you'll hear from students more than any other, I'd guess the question, "What did I miss?" Picture yourself at your desk, right before an afternoon class begins. It's been a long day, and you're getting a little frayed and threadbare. Students are filing into the room, a little too boisterously for your liking, and you're attempting to take roll, seat the kids, and retain your last ounce of sanity. Enter little Suzie, who earnestly implores, "I was sick for the last three days. My mom wants to know what work I have to make up."

You're thinking, "What's the big deal? She's trying to stay on top of things. Why would that drive you crazy, you impatient buffoon?" But you're forgetting something. Suzie is the 25th person to ask you the same thing that day, and you feel like you're going to go mad if you have to repeat yourself one more time. Furthermore, if you forget any part of her make-up work (remember that 29 other kids in the room are trying desperately to get your attention at the same time), it becomes *your* fault because you forgot to tell her.

One of the best things in the world is a homework bulletin board. It's a space that houses a list of assignments for all your classes. Every time homework is announced, you or a designated student should jot that assignment down on the homework bulletin board. As long as you keep it updated and accurate, students will know to head straight to that location to get make-up work. Here's the key benefit of this plan: The responsibility has shifted from you to the student, right where it belongs. This strategy works with kids of all ages; just be careful not to ignore students with special needs, who require more individual attention in such matters.

Choose your words carefully

You want your bulletin boards to convey a lot of meaning in as few words as possible. You already know that. What you may not remember is that kids are practical jokers at heart, and, sometimes, rearranging letters on a bulletin board is simply a temptation they cannot resist. Force yourself into an immature mindset when you create your titles to make sure that you're not providing a canvas for a kid with a dream of instant fame.

Here's an example: One of my former colleagues hated Parents' Night. The whole idea of students coming back to school at night with their parents in tow was repulsive to him. Therefore, each year he called in sick that evening, only to return completely healthy the next morning. "Must've been one of those 90-minute bugs," he'd muse slyly. One Parents' Night he fell victim to the bulletin board title switcheroo. His bulletin board about political writing entitled "The Pen Is Mightier than the Sword" took on a whole new meaning when a student moved the second and third words together.

Choosing a Seating Arrangement

Arranging your seats isn't as hard a decision as you may anticipate; the shape and size of your classroom will usually dictate pretty clearly how your classroom must be arranged (you'd be surprised just how oddly shaped some of the rooms are). Before you get to the business of moving your desks around, have a clear vision of what the room will look like. Be sure to factor in a number of variables that may never have crossed your mind.

Feeling the feng shui

I may sound like Mr. Miagi from that fantastic '80s movie *The Karate Kid* (the wizened, old martial-arts instructor with a love of Zen, bonsai trees, painting fences, and awful sequels), but your room has a certain energy and flow to it. You need to stop and smell the *chi* (or life energy, pronounced *chee*) in your room. (If your room hasn't been cleaned in a while, the chi may smell like old cheese curls.)

Practically speaking, you need to consider the following questions when choosing a seating arrangement:

- **Are you going to do a lot of group work or cooperative learning?** If so, you'll probably want to arrange your seats in clumps or clusters.

✓ **How mobile are you?** If you hate being fenced in while you're teaching, you need a big roaming area built into your design. I prided myself on being an entertainer when I taught, so I preferred a "stage" area up front; I had no need to prowl around the room like a cheetah during class.

✓ **Are you into group discussions?** If so, you don't want debating students only able to look at the backs of each other's scalps. (Unless, of course, you're debating scalp-related issues and other heady matters.) If eye contact is needed, eye contact you should allow.

✓ **Where is the chalkboard in the room?** Even better, how often are you going to use it? As a math teacher, I used my chalkboard every minute of the day, so all my students had to have a clear view of it. If you have multiple points of focus in the room (a chalkboard and perhaps a warm-up or objective board, for instance), students will need to see both of them without dislocating their spines.

✓ **Are there windows in your room?** If there are, do you get a clear, retina-scorching view of the sun at any point during the day? If you arrange your seats facing the windows and the sun is blinding during class, that may prove just a wee bit distracting.

✓ **How do you pass back papers?** Believe it or not, how you return students' papers is a foundational issue to how you'll arrange seats. If you insist upon returning papers one at a time, you have to leave aisles wide enough to accommodate students, desks, and book bags. If your backside is knocking desks out of kilter as you squirm through the rows, you need another plan.

✓ **How many kids have special needs?** You should find out ahead of time if any kids need to be in the front row because of visual or auditory problems. You may also want to seat potential troublemakers in the front of the room or closest to you as a preemptive strike toward establishing class control.

After you've answered these questions, you're ready to pick the seating design that best suits your needs. Don't be afraid to change the students' seats or the overall design during the year, but don't do it too often. Elementary-school teachers tell me that their students love the occasional seating-chart change and the new perspective it brings to them. Secondary students, however, are more territorial and prefer not to have things shaken up after they're used to the routine.

Succeeding with seating

Now, the time's come to draw up a plan and move those seats around. Before you start, make sure that you have enough seats to accommodate the largest class you teach during the day. If you don't, inform the principal and/or the janitor to get additional desks. If you decide to opt for a design other than the traditional, rectangular, row-and-column arrangement, consider one of the following four arrangements, depending on the factors I describe in the previous section.

You can be just as successful a teacher using simple rows and columns. I never deviated from the old standard for my entire teaching career, and it suited me just fine.

The dance-floor seating chart

If lots of student interaction is your cup of tea, the dance-floor-style seating chart, shown in Figure 5-1, is for you. I give it this name because it reminds me of the dance floor at a wedding. All the seats aim toward a central focus point — a large, open space in the middle of the room for activities, meetings, or instructional games (a large part of my teaching style). This arrangement also gives you a little elbowroom if you're claustrophobic.

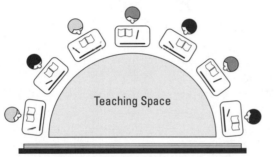

Figure 5-1: The dance-floor seating chart in all its finery.

Teaching Space

Holding class discussions and debates in this type of arrangement is easy because students are able to keep and hold eye contact with one another without constantly having to swing around in their seats. However, this seating chart requires a room with a lot of space in it. Though comfortable and welcoming, this arrangement isn't the way to go with large classes or if you need to economize space.

The runway-model seating chart

If you pace back and forth while speaking, consider using the runway-model seating chart, shown in Figure 5-2, which can put your pacing to good use and keep you from wandering aimlessly. Perhaps you've even dreamed of patrolling a shiny, elevated walkway as a dazzling fashion model, soaking in the adoration and unspoken praise of designers, photographers, and fans alike as they crowd on either side to catch a glimpse of you, but you had to abandon those dreams because you ate more than 400 calories of food a day or gave up the glitzy lifestyle to land the mammoth paychecks of a school teacher. If so, this arrangement is definitely for you. It narrows the space in which the teacher can easily maneuver, but it's extremely effective in rooms that have blackboards on opposite ends of the room.

You'll find this arrangement more often than the dance-floor seating chart because it effectively fits more students into smaller spaces. This seating chart is the most practical (although not most ideal) way to arrange your chairs if class discussion is important to you, because (depending upon where they sit) students can always face at least half the class, and most can see the faces of about 75 percent of their classmates easily. However, as you teach in the center aisle, you may have the unnerving feeling of being surrounded. Some teachers like the security of knowing that no one's behind them.

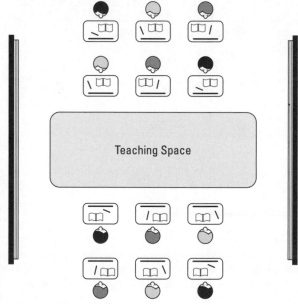

Figure 5-2:
The runway-
model
seating
chart —
very
effective
but very
underrated.

Teaching Space

If you want to implement this style of seating, make sure that you limit the number of rows you use. For example, having three rows of five students is better than having five rows of three. To maximize class interaction, make the rows of students parallel to the center lane as long as possible. Two of my favorite high-school classes, freshman civics and senior English, used this arrangement, and they were the most interactive classes I had.

The independent-nation-state seating chart

If you assign a lot of group work or split your class into teams for games or competitions, you'll probably want to employ the independent-nation-state seating chart, shown in Figure 5-3. I give it this name because, through use of this seating arrangement, you're telling students that you want them to operate independently of the rest of the class, forcibly separating them into small clusters, so that their desks are pushed together and individual teams are able to face one another easily. Keep in mind that students still need to be able to see the chalkboard just by turning their heads to the right or left. Although I don't recommend the independent nation state as a permanent design, it is very useful to teachers who have large tables rather than desks to arrange. If you insist upon using this arrangement for the entire year, offset the isolation it imposes with activities that involve the entire class.

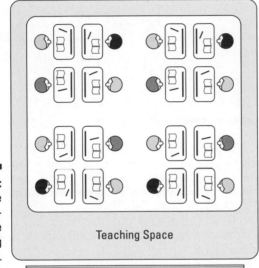

Teaching Space

The farther apart the clusters, the more independent the groups become. I don't suggest using this seating arrangement for the entire school year unless you're willing to mix up the groups every now and then. Otherwise, students become overly familiar with one another, begin to form their own rules, and occasionally think about seceding from the union, which is the class as a whole. Keeping students separated fosters enmity between groups and doesn't promote the unity necessary to provide a welcoming classroom atmosphere.

The Battleship seating chart

Remember that Hasbro board game Battleship? You strategically jammed little plastic ships on pegs into your game board and then spent the next hour or so calling off coordinates in an attempt to sink your enemy's fleet. The game taught many valuable lessons, like the concept of rows and columns and how naval warships were only allowed to move horizontally, vertically, or diagonally. I present to you the Battleship seating chart, gloriously modeled in Figure 5-4. Students sit in groups of two, three, four, and five, arranged as if superimposed on a giant grid. "You sank my reading group!"

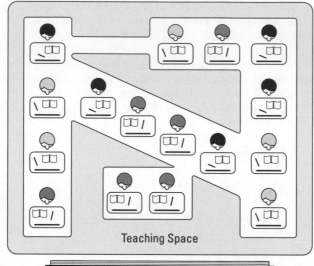

Figure 5-4:
The
Battleship
seating
chart.

Teaching Space

In case you're wondering, no, I don't really see this as a viable long-term seating chart, and I include it more as a joke than anything else. However, it illustrates an important point. If you leave your seats the same way day in and day out, you get into a rut. On the other hand, if students are used to the row-and-column traditional style, and all of a sudden, they walk into your room arranged in a crazy design, their interest will be instantly sparked. A little change does everyone some good.

Establishing an Inviting Classroom

The few days you'll have in your classroom to prepare for school isn't much time at all to get things ready. It's a quick sprint interspersed with all sorts of hurdles along the way. After you get your bulletin boards and seating charts figured out, you still have to do some decorating. Don't forget that you also have to attend lots and lots of meetings during those days as well, so you should plan to spend some evening and weekend time in your room before the school year starts. Though these unpaid hours are only the first drops in an ocean of extra time you'll put in during your career, it's time well spent. You need to have your room decorated, arranged, and organized before the school year starts, or you'll spend the next ten months trying to get caught up.

I'm not going to give you a lot of advice on decorating your room because there's no one correct way to do it. Even better, there's really no wrong way to do it, either. Your overall goal is to make your room a sanctuary, where both you and your kids can feel safe and personally welcomed in a school building that's probably more institutional than friendly.

In my opinion, there are four basic kinds of teachers: fun teachers, smart teachers, organized teachers, and nurturing teachers, classified according to the teacher's strongest positive personality trait. After you figure out where your strengths lie, you can design a room that's a natural manifestation of your personality, which makes the room more comfortable for you and helps the students understand you better. In the following sections, I list the different categories of teachers, describe them (so you can figure out which one you are), and give some decorating tips specific to that group.

Decorating for fun teachers

If you're charismatic, creative, and love to entertain, I classify you as a fun teacher. You have all kinds of unique and crazy ways to keep kids engaged in learning, and they look forward to your class because they never know what to expect. You value relationships with students even more than you do teaching them. You enjoy coming to work not primarily because of your content area but because you like to see kids having fun and enjoying learning for a change. If your school ever rents a dunk tank, you're the first in line to take a plunge. Deep down inside, you wish that other teachers were more fun because kids would like school more. But part of you is glad that they're nothing like you because it makes you a mini-celebrity.

Fun teachers have a reputation to establish and then live up to year after year, consistently doing more exciting and stranger things to keep both their students and themselves engaged. Therefore, their rooms go a little overboard. My first classroom was all decorated according to one theme: *Star Trek*. I was the Trekkie to beat all Trekkies, and my entire room was decorated with a futuristic space theme. During my rookie year, I even gave my students Starfleet rankings according to how much homework they did!

Go a little wild when you pick out the decor for your room, and don't be afraid to bring your personality into it. If you love movies, jam your walls with movie posters. Decorate your classroom like you'd decorate your den at home; in other words, decorate for you rather than the students, and the students will love it all the more. I never had an inch of wall space showing in my classroom, and all the images bombarding me every minute of the day exhilarated me. As a fun teacher, I also reveled in tacky and corny decorations, and the students loved it.

Decorating for smart teachers

Smart teachers have a ton of experience in their chosen field. They may or may not actually possess an education degree because the majority of their training may be in the subject that they're teaching. If you read academic journals, watch *Jeopardy!* and click your tongue when the contestants get wrong answers, or occasionally consider the actions of other teachers a bit juvenile or sophomoric, chances are that you fall into this category.

I'm not saying that smart teachers are condescending. They simply have a very specific view of the way things work, and they signed on as teachers to deepen the understanding of and bring enlightenment to their students. Smart teachers get a lot of respect from their peers, who are usually in awe of the depth and breadth of their subject-matter knowledge. In the same way, students most often choose smart teachers as mentors. Smart teachers are often an inspiration to their students because they embody a noble standard and a personality to strive for.

If you fall into this category, you feel most comfortable when discussing your area of expertise because your knowledge is profound. Your room should contain posters and artifacts pertaining to your specialty area. Steer clear of trite educational and motivational posters with sayings like, "With teamwork, we all succeed," or the cliched kitten hanging from the branch emblazoned with the advice, "Hang in there, baby!" Use genuine elements that bring a sense of the real world into your classroom. If you're a traveler, bring in things you've collected in your exploits and display them proudly. Post appropriate quotes around the room. Too many classroom posters feature Garfield saying things like, "Do your best" or, "I don't do Mondays." Instead, feature insightful and thought-inspiring nuggets of wisdom.

Decorating for organized teachers

Organized teachers are very specific about the way things are done. Papers need to be labeled in a certain way, and assignments and tests have a very rigid schedule. The rules are clear, and those who break the rules must face the consequences. Organized teachers get into education for lots of different reasons and are (underneath all the regulations) very kind people. Although sometimes misunderstood by their students ("I swear she hates me. She's always telling me to stop whatever I'm doing, and it's driving me crazy!") their colleagues know them for who they are. They just want what's best for kids, and they're intent on doing whatever they can to provide the best education possible.

Organized teachers have classes that are polarized. The students who dislike organized teachers are vehement in their dislike, but the students who are mature enough to see the motivation behind the regulation will defend and stick by that teacher with a determination and love that teachers in the other three categories never see.

You need to set up a classroom that will serve as a sanctuary for you. If, three months into the school year, papers are strewn about the room and your organizational system has broken down, things will look bleak. Take steps now to set up a detailed organizational system to handle things such as lists of student make-up work, space for graded papers that need to be returned, attendance and tardy charts, behavioral charts (if you use them), professional memos, and tasks assigned to you by your principal or supervisor. Make sure that you always know exactly where everything is and leave space for your papers in each category to grow.

To help your students get used to you (which is your biggest challenge at the beginning of the school year), make up posters that describe how to comply with your biggest rules. For example, have posters that list important dates or that demonstrate how you want notebooks organized.

Decorating for nurturing teachers

If one of your students gets upset and you have to make a conscious effort not to immediately hug him or her or cry as well, you're a nurturer. This category is unique because every single person in it already knows that he or she is a nurturer. In fact, if you fall into this category, you probably skipped right over the other three teacher types because you have no question in your mind where you belong.

Nurturers love teaching more and more as the years go by. The politics and backdoor dealings of state and local administrators barely bother these people at all. In fact, little discourages nurturers professionally as long as they have strong family structures at home to boost them. Nurturing teachers love kids, and they love being around kids, raising kids, supporting kids, and just about everything else that has anything remotely to do with kids. Most of them even volunteer to teach kids on the weekend in their places of worship — as if dozens of kids a day every day of the workweek isn't enough.

If you're a nurturer, you probably don't need much advice when it comes to room decoration. In fact, most of your room decorations will be student artwork, student photographs, and things that students bring in from home. You live in a student-centered universe, and the world of education would grind to a halt without you — that's no exaggeration. You'll hang up posters with cartoon characters and phrases like, "You can achieve your dreams," but in your room, they won't seem like schlock because everyone knows that you mean the sentiments sincerely.

The best advice I can give you about decorating your room is not to be self-conscious. You have a vision, so don't let anything stand in your way of that vision. Doing so would contradict everything you believe in, and your room wouldn't feel genuine to you. In short, be yourself, and don't be embarrassed about who you are.

Staying Afloat If You're a Floater

Thanks to school overcrowding and the squatting rights of the teachers who came along first, you may find yourself floating for your first year or more of teaching. Some school systems call these poor, tortured souls *roaming teachers,* but a pile of garbage by any other name would still smell as repulsive. Your lot in life is to wander the halls like a homeless, haunted spirit, teaching each of your classes in a different classroom. I salute you, I pity you, and I weep for you, because I was once one of you myself.

Here's your only good news: You don't really have to worry about any of the things I discuss in this chapter. However, you do have special needs and concerns to prepare you for your first day, so here are a few things to think about:

✔ **Try to sign out an empty audiovisual cart from the media center.** This cart will be your educational pack mule, and don't think that you can survive without it, managing with only a briefcase or mammoth tote bag. You need a place to stack papers, store important forms, and keep your office supplies, such as tape, staplers, a hole puncher, chalk and erasers (yes, you need to bring your own), and a 2,000-count bottle of aspirin. To keep your spirits up, you may want to decorate your cart. My little beast of burden was even decked out in holiday lights when Christmastime came around.

✔ **Find a permanent place to lock up your stuff.** A buddy teacher (or a fellow rookie who lucked out and got a room) will be willing to let you park your cart in his or her room and lock it up overnight. Most people will pity you enough to at least allow you a parking space.

✔ **Visit the rooms you'll be teaching in and find out how they're arranged.** You still need to have seating charts and assigned seats when school starts, and to do that, you'll have to know how the seats will be arranged.

Don't even consider moving those seats around, or you'll be brutally murdered by the teacher whose room you're floating into for that period.

As a floater, you'll have to deal with a few additional stresses that your more permanently housed colleagues don't, including dealing with the faculty members who are belligerent toward you because you're floating into *their* room during *their* planning time. I give you some advice for dealing with these annoyances (including coping mechanisms that don't involve violence against those faculty members) in Chapter 14.

Chapter 6

The First Day of School

1 didn't sleep much the night before my first day of school. I was nervous, anxious, scared, and more afraid of riding the bus than anything else, but that's mostly because I was 5 years old and terrified to start kindergarten. Flash forward 16 years, and the mood was much the same. The evening before my first day as a real, bona fide, certified teacher was just as nerve-wracking. I had a lot of the same worries. Would the kids like me? Would I turn out smart or stupid? What if I did something wrong? Where would I put my lunch?

You've spent about 17 years in school to prepare for your life as a teacher. You may very well be a teacher for the next 30 years and live on in the minds and memories of your students as good ol' Mr. or Ms. So-and-so, but all such journeys must begin with a single step, and this step probably feels as significant to you as man's first hops across the moon.

In this chapter, I lead you through your first day, and sprinkle in the advice of a bunch of teachers who've come before you. Think of them as trailblazers, who, through their suggestions and tips, have already cleared away much of the brush and bramble along the path ahead.

Making That Important First Impression

The biggest difference between your first day as a rookie teacher and any other day is that it's your only chance to make a first impression. If you've been on as many blind dates as I have, you know that first impressions mean a whole heck of a lot. In those first few moments, people size each other up.

("Okay, she looks attractive, upper lip is kind of bulbous, though, and, oh my Lord, there's definitely a thick, long hair sticking our of her ear. This isn't going to work out. I can't date someone with thick ear hair. I've got to get out of here, and fast!")

Don't be scared. The first day of school, although important, won't dictate the rest of your school year. If you screw up or feel you didn't give it your best shot, that doesn't mean that the rest of the school year is doomed to failure, you should never have become a teacher, and your parents were right — you just should've become an accountant. This one, six-hour period of time is just a day like any other, with a few tiny differences. This handful of differences, though, is what you can twist to your advantage to ease yourself and your students into the rules and regulations you spent so long creating and tweaking in preparation for the big day.

Students size you up in a different way — they want to know who's going to be in charge. If you show signs of weakness, they know that it'll just be a matter of time until they figure out how to get under your skin (figuratively speaking, or at least I hope so for your sake). This begs the question: What can you do and how can you carry yourself to assert that you're in control of the classroom? That question has lots of answers, and many of them you'll have to come up with yourself. However, I was taught one terrific metaphor for establishing class control on the first day of school; it'll help you visualize the task ahead and give you some positive direction.

Teaching may be a scary job at times, but its inherent danger really doesn't much compare to the profession of lion tamer. Giant, ferocious, feral beasts high on the scent of man's blood surround one, small, proportionally insignificant lion tamer. He's armed with only a whip, perhaps a chair, and the unspoken support and empathy of the thousands in the circus stands surrounding him. Slowly, he walks around the cage, staring down the hulking monsters, which growl menacingly and paw at the air as he walks by.

Suddenly, he cracks his whip, and the lions do all sorts of crazy things. They balance on giant, oversized balls. They jump through flaming hoops. They do political sketch comedy. It's amazing! What keeps these huge cats from realizing that, if they teamed up, the lion tamer would stand no chance against them? What makes them follow the advice and admonition of the teeny little human guy with the whip and the chair? Honestly, what good is a chair versus lions? Not much, except perhaps for the lion tamer to sit down on and make himself more comfortable as he's being mauled beyond recognition.

What you may not notice is that the lion tamer is very deliberate about when he enters and exits the cage. He's always the first in and the last out. Why is this so important? Because he's the first entity in the cage, he's establishing that it's his territory — it belongs to him. When the lions are allowed in later, they enter with the implicit understanding that the tamer is king of the cage, and they're merely guests invited at his whim. If the lions were to enter first, they'd recognize the empty space as theirs and might attack to defend their territory.

If you haven't guessed it, you're the lion tamer in this morality play, and your students are the lions. On the first day of school, you need to be in your room, greeting students as they walk in the door. Don't roam the hallways during class changes or come flying into your classroom as the bell is sounding. You need to show that you're completely in control of what happens in that classroom, from the first minute to the last minute that you share with your students each day.

Take a look at this long list of benefits to being the first in the classroom on that fateful first day:

✔ **You can direct your students to their assigned seats.** You *must* have your seating arrangement ready to go and assigned seats for every student on the first day. The easiest way to assign these seats is alphabetically, for a couple of reasons. First of all, taking roll is easy when seats are in alphabetical order, which is extremely helpful before you learn all your kids' names.

Secondly, seating according to the alphabet is completely impartial. Kids are just like adults in that they want to be close to their friends when entering a completely unknown situation. Your classroom is a total mystery to them, and their knee-jerk reaction will be to try to sit with their friends. By denying them the ability to sit wherever they please, you've made your first statement about who's in charge without making anything personal.

Don't think for a second that students will be fine with this arrangement. Students will surely bellyache about not being able to sit where they want. In fact, you may even get a few alligator tears from the more brazen complainers, but you have to stick to your guns. Simply say, "I'm sorry, but this is the way we're sitting this year." Also, some students have been seated next to each other for years and years because their last names fall close together in the alphabet. Don't hesitate to separate students who look overly comfortable together in the first day of class. If they're chatting amiably minutes after you've seated them, you need to make a mental note to have new seats the next day.

✔ **You can begin to pair names with faces.** Remember that kid everyone warned you about? Pair his name with his face immediately. (Notice that I said "his" because the odds are overwhelming that the few devil spawn you teach in your career are going to be male.)

Learning student names should be your first major objective in the school year. I've often wondered why students respond better when you know their names. Is it because when you know who they are, you also know whose parents to call in the case of a behavior problem? Believe it or not, I don't think it's fear of reprisal from you or their parents. Here's my theory: Students never actually think that you're talking to them, no matter how specific you are.

For example, even the sentence, "The young man in the front row, third seat from my left, with blue eyes and brown hair, weighing approximately 85 pounds with a slim build, dressed in a blue Nintendo T-shirt, blue jeans, and bright red sneakers, please do not look at your neighbor's paper" will fall on deaf ears, although clearly, there's only one student by that description in your class. Red Shoe Boy is thinking, "Maybe he's talking about someone else; my shoes are more of a burgundy." However, when you say, "Jim! Eyes on your own paper, and make it snappy," his self-delusional tendencies are thwarted.

✔ **You can give them clear direction about what you expect.** In earth and space sciences, you learn that nature abhors a vacuum. It's a simple principle — nature rushes to overwhelm any empty space it finds. For example, if you suck the air out of a plastic milk jug, it will collapse upon itself. Nature doesn't like the absence of air in the container, so it collapses the container around it to fill in that space.

Students also abhor living in a vacuum — even more than they hate rules. They want to know what is expected of them at all times during the school day. This, of course, doesn't mean that they'll actually *do* what is expected, but it at least satisfies their curiosity. Nothing bores children more than giving them "free time" in class; after about ten minutes, they're bored out of their minds and begging to do something.

If you're in your classroom before class starts, you can give direction to the students coming in. Most people write on the board warm-ups or (to use fancy-pants educational jargon) an anticipatory set of objectives or questions, so that the students have an immediate goal as soon as they enter your room. You'll often be overrun by paperwork for the first five or ten minutes of class, especially on the first day of school, so listing a simple task on the board gives the students something to focus on while you get your head on straight. It's much better than leaving them to find their own entertainment, because anything that entertains them is bound to cause trouble.

Elementary-school teachers need to use a slightly different tactic. Obviously, some of your students aren't going to be able to read very well, if at all, so listing learning objectives on the board isn't going to do you a heap of good. Be prepared with an activity that students can immediately immerse themselves in. For example, provide paper and crayons, and after all the students are seated, ask them to draw a picture of something they did that summer or perhaps draw a picture of their families. Drawing and coloring are probably familiar activities, so it puts students at ease, while allowing you time to get yourself together.

TIP

How to get a knack for names

What would you say if I told you that you could learn all your students' names the first day of school, make yourself a "cool teacher" in their eyes, and build a sense of community in the classroom in one fell swoop? You'd probably say that I'm crazy. But I'm not. You really can.

I have to credit my Psychology 101 teacher, J. Roy Hopkins from St. Mary's College, with this technique. I'm sure that he's not its inventor, but when he used it in class, it left an impression on me. Most college professors make no point of learning their students' names, so when he spent the first 45 minutes of the first class memorizing ours, I was amazed. Even four years later, he still knew my name, so I decided to try his method in my classes, and it's paid off in spades.

Use this technique the first day of class. Students are expecting an extremely boring first day in all their classes (which most teachers dutifully deliver), so anything you do out of the ordinary will intrigue them. Focus on first names; last names will come in time. Here's what you need to do:

1. **Start at one edge of your classroom and ask the student her first name.** When she tells you, repeat it aloud six or seven times while keeping steady eye contact with the student. (Also ask if she wants to be known by a nickname or middle name, because the name you learn today is what she's going to be stuck with.) Don't try to learn names based on clothing or hairstyle because those things change day to day; focus on the eyes.

2. **Move on to the student behind her.** Find out his name and do the same thing.

3. **Go back and forth a few times between the two of them, repeating their names as you look into their faces.** Do this out loud, as opposed to silently, or the students will get freaked out, wondering why you're staring at them so intently.

4. **Move on to student number 3, repeat the name, and review all the names you've learned so far.** Again, repeat their names as you make eye contact with them. Juggle the order and try to confuse yourself until you're comfortable with the three names you've heard so far.

5. **Repeat this process until you cover the entire class, and then spend some time picking out students at random and trying to remember their names.**

6. **When you feel comfortable with the names, turn your back and ask the students to change desks.** They'll be hesitant, but insist on it: "Come on, hurry. We have places to go, people to see. Pick a new desk and sit there. I'm getting old up here. My clothes are getting even more out of style as I speak!" (A little self-deprecating humor goes a long way.) When the students have rearranged themselves, show off by naming each student, row by row. The students will be impressed, and you'll have earned a lot of points with them. They'll see that you value them more than administrative details because you learned their names before you even talked about one class rule.

Students will probably be paying close attention during this entire process. Many teachers make the erroneous assumption that their students already know each other. Even though some of them have been in the same classes for a year or more, they still refer to each other, in some cases, as "that short boy" or "the weird girl." As you burned names and faces into your brain, they were probably doing the same thing (what else was there to do?). Someone in class will want to show off as well, demonstrating that he also learned all the names. Call him up, have the rest of the class shuffle again, and repeat the process.

Don't Smile until December?

If there's one piece of advice I heard over and over again as I prepared to teach, it was the old standby: "Don't smile until December." In other words, be extra mean at the beginning of the school year and slowly ease up as the year progresses. Believe it or not, this is actually good advice, if applied correctly.

Building a reputation

If you're anything like me, you wish that you didn't have to deal with the discipline issues that arise day to day. It's not that you're bad at discipline, you just wish that you didn't have to deal with it constantly. Sorry to be the bearer of bad news, but you'll deal with more discipline issues in your first three or four months of teaching that you will for the next three or four years. It's all about reputation. The students know which teachers can be pushed around, and which ones stick fast to the rules. They pass the information to each other like spies in a hostile country: "In Mrs. Brown's class, you're allowed to swear (just as long as it's not one of the major swear words), but she hates it when you chew gum. Also, if she's having a bad day, don't even *think* about talking without raising your hand. A kid did that last year and she went completely mental, yelling for like 25 minutes *straight*. She even made a couple of kids cry, and they were on the football team!"

Students are extremely curious creatures; from the first minute they meet you, they're going to try to figure out everything they can, including:

✔ Your first name

✔ How old you are

✔ Where you live

✔ The kind of car you drive (and where you park)

✔ Whether or not you're married

✔ How often you yell and what prompts it

✔ Why you've worn the same pants two days in a row

They'll build their overall impression of you slowly, over the course of the first few weeks, based on how you react to them, what kind of teaching style you use, and how dutifully you stick to both your personal rules and the school rules.

Don't be surprised if all your classes, even the ones you've been warned about in advance, are at least tolerable, if not very well behaved. Very few students will actually challenge you openly in the first few days of school because even they know that that's a poor way to get the year started.

However, very slowly, they'll begin to test you, to see exactly where your boundaries are. This shouldn't surprise you that much — you did the very same things when you were a student.

I now work with a lot of college faculty members, and I constantly see students wheedling them, trying to influence their rules and assignments, especially when it comes to due dates. How many weeks went by in your college courses until someone tried the "We already have a lot of assignments due that week; can't we push this paper back a few days" trick? My personal favorite (which I heard a lot in high school) was, "My Mom doesn't like me doing this much homework; she says that it's just 'busy work.'" Mom was usually surprised to hear herself misquoted whenever I called her to follow up on such a statement.

To avoid future problems, stick to your rules, unless they're completely inappropriate and must be changed. If your notebook-collection rule was a little too eager and it stinks having to gather them up and grade them weekly, too bad. You made that rule; now, stick by it. If you start changing things around midyear, students are going to question every single one of your rules, and the argument "But you changed your grading policy twice already" is going to frustrate your principal, who can't support you unless you stay consistent with the rules you've set.

After a few months of being Mr. or Mrs. By the Book, the students will get the point: You make the rules, and they aren't going to change, so if anything needs changing, it'll be their attitudes and work habits. In essence, you always want to bring students up to your level of expectations rather than lower those expectations to make it easier for your class. By November or December, you can be more jovial and kid around with the students because they already know how it's going to be.

Starting the year relaxed and then trying to introduce discipline later is almost impossible. Beginning the school year as a stickler for the rules and easing up as the school year goes on is much easier. Just about every new teacher I spoke with told me, "I wish I'd been tougher at first, and I definitely will be next year." Being tough from the beginning makes things much less stressful for you because you'll actually be able to focus on teaching rather than constant supervision.

One of my former students, named Laura, gave me a terrific compliment the other day. She's now studying to be a teacher, and one of her professors told her that first-year teachers are historically very bad because they have a lot to learn. Laura told the class about me because she was in my class the first year I taught. "For the first three months, we thought he was mean. He had lots of fun ways to learn stuff, but when it came down to the rules, he was just nasty. Then, one random day in the spring, we suddenly noticed that he was much more relaxed, and everyone was following the rules, and we never even realized what he'd done. Pretty slick."

Overpreparation and sleight of hand

Ever since I was little, I've enjoyed magic. I used to make my family and friends sit through magic show after magic show as I perfected my illusions, and they dutifully sat through every minute, usually oohing and aahing in the right spots. I never did magic professionally, although I did a few magic shows for kids when I was in college under the admittedly poorly chosen stage name of "Mr. Bonkers."

A magician doesn't have any otherworldly skill. He simply attracts your attention away from his hands as he nimbly plucks things from inside his sleeve or coat, or even from between his fingers, where they're hidden. This practice is called *sleight of hand,* and it's the basis for most magic performed up close.

As a teacher, you have your own sleight of hand, and it's called *overpreparation.* You should always have way too much stuff "up your sleeve," because you may get through the material faster than you initially expected. One of the worst things you can do is end a lesson 10 or 15 minutes early and say, "Okay, that's all I have for today. Hang out for the rest of the

period and entertain yourself." Why? Because students will come to expect this behavior from you on a regular basis, and the next time that you try to take up the whole period with (gasp!) instruction, all you'll get are moans, groans, and the wailing and gnashing of teeth. "Why? Can't we stop? I'm so *tired!* I can't *possibly* learn any more!"

Remember that you need to be tough, especially at the beginning of the school year while you're building a reputation. On the other hand, if you end five minutes early in April and allow students a minibreak at the end of class, they'll already know that they'd better not expect anything like that again in the foreseeable future.

Changing your pace and keeping lots of extra material up your sleeve ensnares the students' attention, and (like magic) the period is over before anyone has time to complain. Even if you don't get to the extra stuff, you can always lead off with it in the next class, and that provides for a good refresher and a smooth transition into new material anyway.

Recognizing the difference between friendliness and friendship

You cannot set out with the goal of being your students' friend. That may come in time, as they grow to respect you as a teacher and a professional, but a relationship like that takes months to cultivate. You weren't hired to be their friend. You're there to teach them things about the Ancient Greeks and what parts of speech adverbs modify. You don't have to be the orneriest hombre in the whole school; you just have to be very strict during your first few months of teaching.

You can treat your students with respect, honor their ideas, make learning fun, and be extremely friendly in your interactions with them. Ask them how things are going, why they seem stressed, or why they're extremely happy today. These are friendly remarks that you'd use with co-workers, if you worked in an office. However, when it's time for class, the students should know that roles shift; you're in charge, no matter how nice you are.

Identifying Important First-Day Tasks

Your first day with students is a lot like a first date. In both cases, you don't know each other very well, so conversation is awkward and forced. Therefore, you need to have a full agenda planned so that none of those awkward lulls in conversation cause the chemistry between you to fizzle. You definitely need to learn your students' names (that should also be a pretty high priority on dates, by the way), and you should have assigned seats for them. Other than that, what should you try to accomplish on the first day? Great question.

Addressing administrative tasks

The following tasks need to be accomplished on the first day of school (or the second day at the latest). They may seem boring and routine, but they help the students to better understand what the year is going to be like and to become accustomed to both your teaching style and your expectations:

✔ **Highlight the important rules in your classroom.** In Chapter 4, I discuss how to design rules that suit your personality. Now's the time to address the rules most important to you, including hall-pass rules, dismissal rules, and rules foundational to the way you conduct your class. Any nontraditional rules or procedures need to be addressed so that students get time to acclimate to them.

For example, I gave no credit for any homework assignment that was incomplete, rather than constantly spending time determining how many points partial assignments earned. Because this rule is rather odd and strict, I always highlighted it on the first day. Every year, it caused ripples of panic. "What if I don't understand how to do one of the problems?" was always the outcry. Therefore, I also explained how I wanted students to attempt problems, even if they ultimately got them wrong, instead of just leaving them blank.

✔ **Discuss emergency and safety procedures.** I talk about emergency and safety procedures in Chapter 4 as well. Students need to know what to do in case of fire, earthquake, tornado, hail, and killer-robot-attack drills. You wouldn't want your kids to be annihilated by murderous androids because you never told them to cover their heads and sit underneath their desks, would you?

I will never, never, never forget the safety lecture given to me by my tenth-grade chemistry teacher. During it, she talked about how dangerous it was to wear loose-fitting clothing while performing experiments. As she talked, she walked over to one of the most attractive girls in the class. "You see, if Melissa's nice, expensive shirt caught fire because its sleeves are too loose, I'd be forced, and within my rights, to rip her shirt off to prevent her from becoming burned."

You could hear a pin drop. Every male student's eyes bugged out of his head, trying to conjure up just that image, and every female student groaned inwardly, thinking of the humiliation such a dramatic event would prevail upon an adolescent. In one strike, she got the attention of the guys and the girls, and, at the same time, she got her point across about safety. You may argue that this is borderline sexual harassment, and I don't necessarily disagree. What I'm saying, though, is that it was effective. I still roll up my sleeves even if I just have a fleeting thought about a Bunsen burner.

✔ **Introduce yourself.** Students want to know about you, the person, besides the fact that you're *in charge.* Tell a personal anecdote, talk about your schooling, or be mysterious ("I can't remember anything before my 12th birthday, but lately, I've found that I have the sharply honed skills of a ninja assassin. I think I was genetically engineered to be the perfect killing machine. Anyway, open your books to page 12."). Just don't be boring when you talk about yourself. If you can't make your personal bio interesting, how are you going to make your class interesting?

✔ **Pass out textbooks, even if your students haven't been assigned lockers yet.** Nothing says, "Let's get down to business" better than handing out the textbooks that will burden students for the rest of the year. If they don't have lockers, they'll have to look at those books all day, and every time they do, they'll think about you and shiver a little inside.

You probably have to use a specific inventory form when you pass out books. My school numbered their books so that you could check to see that the book each student turned in at the end of the school year was the same one he was assigned at the beginning. After you fill out that inventory form, put it in a safe place! Your room will go through waves of organization and disarray throughout the year, but you need to be able to put your hands on that form at a moment's notice. Your school year will have a rotten ending if you lose it, because you'll have no way of holding kids accountable for books they lose.

✔ **Explain your grading system.** Whether you use total points, categories, a bell curve, or a blindfold and a dartboard to assign grades, enlighten your students to your computational method as soon as you can. If you expect them to keep a journal or portfolio, explain how you want it organized and how often you'll collect it. Will you allow partial credit, or is it all or nothing? Do you give multiple-choice tests, or are you an essays kind of gal?

Surprises are nice, and they keep things fresh, but you don't ever want your grading system to be a surprise. Parents and administrators alike tend to frown on things like that. For example, if you insist on students using pencil in your class, you'd better let them know before your first assignment and give them time to buy the supplies they need. If you're not sure what kind of grading system to use, skip ahead to Chapter 12, where I discuss some options.

✔ **Collect parental names and phone numbers, as well as any other information you'll need.** I always made it a point to have students fill out information cards for me very early in the school year. On it, I asked for their full name, home address, home phone number, and full names of parents or guardians. I also asked for the home address and phone number of divorced parents who didn't live with the child.

By collecting this data, you're implicitly stating that parental contact is important to you, and that you have no problem calling parents when a student gets out of hand. It's the perfect complement to the name game (as I detailed in the earlier sidebar). Before you start learning names, pass out 3-x-5-inch index cards, and have the list of requested information on the board. Therefore, students who may otherwise complain don't think that the name game is a waste of their time.

Remember that some students' last names are different from their parents', due to divorce, separation, and other traumatic events. Therefore, don't assume that the parent and the kid have last names that match. Also, don't assume that a married woman has the same surname as her husband. This is why I always insisted upon full names on the information cards that I collected. If you begin a conversation by referring to a parent by her ex-husband's name, you're starting with a strike against you, and you could unintentionally unpack some of her emotional baggage before the phone call even starts.

✔ **Discuss any major projects for the year.** If you take some time and outline each of the major projects for the upcoming school year, especially any writing projects, you instill what I call "benevolent panic." Students will realize that you're expecting a lot from them, and that your class isn't going to be a free ride. Don't cause rioting or anything; just tell them enough to make them think, "Oh boy, I'd better start buckling down now, because this class is going to be tough."

✔ **Outline how to go about getting extra help.** You're not only expected to teach students during school hours, but also as requested (on a reasonable basis) after school. In my district, our working hours extended 20 minutes beyond the close of school, and we were expected to tutor any of our students (without cost, of course) who needed help during that time. Realistically, you'll be tutoring longer than that. It really isn't professional to stand up in the middle of a tutoring session and say, "Well, my workday's over; see you later, alligator."

I liked knowing ahead of time when my students were coming. Among the reasons for this was my inability to schedule doctor's appointments.

It was more hassle to miss school to go to the doctor (because of the lesson planning and coverage required) than to simply wait for an appointment after the school day. However, doctors don't work very late, so I'd have to blitz out of the school right at quitting time every once in a while to squeeze in the dentist, doctor, or any other pressing errands in my life (get a haircut, shampoo the dog, or catch a particularly emotional episode of *Oprah,* for instance). Too many times, students would wander in right as I was trying to leave and ask for help.

Eventually, I learned to schedule after-school tutoring. I always told parents, "I'm available every day after school for any kind of tutoring help your child may need, and I don't mind staying as long as it takes. However, your student needs to take the initiative and set up an appointment with me at least 24 hours in advance, so I can rearrange my personal schedule to match." There's nothing rude about asking for a little common courtesy, just as long as you explain your terms up front. I also set up a weekly "Study Buddy Day," which worked very well for me; I describe this in Chapter 17.

You'll have a lot of stuff to cover on the first day, so you may not get to it all. However, I do encourage you to cover each of these topics as soon as you can. Don't take the "Oh, they'll get the picture eventually" approach, or you'll be explaining your rules all year long. Tell them now, and reinforce these procedures all year.

Breaking the ice

By now, you're probably stressed about all the things you'll need to accomplish quickly. Don't forget that you're not the only one making a big adjustment as the school year starts. Kids who have never been in school (I'm looking at you, kindergarten and first-grade teachers) may very well be traumatized. Other young kids may be having a hard time adjusting from one omnipresent teacher to another; the attachments at that age are deep, and there may be a weaning period from "Mrs. Wilson, my last year teacher who was always so nice, and who was my favorite teacher of all time" to you. Don't worry; they'll come around. Younger kids really *want* to like you. Sometime in middle school, though, a big paradigm shift occurs, and the students realize that it's much more fun to begin the school year *not* liking the teacher.

Reassuring the younger kids

Some of the elementary-school teachers I spoke with stressed the importance of finding similarities in your classroom to the students' previous classroom. For example, ask your students what the major components of their last classroom were (a clock, a chalkboard, the teacher's desk) and have them locate these items in your room. You can ask about the important rules they remember from last year and discuss whether or not they apply now.

Many teachers find that reading to their students is very reassuring and helps establish a bond. Most likely, their previous teachers read to them, and their parents read to them, so reading to them links you to people they trust most. I've asked around, and these books are the ones most often recommended to me as good icebreakers for elementary kids on the first day of school:

- ✔ *Oh, the Places You'll Go!* by Dr. Seuss
- ✔ *I Don't Want to Go Back to School* by Marisabina Russo
- ✔ *Never Spit on Your Shoes* by Denys Cazet
- ✔ *Don't Eat the Teacher* by Nick Ward
- ✔ *The Day the Teacher Went Bananas* by James Howe
- ✔ *Emily's First Day of School* by Claire Masurel
- ✔ *First Day Jitters* by Julie Danneberg

If those books are too simple for your classes but you still want to emphasize that going back to school can be a stressful time, I suggest *Integrative Manual Therapy: For the Autonomic Nervous System and Related Disorders: Utilizing Advanced Strain and Counterstrain Technique,* by Thomas Giammatteo and Sharon Weiselfish-Giammatteo. It's a bit more rigorous, but, wow, what a page-turner.

Entertaining the older kids

Older kids aren't nearly as intimidated by the first day of school. In fact, they see it for what it usually is: horribly boring and saturated with handouts that need parent signatures. Your best bet with these guys is to catch them off guard with a fun ice-breaking activity that isn't too painfully corny. Some teachers have kids sit in groups and make lists titled, "What I have in common with my group members," or they have students interview one another and then introduce each other to the rest of the class by means of the interview questions they asked. These ideas are all well and good, but they're a bit too typical for my tastes.

Adolescents will look upon any first-day game with suspicion. The first day is a very important time for them; except for the people who shared classes with them last year, no one this year knows how dorky they really are yet, so they spend most of their time leaning back in their seats and trying to look as cool as possible. They know it's pointless, their friends know it's pointless, and you know it's pointless — but it doesn't matter. I try to break them out of that mindset with a game that makes everyone look equally foolish.

This game, called "What the Heck Is Your Problem," requires that each student have an index card taped to his back. (You prepare the cards ahead of time in a wild, uncontrollable brainstorm session, and later act as the designated taping person.) This index card describes a fictitious (but funny) ailment, achievement, or disorder that the wearer suffers. Here are a few examples:

> ✔ I once made a scale model of the Eiffel Tower entirely out of my own toenail clippings.
>
> ✔ My dreams are haunted by giant pandas arguing in German.
>
> ✔ No one takes me seriously.
>
> ✔ You can't understand a single word I say.

When outfitted with their cards, the students wander about the room and help one another figure out what each other's problems are. However, they aren't allowed to use any of the words written on the card, and students are only allowed to ask each other one question. This way, just about everyone ends up speaking to everyone else in the class. When time is up, students come to the front of the room one at a time and take a guess at their affliction. Because everyone is equally humiliated, this game is a great way to have fun.

On the first day, wacky and unpredictable always beats boring and conventional. However, whatever activity you try, don't be too juvenile. These kids need to try to act cool; they, just like you, are trying to establish a suitable image for themselves for the upcoming school year.

Dressing Appropriately

One final thing to keep in mind on the first day of school: Make sure to dress the part of the grown-up in the room. You won't earn the respect of your students by dressing like them, because in their minds, dress is invariably linked to attitude. Most of today's fashions are popular because they idealize a laid-back, relaxed, "show off as much underwear as you can" attitude. If you dress to be hip and try to enforce discipline, your students will view you as hypocritical because you've broken the cardinal rule of not wearing clothes that match your personality.

Students view clothing as a quick guide to someone's personality; without even saying two words to you, they can tell if you're preppy, grunge, punk, heavy metal, brainy, or whatever the categories are these days. In school, clothes make the man (or the woman), so the teacher's clothes should say, "I mean business, so you'd better do what I say," at least implicitly, if you can't get that exact message printed in tall letters across your shirt.

Guys, this means wearing a tie every day until about December, at which time you can safely switch to sweaters and maybe mix in a golf shirt here and there. Ladies, you probably already know how to dress because (allow me to be stereotypical for a moment) you're more aware of fashion than the average meat-headed fella. However, beware of tops that fit loosely around your neck; you'll be doing a lot of bending over in class and, well, you get the picture.

The Pig Personality Profile

One fun, and easy, icebreaker for older students is the Pig Personality Profile. Although no one is exactly sure who wrote it, it's a very popular and successful activity among professional trainers. Start by asking your students to draw a pig on a blank piece of notebook paper. That's the only instruction, except that they aren't to look at anyone else's pig until time is up. After about three minutes or so, explain that you'll describe their personalities based on how they drew their little porkers. (You may also want to mention that this test is about as unscientific as possible, and that it's all for fun.)

If the pig is drawn

- Toward the top of the paper, you're a positive, optimistic person

- Toward the middle of the paper, you're a realist

- Toward the bottom of the paper, you're a pessimist and have a tendency to be negative

- Facing left, you're traditional, friendly, and good at remembering dates, including birthdays

- Facing forward (or angled forward), you're direct, enjoy playing "the devil's advocate," and neither fear nor avoid discussions

- Facing right, you're innovative and active but don't have a strong sense of family, and you aren't good at remembering dates

- With many details, you're analytical, cautious, and distrustful

- With few details, you're emotional and naïve, care little for details, and are a risk taker

- With four legs showing, you're secure and stubborn and stick to your ideals

- With fewer than four legs, you're insecure or are going through a period of major change

- With large ears, you're a good listener (the larger the ears, the better listener you are)

- With a long tail, you're a loving person (the longer the tail, the more loving you are)

In the original Pig Personality Profile, a long tail is the sign of a good sex life, and the longer the tail, the better. I've taken some liberties to make the test a bit more child friendly, so that you won't get angry parent phone calls and sexual harassment suits filed against you before the second day of classes.

No sweat clothes, no jeans, no flip-flops or sandals, no tennis shoes, and absolutely no shorts (unless you're a gym teacher). If you absolutely *must* wear jeans, start doing so no earlier than January, and make sure that the other parts of your outfit compensate. In other words, guys (I'm talking to you because I know that you need the most help here), wear a dress shirt, tie, and dress shoes if you just can't stay away from your jeans until the weekend. By the way, there is no "casual Friday" for rookies, unless it's a common practice for the entire faculty at your school. You have to be professionally dressed around the clock, until you establish a professional image.

Make sure that your clothes conform to the school's dress code, even though schools don't usually have an enforced faculty dress code. If you're wearing a dress that's too short for student standards or a T-shirt at soccer practice that's sexually suggestive, you're sending the message that the dress code isn't very important, and I'm pretty sure that the administration would disagree with that.

Chapter 7

Keeping Your Kids Under Control

*W*ithout a doubt, brand-new teachers worry more about their class-room-management skills and their ability to discipline their students effectively than they worry about anything else. Deep down, you know that if you can't maintain discipline, you have little hope of getting rehired and eventually receiving tenure.

At it's very heart, effective discipline boils down to three basic skills: motivating your students, confronting inappropriate behavior, and maintaining class discipline after you've established it. In this chapter, I give you some practical advice for each of these skills to help shape you into a fine classroom manager.

Understanding What the Front Office Expects from You

Administrators value good classroom-management skills above everything else when evaluating teachers. They know that before any learning can take place (even that great elementary-school lesson plan you wrote in college about sombreros), you must have an orderly environment. No amount of cooperative learning, discovery-based lessons, or [insert current education buzzword here] can cure the ailments of an undisciplined classroom.

I had that dream again!

Class is underway, and I'm at the board discussing the merits of various techniques for solving quadratic equations in my algebra class. As I look about the room, some students pay attention, while others slowly drift in and out of consciousness. I've tried my best as a rookie teacher to motivate these kids, but I'm finding that it's not so easy. In fact, most students would rather swallow live piranhas than even try to understand what, exactly, a quadratic equation is. That's when the unthinkable happens.

Someone from the right side of the room throws a pencil as I'm writing on the board. The retaliation from the left side of the room is immediate and severe — an algebra book is airborne, and it comes crashing down on the head of an innocent bystander, a girl whose mother is on the board of education. Her boyfriend, outraged at the sight of blood beginning to flow from her scalp, begins throwing punches. He's a maelstrom of destructive force, leaving battered students in his wake. That thin thread of control I once held has snapped, and chaos rules. Just as five more students enter the fray, the door opens, and my principal enters. He's furious, and the veins on his forehead trace a roadmap whose final destination is my unemployment. This vision startles me awake, panting and sweating. It was all a dream — there was no carnage in my classroom. All I can do is lie back down and try to get some sleep.

Rookie teachers can count on their fair share of panic dreams. The theme is always the same: You can't get control of your class, no matter what you do, and everyone can see that you're ineffective as a teacher. Believe it or not, these dreams will become a mainstay of your life. Why so many panic dreams? You're in charge of *every single thing* that happens in the classroom. Yikes!

In most administrators' minds, if you can keep your kids under control, they can help you with anything else. All other small dents in the armor of your teacher preparation can be hammered out, including some early and clumsy lesson plans that don't quite work, just as long you have an orderly classroom.

However, effective class discipline is usually very different in practice than most rookies expect. In my rookie fantasies, I was the facilitator of a small utopian society, where all students respected one another and accepted my leadership. I'd never inhibit their creativity by actually asserting *too much* control. I wouldn't need to. The students would so value learning and the opportunity to be in my class that they'd quickly realize their mistakes when I (kindly but firmly) pointed them out and would quickly correct them, eager to master the knowledge I had to offer. After all, I went to college and struggled through how many education classes? I would be their big Buddha, and they'd (metaphorically) gather at my feet to be blessed by my wisdom. Needless to say, this isn't the way things really work.

Do yourself a favor. Read (or reread) *Lord of the Flies.* That's what really happens when students are left to create their own society — chaos rules, pig heads end up on spears, and the tubby kid in glasses' days are numbered.

No matter how much you may have learned that students crave order and want to be fully functioning parts of a communal classroom, don't believe it for a second. At best, you can work toward that lofty goal throughout the year (and you may even make it halfway there if you're lucky).

At the end of your first day of school, if you followed the recommendations that I give in this chapter and the advice of your buddy teacher (I talk in more detail about buddy teachers in Chapter 4), you established (at least in part) control over your classroom and marked the domain as your own. However, what do you do on the second day of classes, and the third? As long as you keep your students motivated from day to day and consistently enforce all your rules, you shouldn't have any giant problems.

Motivating Students

You can run a classroom a thousand different ways, but all classrooms that run smoothly have one characteristic in common: The students are *motivated.* The way that you interact with students on a daily basis provides the foundation for this motivation.

How can you motivate a student? It's an age-old dilemma, and the question has no simple answer. However, I've found the following three universal truths:

- **Motivated students know that their teacher cares about them individually.** You've already made it a point to learn the names of your kids. Now, find out more about them on a personal basis. As you roam about the room to check homework or pass back assignments, engage in small talk. Though some will be shy at first, others will be itching to talk to you and get to know you better. The other, more reticent students will watch these initial interactions and decide, in time, to trust you enough to share their thoughts and lives as well.

- **Motivated students want to know how they can succeed in your class.** Describing your rules was just the beginning. You also need to explain exactly what you expect in every homework assignment and quiz or test question. If students are constantly thinking, "I have no idea what the heck he's asking here!" or "What can I possibly do to please this teacher?" your expectations are either too vague or too inconsistent day to day.

✔ **Motivated students respect their teachers as consummate professionals.** Your kids know if you're slacking in your teaching responsibilities. They can tell how well you plan for classes based on how comfortable you are with the material, and they want to know just how dedicated you are to doing your job well. If they sense that your lesson plans are thorough, that you're well prepared, and that you're working hard for them, they'll be more willing to work hard for you.

After you've established these three foundational truths in your class, you can do all kinds of more tangible things to motivate your kids. You can go out of your way to make learning fun and add little things to the everyday drudgery of class to spice things up. (I discuss students' expectations in greater detail in Chapter 16 and detail some ways to make learning more fun in Chapter 11.)

Facing Bad Behavior Head On

Eventually, it has to happen. One of your kids is going to break a rule, and you'll have no doubt in your mind that it was intentional and a direct challenge to your authority. No matter how fantastic your rules and how motivated most of your students are, one of them is going to push back to see how you react to it. After you deal with this probing, testing tendency of your students, you'll be well on your way to earning a reputation. The tougher you are on your first offenders, the less time you'll have to spend disciplining kids for the rest of the year — they'll already know exactly where your boundaries lie.

Winning the discipline war

Most rookie teachers wish that they didn't have to deal with discipline and (if they had a choice) would ignore inappropriate behavior. Confrontation causes tension, and you're trying to establish a supportive classroom atmosphere, so disciplining a student almost seems contrary to the goal. Nothing could be farther from the truth. Although discipline is certainly tough and by no means fun, it is an essential component of classroom management.

Kids in your room need to know that if they disrespect you or break a key rule, the consequences are going to be unpleasant. Therefore, you have to know how to effectively confront students when they step out of line. So, remember that even though the easy road may be to ignore bad behavior and hope things work out on their own, they never do. You're going to have to be the one to step in and take control of the situation.

Where teacher education fails

Why is classroom management such a sticking point for rookie teachers, and why does it cause such anxiety? The answer, in my experience, is simple: Most (if not all) teacher-education programs fail to provide you with the training and the skills you need to be the leader in your classroom. They teach you philosophy, they teach you how to create a behavioral objective that can be quantified, and they teach you what order to put multiple-choice questions in when you write a test, but they don't tell you what to do if a student refuses to follow your directions.

Don't shy away from confrontation. Instead of viewing confrontation as something to dread, look at it as an opportunity. Keep in mind, though, that it's an opportunity you need to use *wisely.* Both you and the student (or group) you're chastising are going to be full of adrenaline and very keyed up as soon as you say something like, "John, your talking needs to stop right now." Will the kid get angry? Will he try to save face by being rude to you? You never really know. Many variables can play out in an infinite number of ways, so you want to be sure to approach the situation with a plan.

The three A's of confrontation

Coming up with a practical approach to student confrontation took me a few months. I didn't want to be a monster who was always on edge, waiting for a student to do something wrong so that I could correct him, and I didn't want students who were disciplined in class to feel that I held a grudge after everything was said and done. However, I wanted students to know that I was someone to be reckoned with if push came to shove.

Three key practices will help you confront students when the need arises. I call these the three A's of confrontation:

> ✔ **Anticipate behavioral problems.** Always keep one ear to the ground to listen for oncoming trains. Behavioral problems rarely spring up unexpectedly and are usually the result of days or weeks of pent-up aggravation. Listen to student conversations before and after class, whenever you can eavesdrop from your desk. Most students are very passive-aggressive if they don't like you, and they'll discuss their displeasure with a classmate when they know you can hear them.
>
> For example, if you overhear a student say, "This assignment is really unfair," or "I don't care what she says, I'm going to the bathroom when class starts," that should raise red flags in your mind that confrontation is imminent. If you're careful about watching for the warning signs, you're less likely to be caught unprepared.

If you suspect something, you have to speak with that student individually, away from the rest of the class. If that's not possible, position yourself near that student's desk often during the lesson, so that you can keep an eye on him or her. Most of the time, if that student sees that you're suspicious, that's enough to stifle an in-class argument, allowing you to see that kid after class. Find out what the problem is and talk to the student honestly and openly.

✔ **Assert authority appropriately.** When an important rule is broken, consequences must follow. However, the punishment must fit the crime. Remember that if you start out by shouting at the smallest infractions, you have nowhere to go — you can't up the ante. When I'm in front of a class, I let the students know exactly how I feel, and I make them respond to me rather than telling them specifically what to do. For example, rather than simply barking, "Be quiet!" while a big angry vein pulsates in my forehead, I'll say, "Folks, the room needs to quiet down right now because I'm really losing my patience with you today."

Look at the big differences in those two approaches. The latter gives a valid warning before real confrontation occurs. It gives the students a chance to fix their own behavior before I fix it for them. Also, by explaining how I feel, I open myself up to them as a person and not simply a mindless authority figure. Furthermore, this second approach shows them some respect, because you're not automatically initiating confrontation. With my warning cue, I'm firing a metaphorical warning shot across their bow. Before I start yelling, I'm giving them a chance to avoid the entire unpleasant situation by changing their behavior.

On some days, you're going to be grumpy and tired, and on others, you're going to be chipper and full of excitement. Students need to understand that their actions must correlate with your mood; it's an important lesson in societal interaction, and you're missing the chance to make this connection with students if all you say is, "Shut up, you're too loud."

✔ **Align students as allies after the line has been crossed.** Eventually, you're going to have your fill of nonsense, and your temper will flare. When this happens, don't be apologetic, and don't act as though you regret the temper flare. An angry teacher should make the classroom atmosphere darken as though clouds have moved in and blotted out the sun.

However, after you've gotten the point across, you need to take a deep breath, back away from additional confrontation, and return to business as normal. Don't hold a grudge against students, whether an individual or an entire class. After they've witnessed the consequences of unacceptable behavior, they must be given the opportunity to behave correctly. Some of the students I'm closest to now were the kids I had to discipline repeatedly. Most kids would really rather not be on your bad side, especially when they see how bad that bad side can be, so you must give them the opportunity to cross into the other camp and become your ally.

It's us against them?

Part of everyone's educational preparation regimen in college is a bevy of guest speakers, each of whom gives you a brief, inspirational presentation about the joys of teaching and why every other job pales in comparison. When confronted with these cheesy people intent on inspiring rather than preparing us, I'd often ask, "What don't you like about teaching?" and the answer was always an unqualified, "Nothing," except for one of our speakers, a high-school English teacher from a nearby district.

"It's you against them," he said. "Make no mistake about it. It's war. When you walk into that classroom, they don't want to learn. They want to see you cry. They'll probe you like unforgiving aliens, find your weak spot, and slowly destroy you. Remember that always: It's you against them." The professor who'd invited this speaker quickly attempted to gloss over these statements, but the point had already been made. We all stared at him, openmouthed and unbelieving.

Don't get too freaked out. He was overstating his case a little (okay, more than a little). It's also possible that the speech has gotten a bit rougher around the edges in my memory over time. But the central tenet of his speech held true, more so than any other I heard that semester or since. In order to be an effective teacher, you must first establish control and then command respect. If you think that equating discipline to war is a bit harsh or dramatic, just talk to any rookie teacher who failed to establish an orderly classroom right away. Every day is a battle, and the teacher always loses.

If you've done a good job confronting unacceptable behavior, things won't feel good right away. If the students respect you, they'll probably feel a little guilty, and the room will be quieter than usual. You may even feel bad if you were a little rough.

Too often, new teachers try to compensate for confrontation by joking around or acting apologetic. Don't make this mistake! If you were mad, you were mad. If you were sorely disappointed, the students should feel a little guilty! Let the rest of the class go by quietly, and don't speak any more on the issue. By the next day, class will be back to normal — but with one exception: The students have learned a valuable lesson about who's in charge and what you expect of them.

Recognizing Ineffective Models of Confrontation

Learning the key principles of a good confrontational style and actually implementing them in class are two completely different things. Remembering the three A's that I provide in the previous section doesn't amount to a hill of beans until you apply them, and the application is the hard part. Most rookie teachers get so worked up when confrontation comes along that, even with good intentions, they either go overboard or don't go nearly far enough.

Finding that exact balance between pushover and maniacal dictator can be a little tricky. Therefore, I want to discuss some of these well-intentioned, but completely ineffective, confrontational styles that abound in rookies and seasoned teachers alike. Seeing what *not* to do can help you better understand what you *should* do.

Mr. Sudden Fury

I had a miserable student-teaching experience. It was truly awful, and it was bad enough to nearly drive me away from my teaching career completely before I even started. My "mentor" teacher was an ex-Navy man who (barely) held his kids in check by the pure force of his intimidation. It only took about three days for me to determine his major class-control methodology, which was innately tied to his persona as Mr. Navy Guy.

He didn't mind if kids talked in class. He didn't actually mind very much if kids talked loudly. In fact, he didn't care much if anyone paid attention to him; he was fine with a moderate to heavy noise level. However, he had this mental "high-water level" in his brain. Any noise up to that point was acceptable, but when the noise reached that level, there was hell to pay, and he didn't take credit cards. He would scream furiously, pound his fist on the table, gesticulate wildly, and adopt the glare of a deranged lunatic. Keep in mind that students rarely, if ever, had any warning when that threshold of madness approached!

In other words, he completely ignored all noise in the room, until it became unbearable, and then he completely blew his stack. He might as well have had cartoon steam jets shooting out of his ears. You need to communicate your expectations to your students, so that they're not surprised to find out they've stepped out of bounds. Besides simply punishing students when they misbehave, make sure to let them know when they're getting close to the boundaries of acceptable behavior.

Furthermore, if you are constantly reacting to noise or bad behavior rather than finding ways of preventing it, your work is never done. Remember that kids get a little less threatened and take you a little less seriously with each crazed outburst, and they can't respect you if you can't control yourself, let alone your class.

The Crypt Keeper

On the other end of the scale, you have the Crypt Keeper managerial style. This teacher abhors commotion and thinks any kind of class noise at all inhibits learning and is a sign of poor class control. If you walk into a Crypt Keeper's class, you can tell immediately. Everything is unnaturally silent, and the silence is heavy and oppressive; it feels like you're at a funeral! The kids rarely make eye contact with the teacher or with one another, and the air actually feels a few degrees colder than it does in the hallway outside the classroom. If you happen to catch the eye of a student, he or she looks at you with an empty, glassy expression and the wide-eyed stare of the damned.

When something's in the air . . .

A colleague of mine, Eric Stroh, tells a great story of his rookie year. As is the case with most rookies, Eric was saddled with a very "academically challenged" class, and he was forced to teach them algebra in a small, crowded classroom every afternoon.

This class, however, had a very particular idiosyncrasy: They were vastly amused by flatulence. Now, this fascination is true for most kids (and most of the adults I hang out with as well), but this algebra class was above and beyond the norm. Everyone knows that there's nothing quite so unpleasant as being trapped in a small room packed with people when something so foul is released into the air, but every time it happened during class, he'd just about lose control of his students.

Some students would laugh uproariously, some would gag dramatically, and just about all would flee from the scene of the crime. The result? Desks in disarray, students running about the room overreacting, and one hugely embarrassed kid at the epicenter of all the commotion. You'd think that after it happened a few times, all the hubbub would die down, but it just got worse and worse with each successive (ahem) event.

One day, inspiration struck. He had a discussion with his class. He knew that they'd never be able to ignore the situation if it were to arise again, so he instead opted to offer them a more acceptable behavior to replace the current behavior, which was chaos. "I know that it stinks, and I know that it's gross, but you can't run around the room like lunatics," I can imagine him saying. "Next time it happens, just reach down, grab the collar of your shirt, and pull it up over your nose. Your shirt will help filter out the smell, and I won't get so angry at you for behaving like madmen."

By replacing the undesired behavior with a much more acceptable one, he once again established control of his class. His kids needed help coming up with an alternative to the behavior that was clearly out of line, and he came up with one that kept order while still allowing them to show displeasure at the offensive odor, which they felt compelled to do. After that day, the class was much better behaved, even if portions of the lessons were taught to students whose faces, like the stagecoach bandits of the Wild West, were partially concealed.

Except when it's inappropriate (like a quiz or test situation), students need to feel comfortable talking to one another softly. If you don't believe me, you've never been to a faculty meeting of any kind. Teachers can't keep quiet for one second when the principal is talking. They have to share witty remarks with one another and comment on everything that transpires during the meeting. In fact, the Crypt Keeper teachers are usually the worst offenders at faculty meetings, talking loudly and disruptively, completely unaware of their hypocritical behavior.

Don't hold your students to a standard that you personally can't attain. A little conversation, even if it's not completely about classroom events, is natural. It means that students feel comfortable being themselves in your room. Well-tuned sports cars hum softly as they drive, bees buzz as they go about their business, and even the wind whistles softly through tree branches as you walk outside. Everything has a little noise to it; complete silence is unnatural, and it makes your room uncomfortable.

The Great Debater

Sometimes, the best answer to a student question is no answer at all. Even when they're not openly misbehaving, some students will constantly try to get you to change your mind. "You're going to give us this much homework two nights in a row?" My response to such a challenge is, "Yes, I am. I know, I'm a horrible person and you're going to need counseling when you're done, because of the psychological trauma I'm inflicting upon you at such a young age, but I'm going to assign this homework anyway. It's I who have the greatest burden, having to live with myself after so cruel an assignment." (Humor and occasional sarcasm are great ways to deflect these questions, just as long as you have good rapport with your students and they don't view your sarcasm as condescending.)

Don't make the mistake of justifying an assignment to students unless doing so is necessary. If the homework is bizarre and students can't understand why in the world you're assigning it, by all means, explain yourself. For example, one of my yearly assignments was to go on a 30-minute drive and measure the speed at which the car was traveling at 1-minute intervals. This assignment is a strange thing to ask, so I explained that we'd use the data to try to estimate how far the car drove during that time period, using mathematical methods we'd learn the next day. However, most assignments don't require justification, nor do they require your students' approval. If you think that you're assigning a reasonable amount of homework, that's all the justification you need, unless your school district has some sort of homework policy that you're violating (you should check that out).

If you make a habit of explaining why you do things, your students will get in the habit of always questioning you. They need to know that your classroom, although occasionally fun and always pleasant smelling, is not a democracy — it's a benevolent dictatorship.

The Control Freak

Control Freaks uphold the letter of the law for every person, every circumstance, and every rule infraction. Their lectures sound something like this: "Plant cells, unlike animal cells, have a cell wall. John, stop leaning back in your chair. This feature — Melissa, stop tapping your foot — is similar to what part of an animal cell? Ann, you've been sharpening your pencil for five minutes; sit down. The cell membrane. Sam, face forward."

Even imagining life like that is exhausting. Notice that most of the things the teacher addressed in my example were really not that big of a deal. No one was challenging her authority, and no one was being disrespectful. However, to the Control Freak, that doesn't matter; she needs everything in her classroom to be *exactly the way she wants*. Her list of rules is 5 miles long, and the rules aren't negotiable. Her classes are never much fun for students, and most of the students think that she hates or at least strongly dislikes them.

Some teachers are this way in class because they're also this way at home, and (love it or leave it) being a Control Freak is just part of their personality. If, however, you're a completely different person at home and only act like this in school, it's because you're afraid. You don't feel that you have enough control over your class, and everything that happens during the day could possibly cause your dental-floss-thin reins of control to snap. If you see yourself in this description, you need to master one major skill: how to pick your battles instead of going to war over every single thing. (Knowing how to pick your battles is such an important skill that I dedicate Chapter 8 to it.)

One endangered specimen of Control Freak goes by the name "Captain Ultimatum." When things feel as though they're getting a wee bit out of control, Captain Ultimatum will resort to saying, "If it doesn't get quiet in here in five seconds, no one is allowed to talk for the rest of the semester!" or "Well, if you don't like the way I'm doing it, maybe you'd like to come up here and try it yourself!" Don't ever paint yourself into a corner like this, threatening consequences that you can't enforce or opening yourself up to a situation that you truly can't control.

Getting Discipline Right

It's easy, in retrospect, to see that the Crypt Keeper or Mr. Sudden Fury, as I've described them in the previous section, would not create a very positive classroom atmosphere. How, then, are you supposed to address moderately serious discipline problems? There are two major strategies you can use if things are getting a little hairy in your room: nabbing the ringleader and (as dramatic as it sounds) dropping the atomic bomb.

Nabbing the ringleader

A school administrator once said to me, "Did you ever notice that, when you're driving, one person speeding makes everyone else a little braver? Let's say you're driving down the road and a sports car passes you, going about 80 miles an hour. The people he passes are more likely to speed. Why? Because they figure they can go about 10 miles an hour slower than he's going, and even though that's well over the speed limit, they figure that any cop will go after the guy going fastest first."

That's a very profound observation, because students have the same mentality in the classroom. If someone in your room is really misbehaving and is a huge pain in your posterior, as long as others aren't so obvious or rude in their behavior, they hope to fly under your behavioral radar, undetected. In their minds, as long as someone is acting out worse than they are, they're safe. For all practical purposes, they're right, because if you try to discipline them, they'll feel free to air your dirty laundry. For example, if you turn in a student for being tardy to your class excessively, that student may feel free to tell the principal, "Sure, she's picking on me for being late, but at least I'm not breaking things and throwing books in her class like most of the other kids. I'm late most of the time just because I don't feel safe in there."

The moral of the story is that you have to pick off the fastest speeders first.

Picture this situation. You're driving along, going perhaps a teeny bit too fast, listening to the radio and not really paying much attention to anything except the lyrics of your favorite song. Suddenly, your rearview mirror lights up like Times Square on New Year's Eve. Police lights! How fast were you going? Oh no! Why you? Why today? You pull off the road, trying to remember where your vehicle registration is, all the while trying to come up with a good excuse for speeding, and the police car passes you by. He wasn't trying to pull you over after all! You breathe deeply the scent of pure relief, and you sit for a moment exulting in the fact that *it wasn't you!* For a while, you watch the speed limit a little more closely. You drive defensively, are a bit more courteous, and keep those hands on the wheel at the 10 and 2 position. Your brief brush with the law reminds you that you need to be more careful when you're driving, and you pledge to do just that. You've forgotten all of this within a day or two, of course, but for a small window of time, the policeman's presence was a deterrent to future crime. The only person for whom the experience will be more effective as a deterrent is the person who got caught. He may actually drive slower for a week or so until he again starts wondering just how fast his car can go.

How does this relate to the classroom? If you handle confrontation and discipline appropriately, your stern moments of reproach will have the same effects on your students. Even if they weren't the ones being chastised, they'll still remember the sour odor of your wrath as it was exacted on other people and seek to avoid it in the future, although they won't remember its sting as well as the one against whom the verbal lash was directed.

In practical terms, you should realize that someone in your room will rise to challenge you, like the speeder who tops out his speedometer to see if the road he's traveling has any police presence. If he can drive as fast as he likes, he'll become more daring and brazen during his next trip. Likewise, if you don't punish students when they break the rules, three things happen:

- The unpunished individual will break more-serious rules much more quickly.
- Others in the classroom will begin to test you as well.
- You'll begin an unspoken war of charisma and control with the student who's defying you most openly.

If you don't immediately get control of your class, one of your students is going to try to control it. He or she will openly defy you, and if you consistently shy away from confronting the challenge, students will lose respect for you. Therefore, the question remains: How do I confront bad behavior in my classroom after I've identified the offender or offenders?

Dropping the atomic bomb

In my experience, the best way to deal with confrontation is to make it memorable. In my classroom, aside from the typical, mundane rules, I had three major rules:

- Respect one another.
- Be as kind and as patient as you can.
- Respect the teacher and do what he says without whining.

As much as you want your room to be one big love fest every day, where students are kind, bluebirds perch upon their outstretched fingers, and everyone joins hands and sings, "C'mon people now, smile on your brother, everybody get together, try to love one another right now," that won't happen. In most cases, you won't be able to achieve that, and that's okay. These kids see each other every day for a very long period of time, and they're bound to get on each other's nerves eventually; it's human nature. However, sometimes, students will be extremely disrespectful to you or to one another, or they'll brazenly contradict what you've told them to do.

Throughout this chapter, I discuss lots of inappropriate ways to confront bad behavior, but now I'm going to tell you about the method I used to straighten my students out when they got a little crooked. I call it the "atomic bomb," and it is, without question, the most effective way to tell a class that you've had enough. This technique is the metaphoric equivalent of not only pulling someone over but also handcuffing him and taking him straight to prison. (In Chapter 8, I give you less dramatic methods for dealing with problem behavior, sort of like the verbal warning or the parking ticket.)

In practice, the atomic bomb is exactly what it sounds like: a giant, directed explosion that gets students' attention, tells them exactly what they're doing wrong, and lets them know why it angers you more than anything else you've ever seen in your entire life. It's a reaction that goes overboard, drives the point home, leaves no room for debate, and brings your authority down on top of them with an audible "thump." Let me give you an example.

When I was in fourth grade, I was in the gifted-and-talented program. It was a new program in the school, and it began as a *pull-out program*. I spent half of my school day in a normal classroom, but English, social studies, and science were in a separate classroom next to the library. Thus, every day at about noon, a handful of us would leave our classmates behind and make the short walk to the "smart" classroom for more-advanced instruction.

The more this happened, the more obvious it became to the students who stayed behind that we were different in some way. Because we were the "smart kids," you'd think that we could've found a humble way to explain our other classes. Of course, that didn't happen. We talked about how we needed to go to another class because we were "too smart" for the one they were in, and that we were "special" and deserved more than the teacher could teach "normal kids." Man, were we ever brats!

One day, Ms. Breslin, my teacher, overheard one of our exceedingly insensitive remarks and gave me my first experience in seeing an atomic bomb explode. Her voice climbed a few hundred decibels (she wasn't screaming, but she was, shall we say, speaking forcefully) and her tirade began: "Who do you think you are? *Who do you think you are?* No one in this class is more special than anyone else, no matter what some standardized test says. So you're in some program! Does that make *you* better than he is? Just because you think that you're smarter? Should I list your names on the board in order of I.Q. so that we can all see who the smartest person in the room is? Would it surprise you to find out that, according to the tests you're quoting, the smartest person in this room doesn't even get pulled out? I will never, *ever,* hear talk like that again in this classroom. Ever! No one in here is so special that he's better than anyone else, and don't forget it. I think we'll all remember this better if you sit silently while I try to calm down."

The nuclear explosion was over as quickly as it had begun, but the fallout lasted all year long. The "smart kids" were embarrassed and convicted of their haughty attitudes, and everyone was once again back on an even keel. No one even *thought* of bringing up the topic anymore, and the classroom became a community again within a few days.

Every one of my favorite teachers growing up knew how to drop the bomb effectively, and it's a skill you have to master. However, the atomic bomb is more than simply an outburst of anger. You need to keep a few things in mind as you deliver this verbal explosion:

- ✔ **Your blast must specifically address one issue.** Don't just stand up in front of the room, foaming at the mouth, saying things like, "You kids are driving me crazy!" Instead say, "Can *no one* actually be in a seat when the bell rings? Do you not *know* that the bell is about to ring? Does it not ring at the *same* time every day? Why, then, can you not manage to sit down?!" You're trying to drive home a point, and that point must be clear.

- ✔ **The goal of your outburst is to teach kids a lesson, not scare them.** Students need to know that you're angry because they've misbehaved or upset you; they must understand that they're responsible for what's happening. If you become too angry or scare them, you're out of control. The students can't feel safe in the room if you can't control your temper. Your tirade in the room must be a metaphoric *controlled burn* — a fire that's set intentionally in order to burn away the useless and dead undergrowth and allow for new, healthy plant life to replace it.

- ✔ **The atomic bomb is a last resort, not your first option.** You must first and foremost be a patient person, trying to correct things in other ways. For example, gentle rule reminders or simple commands are usually enough to remind kids who's in charge. You can't drop the bomb more than two or three times on one group of kids during one school year; if you're dropping it more often than that, you're using it too frequently and probably ineffectively. Your students must see you as a reasonable person pushed to the limits by their behavior for the technique to work correctly. If yelling or anger is your status quo, you're not enforcing your rules consistently enough on a day-to-day basis to prevent such pressures from building up a head of steam.

✔ **Vent all your frustration, and take none of it home with you.** If student behavior has gotten to the point where the atomic bomb is your only option, you need to get that frustration out in a healthy way. Reproving your kids is healthy, both for you and for them, because it restores the natural order of things in class — you're in charge and they aren't. I let my frustration run its course before I move on to other things and try to put the event behind me because, otherwise, I go home feeling frustrated and upset, and it's not worth it.

✔ **Yelling is rarely appropriate, even during such a show of force.** Remember that you're not losing your temper, you're simply exerting your authority. Most teachers speak more loudly, more clearly, and with a look of intensity in their gaze as they deliver these speeches, but few actually yell. Yelling (or even worse, screaming) suggests that you've lost control of yourself and of your students, and will actually hurt more than help the situation. As a teacher, you must always be in control of yourself, even when pushed to your outermost boundaries.

✔ **Don't be afraid to use guilt if you've gone out of your way to be patient.** Some of my more effective atomic encounters with students are conducted in a very quiet voice. I pull my chair out from behind my desk, sit in front of the room, and begin with that age-old expression that scares you when your significant other says it: "We need to talk."

For example, after one particularly low-scoring quiz, I said to my students: "You knew when the quiz was going to occur. You knew that I stayed after school to help you if you needed it. I helped you review in class, and I even gave you sample problems to help you know what to expect. Still, you performed badly. Honestly, tell me, what more can I do to help you? Am I not doing everything in my power to help you pass this class? At some point you have to actually decide to do *something* to pass, and stop making me do *everything,* because, clearly, that is not working." The best thing about the guilt approach is that, if you use it sparingly, there is no easy reply to it. You didn't yell, so the students can't get defensive; instead, they'll just shift around uncomfortably in their seats until the guilt fest is over, and I'll bet you they remember your verbal dressing down for a while.

Remember that you must work every day to keep your students in line, and an atomic bomb event must be so rare that it's memorable. When you've employed it effectively, you've taken major strides in establishing a reputation at your school. Word will spread quickly — if you have more than one group of students during the day, the others will hear about it within minutes, and the rest of the student body will be a little less willing to test your boundaries in the future, which is the best possible outcome. Eventually, students will accept your authority without such events, based on your history, and discipline will become much, much easier and far less confrontational.

Chapter 8

Picking Your Fights

● ●

In This Chapter

▶ Drawing the line between acceptable and unacceptable behavior

▶ Modifying student behavior through less confrontational means

▶ Developing a thick skin to counter student criticism

▶ Referring problem students to the school administration effectively

● ●

*Y*ou understand how important it is to establish good discipline on your first day of school and to confront students who challenge your authority. In Chapter 7, I show you a lot of bad ways to handle your class and I talk about effective methods to get your students' attention when they're seriously misbehaving. However, if you're only supposed to atomic bomb your classes on very rare occasions, how are you supposed to keep your kids in line day in and day out? How can you nip bad behavior in the bud? How much of a stickler should you be? At what point do you involve the school administration to help you restore order in your room?

In this chapter, I answer all these questions and help you become an effective classroom manager by giving you practical tips and techniques for confronting less serious, more common behavior issues, such as excessive talking and students struggling to stay awake in class. Dealing with these everyday problems is just as important as thwarting direct challenges to your authority (see Chapter 7), but doing so requires an entirely different approach.

Making the Punishment Fit the Crime

I worked in a local mall as a furniture salesman the summer before I began teaching. I sold that wooden furniture that falls somewhere on the spectrum between extremely uncomfortable and torturously uncomfortable. Because the furniture was as impractical as it was ugly, not many people bought the stuff, and I spent most of that summer sitting behind a desk, putting myself in various situations I'd seen as a student and trying to decide how I'd handle myself as the teacher in just such a circumstance. This exercise was very helpful because it reminded me that I had lots of options when it came to modifying student behavior. I didn't want to become the one-trick pony that so many of my teachers had been, yelling whenever something went wrong. (Who wants a pony that yells all the time anyway? Wouldn't pony rides be a lot less serene and relaxing if the pony were always shouting?)

In Chapter 7, I use the metaphor of a traffic officer occasionally pulling over the most blatant speeders to both punish them and set an example for the drivers around them. When an officer stops your car, he basically has two options: to issue you a traffic ticket (if your offense warranted it) or to issue you a warning, hoping that you'll think twice before committing the same moving violation again.

As a teacher, you have more options than the police officer when it comes to behavior modification, but you don't have the officer's ultimate behavior modifier — the pistol — which is probably a good thing, especially when a student is very disrespectful to you after you've had a really long day.

Addressing minor problems

Making a mountain out of a molehill is a classic rookie error. If a student is off task but not causing a giant disruption in class, be careful not to overreact. If you react too harshly, the student will be stunned, embarrassed, and eventually belligerent. In a student's mind, the punishment must fit the crime, so you should use the methods I describe in this section if the crime is just a "misdemeanor," meaning:

- Talking to a neighbor
- Writing, reading, or passing a note during class
- Daydreaming or beginning to nod off
- Doing other homework or reading non-course materials
- Designing a diabolical weather machine in the hopes of overthrowing the governments of the world and beginning an evil reign of tyrannical terror

Walk toward the student's desk and stand beside him, but don't interrupt class

Sometimes, a student simply needs to know that you see him when he's doing something wrong. As you continue to talk to your class, merely walk over to the student who's off task and stand beside him — you don't even have to make eye contact. This action is a simple way to remind that student where he is and what he should be doing without drawing any attention to him specifically. When I used this tactic, I tried to make it look casual, as though I was just strolling around the room. Only the off-task student and I knew what I was really doing, bringing the lesson right to his desk, so he had no other option but to pay attention.

If the student still doesn't get the picture when you walk over to him, make eye contact, rap on his desk softly with your knuckle, or tap him lightly on the shoulder to get his attention.

Shoot the offender the icy stare of death

If the noninvasive "keep class going" plan doesn't work, abruptly stop talking and stare directly at the student who's off task. Your gaze should convey the message, "If I were allowed to, I would smack you upside the head, so consider yourself lucky." Typically, the sudden halt in the smooth flow of class events will cause the offender to look up at you (his guilty conscience kicks in) and to realize that you're none too pleased. If, however, the student fails to make eye contact while you're staring him down, you can always throw in the annoyed throat-clearing sound: "ah-*hem*." At this point, if the student is still oblivious, a neighbor will usually poke him in the ribs and say, "The teacher's looking right at you!" and you'll wind up getting the point across.

This method works best if the student thinks that he's pulling one over on you, hoping that you're completely oblivious to whatever he's doing. The best way to tell if a student is trying to pull the wool over your eyes is to monitor his eye contact. Students involved in some sort of chicanery will either establish and break eye contact with you in short bursts, quickly looking at you and then backing down to whatever they're doing, or they'll avoid eye contact altogether. This makes mischief-makers easy to spot, and a quick stare down usually brings them back in line.

If, against all odds, the student remains completely oblivious to you as you stare and/or clear your throat to get his attention, punctuate your glare with a quick bark of his name: *"John!"* It should be crisp, sharp, and just a bit louder than your casual speech to make it stand out. This action usually startles the student, who was paying so little attention to his surroundings that being snapped back into reality stings a little bit.

Defuse potential distractions with humor

If a student is off task, but she's usually very attentive, or she's breaking a rule but she's usually very thoughtful and considerate about following the class rules, don't react harshly to her on the rare occasion that she slips up. If, for example, she's daydreaming when you're talking about something very important, you might say, "Hello? Earth to Sarah?" or wave your hands in front of her face to get her attention and say something like, "Doctor, I think we've lost her — pupils are dilated and there's no sign of a pulse." These things should be said with a smile, so the student doesn't feel like the butt of the joke, even if she was off task.

Humor can help defuse other situations as well. Sometimes, you'll feel friction beginning to develop among students in your classes. The older that kids get, the more developed their personalities become, and the more likely they are to get annoyed with one another. It happens. Humor is a great way to let the steam off of any pressure that's forming as a result of student conflict.

For example, I often witnessed increased friction among students after I passed back a quiz or test. More than anything else in the world, students want to know how their scores compare with the scores of the people around them. The moment you begin to pass back papers, you hear the assessment mantra repeated over and over: "Whadjaget? Whadjaget? Whadjaget?"

Grow eyes in the back of your head

If someone has become brazen enough to seriously misbehave while your back is turned (perhaps something was thrown at the board) and you don't know who's responsible for it, you can still do a few things to punish the offender and to prevent it from happening in the future. First, don't start accusing people based merely on suspicion. The worst thing you can do is to accuse someone and be totally wrong. This mistake sends a message of hope to any hoodlums in your classes that they may be able to get away with something.

Second, you still need to meet the disrespectful behavior with an appropriate punishment, and the best way to punish the offender is to punish the entire class, but act as though you really, really regret having to do so. Students will immediately complain that it's not fair that everyone is punished for something that *only one person did*. That's a good sign. It means that they aren't identifying with the guilty party and have decided not to support the perpetrator. Score one for you.

Explain that you agree it's totally unfair. (Do *not* follow it with the statement, "Life is unfair." If

you were going to say that, move to the end of the line. Clichés are never effective in disciplining kids.) Commiserate with the students in a sly way by saying, "If someone decided to act out in a class I was in and I got punished for it, I'd be upset, too. However, you must understand that I can't simply ignore this kind of rude behavior. It has to be punished, or I wouldn't be doing my job, which is making sure that you have a safe and orderly classroom environment. The only person who had a choice about what to do in this scenario is the individual who disrespected everyone by acting so irresponsibly." This little speech tells the kids that you don't hold anything against the innocent individuals personally, but you still won't be pushed around.

If you suspect that the student or students will continue to misbehave, even after that guilt-heavy speech, use an overhead projector to give notes in class. If you write your notes on transparencies and project them onto the board or a screen at the front of the room, you never have to turn your back to the kids.

If a student is particularly disappointed in her score, she may look at a higher achiever's paper and comment, "Another A — and you thought you were going to fail it. Yeah right!" to which the response will inevitably be, "Well, at least I studied." The next line in this oft-repeated drama is usually something to the effect of, "Are you saying I didn't study?" and at this point, you have to step in before things get out of hand. I'd always make an innocuous comment like, "I feel a lot of love in this room right now," or take the hopelessly out-of-date route and say, "Please, your negative energy is really harshing my vibe, dude. Mellow out, man, and feel the love. Give peace a chance!"

This strategy works because the students really aren't angry with one another — they're just letting off steam. A test grade is a big deal to students, and a lot of anticipation usually builds up between test day and the day papers are returned (especially if you were a little slow in getting them graded). Humor keeps them from actually finding reasons to get angry with one another as the steam is released.

Addressing moderate problems

Sometimes, minor problems graduate into bigger problems, and you have to take additional steps to resolve the conflict. Distinguishing moderate problems from the minor ones is easy because students cause moderate behavioral problems in class when they break the rules consciously or act out of defiance. For example, if the students blatantly refuse to follow your directions or are openly hostile to you or one another, you've crossed into more-serious behavior infractions.

Whereas the techniques I address earlier in this chapter help class move smoothly and keep kids involved, the methods I discuss here have a different purpose. They're more punitive in nature and are focused on reestablishing your authority as well as rehabilitating and discouraging further outbreaks of the problem behavior.

As you can see from the sections that follow, you have lots of alternatives to losing your temper. Don't let your students get you angry very often, because they'll figure out what sorts of things annoy you, and they'll save them for days when they feel downright belligerent. Don't let a class figure out how to push your buttons; instead, take deep breaths, keep your cool, and choose an appropriate means to deal with the behavior. When the students find out they can't rattle you, they'll stop trying so often. (Unfortunately, they'll never stop trying altogether, at least not as long as you're a rookie.)

Rearrange your seating chart

When students start to get familiar and comfortable with the people around them, they get braver and more willing to act out in class. The simple act of changing students' seats reasserts your authority and allows you to separate students beginning to ally with one another with the intent of challenging your authority. Redoing your entire seating chart during class isn't a good idea; instead, if you can you should present a new seating chart at the beginning of class, as students are entering, like you did on the first day of school. You will occasionally encounter situations in which you may need to immediately move a student, however.

I always left a student seat empty in the row closest to the chalkboard at the front of the room. During class, I'd use the empty desk to hold my grade book, textbook, attendance book, or papers to be passed back. That way, I was not continuously walking back and forth to my bigger teacher desk, and I could interact more intimately with the students because no large, hulking furniture separated us. Even better, I could easily clear my things off the desk and use it as a place to seat troublemakers if I ever needed to move them during class.

If someone acted out seriously enough, I told her to grab her stuff and move up to the front row, which was just enough embarrassment to get her back in line as well as allow me to keep an eye on her in the much closer seat. Believe it or not, most students eventually thanked me for moving them! Away from their potentially distracting friends, their grades usually improved, and they found out that paying attention wasn't nearly as painful as they imagined.

Threaten the class with the loss of privileges or with additional homework

Elementary-school teachers wield the ultimate weapon: loss of recess. If students don't fall in line, whether the transgressors are individuals or the entire class, nothing hurts quite as much as not being able to run around at recess time. My elementary-school teachers would write a name on the board if that student was in danger of losing recess time, and it usually did the trick. Each time the student continued to act out, the teacher would place a check mark next to her name. Each check mark represented a fixed amount of lost recess time, usually 10 or 15 minutes. Of course, you don't have to single out individuals; you can always penalize the whole class if there are lots of kids turning your hair prematurely gray.

Because secondary students usually aren't allowed recess time, your best course of action is to threaten additional homework. If faced with a misbehaving class, walk to the chalkboard and make a mark in the corner each time you have to stop class. Eventually, the students will ask, "What are you doing? What do those marks mean?" Explain that each mark represents an extra ten minutes of homework for that night, and that you'll continue to make marks on the board at regular intervals until the class is under control.

Some administrators disagree with this practice. They contend that students don't enjoy homework as it is, and portraying extra homework as punishment makes students dislike it even more. To this I say, "Well, *duh*. That's the whole point." Homework is usually not a punishment, and it needs to be a part of your regular routine, because students learn best by doing things themselves at home (or on the bus ten seconds before they get to school). However, by making your assignments longer, you're intruding on students' private time, hitting them where it hurts.

Ruin everyone's day with a pop (unannounced) quiz

You'll have days when trying to teach your students feels like swimming in oatmeal — you work really hard but you don't get anywhere fast. There were days, especially as the weather began to warm up in the late spring and early summer, when my students just refused to pay attention and didn't feel the need to do any homework. I'd stand at the front of the room, trying to give notes, and you couldn't hear me with all the chatting in the room.

Nothing quite reminds everyone you're the boss like the words, "Clear your desks and take out a sheet of paper. It's time for a pop quiz." I still remember how I felt when my teachers made that pronouncement. Cold sweat would break out on my face, and my stomach felt like I had just drunk an entire milk-shake in one gulp.

The best questions for an unannounced quiz are the exact things you were just discussing in class, when no one felt the need to pay attention. Don't ask complicated questions or really try to screw up students' grades. Ask basic things, geared at rewarding students who were paying attention and zonking the people who weren't.

Don't be stingy on detentions

I've heard lots of teachers say that they won't assign detentions after the school day because it punishes the teacher as well as the student; both have to stay late. Let's be realistic for a moment. You're going to be doing some sort of schoolwork most evenings anyway, so what does it matter that you work at school rather than work at home for a little while? There's a whole lot less to distract you at school (no television, no chores, no dinner), so you'll probably get your grading or planning done faster anyway.

Assigning detentions is not a poor reflection on your ability to control your class; it is, instead, a testament to your desire to maintain class control. However, make sure that the detention, itself, is worthwhile. Students shouldn't be allowed to sleep, talk, or do other homework during your detention. (You're not allowing them the same luxury to complete schoolwork before they get home, like you're enjoying.) They should have to do something that makes them think twice about having to serve detention with you again.

Find a punishment that suits you. I used to have students write page-long punishment assignments, detailing what they did wrong, why it was wrong, and what steps they'd take to make sure they wouldn't do it again. When they finished (and if their 45 minutes of detention time wasn't up), they'd clean my chalkboards, wipe down the chalk trays at the bottom of the boards, clean the student desks with Windex and paper towels, straighten the rows of desks in the room, or pick up trash off the floor. If you have boring tasks that need to be done, put their indentured servitude to use. For example, if you have to count textbooks for inventory, alphabetize forms (you'll be doing a lot of that your first few weeks of school), or reorganize and clean your shelves, detained students are a great help.

When you assign a detention, give at least 24 hours' notice (don't assign the detention for the same day) so that parents can arrange to pick the student up if he isn't old enough to drive or doesn't have a car. Make sure to send home to the parents a form explaining why their child received detention, what day the detention will be, and when it will begin and end. (The parent should sign the form to indicate that they've seen it and know what's going on.) Explain to the parent that the child needs to picked up promptly when the detention is over, and list the school's phone number so they can call you if they have any questions. One of the great benefits of detentions is that it gets the parents' attention, because they're inconvenienced as much as, if not more than, the students are. Not many want to go up to their bosses and say, "Sorry I have to leave early today. My kid got in trouble in school, and I have to go pick her up from detention."

Don't feel like you have to go out of your way to make the detention convenient for the student. If he has sports practice after school, and the detention will interfere with it, that's not your problem. In some circumstances (such as away games or planned activities), the coach or sponsor of the event will approach you and ask you to be flexible with your timing. There's nothing wrong with adjusting your timetable to help out a colleague, but don't feel like it's your duty to approach them or to try to make things as easy as possible for the kid. If he screwed up and got detention in your class, it should be his job to clean up any messes that creates.

Call a parent or coach and outline your complaints explicitly

Remember those information cards students filled out on the first day of school? Put them to good use and call their parents when the students do things bad enough to warrant it. If you're a stickler for the rules, you'll be on the phone, calling parents of wayward students every afternoon. At the opposite extreme, I only called when I was really miffed at a kid and felt ready to strangle him. Trust me, when it comes to modifying student behavior, a parent phone call always beats death by strangulation.

The younger the child, the more effective a phone call home usually is. However, when students get involved in extracurricular activities (especially sports) in middle or high school, you have another avenue open to you. If a student athlete in my class was ever disrespectful or didn't do his work, I met with the coach and outlined my concerns. By and large, coaches *love* to hear these sorts of things. Don't be surprised if, after you meet with a coach, your mutual student comes back the next day and says, "I had to do 100 extra pushups," or, "Coach made me run 2 extra miles because you told him I'm talking too much in class." High-school students are more willing to listen to their coaches than their parents, because at that age, most have decided that their parents have *got* to be the stupidest people alive, so punishment from a coach is effective, because it's novel to them.

Send kids who act like jerks to another teacher

Before the school year starts, make an arrangement with a teacher in a room next to yours. If you have a kid you need to send out of the room, send her to that teacher, and return the favor for your colleague when she needs it. The kid is much less likely to misbehave in front of a group of students she doesn't know. However, she still may try. Therefore, you should include this in your speech as you walk that student over to the teacher who will harbor her: "I am completely out of patience with you. You're one step away from the principal's office and a punishment assignment from me that you will *not* enjoy. This is your last chance to start acting like a human being again. If Mrs. So-and-so has any trouble with you — *any at all* — she'll send you right to the office, and it'll get ugly. Got it?"

When I was in school, badly behaving students were sent to the hallway, to "think about what they'd done." This approach is a good idea in theory, because it removes the distraction from the room. Most kids are their worst when in front of an audience of other students. If you send them out, the audience is gone, and so is the need to perform and be cool in front of their peers. One problem with this theory: If the kid is out in the hallway, unsupervised, what stops her from roaming around the building and causing even more problems?

In this day of litigation, you need to make sure that students are supervised at all times. You can always follow the kid into the hallway to talk to her, but now the rest of your class is unsupervised. You can leave the door open so you can keep an eye on them as you speak to the student in the hall, but then her audience is back, and she's more likely to act out. You need another alternative.

Letting Sleeping Dogs Lie

The hardest part of disciplining students for me was knowing when to call it quits. Way back in Chapter 1, I describe teaching as "triage," constantly dealing with immediate needs, and choosing to put your efforts into things that would pay off the biggest rewards. This means that, in some cases, you'll have to give up on a student — to decide that he's not worth all the effort you're putting into trying to motivate him. I know, I know . . . you'll never do that. You'll work with every ounce of your being to show the kids that you care, and you'll leave no child behind. I said all those things, too. But reality has a way of altering your ambitions — and that's not necessarily a bad thing.

Recognizing your limitations

Most people in the teaching profession were good students in school. Even if you weren't the smartest or the sharpest or the most studious person in your classes, you were probably very respectful of the teacher and generally tried to do your best. That's why it's so hard for teachers to understand that not everyone is wired the same way. Some students care more about what they're having for dinner than whether they're going to college. Some are more interested in whether they're buying the right kind of jeans than whether they're going to pass a single one of their classes.

During my first year of teaching, I was a little delusional. I felt pretty smart, considered myself pretty cool, and thought, "Who *wouldn't* want me as a teacher? I try hard, I make class fun when I can, and I want students to do well." Almost immediately I found out that the kids were not all that impressed. *Remember:* They have lots of teachers during the day, and they've had enough new teachers to know that it stinks to be in a new teacher's class when the rookie is still cutting his teeth, so to speak.

One day, I sat with a veteran math-teacher colleague, Kitty Vogel, venting my frustration about a student who wouldn't pay attention, no matter what I did. "This guy Chris never pays attention, never listens, and is constantly falling asleep in class. Plus, when he yawns, it's like, 'YAAAAAARRRRNNN.' He's so loud and obnoxious about it that I want to walk over and kick him right in the shin."

She laughed. "He's always been like that. He was like that in my class, and he's probably been like that since he was in elementary school."

"But I know I can find some way to reach him," I responded earnestly. "Deep down he has to be at least a little curious about learning, right? I just have to find some way to make things relevant to him, and maybe he'll come around."

I will always appreciate what Kitty did just at that moment. She laughed until tears streamed out of her eyes. "What do you think you can do differently than the 50 other teachers who've had him in class? Do you honestly think that you're *so good* that you're going to be able to do something they couldn't do? Forget it!" What an eye-opener.

You're surrounded by other teaching professionals with a lot more experience than you. Learning from them will serve you better than just assuming you're a better teacher than they are.

Surrendering unwinnable battles

You've tried and tried to get a young girl to do her homework, but she won't. It doesn't matter how many times you call home, how many detentions you assign, or how much you threaten and wave your arms around, she just won't do it. At that point, you've done what you can do. Of course, she'll get bad grades, and you have to give her zeros every time she won't turn her homework in, but the blame lies with her, and you have to let it go. She probably hasn't done homework for most of her school career, and her parents probably don't care one way or the other. You can't change her upbringing, you can't reorder her priorities, and you can't be her conscience. All that's left is to provide the negative consequence and concentrate on helping the students who do want to learn and improve their studying skills.

Don't get me wrong. You won't surrender a lot of battles during your career, and the few times that you'll have to wave the white flag won't make you a bad teacher. Even the best teachers need to know when something is beyond their control.

Recognizing an offer you can't refuse

Stacy Karcesky, a colleague of mine, began her teaching career during the week immediately following Thanksgiving. She worked in a school renowned for a troublesome student population; the school's reputation was that it housed the "bad kids," and no one seemed able to get it under control. She was a long-term substitute, waiting for a teaching job to open, and one just happened to open during Thanksgiving break because one of the teachers at that school decided he wasn't coming back. He had no class control, had no idea what he was getting himself into when he decided to teach, and left without telling anyone, sneaking away like a thief in the night.

Needless to say, these are not ideal circumstances under which to begin teaching. Stacy didn't have the opportunity to maximize her first day, didn't have a chance to get the lion-tamer control of the room I discuss in Chapter 6, and faced a pack of students already united in their dislike of the teacher in charge. Furthermore, one of the other teachers at the school approached her before her first class on that first fateful day. "Watch out for Greg," she said. "He's really psycho, and he's completely out of control. If he likes you, he'll make a deal with you before you start teaching. If I were you, I'd take it."

Stacy had no idea who Greg was, or what this "deal" was all about, but she quickly found out. As her seventh-grade class walked in, she was quickly able to guess who Greg was. In this corner, standing 6 feet, 3 inches tall, weighing in at 230 pounds, at the ripe old age of 17, Greg was a sight: a full five years older than his classmates, weighing as much as three of them combined, and possessing a list of criminal offenses that, if laid end to end, would stretch to the outer limits of Neptune and back. In two words, Greg was *bad news*.

He immediately walked up to Stacy, and told her, "I don't want to do anything in class. If you don't make me do anything and let me sleep, I won't interrupt class. Deal?" Without any hesitation, Stacy answered, "Deal," and she never regretted it for a second. Everyone in the class was afraid of Greg, and everyone was much happier if he was asleep at his desk, instead of scouting the crowds for his next victim. One person, however, did not agree with the deal: Stacy's supervisor.

As luck would have it (and luck always does), the supervisor decided to complete his first rated observation of Stacy during this, her worst class. It didn't take him long to see that Greg wasn't participating and that Stacy didn't seem to care. When the lesson ended, he presented her with a good rating, except for the topic "Classroom Management," for which he gave her a grade of "NI," meaning "needs improvement." Beneath the rating, he wrote that Greg had been "off task" during the lesson, and that Stacy had been negligent in her duties as a teacher to engage him in the learning process.

Stacy's response to him was fantastic. "I agree that I can't get him to learn, but this NI does not help me. I don't think he can be part of a proper learning environment, and I won't accept this NI until you come in and show me how it should be done." The supervisor agreed and came in the following week.

Things did not go well at all. Attempt after attempt to wake Greg, the sleeping giant, failed. Finally, after he was aroused, the adamant supervisor teased him, cajoled him, and tried to get him to pay attention. Greg would have no part of it and made no secret of the matter. Then something snapped. The supervisor, frustrated and out of options, picked up chalkboard erasers and began hurling them at Greg. That got his attention. Suddenly, Greg was up and out of his chair, dodging erasers like Keanu Reeves in the movie *The Matrix*. Like a ninja, he pulled the erasers out of the air and flung them back at the shocked supervisor, only much harder and aimed for the face. Moments later, as the supervisor fled the room, he called out, "The NI on your observation will be removed this afternoon." After he was gone, Greg settled back down, and Stacy got back to the job of teaching.

She knew something the supervisor could not accept. In rare and extreme circumstances, you must give up the battle to make kids sit up straight at their desks and learn, possibly for reasons having to do with your own personal safety. Though hard, it was the right decision. The next teacher who yelled at Greg, a substitute who wouldn't accept his "deal," found out why she should have chosen otherwise, when he smashed her over the head with a student desk. She ended up in the hospital, and he ended up in prison, where he got in further trouble for stabbing fellow inmates.

Note that Stacy actually made decisions on two battles in this example. She decided *not* to challenge her student, but she *did* challenge her supervisor. As you can probably tell, there was no clear way to win against Greg, but the situation with the supervisor was win-win. Even if he had succeeded in involving Greg in the lesson, she would have benefited, because she could have used those techniques herself. However, because she was sure he couldn't change Greg's outlook for the better, challenging the supervisor was the most effective way to remove the blemish from her record.

Saying yes to a bathroom request

The battles you'll have to surrender may not be as packed with physical danger, but you must not engage in battles you cannot win. For example, you can never prevail in bathroom and feminine hygiene–related battles. If a girl asks to be excused because of feminine reasons (why do they have to be so graphic I ask you?), let her go. If a kid says he is about to go to the bathroom in his pants, let him go. You can't win by telling these kids that they can't be excused. However, if the behavior becomes repetitive, document the dates and times, and make a call home to discuss the matter with the parents of the dire bathroom abuser. In this case, you'll eventually win the war, even if you have to surrender individual battles.

Taking Things Personally

It would be the greatest understatement in the history of the world to say that I was not very cool in high school. In fact, most other dorky kids looked at me and said, "There but for the grace of God go I." I was little, skinny, into computers, and not the most dapper dresser in the entire world. (I was into bright, solid colors, when everyone else was into black heavy-metal T-shirts depicting scenes of violence and women possessing vastly unrealistic body proportionality.)

From early on, I knew my place in the world of school; I was the quiet, nerdy kid who was funny every once in a while. My hair possessed a mind of its own and would stick out in a different direction every morning, trying to discern the exact direction to the magnetic north pole, perhaps. To make a long story short, I did not pride myself on peer acceptance, because I wasn't posting big points in the looks, athletic skills, or personality departments. Looking back on this sad, sad series of statements, I realize that I was very lucky, because school prepared me well for my eventual career as a teacher.

Teachers don't win popularity contests. Even the most beloved of teachers starts out as a total zero in the school social scene. Even if you were too cool for school back in your own day, to modern students, that day was circa 1742, and you're about as cool as false teeth soaking in a glass of Efferdent. For people used to being popular (that is, people not like me), this comes as quite a shock. I know a teacher who is at her wit's end and ready to quit because her students won't stop making fun of her hair! It sounds petty, but hearing such criticism day after day gets really burdensome.

I remember the young male substitute teacher who sauntered into our school one day wearing pants so tight that it left nothing to the imagination. I mean *nothing*. This was just some average guy, not Fabio mind you, but in his mind, he was Captain Sexpot because of his second-skin slacks. Whatever the reason (perhaps the pants were cutting off oxygen circulation to his brain), he decided these pants were appropriate for school. Needless to say, his kids (and they weren't bad kids) had a field day.

The comments started innocuously enough: "Hey, nice pants," accompanied by chortles and muffled laughter. Eventually, they got more and more creative with the subtle insults until one of them really got a ringer. "Can I borrow a dime to make a call on the pay phone?" the kid asked. The substitute responded that he didn't have any change. "Sure you do," the kid replied. "You have 45 cents; I can see it in your pocket." It's true. His pants were so tight, you could almost make out George Washington's hairdo jutting out of his thigh. Not knowing what else to do, shocked by the kids' constant barbs, he ran from the room, crying hysterically. This, of course, was riotously funny to the class, and he was so humiliated that he never substitute-taught again.

Hindsight is 20/20

Not every personal comment is made as an insult, but that doesn't make things any easier. You still have to know when to pick your fights and when to let it roll like water off a duck's back. During my second year teaching, I was up at the chalkboard one afternoon, in front of a very needy class that presented behavior problem after behavior problem. In fact, they were a buffet of behavior issues including attention deficit disorder, aggression, impulse-control problems, and (most woeful of all) hygiene oversights.

As I wrote a few notes, careful not to turn my back on the class for very long, one young girl suddenly commented loudly, "Mr. Kelley, I know I've never said so before, but I think you have a really nice ass." The room went silent (for the first time all year), as everyone waited on pins and needles to find out how I'd react. Would I yell? Would I take offense?

This young girl wasn't the worst in the class. Her major problem was impulse control and knowing what was appropriate in social situations (obviously!), but I didn't sense any ill intent in the remark. I turned around, and she seemed more embarrassed than anything. It was clear in my mind that she wasn't trying to disrupt class, and that she had merely let slip a comment that probably sounded a whole lot better in her head than it did out loud.

I thought it would do more harm than good to punish her, but I still had to do something. So, I gave my rear end a little wiggle and said, "Any of you can try to deny it, but you all know it's true." Then I went straight back to the lesson. Obviously, I was not coming on to the class; I was just trying to end the expectant silence with a joke in the hopes of continuing class without a scene.

It worked like a charm. Everybody laughed, and we got straight back to work. They actually paid attention, impressed by the fact that I hadn't yelled (this class was used to a lot of yelling from their teachers, believe you me), and the girl looked so visibly relieved, it was comical. I still see her every now and again, since she's graduated, and she always says hi to me instead of pretending she doesn't see me, which is what most kids do when they see a teacher in the wild.

Beware! The students will look for weaknesses in you and try to exploit them for entertainment purposes. You have two ways of coping with this:

- **Make lifestyle adjustments.** Kids are little thermometers of contemporary style. If they're making fun of your clothes, maybe it's time to update the old wardrobe. Most people (myself included) hit their fashion stride in college and have updated few outfits since then. Stop and think: How long ago *was* college? Though mean-spirited, many student comments contain a grain of truth, like it or not. If they call you the Missing Link, guys, cut that hair, shave more than every third day, and try to improve that posture just a little.

- **Make fun of yourself.** It's no fun to make fun of someone who agrees with everything you say. Kids would often tell me, "Mr. Kelley, those pants just don't match that shirt, and they're really tacky." I'd tell them, "I'll show you tacky — wait until tomorrow," and then wear something horribly ugly the next day. Don't take things so personally or seriously. These are kids! Turn their criticism into an opportunity to bond with them; show that, although you're the boss, you can take a little heat without losing your cool.

I had no pride in the classroom; my students would tease me mercilessly, but that gave me the opportunity to tease them back. However, do so good-naturedly. Battling one another with wisecracks and insults has no place in your classroom, especially if you're honestly trying to hurt the student's feelings. *Remember:* You're the adult, and you want to model appropriate behavior. By reacting noncombatively to their remarks, you're showing students how to defuse such criticisms when they encounter them personally.

Passing the Problem (Child) to the Principal: When and How

Most of your discipline issues should be handled within the four walls of your room, and after you internalize the techniques I outline in the past two chapters, you'll be able to do just that. However, you'll occasionally have to refer problem students to the principal or vice-principal. You don't want to do this too often; in fact, you want the administrators in your school to be surprised when you have to refer a student to them. You want them to say, "A child from Mr. Johnson's room? What the heck did you do, kid? Johnson *never* sends people to the office. You must have flubbed up royally."

I know teachers who will send students to the office for just about anything. If the kid doesn't do his homework, he's sent to the office. Talks to his neighbor? Sent to the office. Forgets that the letter *y* can be both a consonant and a vowel? Off to the principal and off with his head. If you send kids up the river for every single thing they do wrong, the folks who get all those refer-rals are going to stop taking you seriously. Furthermore, they'll think you can't control your class on your own.

Before you send a student to the office, make sure you've done all of the following:

- ✔ Talked to the student outside of class about the problem and tried to reach an understanding

- ✔ Called his parents and explained the situation to them

- ✔ Met with his parents and/or guidance counselor in a conference to try to change the behavior pattern

- ✔ Assigned at least one detention as punishment

If none of these strategies work, it's time to refer the child to the main office, and let the principal throw his or her weight around a little bit. When you do, make sure to explain everything the offender did in specifics, citing exact things he said (even if what he said was offensive), and dates and times of all his offenses. Notice that I said *offenses,* plural. Instead of reacting to every little thing, let the mistakes pile up and keep track of them as they do. Document the kid's every bad move and every plan you undertook to make things right; then record all that information on the referral form. If you've documented your case well and tried to mediate the behavior by every means available to you, the principal will be impressed and will punish the kid swiftly and harshly.

Chapter 9

Avoiding Sexual Harassment

In This Chapter

▶ Drawing the line between appropriate and inappropriate behavior

▶ Identifying unhealthy attitudes that already exist at your school

▶ Keeping your nose clean of any sign of impropriety

*N*othing you can be accused of as a teacher is quite so serious as an allegation of sexual harassment. Surprisingly enough, most new teachers don't receive any training or instruction about the topic at all. Too many rookies are under the mistaken impression that sexual harassment boils down to one thing: Teachers should not have sexual relations with students. Well, of course they shouldn't, but the question of sexual harassment is much more complex than that.

I didn't know nearly enough about sexual harassment when I started teaching, because I wasn't nearly as scared of it as I should have been. Don't get me wrong; it's not like I live a wild lifestyle or got into teaching to try to pick up girls ten years younger than I was. However, I never quite realized just how serious a sexual harassment allegation could be.

Sexual harassment is one of the few sins you can commit as a teacher that results in the immediate loss of your job, tenured or not, in the blink of an eye.

In this chapter, I give you some very frank advice about how to handle yourself in this day and age of sexual harassment. This advice goes for both male and female teachers, regardless of the ages of your students. Things do get trickier and more complicated the older the students get, so parts of this chapter are geared toward secondary teachers. However, no matter what grade level you teach, you'll benefit from advice concerning how to conduct yourself beyond reproach so that you never have to worry about being accused of this, the cardinal sin of teaching.

Uncovering Sexual Harassment Shockers

Perhaps I was naïve, but I walked into teaching completely oblivious to what could happen if my character was ever called into question and I faced a sexual harassment suit. What I eventually found out was that such an accusation could come from anywhere at any time, even if the teacher is completely innocent — and that's a very scary thought. It's as though you're standing on a trapdoor every day, and that trapdoor can swing open without notice, catapulting you into regions more horrible than you could ever imagine. I never understood that you always had to be on your guard, actively avoiding situations that could damage your reputation. (If you're wondering how, don't worry — I get to that later on in this chapter.)

Before you're able to take precautionary measures, however, you need to better understand the true nature of sexual harassment at your school. It's a very uncomfortable topic, so most people don't want to talk about it. Unfortunately, this results in many of the misconceptions and myths that plague most rookies, including me, until the scales fell from my eyes and I began to see how things really were.

Every day, you'll probably have to make decisions that involve borderline sexual-harassment issues. No one is immune, and rookie teachers need to be on guard around the clock.

Chances are, some people in your school sexually harass students every day

One day after class, a young girl asked to speak with me. After the other students had filed out, she told me, "Mr. Lang is saying some really inappropriate things to me in class, and I need to talk with someone about it." I told her she could feel free talking to me and that I'd keep things confidential, so she continued. "Today in class, when I was writing on the board, Mr. Lang told me I had a 'cute little butt' that 'really must make my boyfriend very happy.' Only he didn't say 'butt' and he was a little less subtle than I'm being retelling the story."

I couldn't believe it. "Are you sure that's what he said? There's no chance that you could have misheard him?"

"Nope, no chance," she said. "He says stuff like that to the cute girls in class all the time, and it's really gross and not as funny as he seems to think it is."

I asked if she wanted to press charges against the teacher and she said no. She figured that it would only cause trouble, and she was a senior, ready to head out in the world. "At least he doesn't, like, touch any of us. Then it would be a different story." She was happy just being able to talk to me about

How do these things happen?

Why is sexual harassment such a big issue these days? What is it that motivates teachers to form inappropriate relationships with students? I have no clear-cut answers to these questions, but having spent time as a rookie, I can cite some factors that probably contribute to practices teachers end up regretting:

✔ **Most new teachers are very lonely.** The vast majority of rookies have to move when they get a teaching job, and they usually move right before the school year starts. The result: You're a stranger in a strange land with no friends and no family around you. You're working hard all the time and your personal time is chock full of stress about all your classes, responsibilities, and the proposition of being fired or not receiving tenure. It's a recipe for loneliness.

✔ **It's hard to meet people during the school year.** Your job isn't like normal people's jobs. Other adults see and work with adults all day long, and they often end up in relationships with or through people at their office. You, on the other hand, work with children all day long and very rarely even get to interact with adults. Your "co-workers" aren't dating material — they still think burping is the funniest things there is, and they still have to ask you if and when they can go to the bathroom! Add in the hours you'll spend on school-related work or attending school events at night and on the weekends, and meeting someone is nearly impossible. (I was always worried about my reputation as a teacher, so I was very hesitant to cruise the bar scene, for fear of being known as a rummy or a playboy.)

✔ **Some of your students will really like and admire you.** Most teachers were the studious type when in school, to put things nicely. Some of your students, however, probably won't think you're that square, and they may even really like you. Rookies don't always know how to handle that kind of admiration. All too often, respect is either misinterpreted or improperly reciprocated as love, and things get messy fast.

The best thing you can do to avoid getting mixed up in weird relationships is to spend time with adults as much as possible when you're not in school. If you're not married or dating, make it a point to go out with people your own age, and try to build a happy and fulfilling life outside of teaching. When you're able to easily differentiate between your personal and professional lives, the temptation to mix the two together will vastly diminish.

it, knowing someone at the school was aware of it, in case things ever got any worse.

After that incident, I was suddenly aware of sexual harassment everywhere. Teachers I interviewed told me that during cheerleader routines at football games, they occasionally heard school employees softly muttering (so only they and their equally perverse colleagues could hear): "Kick higher! Higher!" so they could see up their skirts! I even remember one of my teachers asking me, when I was a freshman in high school, why I didn't try to have sex with one of my classmates. "I mean look at her!" he persuaded. "You have to take a shot at that!" The moral of the story: Sexual harassment is occurring all the time, at all different levels of visibility, throughout the day.

You may teach some very attractive students of the opposite sex

Before you're angered by this statement, please realize that I'm speaking about much older students. There are a number of adjectives I would use to describe a third-grader (cute, funny, serious, smart, stinky) but *attractive* is not one of them.

You probably won't find this warning in too many teaching books (I sure never heard it) because no one wants to talk about it. However, as soon as I reported to my high-school teaching site, lots and lots of female teachers warned me in advance: "There are a lot of very attractive young ladies who go to school here; don't let that catch you by surprise."

I was 21 when I started teaching full-time in high school, and some of my students were 19. Some of the girls I taught looked older, acted older, and possessed physical attributes of women older than the girls I dated in college! That's the reason they check IDs at bars and nightclubs: Kids don't always look like kids. In fact, some middle-school kids' hormones are already working overtime.

Don't feel guilty if you notice that a student is attractive. However, even though it's okay to admit to yourself that the student is attractive, it's an entirely different matter to be *attracted to* that student. Even if the age separation between you and a student is narrow, even if that person is over 18 and thus "of age" to make decisions about relationships, and even if you think a deeper relationship would definitely be consensual, *forget it!* Students are off limits. Period. Don't even think about it. If the phrase "I know he's young, but he's so mature for his age" ever crosses your mind, you've entered dangerous waters, my friend, and the sound you may hear in the water surrounding you is the snapping of crocodile jaws. You need to paddle your way out of there as soon as humanly possible.

Think of restraint as a mental muscle that needs to be exercised constantly. You must make a conscious distinction in your mind between "casual friend/dating material" and "student," especially when you're out of the classroom and in social circles.

Don't think that this issue is specific to males, who have a bad reputation about anything dating-related to start with. I spoke to numerous new female teachers who admitted they found some of their older male students charismatic and charming, and they had to flex that muscle of restraint to avoid forming crushes or inappropriate emotional attachments, even though they wouldn't have considered acting upon such thoughts in a million years. Even the *thought* of an inappropriate relationship is harmful, so keep your thoughts about your students pure. Just like any other muscle, the muscle of restraint becomes very strong the more you exercise it, and in time, it will become second nature to establish appropriate relationships with all kids.

You're under the microscope every second of every minute

People don't trust teachers as much as they used to. Too many (true) news stories have come out about teachers engaging in sexual relationships with kids for parents to blindly trust you, and you really can't blame them for the hesitation. Therefore, your every action is probably under closer scrutiny than you realize.

I was the head coach of the girls' track team during my first few years teaching. (Read more about what it's like to be required to coach and participate in extracurricular activities as a rookie teacher in Chapter 17.) Coaching is very different from teaching when it comes to physical contact. I had to carry injured girls, catch some when they fainted, help them off the track when they had no energy left, and even provide the occasional hug or arm around the shoulders as consolation or support. This was new to me — I never hugged a kid if she got a bad grade in my calculus class — but it wasn't hard to figure out what to do and when.

At the end of the track season, one of the track moms approached me and said, "I just wanted to thank you for a great year. All the girls loved you and you really helped the team succeed." And then she really got to the point. "I thought it was incredibly inappropriate for a man to coach a group of girls," she said. "Especially since you didn't have any female assistants. It was just you, and I didn't trust you at all. So, I sat in the bleachers at every practice and came to every meet to keep my eye on you to see if you were trustworthy, and I decided, by the end of the season, that you were. So, thanks for being a good coach."

With that statement, said in a tone that implied the tagline "A good coach *for now* — we'll see again next year when I do the exact same thing," I exhaled sharply. If, at any time, she had seen behavior that looked even the tiniest bit questionable from 300 yards away, she was ready to get on the phone and get me fired. That experience left an impression on me to always be extremely cautious — and it's probably the source of my slight paranoia about sexual-harassment suits.

Your students will probably try to woo you with their charms

As students pass through adolescence, they begin to understand that their biological changes are having major effects on the way their classmates treat them. The early bloomers, so to speak, often become the most popular kids, and enjoy extra attention, admiration, and extended periods of openmouthed, drooling stares from their peers. Sometime between the ages of 12 and 17, these kids begin to experiment with this newfound power over others, to determine if they should use it for good or for evil.

In their eyes, you're a safe target, just like the dummies that soldiers of old used to practice their bayoneting on. If your students flirt with you or try to use their powers of pubescent persuasion, don't be afraid. You won't respond (at least you shouldn't), you probably won't get mad, and you'll probably be too embarrassed to say anything about it. For all these reasons, it's open season on teachers.

The more physically attractive you are as a person, the more likely you are to be the target of these student forays into flirting. One teacher I worked with was especially loved by the young ladies and was even asked during class if he was wearing space pants. When he asked what, exactly, that meant, the girl responded, "I was just wondering, because I think your butt is out of this world."

I thought this was a problem only common to older kids, but I found out otherwise when my college roommate, Matt, and I volunteered to teach sign language to elementary-school children for a few afternoons a month. On the first day of class, we lined the kids up and went down the row, teaching them how to sign their name, and as we approached an adorable little girl who couldn't have been more than 8 years old, she gave us both a sidelong glance, grabbed the edge of her skirt, and slowly and suggestively drew it up her thigh! I completely ignored it and thought it had been my imagination, but talking to Matt later, he confirmed my suspicion. I hope she was only modeling what she saw on television or in movies, because it makes me too depressed to think about why else she would have done that. However, we reported it to her teacher, so she could keep an eye on things, in case the child was experiencing more dire and depressing circumstances at home.

More common than the flagrant flirtation is the attempt to play upon the teacher's emotions. If you're a guy, a girl will approach your desk with large, dewy, doe eyes and a quivering lower lip, asking if you could perhaps give her more credit for an answer on the test so that her grade changes from a 78 to an 80 percent. "I've never gotten a C on a quiz before," she'll plead with a pitiful glare that says, "Only *you* have the power to make me happy, you kind, kind man." I've even had girls walk over and put their heads on my shoulder in an attempt to move me or gain my sympathy. When you deny them the grade change, it's amazing how fast those tears tend to dry up as they stomp away, murmuring under their breath.

Young men try the same things. Although they won't approach you with alligator tears, they will try to effect the same change. They'll saunter up to your desk, turn on their 300-watt smiles, maybe put a hand on your shoulder, and say, "There's got to be some way I can get more points for this question." They'll try to make you feel like the slightly overbearing big sister, and the twinkle in their eye tells you that just about everybody falls for this routine. "Come on," they'll say, "It's just one point."

Don't let these students get their way! Teachers give in to attractive and charismatic students all the time, and in doing so, they lose the respect of their other students. Nothing irks students more than a teacher who shows favoritism, especially toward kids who, in their minds, get all the breaks anyway.

Avoiding the Appearance of Evil

It was Friday, the final day before my rookie school year started, and I was running around like a mad person, trying to get things in order so I wouldn't have to spend my entire weekend in the school building getting ready for Monday. As I whirled around, a tornado of motivation, anxiety, and distress, Amy Burke, a young but experienced history teacher from my school, slipped into the room and sat at a desk. "Hey, Kelley," she called out. "Let me talk to you for a second and give you the most important advice you'll hear all week." She proceeded to tell me a story that drove home just how important it was for me to watch how I conducted myself as a teacher.

"Last year, one of the teachers in this school, a guy about your age, was taking roll. As he was calling out the names, he was telling little jokes and getting to know the kids, and the kids were laughing along with him. He got to one girl — let's say her name was Beth Allen. She was wearing these stockings with a plaid design on them, sort of Scottish looking. When he called out her name, and she raised her hand to be recognized, he noticed the stockings and said, 'Maybe I'll call you Beth McAllen, because of your plaid clothes.' A pretty lame joke, to be sure, but she laughed, because he was trying to be nice and everything.

"Later that night, at the dinner table, she told her family the story of the teacher's stupid joke and still laughed a little bit in spite of herself. Her dad, on the other hand, was furious! He called the school the next day and informed the principal that he was suing the teacher for sexual harassment. 'He has no business looking at my daughter's legs and making comments!' the parent exclaimed. 'What kind of a school are you running up there?'

"The moral of the story is this," my colleague continued: "Never say or do anything that can *possibly* be construed as sexual harassment. Lots of people lose their jobs because of false accusations, so you not only have to keep your nose clean, but you have to make sure you don't allow yourself to get into a situation where students (or students' parents) can claim that you harassed them, even though you would never even think to do such a thing."

I still don't know if the story she told me was true, an urban legend, or merely a scare tactic, but she'd gotten my attention. When it comes to sexual harassment, as the saying goes, an ounce of prevention is worth a pound of cure. Amy then gave me a bunch of practical tips to ensure that I looked as innocent as I truly was in these matters, and here, I pass them along to you:

✔ **Keep your hands off students when at all possible.** If you're a touchy-feely person, keep a lid on it. You'll very rarely have any real reason to touch a student, and things are safer for you if you don't. Telling whether a student actually welcomes physical contact is often difficult (they're often too embarrassed to ask you not to touch them), and you don't want to put them on the defensive. I've also found that some faculty members harshly judge their touchy-feely colleagues. Do you really want people to say, "She just can't keep her hands off the boys in her room," about you behind your back?

✔ **Don't drive students around in your car.** Besides the fact that you'll be in a heap of legal trouble if you get into an accident, driving students around eliminates the most important part of a sexual harassment trial: witnesses. No matter how sweet and kind the student you're driving home, what will happen if she decides to say you touched her in your car? It's your word against the student's, and trust me when I say that public opinion is not going to swing your way.

When I was in school, a young male teacher gave a female student a ride home, and days later, in the papers, she was claiming that he forced her to have sexual intercourse with her. All sorts of lurid details were painted in the local newspapers, and his reputation was forever tarnished. Months later, she retracted her statement and admitted that she'd made the whole thing up. However, this retraction wasn't a banner headline in the local news, as the original accusation had been. The truth wasn't nearly as interesting or exciting, so it got buried, and some people still don't know that he's innocent.

✔ **Keep your classroom door open if you have kids with you after school.** When I was in high school and my girlfriend was over, my mom always insisted that, no matter what room we were in, the door to that room would stay open. There's something about an open door that keeps things honest. By leaving your classroom door open, you're announcing that you have nothing to hide; it's a preemptory strike against students accusing you of anything.

✔ **If you're tutoring students outside class time, have another adult in the room with you.** An open door is not enough to completely avoid trouble. You should also make sure that you're never completely alone with one or two students. My friend Rob and I, as new teachers, would always meet with students in the same room after school, so that there were always other people around (again the key word is *witnesses*) and students could never falsely accuse us of anything. If, for some reason, you need to tutor students outside of the school building, do so in a neutral location, like the public library. Never, ever meet a student at his house unless his parent is also there and supervising the visit.

TIP

✔ **Have an administrator of the same sex as the student handle dress-code issues.** Call me crazy, but as a guy, I never felt comfortable walking up to a high-school girl and saying, "I can see your bra through your shirt, and that's against dress code, so go to the office." Despite the fact that enforcing the dress code is my job, making a comment like that to a female student just makes me sound disgusting and lecherous. If I were the girl, I don't know how safe and comfortable I'd feel in a class where the male teacher knew what kind of bra I was wearing. How creepy is that?

However, it's still your job to enforce dress code, so how do you handle it? Whenever I ran across a student of the opposite sex breaking the dress code, I'd write a brief note explaining myself, seal it in an envelope, and send the note with the kid to a female administrator in the office. That way, the rules stay enforced so the administration's happy, and I don't get sued, which makes me happy.

Keep my warnings in mind when you deal with students, even of the same sex, because a little paranoia does a lot of good when it comes to sexual harassment.

The nightmare recommendation

Occasionally, and despite your best-laid plans, you'll probably wind up in a compromising situation. No matter how much time you spend making sure that your every movement is supervised by other adults, being careful what you say in class, and monitoring how much physical contact occurs between you and your students, something unexpected will happen, and you'll need to find a way to maintain your innocent demeanor and behavior record outside school grounds, where the cards aren't stacked in your favor. Here's what happened to me.

I taught a lot of high-school seniors, so one of my daily duties in the fall semester was to write college recommendation letters for a bunch of kids. I tried to write a unique letter for each student, instead of using one or two "standard" letters and just changing the name based on the

requestor. But doing this took time. Most of the kids gave me two weeks' notice, as I requested, so I was pretty good about meeting all my deadlines.

After my first-period class one day, a young girl (who had not given me the prerequisite lead time — her excuse: "But I'm so *busy!*") basically demanded her letter. "I need it today! As it is, my applications are almost late, I have to send them via Federal Express, and the drop-off point near my house closes at 4!" she whined with the practiced tones of a true whining professional. Luckily, I had written her letter the night before, but I hadn't brought it to school, because it needed proofreading.

I told her I would bring it to her tomorrow, and that I was sure everything would be fine, but

(continued)

(continued)

she would have none of it and called her mother. "My mom says you and I can drive to your house, and I can pick up the letter from you there. She can't get off work to come with me, so she said it's okay if I just go with you." That statement set off every warning bell, flag, and whistle in my head. All my precautionary alarms screamed the same message: "You and a student, alone in your house with no witnesses! *No witnesses!* Your wife will still be at work. What's to stop her from saying you tried to grab her if she doesn't like the recommendation letter you wrote?" None of my safety measures were going to work, because we were leaving the school, my safe haven, but the student and the parent were quite insistent. I had to think fast. How could I do this and still keep up honorable appearances? It was a college recommendation, after all, a pretty big deal, and her deadline was looming. I didn't want to be the one to blame if she didn't get accepted.

I had to make a quick plan. First, I talked to her mother on the phone and ensured that this was not only okay with her but also her idea. Then I got an administrator to speak with her as well to confirm it. I tried to get another teacher to come to my house with me, as a witness, but no one was able. So we drove to my house in separate cars, and as soon as we got there, I had her call her mother on my phone and had her stay on the phone with her the entire time, as I printed out the letter as quickly as I possibly could (at that point, proofing it was not an option). As soon as she had the letter, I sent her out and talked to her mother until the student's car was gone.

I don't think I could have been more careful, and although it may seem like overkill, overzealous caution is the only thing you have in the face of a sexual harassment suit.

Part III
Delivering Instruction

The 5th Wave By Rich Tennant

"I wish you wouldn't jot a lesson plan in my dream journal. I spent the morning trying to discern the meaning of radii and polynomials in my life."

In this part . . .

When the school year is grooving along, and your kids know who's the boss (according to the old TV show, it was Tony Danza), you can concentrate on fine-tuning your teaching style. In this part, I help you refine your public-speaking skills, assist you with your lesson plans, and help you connect with your students on a more personal level.

When you get used to lesson planning and feel comfortable in front of your class, it's time to liven things up a bit! Why not throw in some instructional games every once in a while or do something fun to build the sense of community in your room? And speaking of fun, what could be less fun than grading? You need to create a grading system and come up with some solid policies that are clear and make things as easy on you as possible! In this part, I show you how to do all of that. And if you're math-phobic, I even show you how to calculate your grades.

Chapter 10

Finding Your Style

When I was little, my mom told me the story called "The Emperor's New Clothes." It was all about this dignified ruler who was so vain that he always had to have the newest and nicest things. I don't really remember much else about the story until the end. Somehow, the ruler is fooled into walking around naked, blinded by his own pride, and humiliated in front of a lot of people. I didn't really understand the meaning of the story back then, and as a matter of fact, I'm still not 100-percent clear on the moral of it all, but I will acknowledge that it is the first and only story my parents told me that contained full-frontal nudity.

When they consider teaching in front of lots and lots of kids every day, most rookies begin to feel like that emperor — they don't feel clothed by enough preparation. Everything they learned in college seems to run together, and they begin to wonder if they're walking into their teaching job completely naked and unprepared. The truth is that you have more metaphoric clothes in your teaching wardrobe than you'll be able to wear for months and months, even if you put on a different teaching method every day. But although these clothes are numerous, they're wrinkled and musty smelling, rarely having seen the light of day. In this chapter, I help you iron out the little wrinkles in your teaching style and help you avoid the common pitfalls lots of rookies face when they don their teaching duds for the first time.

Creating Lesson Plans

I'll be perfectly frank: Writing lesson plans stinks. That's not very strong language, but this book would receive an R rating if I were completely honest and explicit about how much I dislike lesson planning. Back in my college days, when I envisioned my life as a teacher, I always saw myself in front of a class, instructing, motivating, entertaining, and leading. I never even gave a moment's thought to the hours and hours and *hours* I'd have to spend behind the scenes for each and every class.

Rehearsing your lines

I've said that teaching is a lot like performing, with back-to-back shows every day, except you perform to a captive audience. It makes sense that any entertainer must first learn his lines before the performance can be a success. However, there's no glory in learning lines, just like there's absolutely no glory in lesson planning. No one will appreciate the long nights you spend, eyes sagging with fatigue, propped up at the desk in your apartment, pouring over textbooks for the 127th consecutive night, trying to figure out how to make your lesson ("Cultural Implications of the Religious Beliefs of the Iroquois Indian Tribe") interesting enough so that at least *you* won't fall asleep during your lecture.

Perhaps you already had to swallow the bitter pill of lesson planning when you student-taught. Guess what? It's going to be a whole lot worse now, because you have to plan every lesson for every class every day of every school year from here on out.

Don't even try to console yourself with the thought that "At least I only have to do this once, and I can just use these plans from now on." Trust me — when you look at your first attempts at lesson plans after you've taught for a year, you're going to think, "How did my kids learn *anything* from these plans? Was I actually serious when I was writing these? Was I under the influence of some sort of mind-altering medication?" You'll need a couple years to develop a nice, solid base of lesson plans to teach from, and rest assured that as soon as you develop a good set of lesson plans, they'll either change the curriculum or your textbooks, shooting you right back to square one.

Avoiding common pitfalls

By the time you get to be a full-fledged teacher, you've written more practice lesson plans than you know what to do with. These plans probably vary in their style and in the amount of detail each contains, and by writing lesson plan after lesson plan, you've probably begun to develop your own style, based on your strengths and weaknesses. If, like me, your weakness is organization, you probably use an outline. If, however, your weakness is remembering details in the heat of the moment, you probably have entire portions of your class written out ahead of time. ***Remember:*** Developing the skills of a good lesson planner takes time. In the following sections, I give you a wealth of tips, advice, and warnings to help speed you along the way.

Remember that the more you teach something, the faster you'll get

If you teach the same class more than once during the day, you'll notice that it takes you less and less time as the day goes on to teach the same amount of material. This is due to many reasons, including the following:

- ✔ You're getting more comfortable with the material.
- ✔ You can anticipate student questions based on previous classes.
- ✔ It's getting closer to the end of the day, and you're just as excited to leave as your students are.

You don't want later classes to have free time, so be sure to prepare extra material for each lesson that, although not essential, is interesting. For example, prepare some extra examples, trivia about the topic at hand, or some in-class discussion time. That way, if your lesson is running short, you can insert these extra pieces throughout class to ensure that you fill up the entire class time. Try not to stack these extra things up at the end of class, because your students can sense that the material is just "filler" — they detest anything even remotely resembling busywork, and they'll start to get restless.

Don't be tempted to skip planning, even when you're tired

At some point during the year, after a particularly long school day that left you wondering, "Why don't I just work in a bakery or something?", you'll go home, look at your desk covered in books and papers, and think. "I'm too tired to plan — I'll just wing it tomorrow and not plan anything." Big mistake! Huge mistake! With your luck, that will be the day your principal or supervisor comes to evaluate you, and you'll be completely unprepared.

Nothing says "Please fire me" to an administrator quite like a rookie teacher without a lesson plan. In fact, this exact thing happened to one of the rookie teachers hired at the same time I was. After class was over (a class during which she had improvised quite poorly), her administrator asked to see "Any evidence of lesson planning — any evidence at all." Of course, she had nothing (she was a floater and had even left her textbook in another room), and she was fired on the last day of the school year. Although lesson planning does stink and everyone hates it, everyone still has to do it — so don't cop out, even when the going gets tough.

Assume that your students don't know anything

When you're planning your lesson, if you make the assumption that your students don't know anything, you won't be disappointed when you find out you're absolutely right! All kidding aside, students forget a lot of things from day to day or week to week, and if you expect them to remember something over the summer, forget it! You're more likely to teach a grizzly bear to breakdance than to accomplish such a grand feat.

Don't plan on your planning period

Ah, the planning period. The treasured few moments each day when every teacher is allotted time to run around the building like a mad person, trying to complete all the errands that take ordinary people all day to complete. Call me crazy, but when I was a rookie, I thought I'd be able to use my planning period to prepare the next day's lesson plans. In fact, I thought if I buckled down, I might not even have to do much planning at home. Oh, the bliss of ignorance. . . .

Let me be the first to break the bad news to you: No one holds your planning period sacred but you. The administration will expect you to do all kinds of things during that time, and none of it has anything to do with planning. Furthermore, this is one of the few times during the school day that you can call parents, and you can never gauge how long a parent phone call is going to take.

In practical terms, this means that you should never count on your planning period time to actually make up the day's lesson plans. Always assume that something unexpected is going to surface during that time, so do all your lesson planning at home the night before instead. One of the young rookie teachers I spoke to cited this as the most important revelation of his teaching experience.

"Sometimes I'd get a little distracted at night and never get around to making any lesson plans, but my planning period is early in the day, so I figured I'd just do the plans then and still have a little time to myself in the evening. Guess what? The first time I tried this, my principal decided he wanted to meet with me during my planning period, and it took the whole time! All I could think was, 'Oh, man, am I in trouble. The kids are going to be in my room in ten minutes, and I have no idea what I'm going to do with them.' I thought it was just a fluke, though, so I tried it again the next day, and I had a surprise parent conference during my planning period."

Don't even count on being able to make copies during your planning period. Too many times I strolled into the office with a brilliant worksheet I'd worked hard on the night before, just to find out that all the copiers at the school were broken. Most schools only have one or two copy machines, and they get tons of wear, so they're constantly breaking down. Plus, most schools can only afford copy machines that are approximately 100 years old and are held together by chewing gum, yarn, and the prayers of the teachers who use them.

If at all possible, run off all your handouts for the next day before you leave the school building, and do all your planning before you go to sleep. You never know what can happen the next day.

TIP

If your lesson requires that the students already have another topic mastered, plan on reviewing that topic with them. If you're doing a lesson on adverbs and say, "You already know what an adjective is, right? Well, then, an adverb is sort of like an adjective for verbs and other adverbs," expect your class to look at you with blank stares and mouths agape. Don't get mad when it becomes imminently clear they have no idea what an adjective is. Of course, they'll never admit that they've forgotten. The vast majority of the time, you'll hear the age-old excuse that students have used since the days of the one-room schoolhouse: "Our teacher never taught us that last year." In fact, this reaction is so ingrained and automatic, that they'll even try it if *you* were their teacher last year!

Be patient, and tell them, "Just in case you don't remember, I'll quickly review what an adjective is, but I'm only going to do this once, so listen up." Most students will tune in, because they realize you're giving them another chance to understand, and nobody really wants to be left behind.

Put sufficient detail into your plans

If your plan only consists of a brief outline, it's going to be worthless to you after class starts. Most rookies, even after they've taught for a while, still get a bit nervous in front of a group of students, and nervousness causes you to forget little details. I was a math teacher, and I noticed that I was often unable to work out problems in front of students that I could easily do on my own. I was afraid to make mistakes, because students were copying everything I said and wrote, so I ended up very tense and overcautious during class time. I was afraid that if I made an error, it would make me look bad in front of my kids, so there was always a low-wattage current of panic crackling in my subconscious mind. I found that working the problems out ahead of time, and writing out the steps, made me much more confident in front of the class, because if I were ever to falter or get nervous, I could check my notes and get back on track.

You can tell that you're putting enough detail into your plans when you start to feel like you're beating a dead horse. When creating the lesson plan for the day starts to feel tiresome and repetitive, it's a signal from your brain that you feel comfortable enough with the material to teach it. If you can't seem to shake an uncomfortable sensation as you plan, it means you're not ready yet, so keep at it; go back to the stuff you've already written and beef it up with detail until you completely understand it and feel like an expert on the topic.

Why students don't ask questions — at first

Students don't like to ask questions, especially when they're confused. I don't know the exact reason for this, but I have a couple of suspicions:

✔ By asking a question, students admit that they don't know something or are having trouble understanding, which is perceived by others as weakness.

✔ Asking a question means that you're actually paying attention in class and/or have an interest in the subject. This makes you a nerd, and all nerds must be destroyed by the stronger of the flock — it's just a matter

of natural selection. By asking questions, you're identifying yourself as the weak gazelle in the herd when it's surrounded by cheetahs.

✔ Asking a question makes the class last longer, and none of your students wants to have to pay attention any longer than absolutely necessary.

After you've established rapport with the students, and a classroom atmosphere that isn't hostile to curiosity, they'll feel more comfortable asking questions.

Concerning affairs, domestic and foreign

Elementary-school teacher Sharon Feather told me about a lesson plan she wrote about the presidential election. In it, her students were broken into groups (or "political parties"), and were to formulate, as teams, their party's platform on such topics as the economy and foreign affairs. After a few weeks of preparation in class, parents were invited to attend a mock debate between the two parties, to show off all they'd learned in class. When asked, "What is your stance concerning foreign affairs?" one very earnest student replied, "We think you should be allowed to have an affair with anyone you want, foreign or not." Only then, in front of all the parents, did Sharon realize that the kids had never understood what the term *foreign affairs* actually meant.

You just can't assume students automatically understand you, so you need to strive constantly to make yourself completely clear. Here's another example. One of my students, Megan, came to my math class after a particularly tough history exam. One question in particular had stumped her. The teacher had asked, "What was the major vehicle of the Black Plague?" Megan told me, "I had absolutely no idea at all, so I wrote 'The wheelbarrow.'"

You'll never be able to make yourself 100-percent clear to all your students with each and every class, but make a special effort to inspect your lesson plans and look for words your students may not understand or topics that may be tricky for their age level; strive to express those items as concisely and clearly as possible.

Consider the special needs of your students

In this day and age, tons of kids have Individualized Education Programs (IEPs), which, as I'm sure you know by now, are legal documents designed to help overcome student learning disabilities and handicapping conditions. Make sure that you address their needs in lessons you're planning, because you don't want your instruction to exclude them (most of these kids feel excluded enough already).

One of my favorite kids, Jason, was legally blind in both eyes. He needed to be seated in the front row of class, required substantially enlarged texts, and had to view the chalkboard using a little cone-shaped device he'd hold up to his eye, which would magnify the board enough for him to see it. In addition, he was unable to distinguish between different colors of chalk, which required me to adjust my teaching style. Before Jason entered my class, I often used different colors of chalk to help students visualize my poor drawings. I knew that continuing that practice would exclude Jason, so I had to find different ways to make the pictures clearer, including making them larger, drawing less unnecessary detail, and taking the time to draw neatly. If I screwed up, Jason was always good at saying, "Hey, Kelley, I can't see that at all," but not all students will be as vocal. ***Remember:*** It's your job to teach in a way that accommodates everyone; it's not the students' job to remind you.

Make sure to read your students' IEPs carefully, and adjust your instruction accordingly. Remember that you're legally required to follow through with the accommodations set forth in the IEP, so if you neglect to do so, you not only will be considered careless, but also can be held legally responsible for your negligence in adapting to those accommodations.

Writing lesson plans is sort of like throwing darts in the dark. Even though you may have a general idea where the target may be, you can never be too sure how close you're coming to a bull's-eye. Obviously, the more darts you throw, the more likely you are to hit your target, and the same goes for lesson planning; the more strategies you can come up with to teach your students before they even come in the room, the better off you'll be.

Honing Your Performance

Believe it or not, after you've created organized lesson plans, you still haven't accomplished anything concrete yet. Everyone will evaluate you based on how well you teach the material in the classroom, not on how neatly you wrote your lesson plans or how much time you spent preparing them. Certainly, the more prepared you are, the better the odds that the resulting class will go smoothly, but that's not a guarantee. Even the greatest stars in Hollywood are judged based on the quality of their last performance, and so will you. Tom Hanks never won any Academy Awards for learning his lines in record time — nobody really cares about that, even though it's important to his overall performance. What matters is what happens when the film starts rolling, the curtain goes up, and that final late bell sounds in your classroom. You're on!

You're an entertainer and a showman, and students' opinions of you will be based more on *how* you teach than *what* you teach. Students would much rather be engaged in class and be interested in what you're saying than be bored to death during the most informative lecture ever delivered. Therefore, you have to pay close attention to your delivery, to make sure that it heightens the value of your class notes, instead of seriously detracting from your performance. In the following sections, I provide a few tips to help you make sure that every class is the performance of a lifetime, so that soon enough, you're sure to start raking in those giant movie-star paychecks like Tom Hanks (you can dream, can't you?).

It takes time to find a performance style that suits you and complements your most positive qualities as a teacher. An entertaining teaching style makes up for lots of other little mistakes you're bound to make as a rookie teacher, so making class lively and engaging should be one of your top priorities.

Move around the room as you teach

Whether you're lecturing, monitoring group work, or proctoring a quiz or test, you should move around the room throughout the period. You don't have to be moving constantly, like a spider on a caffeine high; perhaps you'll stay at the chalkboard for 15 or 20 minutes at a time as you give notes, but don't stand up there or lurk behind your desk all period long.

Moving around is unnatural for most rookies — it definitely was for me. I loved to stand in front of the room and pace back and forth, but I forced myself to walk up and down the aisles to check work or answer questions as often as possible. If you don't, your students will start to think of the desk-littered part of the room as "their area" and your desk as "your area." In Chapter 6, I use a lion-tamer analogy, in which I say that, as the lion tamer, you need to claim the entire room as your territory. To make sure that your territory is safe, you need to patrol it occasionally.

If you get too stationary, students will figure out your routine and use it against you. For example, if they don't expect you to ever walk the rows of class during a test, they may get brave enough to "accidentally" leave a page full of notes on their lap during an exam. Besides, if you never come out from behind your desk, how are you ever going to bond with your students?

Your desk is an emotional, as well as a physical, barrier between you and your kids, and you have to breach that barrier to establish a relationship with students. Some days, when my feet or legs were tired, I'd even sit at an empty student desk in my classroom and teach for a while from there. When I did, students were usually very amused and often told me they appreciated it. "It made you more like one of us," a young girl once told me. "I thought it was pretty cool."

Don't carry your lesson plans around with you

If you've prepared well enough at home, you won't need to carry those lesson plans around with you throughout the entire class period or lesson. Think of them as the magic feather that Dumbo the elephant carried around with him in the Disney movie. He thought the feather enabled him to fly, but all it really did was make him look silly — he was able to fly well enough on his own without it.

Most rookie teachers walk around with a spiral or three-ring notebook full of lesson plans with them at all times, as if the notebook were stapled to their forearms or contained medication that kept their hearts beating. Teachers who always have their notes in hand give off the impression that they aren't very knowledgeable about what they're teaching and need cheat sheets throughout the period. Doubts and fears creep into students' subconscious minds: "If *he* can't even remember these notes, then how am *I* supposed to remember them on test days?"

Instead of toting them around, leave your notes on your desk, open to the page you're teaching. If you need to quickly check them, stroll past your desk and consult as necessary. However, after you have your train of thought back on the tracks, move around the room again.

Make eye contact with your students as you teach

Don't read to your students from your lesson plans, as though you were giving a speech, reciting your notes word for word with only occasional glances up to your audience. Eye contact is the only way to truly gauge whether your students are understanding you at all. Because students are usually so hesitant to ask questions, you need to constantly monitor their faces to look for frowns and confused stares that tell you to explain yourself better. Of course, in order to be able to truly watch your students rather than your notes, you'll have to internalize the material you're teaching ahead of time.

Students feel neglected when you don't make eye contact with them. However, they think it's hilarious when you try to *fake* eye contact. I don't know why, but every school has one teacher who is physically unable to make or establish eye contact with students. Almost always a man, this teacher will keep his eyes fixed at some indiscriminate point on the back wall of the classroom at all times as he addresses his students. This point of attention usually floats just above the heads of the all the kids in the class, so no one is ever sure who he's talking to. Students make fun of him mercilessly because, in their book, anyone who can't make eye contact with them can't be trusted.

You can't possibly be an effective teacher if your eyes aren't constantly darting around the room, trying to sense trouble, drawing students into your class, and demonstrating that you're on full alert at all times. In my experience, the easiest approach is just to keep your eyes moving from student to student. As you talk, catch and hold eye contact with individual students for between two and three seconds and then move on. Don't stare at a kid, or she'll begin to get very uncomfortable. Also, try not to always look at the same student or students, even if you like them better than the rest of your class. Try to visually engage everyone in the room each day at least once.

Avoid verbal crutches at all costs

Nothing makes you fair game for harassment faster than a distinct verbal crutch. In case you're not sure what I'm talking about, let me explain. The other day, I was driving to work and listening to a bland sports-radio morning show. The caller, some sports writer I'd never heard of, was trying to explain how likely a Major League Baseball strike would be, and this is how it came out on the air: "Well, the players know that, uh, if the fans, uh, see that the contracts, uh, that, uh, are signed, uh, by the, uh, owners. That, uh, will seal, uh. . . ." The guy sounded like Frankenstein's monster trying to give a post-game interview!

I imagine that, to be a sports writer, this guy probably possesses some measure of intelligence and expertise in his field. However, because of that repeated, guttural, noise, I didn't hear a word he said. All I heard was "uh, uh, uh, uh," causing me not only to miss the whole point of the interview but also to become acutely irritated. However, I must admit that my irritation is akin to the pot calling the proverbial kettle black.

I was pretty proud of myself when I started student teaching, and I was eager for my math-education professor, Dr. Strickland, to come observe me teach. My lesson was excellent; it was firing on all cylinders, engaging, entertaining, insightful, and dynamic. I mean, I was working the room like a Vegas lounge lizard. "So, that's how you add fractions — have you tried the salad bar? It's out of this world. Good night everybody — I'll be here all week!"

As soon as the students left, she walked up to me and said, "Do you realize that you said the word *okay* 97 times? I counted. You were driving me crazy, and I could barely pay attention to the rest of what you were saying because the incessant *okay*s were so distracting. It was all I could do not to scream!"

Speaking to your students is just like holding any other conversation — there will be natural lulls and pauses in the dialogue. Don't try to fill these pauses with awkward and repetitive verbal crutch words; just allow those moments of silence to pass unspoiled. These tiny intermissions give students a chance to catch up to you in their note-taking, to file away what you're saying into their brains, and to mull over the lesson, all very important things.

Stand so your students can see what you're writing on the board

I have to credit my students with helping me in this area. Too many teachers stand right in front of whatever they're writing on the chalkboard, and the entire class has to wait until the teacher moves to see what's going on. This causes class to move slowly, because students are always a couple steps behind you, trying to catch up.

Stand as close as you can to the chalkboard, with your body parallel to the writing surface. Write with your arm stretched away from you, so there is space between your body and your notes. If you're right-handed, begin at the right side of the chalkboard and work your way left so that your body at no time blocks the contents of the board (as shown in Figure 10-1). If you're left-handed, do the opposite: Start at the left side of the board and work right.

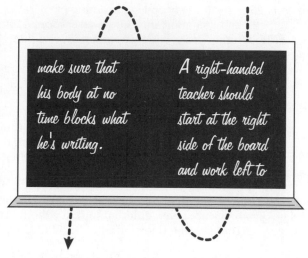

Figure 10-1: How a right-handed teacher should work the chalkboard. Lefties do it the opposite way.

make sure that his body at no time blocks what he's writing.

A right-handed teacher should start at the right side of the board and work left to

By the way, always write your notes on the board while students are in the room. This gives you a chance to explain things as you go along. If you have all your notes on the board when students come in and simply say, "Copy these down," the students will think you're a jerk. An ocean of prewritten notes says one thing: "I'm either too lazy or way too important to write things down more than once." I know a lot of teachers who jam their chalkboards full of notes and then sit at their desks while the students sprain their wrists, silently copying and never understanding. These teachers are lousy and universally disliked by their students, with good reason, in my opinion.

Remember your students' IEPs — not all students are required (or are necessarily able) to take notes on their own. For example, they may have laptop computers to take notes on, if handwriting is the issue. To combat complicated IEPs concerning note-taking, find a kid in your class who both takes great notes and has great handwriting. Ask her (I bet you dollars to doughnuts it'll be a girl) if you can photocopy her notes at the end of each day and give them to the student who cannot takes notes on his own.

Delivering Multicultural Instruction

When I started teaching, multiculturalism was the hot topic. Like a rude awakening, educational institutions realized they were, for the most part, describing history, defining culture, and viewing the world from only one point of view: middle-class white America. The first two weeks of school, I was drafted onto a multiculturalism committee, the goal of which was to pave the way for our school to infuse multiculturalism everywhere it could. Finally, it was time to give authors, poets, playwrights, and philosophers of other cultures a voice! That committee lasted two weeks, and it was never revived. Even though roughly 25 percent of my college teaching-preparation courses discussed multiethnicity and its importance in the classroom, I found that, in the real world, although the idea is widely applauded, you'll rarely find it in practice. There is already so much shoved into the school day that is required by state and federal educational policymakers (like mandated standardized testing and rigid curriculum) that others things, although no less important, get pushed aside.

Is there truly even a need for instruction that covers different ethnic views? Yes there is — don't doubt it for a second. When I was a student, my high-school curriculum was about as bleached white as it could be. In particular, the required reading was probably the same list used by British schools of the early 1800s: nothing written by anyone of color, and almost nothing written by someone who had been alive within the last 50 years. History was not much different. Luckily, things are much different in that school district now, because it finally got caught up in the tide of multicultural change.

The question still remains: What can *you* individually do to be part of the multicultural revolution? You can rarely change the curriculum of your school district, but you can still play a role, as small as it may be:

- ✔ **Choose reading material from multiethnic authors if possible.** Most schools won't allow you to choose what books you're going to teach, so beware of that ahead of time. In fact, the vast majority of school districts insist that you *not* teach from books that aren't on their approved lists. This can be a very sticky legal issue, and it's not worth losing your job over, so make sure to discuss any curricular adjustments you'd like to make with your supervisor first.

  Remember, you're not in charge of curriculum, and this limitation will really inhibit what you'd like to teach in class. Therefore, your best bet, when it comes to being an effective multicultural teacher, is to focus on your students, who are themselves multicultural, rather than the curriculum — unless you feel the curriculum needs a radical change, in which case you should discuss the matter with your subject-area colleagues and approach your supervisor with suggestions.

✓ **If you have students of different ethnic backgrounds in your class, make them feel welcome.** This doesn't just mean "be nice"; instead, you should do all you can to bridge gaps between students of different races, religions, or creeds. Teaching tolerance is one of the most important things you can do during the school year, and it requires you to go out of your way if your school doesn't have a high minority population. Don't try to hide the differences between your students. When time allows, use your classroom as an open forum to discuss differences and highlight similarities between your students.

✓ **Watch your speech for idioms and vernacular if you have students who aren't good English speakers.** One of my favorite students of all time was named Nattapol; he was one of the most diligent and polite students I ever knew, and he happened to be Taiwanese. Although English was not his first language, he was very quick to pick it up from casual speech. However, his entire life experience differed from mine, so I had to alter how I explained things.

I was always one for crazy metaphors and illustrations during class, drawing parallels between equations and Mr. Potato Head or perhaps inequalities and Popeye the Sailor Man. However, these illustrations were completely lost on Nattapol. "What is this Mr. Potato Head you speak of?" he would ask, perplexed. When I explained that it was sort of like a plastic vegetable that you can attach lips and eyes and a nose to, that didn't really help clear up the analogy. When he responded with the sincere question, "Why would you want to put lips on a vegetable?" I knew that I'd have to adjust my examples a bit.

If you have students who aren't native English speakers, like Nattapol, you'll have to monitor your speech. Substitute phrases like "We're finished with this lesson" for less comprehensible (though arguably more colorful) ones like "Stick a fork in this puppy, because it's *finito.*"

You may look at this brief discussion I offer on multiculturalism and think, "Is that it? I learned how to create all these multiculturally sensitive lesson plans for all these years of college and when it all comes down to it, I'm not going to be able to use them?" That's probably right. The best-laid plans you made in college tend to fail in the face of established curriculum and standardized testing.

You'll be judged primarily by the numbers you generate on standardized tests and via your grade distributions, not by the quality or diversity of the education you provide. Therefore, be reasonable and realistic in your approach to involving multiculturalism. Most likely, your school district has already made plenty of changes based on the need to diversify the content of its courses, and those changes will already be built into your curriculum. So you, yourself, don't have to worry about adding content. Instead, by using the tips I offer in this section, focus on making sure that your actions in class reflect a tolerance of multicultural views and needs, especially when you deal with students.

Chapter 11

Making Learning Fun

For my money, nothing is more annoying or boring than predictability. As a student, I used to dread classes that always transpired the same way day in and day out. Routine is one thing, but lack of creativity is another. Students sit in your class for hours and hours a week, and at some level, they want to be entertained. Wouldn't you? Would you want to watch a television show with only one character, always filmed on the same set, with a story line that was nearly identical every episode? Of course not! You thrive on surprise, innovation, and involvement. You want to be wowed, and if at all possible, you'd like to be part of the show. In the old days, people were content to accept teaching passively, but not anymore. Students don't want to be "talked at" every day. They want a teacher who involves them and tries to liven up the material they're learning.

In this chapter, I help you pep up your classes and make things more fun for everyone. I talk in detail about how and when to play games in class and show you things you can do to spark your students' interest. These are the little extra touches that transform people from competent teachers into legendary teachers, respected by parents, appreciated by administrators, and beloved by their students.

Teaching with Class Games

Your students are competing with each other every second of every day. Who will get a higher grade on the test? Who can finish her class work fastest? Who can run faster? Jump higher? Keep his eyes open the longest before he blinks? Stuff the most pieces of cereal into his mouth before the gag reflex kicks in? As an adult, you may forget that most children and adolescents define themselves based on how they stack up against their peers, but you can use that to your advantage as a teacher. Because, at their very core, kids are only slightly less competitive than the typical Olympic athlete, they will drop everything for a class game. If you can harness this natural instinct and accomplish instruction in the meantime, everybody wins. They get to have fun, and they learn something in the process.

In the sections that follow, I describe the games I had the most success with in my classes. We played a lot of games during class time, and I had just as much fun as my students did. But I had a lot less fun the night *before* the games, because they took so unbelievably long to prepare. You have to prepare ahead of time any props you'll need for the game, such as question cards or game boards, and the time commitment required varies based on the game you choose. You also need to make some basic decisions before you even decide which game to play:

✔ **How are you going to break the class into teams?** Should you assign teams randomly? How many teams should there be? Does it matter if the teams are different sizes? These are all tough questions, but the students will usually help you make these decisions. Some classes are adamant that they want to play boys against girls. Other times, they insist on choosing teams on their own. Most of the time, if left alone, students will split into groups fairly and won't leave anyone out.

At the beginning of the year, before students get to know each other and form friendships, assign the teams yourself, or do it randomly. One easy way to do this is to have each student draw a card from a standard deck as he or she enters the room. You can then form two groups by separating the red and black card holders; four groups if you separate by suit (spades, hearts, clubs, or diamonds); or three groups if you separate by even numbers, odd numbers, and face cards (aces count as faces).

✔ **Is there any external motivation to win?** I always think a game is a bit more interesting if something is on the line, like perhaps a few extra percentage points on the winning team's next quiz or test. Be careful, though — as soon as you make the game worth a grade, the competition between students will escalate. Now there's something to lose! You're not playing for some existential award like "the pride of doing a good job." Now we're talking about something concrete to fight over.

As it is, even if the game means nothing in the grand scheme of things, you're bound to have some bickering between students as you play. Stay on top of it and mediate any disagreements before they become arguments. If things get too heated, warn them that perhaps a game isn't worth all the commotion, and they'll probably calm down. If they don't, simply stop the game, demand quiet in the room, and assign work to be completed silently at their desks. In the future, they'll remember to be a little more civil during the competition.

TIP

What time is game time?

Even though games are a nice change of pace, and a fantastic way to drum up student interest, they're usually not a great way to teach new material. After a game begins, it becomes the focus of the class, and it drowns out anything new you try to present — students would rather learn the rules of the game than any content you're trying to introduce.

I found that class games worked best as review for major quizzes and tests. Although they're having fun, students can still see exactly what they do and don't understand for the upcoming exam and can figure out what they need to study.

Don't get caught in the trap of trying to make every class a game, because that's unrealistic. *Remember:* Games require a lot of planning, and you don't want to spoil your class at the expense of every minute of your free time. In addition, because games aren't a great way to teach new things, playing too many games means that you're going to get behind in your curriculum. I found that I could squeeze in, at most, about one game every three or four weeks per class.

After you make these basic decisions, you need to decide what game to play. In the following sections, I outline my favorite class games. Somewhere in this list, I'm sure you'll find something you can play with your students, and perhaps these examples will even inspire you to create some games of your own.

Survivor

Preparation time: Medium

Materials required: Voting box, index cards, soundtrack CD (optional)

Game length: Long

I'm a reality-television fanatic, and the CBS show *Survivor* is the granddaddy of them all. Because the show is such a great combination of skill and luck, it makes a fantastic class game that requires very little preparation but still offers maximum drama for both you and your students. Here's the payoff to grip your kids: By the end of the class period, one of them will have earned five bonus percentage points on his or her next test, but only one person wins — there can only be one ultimate survivor! (By the way, I bought the *Survivor* soundtrack CD and had it playing in the background for the entire class period — it really adds to the fun because the music is so dramatic.)

Before the class starts, come up with a handful of questions on whatever topic you're covering. When the students come in, split them up into groups, or *tribes*. (To make it easy, each row of my seating chart was a separate tribe.) Give each tribe member an index card, upon which each person writes his or her name. Then the game itself begins.

Write three or four rather short questions on the board, one at a time, and have everyone in the class write their answers on a sheet of paper. I usually didn't let tribe members confer with each other, because I wanted to see what each individual knew. After all the questions are complete, give the answers; correct answers are worth 1 point per question per tribe member. For example, if a tribe contains 5 members, you ask 4 questions, and each member gets each question correct, that tribe earns 20 points for the round. The tribe with the most points at the end of the round earns *tribal immunity,* which means the group cannot be eliminated. However, all the other tribes are in jeopardy.

In my game, chance, not the other people in the class, votes you out, so there are no hard feelings. Have each member of the tribes *not* receiving immunity place their index cards into the voting box. (I used an ornately carved wooden box to add to the mystique of the game, but any box will do.) Draw names from the box, one at a time, announcing them as you draw. The first tribe that has three members drawn from the box is eliminated, and you move to Round 2, which includes all the tribes except the one just voted off the island. All immunities are revoked, you ask more questions, calculate points again, assign immunity to the new winning tribe, and then vote yet another tribe out. (I found it easier just to throw out the old names from the box and have students write their names on another card for the second round of voting.)

In the second to last round (when there are only two teams), there's no need to vote one tribe off, because the tribe that does not receive immunity is automatically eliminated. When you're down to one tribe, in the final round, all its members are on their own and voting is a little different — there is no immunity. Hold another question round, just like before, and calculate each tribe member's individual points. Then place each tribe member's name in the box once and then an additional time for each point they earned in the final question round. For instance, if Jack earned three points in the final round, his name would go in once automatically and three bonus times, for a total of four scraps of paper bearing his name in the voting box. After all the sheets are in, draw names from the box until you draw two of the same name; that person is the ultimate survivor, and he or she wins the prize.

The more dramatic you are as you draw the names, the more fun the game will be for students. Be a showman and cue up big announcements with surges in the music to add to the excitement. The toughest part of this game is timing it correctly so that it ends right before class is over. You'll have as many rounds as there are tribes in the game, plus you need some time to explain the rules and get things organized, so split your class period into equal segments numbering one more than your number of tribes. My classes lasted 45 minutes, and I always divided kids into 4 tribes, so I split the class into 5 segments lasting 9 minutes each. Therefore, I made sure the game setup took no more than 9 minutes, Round 1 lasted no more than 9 minutes after that, and so on. Don't run out of time so that no winner is announced during class — finding a winner is the best part of the whole game!

The Box of Death

Preparation time: Short

Materials required: None

Game length: Short to medium

As opposed to Survivor, the game I lovingly refer to as the Box of Death can be thrown in to fill the last ten minutes or so of a class period, but it's not well suited to a larger chunk of time. At its heart, the game is one of survival. Only one winner is named at the end of the game, but you can probably squeeze in two or three games in a short period of time, so even students who are eliminated are back in the action quickly.

To start the game, have everyone stand up next to his or her desk. Because I used a traditional row-and-column seating chart, when all my students stood, their bodies formed a large rectangle, or box — hence the name of the game. Begin at the far left or far right side of the room (flip a coin to decide which) and ask the first person in that column to answer a question. If he gets the answer right, he remains in the game, but if he gets it wrong, he's eliminated and must sit down. The question he answered incorrectly now passes to the person seated behind him, who must in turn get it right or likewise be eliminated. If the second student gets it correct, a new question is asked of the third student, and the process repeats. After everyone in the class has either answered correctly or been eliminated, play returns to the first student not already out of the game until only one person is left.

It's a very simple game with simple rules: If it's not your turn, you can't talk for any reason, and you can't help the person whose turn it is. However, because an incorrectly answered question automatically moves to the next person, this game doesn't work well with true-or-false or multiple-choice questions — if the question requires a yes or no answer, and one student answers "yes" and gets it wrong, the next person doesn't have to be a brain surgeon to get it right.

I originally called this game "The Box," but eventually I modified it when I added my prop: a small plastic model of the Starship Enterprise, of *Star Trek* fame. It was a neat little toy, because if you pushed one of the buttons on it, it made laser sound effects. Thus, if a student answered a question wrong, the spacecraft gunned her down, adding the aspect of "death" to the game. It was very tongue in cheek, and the toy was really cheesy, so the students thought it was pretty funny. If you don't like the idea of even fictitiously murdering your students, you can use a different prop. You can call the game "Kneel Before the King (or Queen)," for example, wear a ridiculous crown (like a paper one from a fast-food restaurant), and if one of your students is eliminated, you can tap her on the shoulder with a royal dismissal scepter or the Rod of Shame.

If you ever have some extra time at the end of class, this a great time filler; it can be a fun way to review the things you talked about in class. Remember that part of the Box of Death's allure is the cornball way it must eliminate its losing contestants, so that kids don't feel embarrassed or self-conscious if they lose. After all, all the attention in the room is on them, so the sillier you make their elimination, the less traumatic it is. Plus, coming up with questions for the game isn't too hard, as long as you stick to what you covered during the class period. (All the material will still be packed into your short-term memory.)

Games based on toys

Preparation time: Medium

Materials required: Fun toy, hotel service bells

Game length: Medium to long

My greatest accomplishment as a rookie teacher was discovering that a silly plastic alligator would make algebra more interesting. One day, as I was walking around a toy store, I found a game called Gator Golf. Designed for kids around 5 years old, this hilarious little plastic alligator about the size of a loaf of bread sits on the ground, mouth agape, waiting for you to putt a plastic golf ball into his mouth. If you're able to hit the target, the mouth clamps shut, the ball rolls to the end of the alligator's tail, and he flips it out, all the while growling and spinning around.

Even though I taught high-school students, they immediately fell in love with the little alligator and the 2-foot-long cheap plastic putters included in the game box. If left to their own defenses, they would have taken turns putting all day long, so I knew if I could create a game based on alligator putting, they'd love it. Then inspiration struck: My game would consist of a question-and-answer portion, during which teams would earn points for correct responses. Those points, in turn, would then translate into the number of putts that team was given to try to hit the smiling reptilian target.

I usually let students pick their own teams. To each team, I passed out what I call the hotel bell. It's that little silver bell you see at hotel desks next to signs that say, "Please ring for service." After the teams were assembled, I'd ask a question orally, write one on the board, or project one on the board using an overhead projector. Just like on a game show, the teams would then have to "buzz in" using the service bell, and the first team to ring in and answer correctly earned one, two, or three points, depending on how difficult I thought the question was.

The question round continued until there were only ten minutes left in the class period, at which time I progressed to the Bonus Alligator Round. I placed the alligator against one wall and marked a line on the floor with masking tape about 40 feet away. Teams then took turns putting for the alligator's mouth from behind the line, one putt for each point they earned in the question round of the game. If they managed to putt down the alligator's throat, they got 25 points; because that was pretty tricky, I also awarded 5 points for every putt that hit the alligator but was not digested by him. The winning team was determined only by the points they earned putting, not according to the points they earned during the question round, so even the team with the fewest points entering the putting portion still had a chance to win.

I bought a new silly plastic toy each year I taught, because the kids eventually wanted some variety, and the bonus round was adjusted accordingly. Here are some of the other toys I used:

- **Chicken Croquet:** Without question, this is my favorite toy of all — a plastic chicken that squats on the ground and clucks electronically when you turn it on. You then try to hit a croquet ball across the room with a flimsy plastic mallet. If you manage to hit the chicken with the ball, he clucks really loudly, hops up, and lays a plastic egg. How fantastic is that? Teams earned 25 points per egg laid and 5 points for glancing blows to the poultry that did not trigger an egg.

- **Toss Across:** You may remember this game from your childhood; it's a plastic tic-tac-toe board that you toss little beanbags at. When the beanbags hit, they turn plastic tumblers in the grid and cause *X*s or *O*s to appear. In the bonus round, students tossed as many beanbags as they had points. Each time they tossed for an *X,* they got 10 points, and if they managed a winning tic-tac-toe combination with *X*s, it was worth 100 points. However, each *O* took 10 points away, and every tic-tac-toe combination made of *O*s subtracted 100 points from their total. It's a little more random that the other games when it comes to scoring, because anything can happen at any time, and no team is ever completely out of the competition.

✔ **Bowling:** Instead of animals or game grids, teams stared down the familiar ten-pin alley during the bonus round. You can buy a set of plastic pins that stand about a foot high and a pair of plastic bowling balls from most toy stores for under $20. The tough part of this game is finding a student willing to be the pinsetter, because it involves crouching on the ground and chasing after errant pins as they spin off between desks. Mark the pin placements on your floor with masking tape before play begins; that way, it makes the already tedious job of the pinsetter a little easier. If no one wants to pin-set for you, guaranteed bonus points to the pinsetter will always find you a volunteer. However, most of the time, you'll have a kid who can't wait to lend a hand to be part of the action.

In my version, teams were allowed to bowl one ball for every point they earned during the question round. Each pin they knocked down earned them one point toward winning the game, and every strike was worth five extra points in addition to that. However, a new set of pins was only set up after they'd knocked down all ten pins, no matter how long it took. This meant that some teams could clear nine pins in one toss but had to take five or six additional turns to try to knock down that last straggler.

Beware! Some students (males especially) are particularly violent in their bowling style, and they even may try to throw the ball at the pins or hurl it with such velocity that the ball could knock down the pins, knock down your classroom wall, and flatten a few tires in the parking lot before it finally stops. Make sure to tell everyone before you start that you'll deduct big points for overzealous throws.

The trickiest part of these games, believe it or not, is trying to figure out who buzzed in first. The bells I described help a lot, but there is still bound to be controversy if two teams buzz in close together. To solve this dilemma, you can use a buzzer system, just like they do on the game shows. Most real buzzer systems, used by school academic quiz teams, cost around $300. Try to find out if your school owns such a system and see if it's possible to borrow it, because buying one is out of the question. You can, as an alternative, buy some New Year's Eve party favors. As long as each makes a different noise, that can help you figure out who rang in first. (If, however, you teach in an open classroom, that may not be the best idea in the world. I can imagine that it may be a little distracting to the teachers around you. . . .)

Reincarnating known games

You saw how, with just a little elbow grease and an obsessive love of reality shows, I turned the show *Survivor* into something I could use in class. If you base a game on a premise students are already familiar with, getting them to buy into it and play along is much easier. Nothing is worse than spending hours creating a game from scratch and then realizing that students hate it. So, if you're stuck for an idea, why not dust off an old (or new) favorite and tweak it up so you can use it in class?

Game shows

Many teachers use the TV show *Jeopardy!* in the classroom. It's really not that much of a stretch, because the show consists of question after question, with dollar values attached. Even though teachers have overdone it, my students still enjoyed the occasional *Jeopardy!* game. However, why not try to come up with a new standard? With just a few adjustments, *Who Wants To Be a Millionaire?* becomes *Who Wants Extra Credit?* Or *Family Feud* can be reborn as the *Language Feud.*

I was a ridiculously big fan of the *Millionaire* show when it first came out, so I was bound and determined to develop it for my classroom. Rather than a succession of 15 fixed dollar amounts for contestants to progress through (from $100 to $1,000,000), I had six levels of prizes that students could win, ranging from a cool pencil to 10 percentage points on a test. I did my best to match everything to the TV show. I even typed up my questions and printed them on overheads so I could project them for everyone to see, just like the questions are displayed for both the contestant and the home audience on the show.

TIP

Look at this studio, full of fabulous prizes!

What's a game show without loads of fantastic prizes? Because your teaching salary and lack of corporate sponsorship prevent you from offering refrigerators, living room sets, and trips to Jamaica, you have to settle for more affordable options. Your students don't expect anything major, but they do appreciate a token prize if they win. These small trinkets become badges of honor and trophies of pride to most students; they're physical evidence of being smart, at least once in their lives. So, what sorts of things can you buy to offer as rewards for a game well played?

✔ **Candy:** As an educator, you qualify for membership in warehouse stores like Sam's Club or B.J.'s. Warehouse stores have vast tubs of candy that aren't too expensive, considering the quantity of sugar-infused treats you get for your dollar. Lollipops were the most popular among my students. Parents of younger children are pickier about what you give their kids to eat, so make sure you have an equally attractive prize alternative for those students whose parents have

them on a strict nonsugar diet. Most middle- and high-school parents don't care what you give their kids to eat, as long as it's not poison (and some wouldn't even blink if you did that). By the time they're teenagers, most kids subsist on a diet of Twinkies and soda anyway.

✔ **Fun, but cheap, plastic toys:** Party-supply catalogs sell all sorts of wild stuff that's incredibly cheap and tacky enough to be really fun for students. What says, "I'm good at spelling," better than a plastic dinosaur-head finger puppet, or a translucent sticky alien that stretches to ten times its original size? What token says, "My teacher values my good study habits," better than a revolting, glow-in-the-dark, sticky eyeball toy? Approximately every two months, I placed an order with the Oriental Trading Company (www.oriental.com), the best prize company around. The prices vary depending on the item, but I bought lots of stuff by the gross (144 pieces) for less than $10. Do yourself a favor: Log onto their Web

(continued)

(continued)

site and sign up for their written catalog. Occasionally, I felt generous and ventured away from catalog shopping, purchasing prizes at department stores (usually cans of Play-Doh or Pez candy dispensers); they went fast — the kids went ape for them.

✔ **Personalized pencils:** If you'd rather give out more academically related prizes than toys and candy, you still have options (although I don't think I'd like to come to your house for Halloween). I had lots of success passing out pencils imprinted with messages I came up with. The best place to buy these is the Oriental Trading Company; for under $5, you can get two dozen pencils in lots of different colors. You can also order them from Current, a stationery store (www.currentcatalog.com). Remember that these take a few weeks to make, so place

your order in the summer if you'd like to use them right away during the school year. Put some thought into the text you'll have stamped onto your pencils. I always chose funny messages, producing pencils that read, "I rule in Mr. Kelley's math class!", "Fear me, I'm a math stud" (for some reason, girls got a big kick out of that one), "My teacher loves me, but in a platonic way," and "I earned this pencil with my big, pulsating brain."

No matter what age they are, kids go nuts for prizes; I always had a desk drawer full of them for game winners or even as rewards for answering particularly difficult questions during class. If everyone's mind was wandering, I could bring the class back into focus with the simple phrase, "How about a prize for the person who answers this tough question correctly?"

They were allowed two lifelines: Poll the Class (during which I'd read the choices and class members would raise their hands to indicate which they thought was right) and Phone a Friend (in which they could ask any student in the class for his or her help on one question). Again to match the show, I included pop-culture questions as well as class-related questions. Although it was a lot of work to prepare (it took about three hours to prepare for a single class period of *Millionaire*), it was a labor of love, because it gave me a chance to do my horrible Regis Philbin impression, which both amused and horrified my classes: "Is that your *final, final, final, final, final, final* answer?"

Board games

If you don't mind straining your creativity muscles a little, you can transform board games your kids already play at home into class games. These come with the additional benefit that you don't have to spend the entire period explaining the rules, because most of the kids either know them already or are willing to help out and explain them to their peers. Here are just a few examples that adapted well to my classroom:

✔ **Taboo:** In this game, one member of a team is given a word or phrase that he must verbally describe to his teammates until the team figures it out. Here's the catch: There's also a list of words he's not allowed to use in his description. For example, let's say you're teaching a biology class, and the student has to get his team to say the word *photosynthesis*. Write this word at the top of an index card and below it, list the words he's not allowed to use in his description — words like *plant, cell, food, green,* and *light.* Create an entire stack of cards like this, and give teams a fixed time limit to see how many they can get right.

✔ **Charades:** This is the classic game where everyone becomes a frantic mime! Before class starts, come up with a stack of index cards, and have a different class topic, vocabulary word, or concept to act out on each one. For fun, throw in some bizarre words that have nothing to do with class every once in a while, like *anvil* or *Bob Vila* and sit back and watch the fun.

✔ **Pictionary:** Just about everyone's played this game, where you draw rather than act words out. Your preparation is essentially the same as with charades — very minimal.

✔ **Scattergories:** In case you've never played this, the object of the game is to create a list based on a given topic; furthermore, you want your list to be completely different from everyone else's, because if you have the same thing written down as another player, neither of you gets points for that answer.

I saw this game implemented best by my middle-school language-arts teacher, Mrs. Momberger. The lesson was about descriptive writing, and she began by saying, "'When the doorbell rang, I ran to the door.' That's a boring sentence. What other words can you substitute for *ran* to make it much more descriptive and interesting?" We had ten minutes to create a list of replacement words or phrases like *bounded* or *catapulted myself.* Students then took turns reading aloud their list; if you had something on your list that was read by another person, you both had to scratch it out.

The whole point of playing games is to be a little unpredictable and change the pace of class a bit. Your students will probably be a little more boisterous or excitable than normal because you've really piqued their interest. Don't overreact to this slight increase in noise level, or you'll ruin everyone's fun. Even though game days take a little extra patience, they're definitely worth it.

Adding the Little Things

Let's face it; the school year really gets long by the time April and May roll around. It's not so bad when the year starts, because there are all sorts of holidays and days off to look forward to, especially Thanksgiving and Christmas break. However, deep in the heart of winter, suddenly there are far fewer holidays, and you're driving either to or from work in total darkness, thanks to the continual shortening of daylight hours. If your school starts early and you stay after normal working hours for extracurricular activities, you may not even see the light of day for months at a time!

The short days of winter are the perfect recipe for getting into a moody funk, and that goes for your students, too. When winter hits, the honeymoon's over; the novelty of returning to school has played out, and kids are counting the 100 or so days until summer rises like the sun in the east. There are lots of strikes against you, inhibiting your ability not only to teach but also to even hold student interest for more than a few minutes at a time. Therefore, doing little things every now and again to spice up class is important, so that both you and your students stay involved and interested throughout the school year. (It'll be just as hard for you as it is for them.) When I taught, I tried a ton of things with that goal in mind, and I share them with you in the following sections.

Talking about personal things before class starts

Lots of things happen to your kids before they even make it into your class-room, and these events can really affect how well they're able to focus for the day. However, if you notice that they're distracted and appear to have some-thing on their minds, allowing them to talk about these things openly before you press on with your lesson for the day not only shows that you care but allows them to unburden themselves enough to actually pay attention.

For example, before class started one November afternoon, I noticed that one of my students, Chelsey, seemed distracted. Whereas most of the other kids were unpacking their book bags and getting started on the day's warm-up activity, she was spaced out, just staring at the chalkboard. "Hey Chels, what's going on?" I asked her, and I noticed that the students around her tensed visibly. Clearly, they knew, and they didn't think it was a good idea that I was asking.

"I got into a car accident yesterday. Nobody got hurt really bad, but I was sit-ting in the back seat, and when we got hit, I flew up into the front of the car headfirst and cracked the windshield with my skull." At this point, she pulled her bangs back and pointed to an angry red cut on her forehead. "The doctor says I have a really hard head for not wearing my seatbelt, but that hard head kept me from getting hurt, so I guess it all evens out," she chuckled uneasily.

As she laughed, the rest of the class exhaled in unison. Everyone (except for me, of course) had heard about the accident but was too nervous to broach the topic with her, because it was weighing so heavily on her mind. When she talked about it aloud, it was as if a heavy weight had been lifted from her and the rest of the class, and things progressed normally for the rest of the day — the ice had been broken. Had I not noticed her distraction and taken those five minutes to let her speak her mind, no one in the room would have remembered a single thing I taught that day.

Speaking from the heart

Very young kids have more fun in class when they feel unconditionally accepted as part of the group, so make a conscious effort to do things that make kids feel welcomed and loved in your class. Games are a good way to do this, but you also need to provide more straightforward activities whose sole purpose is to build the children's self-esteem and show them that they are a valued member of your class.

One elementary-school teacher, Sharon Feather, described a great activity she did every year with her elementary-school classes. One of her bulletin boards contained a cutout construction-paper heart for each of her kids, and on each

heart was glued a picture of that student. Whenever the students thought of something they really liked about one of their classmates, or wanted to encourage each other, they'd write little notes on slips of paper and place them in the student's heart.

Sharon said that since she introduced the activity, she's made it a permanent fixture in her room. It gives her class a forum for expressing positive things to one another in a comfortable way, which means they can bond together even if they're shy and would lack the courage to approach another student face to face.

Allow your kids to unpack any baggage they feel they need to (even if it's about another teacher — just don't take sides if they're venting about a colleague), because you'll get more accomplished in the class period even though you'll lose a few minutes as they blow off steam.

Acknowledging achievement in fun ways

Even though they don't act like it, kids want to be smart — it's the one thing they want and fear the most, because standing apart from their classmates is both good and bad. I tried mixing looking smart and looking silly together, so that students wouldn't fear looking intelligent in front of the class, thanks to an innovation I called The Big Pants. Actually, when I say "big," I actually mean *gargantuan*.

One afternoon, on my way home from school, I stopped by a local department store and made my way to the menswear section, intent on finding an inexpensive pair of pants with the largest waistline they sold. After some digging, I was able to find thin, gray dress slacks with a 64-inch waist. Now those are some big pants! While I was there, I also picked up a pair of suspenders (because I doubted that any of my students would be able to wear the pants without them). Little did I know that these mammoth pants would become legendary among my students.

During class the next day, I asked a pretty tough question during class — one that stumped everyone, but that everybody (from the biggest nerd to the lowliest dweeb) would have a shot at if they took a lucky guess. To spark their interest, I called it a "Big Pants question" but refused to explain what the heck I was talking about. After some head scratching, one of the shyest students in class raised her hand and nailed the answer right on the head. "Congratulations," I said. "To reward you for answering one of the hardest questions all year, I bestow upon you the honor of donning the Big Pants for 24 hours. Wear them around the school and at home proudly, as a symbol of your academic prowess."

I didn't know if she would go for the whole concept of wearing enormous pants as a *reward,* but she surprised me by calmly walking to the front of the room, stepping into the giant pants, adjusting the suspenders, and striding proudly back to her desk. I saw her throughout the school day, walking between her classes in the hallways, sporting those pants that came up nearly as high as her chin, pants she could have worn simultaneously with three or four of her closest friends. For her, they were a status symbol, and because of her willingness to play along with my silly idea, those pants became a much desired trophy of academic excellence. Even administrators would high-five students in the hallway who passed them wearing the big pants!

Having your own awards assembly

At the end of every school year, I held the Kelley Awards. In essence, it was the academic equivalent of the Emmy Awards, but just for the students in my classroom. The ceremony began very humbly during my rookie year: I took 15 minutes out of each class and passed out certificates for the top ten students in that class (by grade) and the most improved student (from the first to the final marking period).

As the coup de grâce, I had a plaque made for each of the top 2 students from the entire group of 150 that I taught; it was the ultimate honor, which I named the Kelley Award. Additionally, I had their names carved into a plaque I hung on my classroom wall; it was one of those Employee of the Month–type plaques, displaying lots of little plates, onto which I engraved the names of each successive year's Kelley Award winners.

Year by year, the little ceremony grew, and the Kelley Awards gained a reputation in the school. By its fourth year, students actually brought in formal clothes to attend the in-class event (tuxedos and formal gowns that they were also wearing to the prom, if you can believe that!) and the ceremony featured musical performances. One year, I even had a barbershop quartet comprised of my students, the choir director, and me (struggling but) singing the lead.

I upped the number and types of awards each year, including several annual awards named after my outstanding students of the past, and gave funny special awards like Most Likely to Become a Supervillain and Most Likely to Spell His Own Name Wrong on a Test. I even had other faculty members come in as guest presenters on their planning periods, decked out in their finest clothes. The students really enjoyed those awards and took them very seriously — it even became common for the valedictorian or salutatorian of the school to list the Kelley Award among their most outstanding achievements, which were announced before they spoke at graduation.

Making class T-shirts

At the end of every year, most of my classes had to take a big, nationwide, standardized test. If they passed that test, the students actually received college credit for the calculus course I was teaching, but the test was sort of expensive, and, because so much was riding on it, the exam made them as nervous as turkeys in late November. Most years, the test started at 8:00 a.m., and because school started at 7:30, that gave the kids a good half-hour to panic and stress out beforehand.

To help alleviate that stress, I wanted to serve them a huge breakfast and fill up that pesky 30-minute freakout period with donuts, bagels, fruit, milk, and juice. However, such a cornucopia of catered food carried a price tag of nearly $300, and I didn't have that kind of money to throw around. The students and I brainstormed, and we decided to hold a T-shirt design competition. Any student in any of my six classes was allowed to turn in a design for a class T-shirt on a regular sheet of office paper. Each submission would receive a small amount of extra credit (for the effort, and to help drum up the number of entries), and I narrowed the entries down to ten finalists (who received slightly more extra credit.) Students then voted on those ten finalists to determine the winner.

I contacted local printing companies and was always able to find someone willing to cut me a price break on screening the T-shirts, because I worked for the school system. Therefore, I was usually able to offer the shirts to students for under $15, and all the profit went to paying for their breakfast. Even though some students only wore their shirts that day (they were math shirts after all), some wore them for years to come.

Writing letters as a class project

My mom was an elementary-school teacher before I came along, and one year her elementary-school class wrote to hospitalized Broadway star, television icon, and snack-cracker spokesperson Sandy Duncan; they even got a kind, lengthy personal response back! This inspired me to do the same on a much larger scale. Every few years, my students would write to hundreds of celebrities, asking for two things:

- ✔ An autographed picture.

- ✔ Some wisdom, specifically, "What one piece of advice would you give a teenager of today?"

After a few months, we'd get a few response letters back every day, and these brief brushes with fame really excited my students, and helped those long winter days go by so much faster. The big problem, of course, was figuring out how to get in touch with these folks, but here are the two best sources for celebrity addresses:

- ✔ **Michael Levine's *The Address Book: How to Reach Anyone Who Is Anyone.*** Levine releases a new edition every few years, so make sure to get the most recent one, because celebrities seem to change addresses more often than they change their clothes. Even with the newest edition, expect to have about 25 percent of your letters marked undeliverable.

- ✔ **The Star Archive (www.stararchive.com).** For the most up-to-the-minute information, you can't do better than The Star Archive Web site. Not only does it have a ton of addresses, it also lists every address associated with every celebrity, and it even verifies which ones actually reach the people, which ones are undeliverable, and how long it took the celebrity to respond.

Whereas our celebrity mail was always addressed to the whole class, you can opt for more personal correspondence with pen pals. Lots of elementary schools have programs in which students correspond with other classes from far-off parts of the United States or even other countries. If your school doesn't already have a program in place, think about striking up a relationship with a school in a foreign nation so that your students can broaden their horizons by learning firsthand what life is like for someone their age far away.

There are a few Web sites out there that can help you contact a school to pair up with, the crucial first step. Here are a few of the most popular sites dedicated to pairing up students with pen pals:

- ✔ www.pen-pal.com
- ✔ www.world-pen-pals.com
- ✔ www.epals.com

Looking to the stars for guidance

My celebrity-correspondence project was one of my most popular. Even though it didn't directly relate to my algebra curriculum, it was worth the small in-class time investment. Honestly, by the 130th consecutive day of algebra, even *I* was ready to go crazy. However, when the letters started rolling in, my kids came to class excited by the possibility of having received celebrity mail.

There were lots of practical issues to deal with. Postage was the big one. It costs quite a bit to mail out 300 or 400 letters, but I passed around the hat, and students contributed to help the cause. Most of my kids had jobs and were willing to chip in $1 each; elementary parents may be just as willing to do so if you explain the nature of the project ahead of time.

Many celebrities won't respond to you, some because the letter never reaches them (constantly changing addresses is one way to avoid having to answer fan mail I suppose) and others because they just don't have the time to answer. Of the 400 letters I sent, I got about 50 personal replies, 100 signed photos with no personal reply, and 250 returned or unanswered letters, so make sure you're up front with your students before you even start — most people aren't going to write back.

Of course, the more personal the letter, the more likely you are to get a reply. I didn't want to waste too much class time on the letter-writing process (because mine was a math class after all), so I sent out the same, relatively generic letter to each celebrity, but I found that having all the students sign the back of the letters motivated more stars to reply. Because we asked for life advice, I thought you might be interested to hear some of the more interesting responses:

"Read, read, read." (Meg Ryan)

"Be nice to people and stay out of debt!" (Andy Richter)

"You are the master of your mind!" (Bill Cosby)

"Master the English language — the most important tool you'll own." (Colin Powell)

"Never take anybody too seriously, especially yourself." (Dave Barry)

"Always think for yourself." (Bill Maher)

"There are no limits to what you can achieve and accomplish in your life, save the ones you impose on yourself." (LeVar Burton)

"Choose your dreams carefully, so you can grow with them all your life." (Yo-Yo Ma)

"People become really quite remarkable when they start thinking they can do things. When they believe in themselves, they have the first secret of success." (Donald Trump)

"[Remember that] Elmo is always your friend." (Elmo)

"I think I'll have a hamburger, some golden French fries, and a creamy chocolate shake." (Ronald McDonald)

After everyone got a chance to see them, I laminated each photograph and hung it at the front of the room, and it wasn't long before my room looked like the office of a Hollywood casting agent.

Because you'll be seeking pen pals as a class (as opposed to seeking them individually, student by student), you should send an e-mail to the site and request class rates. In addition, you should be ready to provide parent permission forms in order to assure that your students will be allowed to participate.

Too many teachers are so intent upon finishing the curriculum or caught up in preparing detailed lesson plans that they forget to make their students feel welcome in their room. **_Remember:_** Kids are not machines, and they're going to need a break from the repetitiveness of the school's prison-like fixed time schedule. These are little things you can do that raise the morale of your classes without requiring a big-time commitment, so you're able to keep the kids interested and still accomplish everything you need to. Everybody wins.

Chapter 12

Managing Assessment

● ●

In This Chapter

▶ Determining what sort of grading system to use

▶ Calculating your grades

▶ Surviving the crushing weight of all those papers you have to check

▶ Writing good quizzes and tests

▶ Developing sound grading policies

● ●

*B*y the time I was in third grade, I was positive that I wanted to be a teacher. Of course, school was really the only world I had known up to that point, but the stark differences between the lowly student and the almighty teacher were beginning to dawn on me. For one thing, the teacher had a much larger book than I did, and (even better) the teacher's book had all the answers written in it! Even better, though, the teacher held the power of the red pen, and the crimson ink contained therein was imbued with great power — the power to praise, the power to destroy, and the power to convince your parents that you should be grounded for not studying. With one stroke, a happy face on a homework assignment became an unhappy face, but the implications of that single stroke were staggering.

When I became a teacher, the excitement and intrigue about grading lasted all of about 15 minutes; it was then that I realized what grading truly was: an excruciating chore that would haunt me until I died. (Sometimes, I would have preferred the warm embrace of death to grading a stack of 100 short-answer and essay tests.) In this chapter, I help you with the major tasks you'll face when it comes to assessment: figuring out how you're going to grade, how often you're going to grade, what those grades will consist of, and how to make sure that your grading system is sound enough to stand up to administrative or parental scrutiny.

Establishing a Grading System

Grading is unique in that it represents a very small percentage of what you do in the classroom, but an incredibly large percentage of what you do at home.

To make things worse, even though grades are arguably the most important thing to students and parents; for you, grades are merely an annoying afterthought to instruction.

Even though that sentiment is completely understandable, let me give you one word of caution: If you don't carefully craft your grading system before school starts, your dislike of quizzes, tests, percents, and averages will progress from "annoyed" to "crazed." You need a set plan ahead of time, so that you can handle student questions, parental complaints, and administrative inquiries, when they arise. (Notice I said *when*, not *if*. Having your grades questioned on a regular basis is just a fact of life.) Make sure you have a very specific grading system set before the school year begins.

If you've never set up a grading system before, it can be a daunting task. There are lots of different grading styles out there to choose from. One thing they all have in common: They result in a clear, indisputable numeric grade. You may have dealt with hazy grading in college (that is, "You deserve, oh I don't know, how about a B?"), but that won't fly outside the university. You need to be able to stand firmly behind any grade you assign, and nothing is more concrete than a solid number based on a well-conceived mathematical formula. There are two major grading systems that most people use. In the following sections, I explain them both, along with their strengths and weaknesses, so that you can decide which one suits you best.

The total-points method

The total-points technique is, by far, the quickest way to both assign and calculate grades, as long as you're not too concerned with weighting different categories of assignments precisely (and most people aren't). In this system, each assignment is worth a certain number of points, and you record how many points (out of the total possible) each student earns on each assignment. Typically, the more important an assignment is, the more points it's worth.

If you use the total-points method of grading, you may say that all your homework assignments will range between 5 and 15 points (depending on how long each was or how many parts it had), all your quizzes are worth somewhere around 50 points, and all your tests are worth about 100 points.

One downfall of this method is that students (especially younger ones) may have a hard time interpreting a score of 37 on a 50-point quiz. Is that a good score, or not? To help them, you may want to write the percentage on their paper as well, or, if you're more mathematically inclined, you can teach them how to calculate the correct percentage.

The total-points method is very flexible, because you can adjust things on the fly. If you think one quiz is more important than another, you can tweak the points accordingly. Furthermore, there's no hard and fast rule about how many points everything is worth. If you give a 50-question multiple-choice test, it could be worth 50, 100, or maybe 150 points, depending upon how much each question is worth. It gives you the freedom to adjust scores without looking like a pushover.

For example, let's say that this 50-point test I mentioned turned out to be a lot harder than you intended it to be (I always wrote really hard tests late at night, cranky that I was up late, lesson planning my pants off) and most of your students fail it. You can't just throw out the test and say it doesn't count, because your students will then beg you to do the same thing on every test for the rest of the year. Instead, make each question worth 1 point. As you pass the tests back, express disappointment in the scores, but explain that you're willing to give everyone a second chance. Review the material in class again and then give another test, but make the second worth 100 points! That way, the new scores will be worth twice as much as the old (in the context of the entire marking period), and you've effectively diluted the bad scores, retaught the material, and come out looking like the good guy all in one fell swoop. Pretty slick, eh?

At the end of the marking period, calculating your grades is a piece of cake. Let's say one of your students, Ida Studiedmore, got the following grades (each is in the form *points earned/total points possible*): 5/5, 7/10, 23/35, 89/100, 112/132. (By the way, you should have many more grades than this each marking period, but this is just for example purposes.) To calculate Ida's grade, add up all the points she earned and the total points that she could have earned separately:

Points Earned: 5 + 7 + 23 + 89 + 112 = 236

Points Available: 5 + 10 + 35 + 100 + 132 = 282

Now divide her total points (236) by the total possible (282) to get approximately 0.8369, which translates into either 83 or 84 percent, depending on whether you want to round up your scores (see the nearby sidebar "To round or not to round? That is the question"). Notice how each of Ida's assignments was worth a different number of points, and calculating her final grade wasn't difficult.

You can adjust the total-points method to use letter grades if you'd rather assign an A or B+ rather than a fixed numeric value. Just assign letter grades throughout the marking period, and when it comes time to calculate grades, translate the letters into numeric values. In most school systems, an A corresponds to the numeric range of 90 to 100 percent. So, translate A– into 90 percent, A into 95 percent, and A+ into 100 percent, and do something similar for Bs, Cs, and Ds.

To round or not to round? That is the question

Lots of things differentiate teachers: the nice ones versus the mean ones, the strict ones versus the lenient ones, the interesting ones versus the boring ones. However, no difference is quite so dramatic or religiously entrenched in people as the separation between those who round up grades and those who do not. If a student in your class ends up with an 89.5 percent, do you consider that an 89 or a 90?

There is a contingent of people who say that an 89.5 is less than a 90, so that student has not earned the higher grade, and they routinely refuse to "bump the grade up" higher than it should be. Some of these people are absolute extremists (read "just plain mean") and won't even round up an 89.99 to a 90. On the opposite end of the spectrum, there are teachers who say that 89.5 percent is just as close to 90 as it is to 89, so why not give the benefit of the doubt? They think the tie should go to the student, and assign the higher grade.

Between the two extremes, you have your fence sitters, who decide whether or not to assign the higher grade based upon how much effort the student has shown. For example, the teacher will be much more willing to round up for a nice student who does all his homework than an irritating student who likes to fall asleep

in class. According to these teachers, "You scratch my back, I scratch yours" is the rule. In other words, a little respect and effort pays off in the end.

Where do I fall in the spectrum? I round up 0.5 and above for every student, with no exception, because I think it's the only fair thing to do. As much as I'd like to think that my grading is 100-percent accurate, I know that it never is. I may take off 2 points on one kid's quiz for a mistake, but 4 points off another kid's quiz for the same mistake; though I wish it weren't true, I fully recognize that I'm not perfect. The way I look at it, assuming that a grade of 89.5 must be *exactly* 89.5 is completely ridiculous. In reality, the true grade probably ranges somewhere between 89 and 91, so I give the benefit of the doubt to the student — you get a lot fewer angry phone calls that way, and it's a battle not worth fighting. After all, it's only half of a percentage point!

Don't ever round up one student's grade but not another's, based on subjective things like "effort." If you insist on rounding up only selected grades, make sure you do it based on something concrete, like having an A average in homework, and make sure you share any selective criteria like that ahead of time, so that you're not playing favorites.

Don't make an F equal to 0 percent, or your grades will get skewed too low; instead, make an F equal to 40 or 50 percent, depending upon how mean you are. Of course, any missing assignments should receive a 0, rather than an F, because missing assignments should bring the grade way down.

After you've transformed all the letters into numbers, calculate a simple average of all the numbers together to come up with the final grade. *Remember:* Even letter grades must result in a fixed, numeric grade at the end of the marking period, in case the student wants to debate you about it.

The category method

I assigned grades using categories, because I was very picky about how much I thought different kinds of grades should be worth. For example, I taught high-school seniors, and I wanted to impress upon them how important good test grades were in college (because most of your final grades in college are based on how well you perform on tests). So I wanted test scores to be really important, whereas homework scores (although important) were less influential.

If you grade according to total points, you don't have this fine control, and most total-point people don't even realize this. If you have a lot of homework assignments worth lots of points, they can drown out quiz and test grades. For example, by the end of the quarter, you may have assigned 300 points' worth of homework, but only 200 in tests, effectively giving a student a lowest possible score of 60 percent if they do all their homework but get every single test question wrong for the entire marking period.

In the category method of grading, your first objective is to choose what categories of grades you'll collect and how much weight each category will be worth. (When you're done, all those category weights added together need to equal 100.) Here are the categories from my algebra class as an example:

> Homework/class-work assignments: 25 percent

> Quizzes (announced and unannounced): 35 percent

> Tests: 40 percent

You can add all sorts of other categories to your grading system; some people lump quizzes and tests together as one category and add categories like "Projects" or "Notebooks." No matter how many categories you choose, calculating grades is done in a similar fashion.

Here's how you calculate a student's grade (let's call him Willie Pass) with the category method. This marking period, Willie had two homework grades (7/10 and 15/25), two quiz grades (89/100 and 67/100), and two test grades (91/100 and 87/100). To figure out his final grade, you first have to calculate his percentages in each category separately. Therefore, in each category, divide his total points earned by the total points possible. For instance, Willie earned 22 total points on homework, out of a possible 35. Divide 22 by 35 to get a homework grade of 0.62857. (To be as accurate as possible, keep 4 or 5 decimal places if the actual decimal is long and ugly, because the more you round as you calculate, the more inaccurate your final result will be.) Do the same thing for Willie's quiz grades (156 ÷ 200 = 0.78) and test grades (178 ÷ 200 = 0.89).

Now it's time to get the final grade. The trick is to multiply the decimal score in each category (which you just figured out) by the corresponding category weight in decimal form (using the category weights from my algebra class, the homework weight, 25 percent, is 0.25 in decimal form; the quiz weight in decimal form is 0.35; and — you guessed it — the decimal form of the test weight is 0.40). So, if you do the multiplication correctly you get:

Homework: $0.62857 \times 0.25 = 0.15714$

Quizzes: $0.78 \times 0.35 = 0.273$

Tests: $0.89 \times 0.40 = 0.356$

You're almost done! All that's left to do is add up the numbers you just got, and that'll be your final grade: $0.15714 + 0.273 + 0.356 = 0.78614$. Therefore, Willie's grade will be 78.6 percent. He did pass after all!

How valuable is class participation?

Most rookie teachers who use the category method of calculating grades are very tempted to include a class-participation grade. After all, most of their college classes had it, and new teachers want students to participate in class, so it seems like the perfect idea. Unfortunately, it's not. In fact, there's no good reason to have such a category in your grading scheme.

You're on very shaky ground when you introduce subjective categories into your grades. If you can't open up your grade book and show an administrator *exactly* how you assign a grade, then you shouldn't use that grading technique. What if Ida's mom calls up and complains that her daughter got the same grades as Willie, but Ida got a different letter grade on her report card? If that grade difference is due to that troubling Class Participation category, can you justify yourself? You'll need careful records and hard evidence, not just an overall sense that "Ida seemed to talk less in class," which brings me to my second argument against subjective grading.

If you insist upon using a Class Participation category, commit yourself to keeping careful records. You'll have to document both how often students participate and the significance of their participation (that is, did they offer a significant insight or just ask if they were allowed to do the assignment in pencil?).

Class participation is a record-keeping nightmare, and even with those records, you can still be challenged. Parents may even accuse you of using your subjective category to help the students you like and punish the ones you don't. And the truth is, you'll be tempted to do just that. At the end of the marking period, kids you absolutely love are going to get low grades, and kids who annoy you are going to get grades higher than you want them to — a little voice will say, "I can tweak that participation score and they'll get what they deserve!" Ignore that voice. There's nothing you can do, aside from offering the low achievers extra-credit opportunities.

Because of the heavy documentation involved and its overall subjective nature, class-participation grades are generally a bad idea. In fact, they're outlawed by some school systems, which have learned that such grades are difficult to justify legally. Do yourself a favor and keep all your grades based on concrete and easily verified grades.

I know, that seems like an awful lot of calculating, and compared to the total-points method, it definitely is. However, the category method offers an additional advantage that you may have noticed as I led you through that example. Before you multiply the weights in, you have three numbers — 0.62857, 0.78, and 0.89 — which are the homework, quiz, and test category scores individually. If Willie complains about his grade, and insists that he should have gotten at least a B on his report card, you can easily show him that his homework score (62.8 percent) is the culprit. Knowing how quiz grades compare to test grades, or even how individual category scores vary from marking period to marking period is valuable information for you.

You may wonder why I showed you how to calculate these grades by hand when there are lots of computer programs out there that will do all the number crunching for you. You have to be able to calculate grades by hand to answer questions like, "What would happen if John gets a B on his next test?" If you can't explain to parents where your grades come from or how you arrive at your final numbers, they'll doubt your intelligence and professional ability.

Mastering the Tricks of the Trade

If you only had to worry about grades a few times a year when report cards came out, you'd probably be a happier person. I know I would have been. The constant burden of grading haunted me like an angry dead relative, and no matter how I tried to placate the spirit, nothing worked. I knew that grading was going to be a chore, but I had no idea that, in no time at all, it could become completely overwhelming as well. You have to think of grading as a natural and unavoidable part of your day, just as unpleasant but necessary as a long commute to work would be. Even though you can find ways to lighten your burden and make things easier on yourself, nothing can lift that constant weight of grading from your shoulders.

Some college professors have it good — they have graduate students or teaching assistants whose job it is to grade their papers for them. All they have to do is worry about teaching! You, on the other hand, have to do it all, and many rookies have told me that this dark side of teaching really sours them. "I have enough to do without checking 60 papers a night and triple that on the weekends!" I know how it is. I spent many a night grading until the wee hours of the morning, banging my fists on the kitchen table in sleep-deprived frustration. Luckily, frustration breeds inventiveness, and all the hardships I faced trying to understand how to handle assessment forced me to reinvent my policies and made me rethink how I was doing things. In the remainder of this chapter, I share those insights with you in the hope that your fists (and table) need not undergo the same torture.

Preparing practical policies

Any grading policies you have, or plan to have, in place are probably based on your experience in other teachers' classrooms, either the teachers you were paired with in college, or the teachers you had when you were in school. What you don't realize is that these people probably had all kinds of subtle and unspoken policies in place that you never even realized were there. These subtle practices help you save time, save face in front of your students, and avert both teacher-student and teacher-parent disagreements about grades before they even start.

Don't check every single assignment for correctness

When I started teaching, I was tempted to check every answer of every homework question every student turned in, for two reasons. First, I wanted to make sure that I could monitor the evolution of each student's understanding. Second, I was wildly insane. If you check every homework, every quiz, and every test, you will never have a moment to yourself; it's the fast track to teacher burnout, and I've seen it happen. Instead of grading every homework, do a "spot check" to see if students completed their assignments, and give credit based on the *completeness* of the homework rather than the *correctness*.

One word of caution: Don't just glance at the assignment; take a moment and read pieces of it to make sure that the student has actually tried it and isn't just trying to get credit for free. I occasionally caught a student whose assignment read, "I did not do this homework and am only writing this to make it look like I did. Ha ha. You're going to give me credit even though I didn't do squat." Hmmm. Turns out he was wrong about that one. An assignment like that smells like a 0 and a detention for general jerkiness.

Don't promise a fixed turnaround time for grading papers

When I was a student, sometimes it took teachers three or four weeks to grade papers and return them to us, and I hated that. I was adamant that I'd return papers much faster. On the first day of school, I even told my students, "I know how hard you study for these quizzes and tests, and I don't want to disrespect you by returning them to you after taking my sweet time grading them. I will always return papers to you within two days of any assignment, so you'll always know exactly how you're doing."

The kids loved it, and appreciated how hard I was working. Needless to say, they were miffed when I completely reversed my policy during the second week of school. I believe the retraction went something like this: "I now understand why teachers return papers late. It's because I'm so busy that some days I have to choose between grading papers and showering, and lucky for you, showering has been winning out. Every night you should pray that it stays that way, because it's hot in this room." With that said, try to grade papers as quickly as you can; students tend to learn more from a test if they can remember having taken it in the first place. If you're constantly hearing, "When did we take this test?" you may need to put those papers a little higher on your priority list.

Make sure your grading policies are fair

The more complex your grading system, the easier it is for kids to find loopholes in it to exploit. Before you introduce any untested innovations into your assessment scheme, you have to consider every possible angle and be ready to justify your plan to parents and administrators alike. For instance, I spoke to one teacher who invented a policy in college and couldn't wait to implement it when he got into teaching, only to find out that it was a bad idea.

His revolutionary idea: If a student got a poor grade on a quiz (below 70 percent), he should be allowed another chance at the quiz — a retake. During his student teaching, he saw a lot of students do badly on quizzes and tests because of severe test anxiety, and he created the retake policy so that these students could achieve the grades they deserved, instead of punishing them for being extra nervous on test day. According to the policy, the student would come after school, retake the quiz or test on his own time, and the new grade would replace the previous, nerve-addled one.

Can you spot the loophole in this policy? Let's say the two students I introduce earlier in this chapter, Ida Studiedmore and Willie Pass, take a major test in this class. Ida gets a 69 percent (which translates to a D) and Willie ekes out a 71 percent, a low C. Both of the students usually get As or Bs on tests without having to study much, so both are shocked at their grades. Lucky for Ida, her grade qualifies for the retake policy, so she goes home, studies hard, and retakes the quiz, this time receiving a 95 percent. Her D is obliterated from the record, and she moves back to the head of the class, leaving poor Willie in the dust with his meager 71. What motivation does Ida have to study for a quiz in the first place? Why not bomb it on purpose, find out what the questions will be, and then retake it after she's looked up all the answers?

Make sure students and their parents know what their grade looks like before report cards come out

In this day and age, electronic grade books abound. Many school systems require you to submit your grades electronically, via the software they already have in place, but even if you're not required to store or calculate your grades electronically, you should. This way, you can print out progress reports for students every couple of weeks, and either pass them out or post them on the wall, so that students always have a good idea of how they're faring in your class. It would be too much to ask teachers to constantly calculate these grades by hand, but now that the computer can do it for you in the blink of an eye, there's no excuse for not keeping students informed.

Should students grade each other's papers?

One easy way to stem the tide of grading is to allow students to check one another's work every once in a while. I had students check their classmates' work all the time, and it was enormously helpful. Rather than spending hours at home, laboring over stacks and stacks of work, I'd spend 15 to 20 minutes in class, discussing questions, explaining how to grade them, and having students call out grades when we were done, so that I could record them in my grade book.

Not only do students get immediate feedback about how they did on their assignments, they also get a behind-the-scenes look into how you assign points when you grade. Some students complain that they never know what the teacher is "looking for" when she grades, and this practice helps address that issue.

Of course, there are negatives as well. Can you trust your kids to grade one another's papers honestly? Will they give points to their friends, just to be nice, and will they cut the test taker slack when he doesn't deserve it? These are all good questions, and they all speak to one central issue: You have to be able to trust your students in order to grade papers in class. I always found that a stern warning helps motivate students to stick to the straight-and-narrow path.

Each year, before we graded papers in class for the first time, I told this story: "During my rookie year teaching, two seniors, a boy and a girl who had a crush on one another, always graded each other's work. I eventually found out that they were inflating each other's grades by being extra lenient and even marking things right that were definitely wrong. When I found out, I made

them pull out all those quizzes and I regraded each of them myself. If their final grade differed from mine *by even one point*, I gave them both a 0 for that quiz, and they both ended up not graduating because of it. The moral of the story: Don't even think about cheating, because I will fail you and the person whose paper you're grading, just like I failed those seniors."

This story was, and remains, a total fabrication. I made it up to scare my students enough to be honest while they were grading, and it worked like a charm. It's not as though I harped on it all the time or was a jerk, constantly threatening them. However, that one stern warning, mentioned in passing, hung around their subconscious minds all year long. I regularly compared quiz grades that we checked in class against papers that I graded at home, to make sure there were no disparities, and I never found any. In fact, I found that my students graded each other more harshly than I graded them!

By the way, having students grade one another's papers in class and call out the results to the teacher is completely legal. In 2001, a mother named Kristja Falvo took her local Oklahoma school district to court, challenging the practice, and the case went all the way to the Supreme Court, where it was unanimously decided that peer grading does not violate students' Family Educational Rights and Privacy Act (FERPA) rights. However, some students may be sensitive to hearing their grades announced in class, so you should probably make sure to check with an administrator, to save yourself parent phone calls and headaches later.

If you think a student is in danger of failing your class, both she and her parents need to know *while she still has time to do something about it*. In some school districts, you have a fixed number of weeks before the marking period ends, before which you have to warn the student and her parents in writing if there is a chance the student may not pass; if you fail to provide that written warning, you aren't permitted to fail her for that marking period! Therefore, you need to stay constantly vigilant when it comes to monitoring your kids' grades. It's not enough just to say, "You know what you've gotten this marking period and how I calculate grades — figure it out yourself!"

If you plan on hanging the grades on the wall or posting them in any public location, obviously, you don't want to list the student names next to the grades. Not only does that cause potential conflict ("Hey, Frank, congratulations! You're the stupidest kid in this class!"), it's also illegal, according to the Family Educational Rights and Privacy Act (FERPA). In essence, FERPA prohibits you from disclosing student grades and other educational records to others. In fact, you can't even post grades by social security number, birth date, height, weight, hair color, or number of times they've seen the movie *Star Wars*. Anything that is personally identifiable is a no-no.

Your best bet is to assign unique codes or randomly assigned student numbers for your class and then post the grades showing those codes in lieu of names. Be clever about it. Don't just assign students numbers in alphabetical order, so that in your class of 30, Brian Aardvark is obviously Student 1 and Stacey Zucker is 30. Only you and the student should know under what code his grade is listed.

When it comes to grading, every little thing you can do to lessen your burden and avoid potential problems is worth it. The perfect set of grading policies works so well that most students don't understand just how many factors are at work within it.

Absorbing assessment advice

Before I wrap up this chapter on how to handle assessment, I want to throw in a few tips about actually preparing and administering quizzes and tests. When I started teaching, I thought I did a pretty good job of getting my classes under control and presenting material in an interesting way; my biggest weakness was knowing how often to quiz my students and how to create quizzes that took a reasonable amount of time to grade. You may find out, as I did, that testing is much different from what your college classes told you it would be.

There is nothing wrong with having multiple-choice questions on exams

Of course, you can't only give multiple-choice tests; the big push these days is to make sure students are effective writers, so you need to include essay questions or short-answer questions here and there no matter what subject you teach. However, if you create a test that is only short-answer and essay questions, grading those papers will suck away your will to live.

I was taught in college that multiple-choice or fill-in-the-blank questions address only low-cognitive-level skills, so most of your questions should be more metacognitive in nature. For example, they say that asking the question "When did the Civil War begin?" is a next-to-worthless assessment item, because it involves only recall skills. On the other hand, education experts are enamored of the question, "If you were Abraham Lincoln, how would you feel about the Civil War?" because it requires you to form your own opinion and justify it. Call me old school, but I think knowing facts is as important as having opinions. Has the Daily Double on *Jeopardy!* ever been, "How would you feel if you were the nucleus of a cell?" (The correct response is: "What is claustrophobic, Alex?")

Your best bet is to have some questions on every test that are simple to grade (matching, multiple-choice, true/false, fill-in-the-blank) and some that will require you to make a partial credit judgment. This way, administrators are happy, and you don't spend the next 30 years of your life up to your armpits in ungraded test papers.

Premade tests and quizzes are almost always awful

Even though your textbook probably comes with a whole set of supplemental premade tests and worksheets (or *black-line masters*), don't plan on using them exclusively. Here's one example of a question my wife found in a very popular contemporary math textbook's accompanying set of premade tests: "What do the numbers 3, 7, 11, and 16 have in common?" Think about that one for a second — I defy you to come up with an answer! Here's the answer the book gave: "These numbers are not multiples of 5." Have you ever seen a more ridiculous question? The answer may as well have been, "They aren't letters"! Of course, not all the questions are that bad, but you have to read through them and pull out the horrible ones.

Another reason to think twice about a prewritten test is that it rarely reflects your teaching style. You probably stressed different things than the test does, and the exam probably words questions differently than you would, so most of the time you'll need to make up your own exams. Plus, if you're constantly using prefabricated exams, kids and parents will think you're too lazy to create your own. If you're not good at coming up with your own questions, pull the best ones from the preprinted masters and scan other sources (like other textbooks or workbooks) for additional questions.

Make sure you have at least one significant grade every week for each student in each subject you teach

This was my biggest mistake. As long as each class day seems (especially as the year lingers on), each class period flies by before you even realize it. You need to make it a point to have at least one weekly quiz or test, so that you build up a good base of grades, or else days will slip into weeks, and you'll wind up at the end of the marking period with one or two grades. When I say "significant grade," I mean something that was graded for correctness, not something that was just spot-checked — it needs to somehow measure the student's mastery of what you're covering in class.

One rookie teacher I knew only got around to assigning one quiz and one test during his first marking period and he only graded the test! Big mistake — parents called and complained that he was assigning grades based on hardly any information, and he was in trouble deep. To make sure I had one significant grade per week, I gave quizzes or tests every Friday, but only on Fridays. I consider it the greatest idea I ever came up with as a teacher, because of all the benefits:

✔ Every week, students could tell exactly what they did and did not understand.

✔ Because they were in a routine, no one could ever say she forgot to study.

✔ Kids are the most rambunctious and wound up on Fridays, and keeping class control is a lot less tiring when you're testing than when you're teaching.

✔ Even though it stinks to spend the weekend grading, it stinks worse to spend your weekday evenings grading, when you'd rather be doing things like eating and sleeping.

Of course, I taught high school, and this tip does not work so well for elementary-school teachers. Can you imagine a 7-year-old having to sit still and take tests in every class every Friday? The good news is that tests designed for very young children usually don't take that long to grade. In fact, some teachers are able to grade the majority of their papers during class time! As the students finish, have them bring their papers up to your desk, and start grading them right on the spot. By the time the last few kids finish, you'll probably have at least half of the papers graded, and you can easily knock the rest out during a planning period or later at home.

When I started my Friday testing plan, I started looking forward to the end of the week, because I knew it would be time to finally get off my feet and not have to perform. Because the exams were back to back, when I got my second class of the day started on its test, I could start grading the tests from the first class. This greatly reduced the amount of take-home grading that always occurred when I tested different classes on different days — it just never gave me the opportunity to sit down for very long and actually get knee-deep into grading.

As much as I detested grading papers, I was always amazed how interested people are in a teacher marking a stack of tests. Whether in the Laundromat, doctor's office, or any other spot where I could whip out a stack of work and the Red Teacher Pen, I always drew a crowd. "What are you doing there?"

they'd ask, "Grading papers?" If you follow my tips, your grading won't be so overwhelming, and you won't have to bring it with you wherever you go. You can do what people are meant to do at the Laundromat: Stare at each other's underpants in the dryers and wrestle other patrons over who gets to use the washers next.

Part IV
Meet the Supporting Cast

In this part . . .

Teachers are in the spotlight from the first minute of the school day until long after all the kids have gone home and already forgotten to do their homework. Even though you're the star of the show, there are all sorts of other people on the set and behind the scenes. Of course, you're surrounded by students for the vast majority of the day, and the brief moments you're free of them you'll spend with your colleagues and administrators. If you're going to be around these people all the time, you may as well get to know them better, because they all expect different things from you. In this part, I take you on a tour of all the major and minor players at your school, and give you some tips to help you establish relationships and thrive in this unique social environment.

Chapter 13

Getting to Know Your Administrators

- -

In This Chapter

▶ Differentiating between the types of administrators you'll meet

▶ Meeting expectations of both principals and supervisors

▶ Clearing up common misconceptions about the folks in the main office

▶ Understanding what administrators want to see when they formally observe you

- -

Administrators are hard to figure out. Even after years of having interacted with them in their natural habitat, I still find myself mystified by the species. What sort of person would take tons and tons of graduate classes in administration (with such exciting titles as "Contemporary Assessment Methods as They Concern Instructional Leadership and School Improvement"), just so she could work eight more weeks every year than she did as a teacher, for a marginally higher salary? Who would want to spend his entire day dealing with the worst students in the school, divvying out punishments, dealing with irate parents, and (more often than not) looking like the bad guy?

I have no idea, so I met with a bunch of administrators and asked them all sorts of questions to try to figure out the answer to the quandary that plagues all teachers at one point in their career: Who are you and what do you want from me? In this chapter, I introduce you to the different kinds of administrators you'll meet, both at the school level and at the local board of education, and try to communicate the wishes and expectations of this strange species, so that you and they can peacefully coexist.

A Field Guide to Administrators

You'll find just as many awful administrators out there as you'll find good ones, and even the best administrators have little quirks that make them difficult to deal with at times. Your school probably has a handful of principals and vice-principals, each of whom has a different personality, a different way of handling conflict, and different priorities. It's very confusing, and to make things worse, these powerful people can be very intimidating to a rookie. What one person may expect from you, another person may not.

The expectations set forth by your different supervisors are deeply rooted in their educational philosophies, their personal credos, and whether they had time to eat breakfast that morning. I swear to you, administrators are some of the moodiest people I have ever met in my life, and trying to discern what motivates them and why they do the things they do is a difficult, if not impossible, task. Therefore, I've compiled the following field guide, based on my experience as a teacher. Just like a wildlife field guide (which will help you differentiate between types of snakes you'll see on a nature walk), this field guide will help you spot different kinds of administrators, give you insight into their personalities, and let you know which (like the snakes) are poisonous.

The Dictator

One of the most common species of administrator, the Dictator is also the easiest to spot. His list of rules and regulations for the school are a mile long, and he expects each one of them to be followed. In his world, teachers and students blend together into one hazy mass called "people who'd better do what I say or I'll grind their bones and use the powder to make my bread." There is no gray in the sight of the Dictator, because he possesses an educational astigmatism that only allows him to see black and white.

In the lair of the Dictator, teachers are held to the *exact* same standard as students. One teacher I spoke to grieved under the oppressive weight of her Dictator principal. "Sometimes when I'm up in front of the class," the teacher confided, "My feet start to hurt, so I'll hop up on a student desk and teach from there for a while. The principal walked in on me once, while I was seated on the desk, and reamed me out for it! She told me 'Students aren't allowed to sit on desks. What sort of message do you think you're sending if *you* do?' I mean, honestly, I got in trouble for *sitting* wrong."

There are good things about the Dictator. Students are generally well behaved in a Dictator's school. Even though their behavior is probably motivated by fear rather than a healthy desire to be a good citizen, at least there are some positives. The biggest negative, however, is the morale at the school, because teachers are not treated as adults. Almost all administrators were, at one time, teachers, and they developed their leadership skills while supervising children. Some administrators aren't able to change their tactics when they're in charge of adults, and they expect the same sort of unquestioning obedience that they did from their kids, which doesn't sit well with most faculty.

Zen and the Art of Supervisor Maintenance

It's almost certain that, at some point, you're going to clash with one of your administrators. Either the administrator will go easy on a kid when you wanted the book thrown at him, or perhaps after an observation, she'll come down hard on you for something that seems like no big deal at all. At first, these episodes really upset me, and I'd beat myself up about what I could have done better to try to avoid getting chastised again. I was afraid of not getting tenure and having to walk the streets unemployed — I spent all of college preparing for an education career, and I wasn't keen on returning there to start over from scratch with a new profession.

I remember exactly when I stopped fearing my supervisors. I was driving home from school around 7 p.m., more than four hours after school was over for the day. It was my second year teaching, and I'd stayed late to decorate my room for the holidays — I wanted to surprise my kids, so I waited until everyone had gone home before I got started. About halfway through my 30-minute commute, a car pulled out in front of me unexpectedly, and I rammed into it at about 60 miles per hour.

I spent about two hours strapped to a wooden board in the emergency room and then another two hours lying around, waiting to be cleared to leave. As soon as I got home, I called the vice-principal in charge of assigning substitutes to tell him that I wasn't going to be able to come in the next day. His response was, "We have a lot of teachers out tomorrow, and we don't have a lot of subs; you can't take off." I was mortified — I had barely taken any leave for two years, and I was in no shape to teach. "I spent all night in the hospital," I explained. "I have no way to get to work even if I wanted to — my car is destroyed and I'm hopped up on pain medicine."

"We all have our problems," was the measured reply. "You still need to come in." That was it. I had had enough. "I'm sorry to make things hard on you," I snapped sarcastically, "But if a car accident isn't reason enough to miss a day of work, I don't know what is. If you have a problem with my absence tomorrow, I suggest you take it up with the principal." With that, I hung up the phone and went to bed.

When I returned to school two days later, no one mentioned anything about my absence, and I had learned a valuable lesson: Sometimes administrators are unreasonable, so if you conflict with them, it's not always your fault. I pass on to you the advice one veteran teacher gave me upon hearing that story: Teachers are like rocks in the bed of a stream; though the tide may come and go and the river's course may alter, the rocks always remain. No matter how much you may conflict with an administrator, don't try to fight the current. Administrations change quickly, and before you know it, the administrator will be gone, but you'll still be there. Stick with what you know works in your classroom, and patiently wait for the tide to change.

The best way to deal with a Dictator principal or supervisor is simply to comply with his or her wishes, unless you're ready for battle. As soon as you identify yourself as a conscientious objector to the Dictator's plans, you're branded for life, and you'll find out how a disgruntled supervisor can make every day miserable for you. Rookie teachers don't need enemies, especially enemies who will ultimately decide if they'll be rehired. So try your best to follow the rules, even the stupid ones (especially when the Dictator is watching), thereby identifying yourself as an ally. When the Dictator trusts you, he'll view you as an adult and will be more willing to cut you some slack.

The Political Animal

People have all kinds of reasons for wanting to become administrators. Some people have just had their fill of creating lesson plans, checking papers, and calculating grades, and they need a career change. However, most school systems won't reimburse you for graduate classes that are unrelated to the field of education, so most teachers seeking new employment end up being funneled into one of two professions: administrator or guidance counselor. Because they bring so much classroom experience to their new jobs, they understand how things work in education and are usually very good at what they do; they know how teachers think, what students want, what parents expect, and they're able to make decisions that work well for everyone concerned.

On the other hand, some people get into administration because they see it as their ticket to bigger and better things. Not content to serve as merely a school-based principal or vice-principal, these folks have their eyes on a much greater prize: superintendent, state department of education bigwig, or politician. They hop from job to job as quickly as possible, amassing titles, gathering momentum, and stepping on lots of people along the way.

The Political Animal is not quite as easy to spot as the Dictator, because she's slick. She wants to be everyone's friend, at least on the surface, because subconsciously she's always trying to build a platform of supporters in her march toward fame and recognition. The best way to track down the Political Animal is to find out who's participating in the most committees, initiatives, school-improvement groups, state directives, and national action groups. For her, being a good administrator is about *looking* involved, although she's on so many committees that you rarely even see her in her office.

She doesn't do a very good job disciplining students, because she dislikes it, and she doesn't practice discipline enough to develop any skills. She has no backbone, will not support her teachers when they try to punish wrongdoers, and will instantly cave in to parents when they call and complain. In her mind, students are your job, and things like long-term planning, drafting vision statements, and writing grant proposals are her job.

The best way to deal with this type of administrator is to always be on your guard, because the Political Animal is not tame by any means. ***Remember:*** She's interested in appearances first and foremost, and if you, as her subordinate, make her look bad, she'll turn on you in a second. If you're interested in getting into her good graces, design a lesson plan involving all the latest strategies dreamed up by the multiple committees she's on and invite her to attend the lesson. However, don't make it your goal in life to please her, because she'll never be completely happy with you. Her life is lived in a constant state of flux, always trying to fit more into the day, so that her list of achievements grows long enough to lead her to the next rung up the administrative ladder. Like her or hate her, she'll be gone before you know it, so the best thing to do is to keep your nose clean and throw her a bone every now and again so that you don't become her prey.

The Pushover

At some level, kids are supposed to have a healthy fear of the main office. It's a place that should conjure up images of harsh discipline, consequence, and regret. Unless they've been there a lot and have no respect for the school system at all, most kids do in fact hate being sent to the office. At the very least, it means a stern conversation, a confessional phone call to their parents, and maybe even detention or suspension. However, if you have an administrator who's a Pushover, kids are just itching to go to the office, because they know not only won't they get in trouble, but it's very likely that the teacher will be lectured instead.

The Pushover is usually a very nice guy at heart. He likes kids, he loved teaching, and he really gets a kick out of his job. The only problem is that he tends to believe students' accounts of what happens in the classroom rather than the teachers'. It's even worse for you, as a rookie teacher, because you have no history in the school, and the Pushover has a history with all the bad kids.

For example, say you have an obnoxious kid in your class named Tommy. One day, you ask the students to work in groups, and he refuses. When pressed to do as you ask, he becomes rude, and when pressed harder, he becomes belligerent. You threaten to send him to the office, and still he ignores you. Because Tommy is becoming a huge distraction to the other students and is disruptive, you send him down to the office to get him out of your hair, expecting to sit down and write a referral report detailing the incident when class is over, to follow up with the administrator in charge.

As soon as Tommy gets to the main office, he heads straight for the Pushover. "Mr. Kelley was really rude and disrespectful to me in class; he won't even listen to me when I try to talk to him," he confides. "I try to be good in his class. You know how bad I used to be and how I'm trying to be good now, but he makes me so mad, because he doesn't even care." Tommy knows exactly what words to say. He plays upon the relationship he has with the administrator, and in a few minutes, the Pushover is standing in your doorway, asking to speak with you. "Why can't you work with Tommy?" he asks. "He's come a long way, and we're making good progress with him. What's your problem?"

There's only one thing you can do when faced with this administrator: Make a point of getting to know him. Stop by his office in the morning and make non-work-related small talk. Ask about the family, what he did on the weekend, and how his favorite sports team is doing. Let him get to know you as a nice person, who has reasonable expectations and who works hard. Share stories about successes you've had with kids, and ask for his advice occasionally, even if you don't really need it. When he gets to know you, he'll be less willing to believe false stories offered up by desperate students.

The Charity Case

Have you ever wondered, "How did that guy ever become an administrator?" He has poor management skills, is almost universally incompetent, doesn't know much about or care much about educational theory, but seems to keep climbing up the corporate ladder, passing by scores of people who could do a much, much better job? If so, you've met a Charity Case. These people, who succeed and are endlessly promoted due to their connections rather than any tangible skill, are not unique to the field of education. They are the tiny group of people in management, the exception rather than the rule, who give the rest of the group a bad name.

Even though I know these people are out there in every business, it frustrates me that they're so prevalent in school administration. Your first encounter with a Charity Case is bound to be a shock, because you probably think that those in education should be held to a higher standard. Unfortunately, the worse some people screw up in the classroom, the quicker they're moved to a supervisory job (as long as they have those connections).

One young teacher relayed to me her first experience and how much it upset her: "I had this teacher in high school who was just terrible. He had been around forever, and he did everything they told us, as teacher candidates in college, never to do. First of all, he only taught about 10 percent of the days we were in class. The other 90 percent, he sat in his separate office and chatted in there with the cute girls from class, while the rest of us just sat and waited for the period to end. Second, he was making *constant* racial slurs against students in our class, and really upsetting the African-American and Latino students. Finally, he cursed at us all the time, and not just casual swearing — he called us obscene names. I know we were in high school and not little kids, but still that's just inappropriate. I won't even get into how he talked about sex all the time; I don't even want to think about it. In college, I thought it would be fun to student-teach at the high school I went to, so I made all the arrangements and was glad to see that he no longer taught there. Some of the faculty I talked to told me that all he'd done had finally caught up with him, and the board of education had to pull him out of the classroom. I was so thankful and relieved — until I found out what they did with him: They made him the district supervisor of the subject he taught! He was such good friends with the uppity-ups that they gave him a raise, more responsibility, and influence over thousands of kids."

If your supervisor is a Charity Case, don't expect any support or constructive advice. Deep down, these administrators know they don't deserve to be where they are, and they're afraid to take a stand on anything. They owe so many different people so much that they're not in a position to back you up or fight for you when you need it. Because most Charity Cases work at the local board of education, alongside your supervisor, your best bet is to seek the support you need from your principal or other school-based administrators.

The Ideal Administrator

Here's a novel idea: How about an administrator who actually sits back and lets you teach, without imposing her personal agenda? One supervisor I spoke to said the words you rarely hear, but always long to, from your boss: "I spend a lot of time interviewing, observing, and choosing new teachers to hire, so when they get into the classroom, I'm confident they possess the skills they need to do a good job. I'm happy to let them do their thing and step in and help whenever they ask for it. They don't need me constantly criticizing or second-guessing them, or always telling them when they do little things wrong. They'll figure it out for themselves." The Ideal Administrator believes you innocent of professional incompetence until proven guilty, instead of automatically assuming the worst. She supports you before she finds fault, always gives you the benefit of the doubt, and makes you feel better after you've met with her, instead of draining away all your confidence.

Too many administrators think that their job is to nitpick every tiny aspect of your lesson, to assert their expertise, and to consistently prove to you why they're in charge. However, there are some good administrators out there. They understand that the most important people in a school system are the teachers, fighting it out in the trenches every day, and making the changes in kids' lives that inspire success.

Dealing with Dueling Bosses

One of the weirdest things for new teachers to cope with is the multitude of people supervising them. Most jobs only have one boss, and even though that boss has a boss and the boss's boss has a boss, those uppity-ups usually don't even know you're alive, let alone actively tell you what you're doing wrong. Teachers, however, have building supervisors and school-board supervisors as well, and both of them have their own ideas about what you should be doing in your classroom.

Luckily, all these supervisors are usually worried about different kinds of things, so you'll rarely feel caught in the middle, unsure about whose advice to follow. If they do have conflicting expectations, though, it's not your job to straighten that conflict out! For example, if your principal thinks teachers should be assigning homework every day and the subject specialist thinks that's too much work for you to be handing out, go straight to your principal, explain the confusion, and let him work things out with your other boss. You have enough to do without mediating disagreements between the people supervising you.

To make working under the scrutiny of two sets of eyeballs easier for you, in the following sections I briefly discuss what the owner of each pair of eyeballs values most from his employees. After all, you're not a mind reader! How can you possibly meet those expectations if you don't even know what they are?

Pleasing your principal

Most important of all, you should know that your principal thinks you have a lot of potential — she hired you, after all! Even though school districts help narrow the body of applicants for jobs, it's usually the principals of the individual schools who have the final decision about who gets to work in their buildings. That should be a vote of confidence — she picked you out of all the other people, so even if you're not the best teacher in the world just yet, at least she thinks you have the most potential!

The primary job of the principal is simple: Make sure every single person in the school is fulfilling his role in the educational process every minute of the day. It's a simple concept, sure, but it's an incredibly hard job. Therefore, it's most important to a principal that you help keep the building running smoothly and see to all your responsibilities, including:

- ✔ Enforcing school rules and policies in all your classes

- ✔ Maintaining control of your students without constantly needing to send kids to the office

- ✔ Performing your assigned duties (such as supervising and/or patrolling the cafeteria, hallways, parking lots, study hall, detention, or another teacher's classroom if needed), no matter how unpleasant

The more thorough and dedicated you are to all the parts of your job, especially the parts that don't involve teaching, the more willing your principal will be to support you, so don't complain about menial tasks she assigns.

Asking permission versus asking forgiveness

You may have heard the expression, "It's always easier to ask for forgiveness than to ask for permission." In other words, instead of always asking your supervisors whether you're allowed to do this or that, just do it, and if things go badly or you get in trouble, apologize. In the field of education, people are nervous about change, and if you plan on teaching things in a new and novel way, it's bound to cause a little apprehension, especially from parents, who are well known for the quote, "That's not the way I learned [insert your subject here]."

For example, I assigned creative-writing projects in my algebra classes during my rookie year. The guidelines about the project were very flexible: Take a mathematical topic we've discussed this year, and write a story, poem, or short play about it, the length of which is at least one page. It was not a major project, worth about as much as a quiz, but I wanted to give students the ability to flex a little creative muscle in a math class for a change. I had a lot of artsy students in my classes who didn't enjoy the black-and-white, all-right or all-wrong nature of math, and I thought this would be a good way to grab their interest. Plus, we were supposed to include more writing in math, so I thought I'd introduce writing in a nonthreatening way. Indeed, it worked well and didn't prevent me from completing the required algebra curriculum.

Had I asked if it was okay to assign such a bizarre project, I would likely have been told no. In fact, my supervisor called me when he found out and explained his disapproval of the assignment.

However, I found out that my principal was a huge fan of it, and he supported me 100 percent. Therefore, I was able to go forward with it, which would not have happened had I asked both administrators. When the project was already up and running, seeing that the pros outnumbered the cons was easy.

Here's another example from my teaching experience that proves action beats prior approval. I love the Christmas holiday season, especially all the lights and decorations. Therefore, the first year I had a classroom of my own, I was determined to decorate it to the hilt during the holidays. Right after Thanksgiving that year, I invited students to stay after school and help me put up innumerable strings of holiday lights, tons of tinsel, and all the (religiously ambiguous) finery I could find. Fifty students stayed after school and worked for hours until the room was dazzling, in a gaudy Las Vegas way. Even so, the kids loved it, and students from all over the building came to see it during class changes.

The principal found me later and told me it was against school district policy to have decorative lights in classrooms, and that had I asked permission, he would have had to tell me no. "But now that all those lights are up, I'd be a real grinch to make you take them down, wouldn't I?" he said with a wink and a smile, not unlike St. Nick himself. From then on, my school administrators chose to look the other way as students gathered in my room every year to create the inspiring, if not seizure-inducing, array of blinking holiday lights.

Satisfying your supervisor

Whereas your principal is more worried about the role you play in the school building, your early-education or subject supervisor values your professional knowledge and teaching methods more. Principals value practical class-control skills and usually are pretty flexible about what you do in class, just as long as students are learning and on task, but supervisors aren't quite so compromising. The sad truth is that many supervisors are so far removed from the years they spent teaching that they've forgotten what's important. They value numbers, grades, and standardized test scores more than class control, instructional leadership, and dedication to your students.

I was observed many times by many different administrators, at all different levels of political influence at the local school district. Not only did I never receive a bad rating from an administrator at my school, I never even received a single comment in the portion of the teacher evaluation form labeled "Suggestions for improvement." In fact, no principal or vice-principal ever saw fit to even hold a conference after an evaluation; they simply congratulated me on a good lesson and asked me to sign the evaluation form. I tell you this not because I think I was the greatest teacher ever, but because this is the experience most teachers have with their school-based administrators. However, people almost unanimously relate a different experience when it comes to supervisor evaluations.

No matter how stupendous your class was, count on your supervisor finding at least a couple things wrong with it, or at least offering some suggestions to improve things the next go 'round. One new teacher told me "I taught the lesson of my life, infused all the new teaching methods my supervisor described at the beginning-of-the-year in-service meetings, involved students, moved around the room, and did everything like I was taught in college. When class was over and all my students left, he reamed me out for 45 minutes about how I spent too much time going over homework! I told him I only spent 15 minutes talking about it, and he said, 'Well, then I guess it should have been 10.' I have the worst kids in the school, and they all behaved, participated, and learned, but all he wants to talk about is how he thinks I spent 5 minutes too many on homework review! These kids don't even *do* homework in their other classes!"

I often felt the same way after my observations; it's almost as though your supervisor feels he needs to find *something* wrong or needing improvement with your lesson to justify having to drive all the way up to your school and observe you in the first place. I never was good at handling that unexpected criticism, especially because its message was so opposite what I was hearing from students, parents, and administrators at my school.

Surprisingly, all veteran teachers give the same advice when it comes to dealing with superfluous criticism: Completely ignore it. One faculty member I spoke to expressed it well: "These supervisors hardly ever see you in the classroom, but when they come in, they act like they know everything about you. No matter what they tell you in the meeting following your observation, just agree with them. Don't fight — it's not worth it, and they'll always win. Instead, as soon as they leave, just go back to teaching the way you always did, the way that everyone else seems to think is just fine."

Of course, each time your supervisor observes you, you should act like you follow his advice all the time. ("See that? I limited myself to ten minutes of homework review! What a great suggestion that was!") Sure, it's an act, but you don't want to be openly antagonistic toward your boss, no matter how misguided you may consider his advice. In fact, following the advice of your supervisor is sort of like housecleaning — most people only do a really thorough job when they know somebody's coming over. However, you can only pull off this scam when the advice your supervisor gives is truly insignificant, and I explain why in the next section of this chapter.

I'm not telling you to ignore anyone's constructive criticism, especially when you're new. You have a lot to learn, and you won't get better without making your fair share of mistakes. But I recommend giving more weight to the opinions and suggestions offered up by the teachers and administrators at your school, who know you and see what you do on a regular basis, than you give to those who only get a brief snapshot of your teaching ability every couple of months.

Overcoming Observations

In my opinion, no job even remotely resembles teaching. Forget for a moment about the high expectations, low wages, and hours you spend grading papers until your hand resembles a twisted claw; no other job requires you to dedicate yourself so completely. You spend ages and ages designing personalized lesson plans, educating children, entertaining your classes, developing a strong relationship with and among your students, and even hanging around after school in case anyone needs a shoulder to cry on or simply someone to listen. Teaching is not just a job, it's a lifestyle choice — and you have to pour everything you have into it every day. That's why most rookies have such a hard time when they have to face formal observations and ratings.

And face them they will. During my rookie year, it felt like I was being observed every other day, by every conceivable person even remotely involved in the school system. I was observed by the principal, all the vice-principals, my school mathematics administrator, my district supervisor, the director for secondary education, the director of curriculum, the superintendent, and even the guy who slices cold cuts behind the deli counter at the grocery store down the street. They all did the same thing: Sit at a student desk, and write, write, write until their fingers bled.

Not long after that monsoon of observations begins, you'll get used to them. With each observation, you'll become less and less nervous, and by the end you may even be able to act normal during an observation. The nerves don't ever completely go away, however. Deep down in your very being, next to the macaroni and cheese you ate for lunch, you know that observations go into your permanent record, and you can't have a pockmarked and scarred permanent record if you're going to get tenure.

Who is that masked man?

Class feels different when someone is in your room observing you, and the students can tell. You're more nervous than normal, for one thing, but even more obviously, there's a complete stranger sitting in the room! The presence of this unnamed intruder has different effects on students depending on how old they are.

Young students are usually quieter than normal and uneasy when someone they don't know, clad in shirt and tie or pantsuit, appears without warning and sits at the rear of the class, hovering dangerously out of sight (especially if the administrator in question is not from the main office). To ease their minds (and return your class to some semblance of normalcy), you should introduce your supervisor. There's no need to explain that the visitor will decide the fate of your professional career, or try to describe what his job is. Instead, introduce him as "another teacher from the school district who heard about all the good things we're doing in class, so he wanted to come by and see how much you've learned already this year." This helps turn student unease into excitement — little kids love showing off what they know.

As students get older, they figure out what's what, so you don't have to explain the presence of the administrator. However, they're still a bit uneasy, because the new person always puts a damper on the usual chemistry in the room. I've found that the best way to make the students more comfortable is to plan a cooperative-learning lesson for announced observation days. This gives students a chance to interact with one another in a normal way, and it helps compensate for the weirdness of the extra person in the room.

If he's game, include your supervisor in one of the cooperative learning groups. *Remember:* Supervisors used to be teachers, and the one thing they probably miss the most from their chalk-dust days is interacting with kids. This exercise gives your supervisor the chance to relive some of his best memories and keeps him plenty busy in the meantime — too busy to write down every single thing he would have done differently if he were the teacher. You'll get your best teacher ratings when the supervisor feels like he's part of the class, rather than an unwelcome outsider.

Before you start panicking about these observations, remember that almost all teachers get tenure. In fact, the only ones who don't are so awful at teaching that if they actually got tenure and ended up teaching their whole lives, they'd be miserable anyway. It's rare, if not unheard of, for a teacher to be denied tenure because of an unfair evaluation or a rating that was conducted on a bad day. Finding teachers out there is hard enough; your school district will probably do everything in its power to keep you on board and in the classroom. In fact, one principal I spoke to told me that if he's formally evaluating a teacher and it's not going well, he automatically downgrades it to an informal observation (which is for informational, not rating purposes), works with the teacher on ways to improve, and reschedules the formal observation after the teacher has had a chance to make those improvements. "I'm here to help, not to try to ruin people's careers," he said.

TIP

This observation is rated R for adult content

For some reason or another, my best teaching ideas occur to me when I'm in the shower; in fact, by now I should know to leave a pad of paper sitting on the toilet tank so that I can jot notes to myself while drying off, rather than running through the house soaking wet while trying to find a pen. During one particularly long shower, I was trying to figure out how to teach basic statistics to my algebra students without it being boring. Then inspiration struck: I would have the kids watch TV at home for three hours during a one-week period, and they'd keep track of how often they saw various things. Feeling like a modern-day Archimedes, who once ran nude from his local bathhouse through the streets shouting, "Eureka!" because he'd solved a complex problem posed by the king, I leapt from the shower once again in search of a writing implement.

For the next few hours, I mulled over the basic logistics of the project. The students would watch both television shows and the commercials they contained three times for an hour at a time. During that hour, they were to keep track of how many times they saw or heard references to sexual content, violence, murder, soda commercials, and car commercials, among other things. Based on this data, we'd be able to predict things like how often, during one lifetime, they were likely to see a murder on television, based on the kinds of shows they personally watched.

I was so excited about my idea that I told my principal about it and invited him to come in and observe the kickoff lesson for the project. During that class, I would explain the project, answer any questions, and then pass out the tally sheets we'd be using. Because I wanted all our results to be similar, I planned to do a practice run with them, so the night before, I taped the television show *Mad About You,* starring Paul Reiser and Helen Hunt (a good, wholesome family comedy about a man, his wife, and their zany adventures). My plan was to watch the show and all its commercials in class so that students could practice spotting the various elements.

As soon as class began, I knew that I had hooked them — a class project that required watching television seemed too good to be true. The principal had actually found time to observe the class, and he was going to do a formal observation. I was pumped; the class was excited about watching TV in class and was interested in the nature of the project, and the principal was impressed. After all the preliminary explanation was done, I strode confidently to the VCR and pressed the Play button.

Immediately, I knew I should have previewed the episode. The usually family-friendly show was not so friendly this time — it was all about the main characters having exceptionally good sex and discussing it in detail for the entire show. They were saying things like, "He was an animal; at one point the bed was banging against the end table so hard, the alarm clock broke." At that moment, a student raised her hand and asked, "What happens if we run out of room in the 'sexual content' box?" I thought I was going to be fired for not previewing the tape, but that's when the principal started laughing uproariously. "Mr. Kelley," he said, "I didn't know this was going to be one of *those* kinds of classes." I had learned a valuable lesson, thankfully not at the expense of my future employment — always preview anything you're going to show to your class.

If you're like me, those gentle reassurances aren't enough. I'm still going to be nervous about observations because I want to do well, even if my job isn't always on the line. With that in mind, I've compiled some tips from teachers and administrators alike to help you not only survive those observations but also to come out smelling like a rose (unless you're a guy and you'd rather smell like something more manly, like maybe concrete):

- ✔ **Make sure your lesson includes any elements required by your school district.** You're usually required to post an objective and a warm-up activity on the board; however, your system may require additional elements as well. For example, some systems require that each lesson end with a summary and review portion, during which you rehash the major points you covered during the class. Ask your supervisor or principal exactly which elements are mandated well before your observation takes place so you have time to get used to them and work them into your lessons.

- ✔ **Showcase your best material.** Most supervisors will tell you that you shouldn't prepare anything special on a day you know you'll be observed. This is roughly equivalent to the person you're dating telling you not to get them anything for their birthday; in other words, they're lying, and they expect you to understand that they're lying. Beware if your supervisor tells you ahead of time that she wants to see quality instruction during your observation, because that's even worse. It actually means that you should pull out all the stops and perform a full-fledged dog-and-pony show, or she'll be disappointed.

Administrators understand that having to produce a whiz-bang lesson plan each day that entertains, informs, involves, and inspires is a nearly impossible task. However, that doesn't mean that some don't want you to do just that every time they come into your classroom. Others are more realistic. "Anybody can put on a spectacular show once or twice; I'm looking for good, solid teaching on a daily basis, not a Broadway play when I walk in the room," one principal told me. In either case, they want you to impress them as a classroom leader, and it's hard to do that if your lesson plan consists of having the students fill out a crossword puzzle, so spend extra time preparing quality lesson plans for that day.

The easiest way to tell how sensational a lesson plan your administrator expects is to pay special attention to how long ahead of time he tells you he's coming in to see you. If he stops you in the hallway in the beginning of the day and says, "Mind if I stick my head in around noon?", then all he wants to see is that your kids listen to you, that you prepared appropriate lesson plans, and that your lesson fills up the whole period, not leaving time for off-task behavior. If, on the other hand, your supervisor tells you, "I'm going to come observe you in three weeks, so you'd better not schedule a quiz or test for that day, because I want to see a lesson," you have your work cut out for you. He wants to see innovative teaching with hands-on student participation (in other words, a lesson that will live on in his mind until his dying day).

✔ **Don't make any dramatic changes to your class on observation day.** If your school district requires you to post warm-up activities on the board before every lesson, fulfilling this requirement for the first time when you're being observed isn't a good idea. In other words, if you've been lazy all along, your supervisor will figure it out, because your kids will always slip up and give away your secret. ("What's that on the chalk-board? We've never had to do a warm-up in here before!") Whether they're young kids and don't know why the observer is in the room, or older kids who know they can really make things hard for you if they mis-behave in front of the visitor, trying to fool your supervisor into thinking you follow rules you really don't when he's not around is a bad idea.

Earlier in this chapter, I mention that ignoring the superfluous advice of your district-level supervisor is usually safe, as long as he isn't in the room. That's only true if the advice he gave you was, indeed, anecdotal. If, however, his advice is serious, like, "Dress like a professional," or it addresses a major aspect of the way you run class, like, "Walk around the room more, instead of standing in one place the whole time," you can't just change those things on the fly without students noticing. Whether it's intentional or not, they'll always give your secret away ("Wow, you really dressed up today, Mr. Kelley. Are you going to a funeral or something after school?") and your supervisor will be none too pleased.

✔ **Demonstrate your relationship with students.** If you've truly spent the time and established a strong relationship with your kids, you should highlight it. Before class, don't stand stiffly and nervously behind your desk, pawing through your lesson plans one more time with sweaty hands. Instead, walk around the room and chat with your kids: "Hey there, Melissa, how's play practice coming along? Were you able to learn those lines? I told you you'd be able to do it!" Early in the school year, you may not yet have this sort of relationship, because the students are still seeing the meaner, stricter version of you that enforces the rules to the letter, but don't worry. By the end of the school year, as you're able to ease up a bit, this sort of interaction will become natural.

✔ **Don't worry about a little bit of noise in the room.** No one expects your room to be silent, especially before class begins. Even after years of observations, you'll still be a little nervous when an administrator walks through the door, especially if her visit is unannounced. This nervous-ness causes most teachers to be hypersensitive to noise or off-task behavior, but don't let it happen to you. Kids talk to each other a lot, especially when they feel comfortable in a classroom, and conversation is not a bad thing. Your supervisor probably won't care if your students chat, especially before class starts; what she wants to see is that they quiet down and focus when you ask them to.

✔ **Try to involve all your kids in the lesson.** Don't fall into the trap of always calling on the same kids when you ask a question. There are lots of kids in the room, and they all deserve an equal chance to participate, even the ones who are shy and would really rather not. Your supervisor is going to watch who you communicate with. Mostly boys? Mostly girls? More students on the left side of the room than the right? Spread your questions around and try to speak to every student at least once, if at all possible. By the way, this is a good idea all the time, not just during observations — but on observation days it's critical.

Additionally, keep your eyes always roaming around the room, looking for kids whose minds are wandering. Your supervisor will be doing the same thing, and if he catches a kid off-task whom you miss, you'll hear about it later. Heaven help you if a kid falls asleep in your class and you don't notice or do something about it.

Keep in mind that you're being observed even when administrators aren't in your room. If the principal calls your room on the intercom system to speak with you, be assured that he's also listening to see if your kids are working. In fact, he has lots of ways to check up on you. For example, it's not uncommon for principals to pause outside your door, out of sight, as they make their rounds throughout the day. They're listening to see if you're using time effectively and to see how well you've established control of your classes. Most of all, the principal will keep his ears open to conversation as he walks through the halls and the cafeteria. There are no secrets in a school, and it won't be long before he finds out what the kids and other teachers think of you.

Chapter 14

Getting to Know Your Co-Workers

- -

In This Chapter

▶ Introducing types of faculty members you'll meet and have to work with

▶ Earning the respect of your colleagues

▶ Developing good relationships with the staff at your school

▶ Dealing with the trials and tribulations of floating between classrooms

- -

*W*hen you first get started as a rookie teacher, you have a lot of stuff on your mind. You have to learn tons of school rules and policies, figure out how you're going to run your classroom, absorb a crazy amount of knowledge every single night to prepare for the next day's lessons, construct lesson plans to mold that knowledge into bite-sized and easily digestible chunks, grade until your eyeballs dry up and fall out, and every evening run past your landlord's Doberman pinscher, whose nose is a groin-seeking missile fired at a very high speed. (Perhaps that last one only applies to me, but you get the idea.) The last thing that ever crosses your mind is the thought of dealing with a co-worker.

Although your career and personal foray into the wilds of professional teaching is just beginning, most of the people you'll work with have been at it for a while. Don't fall into the trap most rookies stumble upon: ignoring the other adults in the building and focusing all your energy on your kids. In this chapter, I give some advice about interacting and dealing with the handful of adults you'll see every day, because bonding with them is much trickier than bonding with your students.

A Field Guide to Co-Workers

Most of the teachers you'll work with are a lot like you, only older, wiser, and a little more stable in the income department. All too often, rookies try to define themselves based on how *different* they are from their colleagues, such as, "I'm much nicer to my students than she is," or, "He isn't very patient when kids ask questions." Don't do this — you need the support and acceptance of your fellow employees, or your work life is going to be miserable.

You need adult interaction on a daily basis with people who accept you and don't feel that you're judging them. (Especially because you're new, veteran teachers don't take kindly to criticism from rookies.)

With that said, I want to warn you about a few species of teachers whom you may not be familiar with. As a rookie, I didn't even know that some of these species existed, so I had no idea how to deal with them. Although most teachers fall into the wider, less specific category of "underappreciated hard workers," the following teachers are found at every school, and they definitely deserve special mention.

The Coach

There is a secret and exclusive club in every school building — the fraternity of coaches. Although I use the term *fraternity,* it isn't exclusive to male teachers, although they usually account for the majority of the membership. They don't have a secret handshake or wear a pinkie ring that allows them to decode top-secret messages related to athletics ("Two dodge balls have been stolen! Stay tuned for developments!"), but they do have their own parties and special meetings, which are just like regular teacher parties and meetings, only with more drinking. They rarely refer to each other by name, preferring the simpler and affectionate title "Coach," as in, "Good morning, Coach," "Heard you guys had a rough game last night, Coach," or "I'm sorry to hear about the mounting tensions in the Middle East, Coach." If forced to call another club member by name, they'll never use the first name — only the last — and will always precede that last name by "Coach."

In case you haven't figured it out, coaching is a big deal to these people; in fact, some love coaching much more than they love teaching. This causes automatic tension with the other faculty members of the school, who automatically assume two things:

✔ Coaches care more about athletics than academics.

✔ Coaches get more breaks than "regular" teachers if they're good at coaching.

Whether or not those assumptions are true, they cause an unspoken rift between teachers who are athletically inclined and those who are not. It's the ages-old jocks-versus-nerds struggle, made weird by the fact that some teachers can be both at the same time. Don't automatically assume that a coach is not also a smart and dedicated teacher, but don't expect to become a member of his club either, unless you're willing to don the whistle and stopwatch.

To unionize or not to unionize

Not long after you begin work as a new teacher, you'll be approached by teachers' union representatives, and pressured to join up. With freebies like pens, pencils, apple-shaped notepads, apple-shaped calendars, apple-shaped insulin dispensers, and apple-shaped apples, they will do their best to get you to join their ranks, and you need to decide ahead of time what you want to do.

Joining the teachers' union has some definite advantages, and the best by far is the legal protection unions provide to their members. If you're ever sued by a student or parent, the union will provide good representation for you for free; this is the reason that most people join the union, at lest initially. A lawsuit can destroy your credibility, reputation, career, and financial well-being all at once, and in comparison, annual dues seem a small price to pay for such security.

Most unions are also tied to a credit union, which can provide loans with good interest rates; this is good news if you need to buy a reliable car (not the rusty boat you drove around in college) or decide to take the plunge and become a homeowner. You can even get low-cost life insurance, and if you flash your membership card at the drive-thru window at Arby's, they'll give you extra curly fries.

There are disadvantages to membership as well. Unions are very political beasts, and the vast majority of your money goes into lobbying Congress and other intangible things. We're not talking about $35 in annual dues, either. Most unions charge between $400 and $500 every year for membership, and it's rare that you'll see anything concrete that results from the money you've invested. It can feel like throwing your money into a big, dark hole every year — but I was always happy to toss my money in, knowing that I had legal protection if I needed it.

Here's what they don't tell you: The union may support you legally even if you're not a member, because any legal issues that affect you as a teacher will probably affect their members as well, so they want to be involved whenever legal precedent is set. I became a bit disenfranchised with my union when I saw them support teachers who weren't members, because I kept thinking, "These teachers involved in legal wrangling are much older and wealthier than I am, so why are they getting legal help for free, while I'm paying dues even though I can barely afford my rent?"

Before you make your decision one way or the other, remember that unions are often responsible for contract negotiations, so if they negotiate raises or benefits, it's due in large part to the work of the people you're supporting with your dues. Most teachers who aren't union members still get the pay raises anyway (some have to pay a fee for the right to earn the new salary), but you may get labeled as a freeloader if you take the pay raise without investing in the union. However, you should know that excluding you from a union-negotiated contract, even if you're not a member of the union, is illegal.

The easiest thing to do is to simply join the union when you start teaching. I actually withdrew after a few years, frustrated that I could see no tangible benefit other than a deluge of apple-themed junk. However, the year I withdrew, there was a huge contract negotiation, and I felt really guilty, because the union was instrumental in making sure teachers' medical benefits were not eliminated. There's really no harm in joining the union — you'd just spend dues money on junk food anyway, so you may as well join.

The Grouch

Teaching requires a lot of personal investment, and if you don't feel as though you're getting a good return on that investment, it takes quite a toll on you. Among the veteran teachers at your school, you're bound to find the Grouch, a teacher who has been at his job for a long time and has become bitter, if not angry and confrontational. The Grouch is not evil and doesn't hate the kids in his classes, contrary to popular belief; he just feels underappreciated, and over time, that unsatisfied desire to be valued festers, turning into callousness and disrespect for those in authority.

People who have known the Grouch for a long time, or who have taken the time to get to know him personally outside of the school building, tell you that he cares on the inside, and that the rough exterior is just a mask for his true feelings. The educational system has mistreated him, his principals give him all the worst classes, and no matter what he does, he's always criticized. Waiting for retirement, he's happy to do the bare minimum in his classes to get by, and he'll spend the majority of his time sitting in the teacher's lounge complaining about whatever happens to be on his mind at the time.

When I was a rookie, I knew a few Grouches, and despite their rude exterior, I thought I saw some good in them. After all, they'd been teaching for quite some time and probably had some wisdom to offer, though it was probably colored by years of resentment and hostility. I made it my goal to try to get through to them, to use my fresh, rookie eyesight to help them see through the cataracts forming over their professional outlook.

My efforts were a complete waste of time. The Grouch isn't interested in changing his point of view. In his mind, he's a misunderstood genius surrounded by fools, and there's no way you'll be able to convince him to change his ways. He's a sinking ship, burned out on work and unhappy with his life, and if you're not careful, he'll take you down with him.

If you choose to associate with a Grouch, he's going to rub off on you; furthermore, if you make the mistake of sharing your personal frustrations with a Grouch, you can count on that information becoming public as soon as you turn your back. "The rookie teacher agrees with me," he'll boast. "This administration is nothing but a screw-up."

It won't take you more than a few days to figure out who the Grouches are at your school, and when you do, avoid them. If they talk to you, be polite but noncommittal, and exit the conversation at your earliest convenience. Don't agree or disagree with anything said, or you're going to get caught up in a long, drawn-out conversation that ends in nothing but frustration.

The Golden Boy

Some days you're going to feel like the entire world is against you. No matter how hard you plan and how good you are at classroom management, there are days when you make all kinds of mistakes while you're teaching, and nothing you do seems to go right. Your kids are antsy, you're distracted, and it feels as though the entire day has been a complete waste of everyone's time. In fact, you almost feel as though the kids may have learned more if you'd just stayed home and let them watch movies with a substitute all day. Right at your lowest moment, when you're ready to give up on teaching and throw yourself through the window, you overhear a kid whisper, "I wish this class was more like Mr. Halstead's class. He's a much better teacher."

Whether or not the kid intended you to hear, it's not breaking news. Every time you hear anybody talk about Mr. Halstead's class, all they do is rave about it. "Mr. Halstead's funny," "I laugh every day in Mr. Halstead's class," "Mr. Halstead is the smartest teacher I've ever had," and, "I wish Mr. Halstead was my dad" is all you hear all day long from kids all over the building. In fact, you're beginning to feel like Mr. Halstead could do anything and the kids would love him for it. ("Today, Mr. Halstead fell down, and I swear, I've never learned so much about gravity.")

Your kids aren't going to love you (in fact, they really shouldn't) while you're still establishing your authority in the room. You're a new teacher no one really knows, whereas Halstead probably has a reputation that extends a decade or more. The kids know who's in charge when they walk into that room, so there's no need for him to be as mean at the beginning of the school year. He has the luxury of immediately being nice. Give it time, and eventually you can earn that same reputation and frustrate future rookie teachers.

If you're not willing to wait years and years to try to reach your kids in a personal way, there is one thing you can do: Occasionally pull back the curtain from your professional life and tell some stories about things that happen to you when you're not teaching. Did you have a great weekend? Take up the first five minutes of class telling your kids how great your weekend was; let them see that you're a real person. Of course, you always take a risk when you reveal personal things to anyone, but there's nothing you can do to build your relationship faster.

Paying Your Dues

Did you see that horrible video they played on one of those investigative television shows a few years back, documenting a Marine Corps ceremony called the pinning of the blood wings? It showed a line of new recruits, bare-chested, standing against a wall. Each had reached a milestone in his training, and was about to receive his "wings" — a pin commemorating the event. What made the ceremony scandalous was how the pin was awarded to the recruit. It wasn't presented in a velvet jewelry box or pinned to his uniform by a high-ranking officer amid pomp and circumstance. Instead, it was hammered, point first, into the recruit's chest by the fists of other soldiers. This brutal act initiated the poundee into the Corps, promoting him from "new guy" to "just one of the guys."

There is no parallel practice for public-school teachers. You won't suddenly be surrounded by colleagues and have a stick of chalk rammed up your nose or be forced to sniff dry-erase markers until you pass out, but there were times as a rookie when I wished that there were some sort of hazing ritual. Why? Although unpleasant, hazing is fast and immediately earns you a place among your peers. Instead, as a new teacher, you usually need years and years to earn the respect of your co-workers, in a painful (though less bloody) process called "paying your dues."

During your first year or so of teaching, most of the other faculty members at your school aren't going to go out of their way to be nice to you. It's not that they'll be mean or try to take a swing at you if they see you in the hallway, but they aren't as excited to get to know you as you probably are to meet and establish relationships with them.

This isn't true of *all* teachers, of course. Among the faculty in your grade level or department, you'll find one or two people who will bend over backwards to help you, no matter how much help you need and how often you ask them for it. The rest of the faculty will eventually soften to you, but only after they feel you've earned their respect — and that takes time. They want to know that you didn't have anything handed to you on a silver platter, but instead had to claw your way up from the bottom of the ranks, just like each and every one of them had to. You may feel like the odds are stacked against you, like I discuss in Chapter 1, but the majority of your colleagues need to see you handle adversity before they deem you worthy of acceptance.

Don't get discouraged — all rookies are initiated like this, and like it or not, you're probably going to wind up doing the same thing to rookies who come after you. To help you through this time of trial, I've compiled some tips that will expedite the process and guarantee that your dues will be paid in full, just as quickly as possible:

> ✔ **Keep your opinions to yourself.** If you're in the faculty lounge and a debate breaks out about teaching styles, don't pipe in with your own two cents, no matter how strongly you feel about the issue. Even if the

other faculty members politely listen to you, I guarantee that the only thing running through their minds is, "How dare you even have an opinion? I've been teaching longer than you've been alive! I have bookmarks older than you!" Until you've been at the school for a while and have a proven, successful, and undeniable track record, no one is interested in your opinions about teaching.

✓ **Don't expect other faculty members to go out of their way to get to know you.** One rookie teacher at my school made every mistake in the book when it came to paying his dues. I remember one day, he stormed into my room during his planning period and said, "No one in this school talks to me! I'm new here, and only one or two people have come by my room and welcomed me and introduced themselves! What kind of place is this?"

I tried to explain that he was really lucky to even have that many people stop by his classroom. I said, "You have to understand that there are almost 20 new faculty members here this year, and there were just as many last year. So many new people quit each year that most faculty members aren't going to invest the time to get to know rookies. If you want to make friends, you're going to have to take the initiative. Walk around the building and introduce yourself to people. Stick your head in their classrooms after school and make a little small talk. You have to go to them, because they won't come to you."

✓ **Don't be pushy and try to teach the good kids or the smart kids.** Even though you're fresh out of college classes or a career that makes you extremely knowledgeable, that doesn't mean you deserve the best and the brightest kids in the school. Even if, and this is unlikely, you're the smartest person in your department, that doesn't automatically earn you the better classes. In most schools, seniority means more than anything when it comes time to hammer out teachers' schedules, so you're probably not going to teach what you want for some time.

Everybody starts with the "less than ideal" classes, and if you lobby for better classes, you'll be labeled as a spoiled brat by your colleagues. No one gets the best schedule handed to him for the first few years he teaches; trust me, you wouldn't want those classes as a rookie, anyway. Think about it — if you start with great classes, there's nowhere to go but down for the rest of your career. On the other hand, when you start at the bottom, every small step up is an improvement.

✓ **Remember that you're probably not going to win any teaching awards as a rookie.** No matter how successful you are, don't expect to receive any awards for a couple of years, even if you're the best teacher for miles around. Most teaching awards honor people based on skill and endurance, even if that's not an explicit condition of the award. In other words, someone who's been teaching for 25 years is much more likely to get a teaching award than someone who's only been at it for 2, because awards committees tend to respect those who've run a marathon in their professional career, rather than those who are merely good sprinters, no matter how exceptional a job you've done in your short time in the classroom.

I taught for seven years, and beginning my second year, I was a finalist for "Teacher of the Year" honors at my school for six consecutive times. Each year, almost every other finalist was different, but no matter who else I was up against, I always lost, because it always went to the person who'd been teaching the longest. I was the Susan Lucci of teacher awards, always nominated but never a winner. Though there are sometimes exceptions to this rule, I wish someone had told me not to get my hopes up, and warned me that veterans are always the heavy favorites when it comes to professional recognition.

✔ **Participate in a wide variety of after-school activities.** Nothing is more valuable than your free time; if veteran teachers and administrators see you around the school when regular working hours are over, they'll know that you're a team player. In their minds, people who work past the hours specified by their contract are dedicated and care about the school. However, if you're going to invest free time back into your school, make sure you get some benefit out of it — be visible. Although working late into the evening holed up in your room and bent over your desk may ease the burden of your lesson planning, no one can appreciate how late you're staying if they don't see you do it.

Pay attention to the announcements at faculty meetings. Your colleagues are constantly asking for volunteers and assistants in extracurricular clubs or school events; find one that interests you, and help out, even if you're bogged down by work. Most rookies complain that they can't find the time to help out or sponsor activities at school, because they spend so much time at home preparing for the next day. Even though you're busy, you need to find time anyway; the more excuses you make to avoid helping out now, the less likely you'll be to help out even when you have lots of free time. You're not going to get to know your fellow co-workers unless you make an effort, and helping with activities is the best way.

Paying your dues is an important part of acclimating to your school. You're showing other people that you're not above rolling up your sleeves and helping out, and that you're not so full of yourself that you think you're always right. Before the majority of your colleagues will form personal relationships with you, they want to see that you're a humble person, willing to do the grunt work when necessary, and willing to help out a fellow teacher in need.

The prodigal son returns

When it came time to apply for jobs, I cast a huge net. Like most teacher candidates, I was scared to death that I wouldn't be able to find gainful employment, so I was convinced that if I had to be unemployed, it wouldn't be for lack of trying. I applied for a teaching job in all 24 school districts in the state of Maryland, attended job fairs, sent out résumés, drove all over the state for job interviews, and did everything short of holding a parade in my own honor to try to get my name out there to potential employers.

When all the dust settled, I ended up with a job in the same school district I'd grown up in. In fact, I taught in a school not 10 miles from the hospital in which I was born and all the schools I attended growing up. To be perfectly honest, it was the last place in the world I wanted to teach. In fact, when I was offered the job, I hemmed and hawed until the very last minute, when they told me it was my last chance to decide. I had wanted to get out of my town, move somewhere new, and start the adventure of my adult life with a blank slate; suddenly, I was going to be teaching alongside all the people who'd seen me grow up, who'd known me when I was at my nerdiest and gangliest. (If you've ever known anyone who wasn't goofy and stretched-out looking when he was 12, I'd like to meet him.)

There aren't many high schools in my district. In fact, when I was interviewing, there were only two: the high school I attended and its fierce rival. In my third and final interview, the principals from both of the high schools and the math supervisor grilled me for close to an hour, and then I was off to wait to hear what resulted. My former high school had a chance to hire me and decided not to, because (and this is true, I swear) I did not wear a sport coat to my interview.

Fate had spoken, and I ended up teaching at the school up the road. It was the best thing that could have happened. I rarely saw the teachers I'd had in high school, except at district-wide teacher in-service meetings, and those teachers never really knew how to talk to or react to me. Although they tried, they had a hard time seeing me as an adult; I had only been out of high school for four years, and suddenly I was back, only this time wearing ugly ties. They cringed when I called them by their first names, and no matter how often I tried to initiate professional dialog, it was always like talking to friends of my parents whom I barely knew. Conversations were short, polite, and uncomfortable.

Things only got worse when, years down the road, I happened to disagree with some of their educational philosophies. Out of nowhere, and without provocation, my favorite high-school math teacher began screaming at me at the top of her lungs. She accused me of all sorts of things in a voice that quivered with rage and righteous indignation, including oversimplifying my curriculum and inflating my grades, and she ranted about how my students would fail college because of me and the way I taught things in my class. In her mind, I had no right to an opinion and teaching style of my own; she was unable to see me as a professional or a colleague, and her outburst, held right in the middle of the meeting for all to see and hear, was hurtful and just plain nasty.

If you can help it, don't teach in any of the schools you attended as a student. You don't have to move to the other side of the world to teach — I was very happy a mere 20-minute drive down the road. Though some of your teachers will welcome your return, some will refuse to acknowledge that you ever grew up, and criticism from the teachers you used to respect and look up to really stings, take it from me.

Understanding Staff Members

There's no doubt about it: Teachers are some of the most underappreciated people in the world. We instruct the leaders of tomorrow, teaching them the information and providing the skills that they'll one day use to succeed, and very rarely are we remembered, let alone given any credit, when those successes begin to blossom. However, before you start feeling too sorry for yourself and have to reach for one of those self-esteem-building self-help books like *What Color Parachute Is My Cheese Wearing?* or *100 Mistakes Women Make While Mistaking Their True Mistakes for Mistaken Behavior,* you should know that you're not part of the most underappreciated group of people in the educational system.

Beneath you in the food chain of neglect are all the people at your school who aren't teachers. Not only are they dismissed by parents and students, they're all too often ignored by teachers. Although they may not ever check homework or have to grade papers, they form the backbone of the school, and you'd be lost without them. Sure, your job as a teacher is important, but without the support staff at your school, you wouldn't be able to get your job done.

As you go about meeting other faculty members and forming relationships, make it a point to meet staff members as well; learn their names, and let them know they're doing a good job. They probably only get about half as much positive feedback as you do from students and parents, and half of next to nothing sure ain't much.

In the following list, I summarize the key members of your staff and give you a few tips to get to know them better:

- **Secretaries and administrative assistants:** Imagine having to look at the worst kids in the school all day long, and forcing them to stay seated and quiet while waiting for an administrator. Now, add to that a principal who needs something done urgently about every 20 minutes, telephones that don't stop ringing until late into the night, a pile of typing and word processing that always needs done, the responsibility of manning the intercom system, and the unspoken expectation that you must always be chipper and friendly to anyone who comes into the office.

    It's a recipe for madness, but somehow secretaries manage, and all they ask is that you make eye contact with them and talk to them as you pass through the office. Don't avert your eyes or pretend you're deep in thought as you walk by so that you don't have to speak with them, because they're usually the nicest, friendliest, and most patient people at your school. Keep in mind that, on top of everything else, they're the central points through which all the gossip passes. If you're doing something wrong, they're the first to know, so they make better allies than enemies, and if they like you, they'll go out of their way to help you out whenever they can.

- **Custodial staff:** Whenever a custodian comes into your room for the first time, make it a priority to introduce yourself. Find out her name, and always call her by name when you see her in the hallway or in the cafeteria. Custodians are by far the most ignored and overlooked people in a school, usually because they're quiet, and because too many teachers view them as the "hired help," rather than colleagues.

  Custodians are employed to _sanitize_ the school, not to clean up after you and your students, so do your part to clean up before they get to your room. Don't let your students get into the habit of leaving scraps of paper or trash on the floor, thinking "they pay people to clean up, so I'm not going to do it." Make it your students' responsibility to keep their area clean, so that custodians can take time to actually make the room really clean without having to first make it neat. Custodians have a hard enough job already — would you want to be the one who has to grab the sawdust bag every time a student throws up? No thanks.

- **Office and instructional aides:** If you're lucky enough to have an aide assigned to your grade or department, consider yourself extremely lucky. However, don't look at these hardworking folks as an opportunity to slack off. For example, asking them to do your copying is fine — they have access to the machines for longer periods of time during the day, and they can complete your jobs when those machines aren't in high demand. On the other hand, don't ask them to do things like typing, which you can easily do yourself but just don't want to. If you don't know how to work a word processor in this day and age, then take a class or have someone show you how.

The best advice to remember when working with a staff member is that you're not the only person in the school building who has needs. Sometimes, in the hustle and bustle of the day, with deadlines pending and student confrontations weighing heavily on your mind, you'll tend to lose perspective and get pushy or impatient. Staff members have priorities and deadlines of their own, and you can't always be at the top of the list. No teacher is so important that a staff member should drop what they're doing to attend to his needs immediately. Above all, let staff members know how much you need them, how glad you are to work with them, and how great a job they do. Not only will it give them the positive feedback they so rarely receive, but when they like you, they're more likely to bump your needs up on their priority lists.

Facing the Facts If You're Floating

There's something about having to carry all your worldly possessions with you as you pass between classes that is profoundly depressing. In fact, when you're forced to float, you don't feel like a real teacher at all, but rather a placeholder, someone who is needed because of class sizes, but not worth actual space of his or her own. When I was a rookie, I was told that I'd get a classroom "just as soon as some old rooms were renovated." Supposedly, it was only going to take three months, and I'd be into a classroom and settled before Christmas break. It wasn't until late April that I finally was able to abandon my squeaky-wheeled cart (which by then housed a small fish tank and carried a sign that read "Home Is Where the Cart Is") for more permanent digs, but by then I had already seen the dark side of my colleagues.

People don't like it when you squeak your way into their rooms, whether it's during their planning period or lunch (and God help you if you're actually displacing a class they're teaching, forcing *them* to float for a period as well). You'd think people would go out of their way to be nice to you, the second class citizen, unable to own anything larger than a three-hole punch, but all too often they aren't. In fact, many rookies discover that the rooms they float into are hostile environments. If you have to float, you have a whole set of rules unique to you when it comes to dealing with colleagues. Here are a few obstacles you'll face and some tips on how to deal with the ornery veterans who (purposefully or not) toss them in your way:

- **Bring all the office supplies you'll need with you.** Never assume that the office supplies in your rooms will be available to you. They may be missing or difficult to find. One of my host teachers (I call them *host* teachers because they viewed me as a parasite) used to keep his chalk precariously balanced on the top of his chalkboard rather than leave it in the chalk tray, like most normal people. "I don't like my chalk getting all dusty and dirty," he responded when I asked him about it months into the school year, when I'd finally found his chalk treasure trove.

  What he meant to say is, "Don't ever touch anything that belongs to me or I'll gut you like a fish," which brings me to my second reason: Most host teachers don't like you touching their stuff, even things as mundane as paper clips and notebook paper. As a rookie, I was occasionally yelled at by veterans if I used their stapler and didn't return it to the *exact* spot on the desk where I'd found it. Don't even *think* about looking in another teacher's desk for any reason at all, even if you're just looking for staples to refill their stapler for them. You're just asking to be branded as a thief.

  What sorts of supplies should all floating teachers carry with them? Here's a brief checklist:

  - Pencils, pens, and rubber erasers

  - A stapler with extra staples

  - A three-hole punch

  - Correction fluid, like Liquid Paper or Wite-Out

  - A ream of blank white paper for creating quizzes and tests

  - Paper clips

- Rubber bands

- Scissors

- Chalk (white and multicolored)

- Chalkboard erasers (I've had spiteful teachers hide theirs from me!)

- Aspirin (I prefer Excedrin, but if the year's going badly, there's always cyanide)

Also bring all the forms you'll need, including hall passes and referral forms. When host teachers see that you come prepared, they're less likely to lock the place down when they leave for fear of you stealing their wallets or doing something even worse, like leaving a box of thumbtacks open. By the way, it's not a bad idea to plaster your name on your stuff so it doesn't disappear.

✔ **Beware of limited board space.** I constantly wrote on the board — most math teachers do, and they possess chalkboards so thick with dust at the end of the school day that it's hard to see where the chalk stops and the board begins. Imagine my chagrin during the last class period of my rookie year, when the host teacher warned me, "Never erase anything that I write on the board. I'll try to leave you enough space, but I like keeping my notes on the board." *Remember:* This is the last period of the day, so he's already finished teaching by the time I walk into the room!

I didn't want to rock the proverbial boat, especially because he usually only had one or two sentences on the board, usually his objectives for the next day. As the weeks went on, however, the space left for me became progressively smaller and smaller until (and this is no exaggeration) it was a small rectangle, 2 feet long by 1 foot tall. That was the last straw — a small rectangle floating like driftwood right in the middle of a note-cluttered sea.

A lot of floaters I've talked to had the same experience with the amazing, incredible, shrinking-board-space phenomenon. It's the host teacher's way of passive-aggressively getting back at you for taking over his room during his planning period. ("They can force me out of my room, but they can't force me to make it easy on the chump who's going to be in there.") Basically, you have two options for dealing with it:

- Write your notes on overhead projector transparencies, before or during class, and project them on a pull-down screen. Of course, this means that the host teacher has to have both the screen and the projector in his room already — there's no way you're going to be able to wheel both your cart and a projector cart in the hall-ways between classes.

- Ignore the bum and erase his boards anyway, if you're not afraid of a little confrontation.

I (and just about all the rookies I talked to) tended to follow the second course of action. Just erase the boards if the host is being unreasonable and go to the principal (or administrator who's been most sympathetic with you) at your earliest convenience and explain yourself. No one's going to take the other teacher's side if he's being unreasonable, and it felt good to take a stand for myself when it happened to me. Your life is tough enough as a floater without having restrictions placed on you at every port of call.

✔ **Prepare yourself for some unannounced observations.** There were times when I floated that the host teacher never left the room; instead, she just sat to one side and graded papers, read a newspaper, or merely milled about in her cabinets. This makes things very uncomfortable for you, because it feels like the host teacher is watching you and judging you based on every little thing your kids say and do. (By the way, that's exactly what she's doing — your worst fears are true!) This is unacceptable. The host teacher should scuttle off to the faculty lounge if you're using her room, not sit in there and confuse the kids about who's in charge.

If your host teacher won't get lost when you're in her room, go to your principal (or, once again, the administrator who has been most supportive of you) after it's happened a few times. There's no way you can ask her to leave without ruffling her feathers, and it's not your job. Asking for the classroom to yourself if you can't have a classroom of your own isn't an unreasonable request, so don't be shy.

Unless you have a kind and supportive host teacher (they do exist — the best host teachers once had to float themselves, so they understand your plight), you almost have to treat the host teacher like a student: Hope for the best, prepare for the worst, and don't get bossed around. If you're teaching in that room, you have just as much right to it as, if not more than, the host during that time period. Act like it's your room, not borrowed property, because as far as that class is concerned, it *is* your room — what happens inside it the rest of the day is irrelevant.

Chapter 15

Getting to Know Parents

• •

In This Chapter

▶ Previewing parental personality types

▶ Handling parent phone calls like a pro

▶ Managing parent conferences

• •

*W*hen a student screws up in school, teachers and parents have a very hard time communicating with one another. It's not because they don't want to be cordial or to work together for the benefit of the mutual child, it's just that so many emotions and defense mechanisms are at work that establishing a solid relationship is tricky. After all, if the student in question is acting up in your class, then surely, someone is to blame. Is it the parent, who didn't do a good job raising the child, or is it the teacher, who has no control over his class? When I say it like that, the answer is obvious: Neither is to blame, at least not to the degree I suggested, but that doesn't stop each party involved from being suspicious of the other.

When I was a rookie, a veteran teacher once told me, "Be careful how you deal with parents. If you're criticizing their kid, they think you're automatically criticizing them, because that kid represents their best effort at parenting. If he's misbehaving in your class, parents assume you're suggesting that their best effort isn't good enough, and they take offense at that, especially from a rookie." He raises a good point: How could I, as a 21-year-old teacher, offer parenting advice when I hadn't even managed to keep a goldfish alive for more than 48 hours?

In this chapter, I explain what parents want, how to deal with those expectations, and how to handle yourself when you talk to them, even during parent conferences that get ugly.

A Field Guide to Parents

Receiving a call at work and finding out that your child is misbehaving is roughly the equivalent of getting a call from your doctor's office and finding out that you've been diagnosed with a strange disease. The first question that comes to mind is, "How serious is it?" followed closely by, "Is there anything I can do about it?" This is really the best-case scenario for the doctor. Clearly, the patient is willing to accept the diagnosis and wants to do whatever he can to get better as soon as possible. As a teacher, you'll relish the calls when parents react the same way. "He's not doing his homework? How often do you assign homework? Is there any way I can find out what homework you've assigned to follow up with him? What do you suggest we do to get through to him?"

Later on in this chapter, I let you know how to handle these initial parent phone calls, during which you address the illness and prescribe a course of medicine to knock out that runny nose before it becomes full-blown pneumonia. For now, I'll tell you about the different ways parents will respond to your diagnosis; parents' reactions help you to understand their personalities, and that's important, because each different personality requires its own special bedside manner.

The Short Fuse

"What do you mean Sarah talked back to you in class? She's never mouthed off to a teacher before! She's always been very respectful to her teachers, so clearly, you must be the problem. What did you do to set her off? She's mentioned to me that you're not a very good teacher, but I always told her to give you the benefit of the doubt. Now, however, I'm beginning to see just how unreasonable you are!" Welcome to the land of Denial: population, one very miffed parent. All you did was call and say one thing, and before you're even able to describe the circumstances surrounding the problem or give any details, suddenly you're the Grand Marshall of the Macy's Frustration Day parade.

The key to handling the Short Fuse parent is something I call "reasonable patience." You have to remember that your call is a bombshell upsetting a parent's day, and if you caught him at a particularly bad moment, the shrapnel is gonna fly, baby. Sometimes, parents just need a few minutes to blow off steam, especially when they're completely caught off guard. As the parent vents, don't speak; don't even offer grunts or guttural verbal cues like "hmm" or "uh huh" — if you do, that will only encourage him to continue and dominate the conversation. Wait until he's done and then continue as though the outburst never happened. Most likely, he overreacted and realizes it but is hesitant to apologize to someone he doesn't yet know or trust, and it won't do you any good to remind him how rude he just was. (Taglines such as, "Are you just about done now?" or, "Are you going to let me speak for even one minute without cutting me off, you obnoxious jerk?" are not the best rejoinders, even though you'll be surprised just how tempted you are to use them.)

Explain exactly what happened in class, citing specifically what the child did that was against the rules, and explain why you have those rules, if they're not traditional. Tell the parent how many times you warned his child, how patient you were, and how none of these things changed the child's behavior. Eventually, most parents begin to react in a reasonable manner and understand that you're not putting them on trial for giving birth to and raising a menace to society. In fact, most Short Fuse parents will begin to turn their wrath toward their child as the conversation progresses. For these folks, anger or frustration alone provides the impetus for change, so you have to allow them their anger if you want them to take you seriously and discipline the child appropriately.

Sometimes, the parent's wrath will not diminish as the call goes on and on. In fact, they just get themselves worked into a frenzy, gnashing their teeth and attempting to call fire down from the sky to consume you in the tiny cubicle that houses the only private phone in your building. If they're not letting up, you don't have to sit and listen to the mad ranting. Give it ten minutes, and if things aren't getting rosier or more congenial, attempt to break into the lunatic rambling with the phrase, "Clearly, this phone call is accomplishing nothing; I suggest that we set up a conference with you, your child, his guidance counselor, the principal, and me, and perhaps cooler heads will prevail." This is a polite way of saying, "I'm tired of being your punching bag, you jerk, so let's hear you scream at me in front of the principal and see how many friends that wins you."

If he still won't stop his incessant hollering, or he won't let you break into the conversation, hang up. He deserves it, and you don't earn any bonus points for staying on the line. However, this will *really* get him angry, so you can count on his next call going straight to the principal. Therefore, as soon as you hang up on the parent, march right down to the principal and tell her what happened — how you were tired of getting yelled at and tried to set up an administrative conference but failed — and your principal will usually be more than happy to handle the situation. Make sure the principal hears your side of the story first, because the parent will try to make you look like Satan in khakis.

The Deathly Silent

At the other extreme of the confrontation continuum, far, far away from the Short Fuse, you find the Deathly Silent parent. Talking to the Deathly Silent parent is really tough, because you do almost all, if not all, of the talking. Here's how a typical phone call would go: "Hello, Mrs. Burke? Hi. It's Mike Kelley from your daughter's school calling. I'm her math teacher, and I have some concerns I'd like to discuss with you." What follows is a silence, as though the parent is sitting in the middle of deep space. Perhaps you hear a cough or a throat-clearing sound, but not much else. After a few beats, the parent will respond with a murmured "uh huh" or "okay," but clearly she is terrified by your call, shocked that her child has misbehaved, or unable to speak because she's being squeezed to death by a boa constrictor (though the last case is the least likely of the three).

Teaching other teachers' kids

When a kid gets in trouble in your class, it takes only moments for the entire school to find out about it, especially if it happens right before the lunch shifts start. The cafeteria is a breeding ground for rumors, gossip, and also mold (if you look on the underside of the tables), and nothing is sacred. I remember one day a gym teacher at my school caught a young girl trying to sneak out to the parking lot to cut classes. He led her into the main office, the principal called her parents, and she got suspended. A typical story, if not a very interesting one.

However, because it happened right before lunch, it was late-breaking news to the hordes of rampaging students. "Flash! We interrupt your ham sandwich with this news update: Jenna Travis has been apprehended in a foiled attempt to escape the premises!" The story got all twisted around in a few short hours, and by the end of the day, the teacher's capture of the runaway was an epic and harrowing tale.

In the updated, and completely false, version, Jenna snuck out of class with a forged hall pass, crept through the hallways with the stealth of a puma, and hit the exit doors at a full run, hoping to make for the safe harbor of the student parking lot. As luck would have it, Mr. Clemens was patrolling the lot and saw her coming. In a desperate attempt to prevent her from escaping mandatory schooling, he tried to tackle her, but she was too fast. As Clemens leapt toward her, she spun around and, with the grace of a ballerina (and the brawling prowess of a street fighter), kicked him square in the groin. They grappled, and fisticuffs ensued. With a lucky strike, she bloodied his nose, and

he became enraged. Cursing, he dragged her into the building, kicking and screaming, a trail of blood and mashed nose bits strewn in their wake, like bread crumbs leading to a horrific gingerbread house.

What *really* happened? Nothing. She got caught and, at his request, followed him to the office with not so much as a word of protest. No matter how boring the story, or how few the grains of truth, when that grain is ground into flour by the rumor mill, all kinds of fallacious delicacies are baked and served fresh all day. You may already know this, but you're probably wondering why I am bringing it up now, in a chapter about parents.

Knowing that rumors persist and stories get blown out of proportion, you should take extra caution if you teach a child whose mom or dad works at your school. Let's say you catch a colleague's child cheating in your class. Try not to make a big deal about it when you report it to the principal — there's no need to draw the attention of students or other teachers to it, because that's just going to make things harder for the teacher, who will probably have to deal with it for weeks after the incident is over. It's bad enough for your child to misbehave, but to do so in your workplace, where everyone knows about it, is much worse. If you can, be sure to talk to that teacher immediately, so that he finds out about the incident from you rather than through the grapevine; call it professional courtesy. I'm not suggesting you ignore the cheating or let the kid slide — just be thoughtful of the difficult situation it places the parent in, and be considerate.

Unlike the Short Fuse (whose response to your call is so infuriating that you'll be possessed to try to punch through the cinder-block wall of your school building), the Deathly Silent parent evokes immediate feelings of sympathy. You, the big mean old teacher, just walked up to the beautiful landscape of her life and tramped down her tulips. Your first instinct will be to get off the phone as soon as you can, both because you feel as though you traumatized the parent and because talking to someone on the phone who is as chatty as a mime is uncomfortable. However painful the conversation may be, you need to be sure to make your case, instead of just blurting out a few words and racing off the phone as soon as you can.

Take your time, and make sure to explain everything to the parent in detail, even though she won't respond or indicate that she's heard you in any way. Don't beat around the bush, apologize, or draw out the conversation longer than necessary (as uncomfortable as you probably feel, she's far more uncomfortable), but don't rush either. When you feel as though you've presented the necessary facts and discussed ways to remedy the situation, give the parent your contact information, so that she can call you back after she's had time to digest the situation, in case she wants to talk to you again after the proverbial cat has returned her tongue.

Just because the conversation was awkward, don't assume that the Deathly Silent parent won't take action after you've hung up the phone. She's probably silent because her brain is working overtime, trying to figure out what she can do, and how to get a handle on the situation. Quiet parents, in my experience, work more diligently with their children to address your concerns. The fact that she didn't argue with you from the first moment of contact is a good sign — she accepts your professional opinion at face value and wants to work with you to make everybody happy again.

The Lost Cause

Imagine this situation: You're on the phone, talking to a parent, trying to convince her that her daughter is unmotivated, lazy, and "attitudinal." No matter what you ask the girl to do, she rolls her eyes, sighs, and mumbles something under her breath about where she thinks you should store your grade book (and she's not talking about jamming it in your desk drawer, either). She's not a threat to the safety of the other students, or even the worst-behaved kid you'll face; she's just lazy, rude, and spoiled. You try to get this across to her mother, who responds: "That's just the way she is — a little moody." You suggest that, perhaps, a loss of privileges or grounding her may be in order, and you're floored by the response. "Well, she's going skiing with her friends this weekend, and she's really been looking forward to that — but maybe when she comes back, I can talk to her or something."

I'm not making that conversation up — it actually happened to a colleague of mine, who was justifiably enraged by the parent's noncommittal and clearly wishy-washy attitude toward discipline and confrontation. "That woman just doesn't seem to understand that the main reason her daughter is such a pain in the neck is that she gets away with anything. How am I supposed to discipline this child when her own parents are too busy to do it? Honestly, how many years has this kid been allowed to live consequence-free, and how am I supposed to get her to behave during the nine months she'll be in my class?"

The Lost Cause parent has absolutely no idea how to control her child. You'd probably associate this parental shortcoming with kids who have big, obvious behavior problems, like bullies or defiant class clowns, but the truth is you'll find kids of Lost Cause parents along every shade of the behavioral spectrum. Of course, you'll have your student hooligans who contradict you every chance they get, and when you call their parents to try to effect a behavior change, you may get the response all teachers get at one point but dread nonetheless: "Now you see what I go through every day. I have no idea how to control him, but at least he's not my problem while he's in school — he's your problem." You'll also teach the "good" kids who have their parents completely fooled and wrapped around their fingers tighter than class rings. "I know that my son has skipped school a couple of times," the parent will say, "but he works so hard — I think he just needs to blow off steam."

By the time you have to call a parent to report bad behavior, you expect action. You've tried everything you can to remedy the situation, and you're admitting that you, alone, cannot fix everything. You need parents to deliver the same message at home: "Respect those in authority, and be prepared to pay the price if you disobey your parents or teachers." However, the Lost Cause parent will never be able to deliver that message. Either you're going to have to establish and model an appropriate adult-child relationship with that student (because the children of Lost Cause parents inevitably feel as though they should be treated as adults) or turn the behavior problems over to the guidance counselors or administrators, who have more time, patience, and experience dealing with such parents.

The Quick Fixer

Earlier in this chapter, I say that making a parent phone call about a misbehaving student is about the same as informing someone that they have a disease. The Quick Fixer parent would respond to such a call from the doctor like this: "You say I have 95-percent blockage in all the blood vessels of my heart and that if I so much as dial a phone too fast, I could have a massive heart attack? Yikes. That's bad news. I know what I'll do. I'll start eating more broccoli with my lunch. Thanks for the call. Bye now!"

Clearly, there are a lot more things at work here than insufficient broccoli consumption. Adding one food, no matter how disgusting it tastes, is not enough to turn the tide of a potential coronary explosion. First of all, it's bypass or angioplasty time — the blockage must be removed so that the patient survives. Second, a new diet and exercise regimen must be designed and put in place so that the situation does not recur.

Student behavior problems are like medical problems in that there is no immediate fix, because diagnosis is rarely simple. Repairing a bad attitude is not the same as fixing a broken ignition system in a car or changing a flat tire. Most of the time, you'll have to try a number of different approaches to address the problem before something works. Certainly, it's embarrassing, distressing, and aggravating for a parent to find out that his child is misbehaving in school, and it's understandable for that parent to try to fix what's wrong as soon as he can, so that his life can return to normal quickly. "So, Sarah didn't do her homework? Well, guess who's not going to be talking on the phone for the next three months?"

Help Quick Fixer parents probe and diagnose the problem. Why would Sarah fail to do her homework? You (and her parent) can't automatically assume that she's fallen in with Satanic cult members and that her dark rituals are taking away from homework time, or that Sarah is part of a street gang preying on the elderly and eating puppies. It's important that the Quick Fixer not overreact. Maybe Sarah's involved in too many clubs or extracurricular activities. Perhaps she's frustrated in class because she's having a hard time understanding, and she's too embarrassed to ask for help. I had a really good student who refused to do his homework, because his parents' expectations were very high. "This way, if I don't get an A in your class, I can say it's because I was too busy in student council to do homework, and they won't have to face the fact that I'm not as smart as they think I am," he explained.

When faced with a Quick Fixer, your job is conversational angioplasty. In most cases, the communication between student and parent has become restricted, and you must stress to the parent the importance of talking to his child. Stress to him that finding out *why* his daughter isn't doing her homework is more important than focusing solely on how he will punish her.

Phoning Home

Now that you know how various types of parents will react when you call them, it's time to start thinking about how, exactly, you should handle those phone calls. When you get used to making them, you'll find out that these phone conversations are one of the most powerful weapons in your behavioral arsenal. Parents would much rather be told by a teacher that their child is misbehaving, and have time to discuss options to fix the situation before it escalates and has to be addressed by the principal. However, if you don't handle yourself well during these calls, you can make a bad situation much, much worse. To help keep you firmly in the frying pan (but out of the fire), you should first and foremost have a plan before you start dialing.

Dialogue dissected

The most successful parental phone calls have four distinct parts: the introduction, the explanation, the treatment, and the follow-up, and they must occur in that order. If you jump right into the meat of the call before you fully introduce yourself, the parent is going to be confused, overwhelmed, and probably defensive. On the other hand, if you explain who you are and why you're calling, but have no plan of action prepared or fail to ever talk to the parents again, they'll feel like you're going through the motions but aren't really interested in helping their children.

It takes time to figure out how to constructively criticize a child without backing parents into a corner; in fact, it took me three or four years before I was good at phone conferences. By then, I was not only able to call parents without anxiety and attacks of nerves, but both the parents and I actually felt better by the end of the phone call. Even though we'd both admitted there was a problem, we both felt good about our ability to work together to find a solution. The key to success is understanding that each of the four phases of a phone conference has its own hoops to be jumped through and pitfalls to be avoided.

Stage 1: The Introduction

As you dial the parent's number, remember that she has no idea that you're calling and that she may not even really know who you are at first. In the first two or three minutes of the call, you need to explain who you are and where you work. As soon as you identify yourself as a school employee, the first thing the parent will think is, "Oh no, what the heck happened?" Therefore, your primary concern is to get into the meat of the conversation as soon as possible after you've properly identified yourself.

By the way, if a secretary or co-worker of the parent answers the phone, there's no reason to say, "This is her son's teacher calling; her kid acted like a moron in class, and I'm calling to ruin the parent's day." Just give your name if you're asked to identify yourself and save the juicy details for the parent — she'll be miffed if she thinks you're discussing private things with other people, especially the people she has to work with. ("Hey Kate, heard your kid can't keep his mouth shut in class; I've never had any trouble like that with my Veronica. She's such a great kid, not to toot my own horn or anything.")

Avoid the temptation to engage in small talk at this critical introductory point in the conversation. As soon as parents get the picture that you're their child's teacher, they're simply waiting for the other shoe to drop. Clearly, something happened worthy of taking the time to make a phone call, so what is it? Did my kid fail a test? Get caught cheating? Get into a fight? Break the school record in the 100-meter dash? What!? Small talk only heightens the parent's anxiety level, because she knows something bad is coming. Before you get into all the details, you need to have a nonthreatening summary statement prepared, such as, "I've observed some behavior in class that concerns me." The statement allows the parent a moment to mentally prepare herself for the news you're about to deliver and is a natural segue into the second phase of the conversation.

Stage 2: The Explanation

Now's the time to get down to the nitty-gritty and tell the parent why you're calling her in the first place. You should begin with what I call a fishing expedition: Throw out a wide net and see if you catch anything. You want to see if there are any obvious things that can be causing the undesired behavior before you start offering up your own thoughts or suspicions. For example, if Dave isn't paying attention in class, you may want to begin with: "I've noticed that Dave seems distracted in class lately, and I was wondering if you noticed anything different in his behavior or personality at home." This gives the parent a chance to participate in the conversation and inform you of things you'd otherwise have no way of knowing.

You may be surprised by what you find out. During one fishing expedition, a mother told me, "Dave's dad got really sick two nights ago and had to be hospitalized. He has serious heart trouble and collapsed at a softball game. Things are beginning to stabilize now, but it was touch and go there for a while." Bingo. Behavior problem solved, and there's no need to cause this family any more trauma right now. If the parent has no obvious explanation for the inappropriate behavior, you need to describe exactly what the child is doing; most parents want to get as much information as possible so they can talk to their child as soon as they get home that evening.

At this stage, it's important to tell the parent that the bad behavior is a change from the norm, because students will immediately assume that you don't like them if you have to discipline them in class. They're apt to go home and complain that "He just doesn't like me — I have no idea why he yelled, because I didn't do anything wrong!" (Even though you may have a good relationship with the student, remember that most students are instantly defensive when they screw up, and they'll go right into "damage control" mode with their parents, even if it's unnecessary.) I once had a student who was a good guy and always congenial, even if he wasn't the sharpest crayon in the box, so to speak, until one day, when he screamed at the top of his lungs at me, got red in the face, and mumbled some unpleasant things under his breath. I was angry at the outburst, and sent him out of the room until I had time to calm down. When I was able to breathe normally, I went to talk to him, but he wasn't interested. He wouldn't even make eye contact with me.

That afternoon, I called his mom and found out that his coach had yelled at him the day before, and it had really upset him. I stressed that he usually was a really nice guy, and that I'd never had any previous trouble with him in the classroom. Parents need to hear that; they want to know that bad behavior is the exception rather than the rule. If they think that you usually like their kid (even if you can't stand the sight of him), it helps the rest of the medicine in the conversation go down a little easier.

TIP

Honesty is the best policy

If you somehow instigated a confrontation with a student, or behaved unprofessionally during it, you have to admit it to the parent when you call him. It's an easy mistake to make. In the heat of the moment, students spew all sorts of hurtful and untrue accusations, and as the teacher, you have to let them roll right off your back. Of course, being dressed down by a 9-year-old in front of your class for no reason other than you asked him to stop talking while you're talking is enough to enrage even the most patient person.

You're bound to lose your temper and say things you shouldn't, and you'll know you've goofed just as soon as those words slip out of your mouth. One year, I had a very young, immature, academically challenged class (the non-politically-correct term here is *thugs*) that required infinite patience, resolve, and aspirin in equal amounts. After months, I felt as though I was finally getting through to them, especially the ringleader, a defiant young lad in a crew cut who was ready to fight verbally or physically at a moment's notice.

I felt as though we were connecting until the day he stood up and said, "Hey, darn you" at the top of his lungs. Rather than *darn,* though, he used the F-word, the mother of all swears, and my body temperature went from a calm 98.6 degrees to approximately the temperature on the surface of the planet Mercury in about three seconds. My response was immediate: "Get the hell out of this room and go straight to the office." When he left, I knew I had messed up. I cursed too! Sure *hell* isn't as bad as the word he used, but it's still not good. Clearly, I had to call the parent to explain what the kid had done in class, and I had to come clean about my own behavior as well.

"Mr. Rankin, when your son hit me with that outburst, I have to admit I lost my temper a little," I remember saying. "I told him to get the hell out of the room, and I regret using the word *hell.* Even though I was upset, it didn't excuse my language, and I want to apologize to you for speaking to him like that. Just because he incited me doesn't make it right for me to react like that." I held my breath to find out how he'd respond. "I'd have cursed a lot worse if he had said that to me," Mr. Rankin said. "Don't apologize to me; he should be apologizing to you for making you that angry."

If you try to deny or cover up things you do in class, it'll come back to haunt you, because everything happens in a room full of witnesses who may not be able to remember a single thing you teach but can recite verbatim the things you say in anger. Be honest so that the kid doesn't trap you in a lie.

Stage 3: The Treatment

When the problem is out in the open, and you've rattled all the child's behavioral skeletons out of the closet, you and the parent have to figure out what you're going to do about it. If the parent is going to cry, now will be the time, so steel yourself if her voice has been quivery during your conversation. If things are getting emotional, make sure that whatever disciplinary action is decided upon actually fits the crime. Reassure the parent that the problems you've discussed with her are not the worst things you've ever experienced, nor are they uncommon, so that cooler heads can prevail. If, on the other hand, the parent is stoic or unemotional, you could be dealing with a completely different kind of problem.

Stoicism or emotional flatness is a good indication that the parent may be entering the "Ah, so what?" mindset. She begins to get used to the idea that her kid misbehaved, and the shock of it begins to die down. In fact, she may start to think, "I really can't blame him for the way he acted; I'm not sure I would have acted any differently in his place." Therefore, it's very important to stress to this parent that even if inappropriate behavior is *understandable* in a certain circumstance, that does not make it *acceptable*.

For example, a number of students have tried to cheat on my tests. In fact, I found that the smarter the kids I taught, the more likely they were to try to cheat. Smart kids are used to doing well in school and are willing to go to extreme means to get good grades, even if those means lie outside the law. Although parents are usually very supportive of a teacher who catches their child cheating, I actually had a parent tell me, "It's so hard to get into college these days, what with skyrocketing grade point averages and mammoth SAT score requirements, I'm glad she cheated. It tells me that she cares about getting into college, and I'll encourage her to cheat again, to get every possible academic advantage she can muster."

Clearly, having to perform well academically is a stress, and cheating is one way to relieve that stress (look at all the time you're just throwing away when you study, after all!). Although the motivations are clear and I empathize with the stress students shoulder, cheating is not the answer. The same goes for tardiness, not doing homework, and failing to do assigned projects because you're "just too busy." The fact that the student had reasons for failing to do what's expected doesn't excuse the behavior.

The best way to discipline a child is to partner up with parents. There have to be repercussions both at school and at home for misbehaving at school. You can't just trust the parent alone to handle the situation, because the offense occurred in your room. The child owes a debt to you for breaking the rules, and you need to collect payment. However, the parent must follow up with punishment at home as well, because otherwise you run the risk of forming an us-against-them mentality that pits you against the families of your students. "Sure, that mean old teacher made you stay after and clap erasers during detention, but Mommy and Daddy think that inhaling eraser dust is punishment enough, so go have some extra ice cream." When kids know that *all* the adults in their life are out to get them if they step out of line, the prospect of screwing up is much less attractive.

At the elementary level, it is important to meet the parents or talk to them on the phone at the beginning of the school year *before* anything happens, just to introduce yourself and say, "I'm so glad Josh is in my room." Partnering up with parents from the start is a big help. Always think of something nice to say about the child. "Tricia has beautiful handwriting," "Sheldon has a great sense of humor," or "Mike seems to have a good sense of balance, despite his oversized head." (I include that last one because it was most appropriate for me as a child.)

Stage 4: The Follow-Up

By far, this stage is the most neglected. It's not enough just to call a parent, explain what's wrong, and assume that things will get better just because you had a heart-to-heart talk. As stressful as these conversations are, and as hard as they are to squeeze into your schedule, you have to set aside time in the near future to call the parent back and see how things are going. Most likely, they're trying to shake things up at home and need to know if it's having any effect on the kid's behavior in school.

Before you wrap up the conversation, tell the parent that you'd like to touch base with her in about a week to update her on what's going on in class and to get the lowdown on what's happening at home. Jot it down on your calendar and don't forget! Decide what day would be the best for you and make sure you tell her about what time you'll be calling. (To be safe, you should call right after school, just in case things pop up during your lunch or planning period that prevent you from keeping your phone appointment.)

One word of caution: If a parent says, "Do me a favor and call me if anything changes," don't just automatically agree. Instead, say, "I'll do my best, but I have to warn you that I can't be as tuned in to subtle behavior changes as you can." I hesitate to guarantee parents I'll call them immediately, because it's impossible for me to notice everything simply because of the number of kids I see during the day. "Of course, rest assured that if anything major comes up, I will call immediately." This places some responsibility back on the parent, which is very important. Otherwise, she could just call the principal and say, "I had no idea there was still a problem. Mr. Kelley told me he'd call if anything changed and he never called, so how was I supposed to know?"

Most of the time, your conversation with parents will result in a change in the child's behavior. Sometimes it won't work, you'll have to involve the principal, and things will get messy, but that's rare. Therefore, you're bound to get good news when you follow up with parents. Even if the child from hell is now an angel from heaven, don't neglect that follow-up call. Parents want to see that you'll follow through, and they're much happier to talk to you than they were before. For one thing, it's not a surprise this time, but more importantly, it's a chance for the two of you to pat each other on the back and talk about what a great job you did.

Successful strategies

Now that you have a good idea about what makes up an effective parent phone conference, you can handle just about anything that comes your way over the phone. Faced with happy parents, angry parents, or clueless parents, you have a strategy for each, and your skills will only improve with time. So far in this chapter, I've focused on the kinds of people you'll meet and what to do when you're on the phone, but that's only part of the picture. In the following sections, I provide a few very practical tips about when and how to make those calls so they can be as effective as possible.

Always get to the parent before the student does

Students these days have a lot of skills, but none is so honed as their ability to make excuses on demand. Let's say that, during a test, you catch a student brazenly looking at his neighbor's paper. We're not talking subtlety here — he's craning his neck and leaning so far over to see that his desk is tilted onto two legs. "Scott, stop looking at her paper," you say, and in response his desk loudly slams back to all four legs. "I wasn't cheating," he states, eyes wide with fear and feigned innocence. "I was just trying to look at her watch and see what time it is." Notice I said that students were good at *making* excuses, not that their excuses were particularly *good*.

In your mind, there's no doubt Scott was cheating, so you take his test paper away, give him detention, and tell him you'll decide if he's going to take a 0 for the test when you meet with him after school. Even if you read contrition in his eyes, here's what he's really thinking: "I have to call my mom as soon as possible and lie like there's no tomorrow, because if she hears about this before I get a chance to make up my side of the story, I'm in big trouble." Therefore, you need to call the parents first. As soon as class is over, you need to dart to the phone, so that the true side of the story reaches their ears first. If Scott gets a chance to try to soften the blow before you call, his mom will be more hesitant to believe you, because in the case of a he-said, she-said game, her own kid gets home-field advantage.

If, however, Scott tries to spin a tall tale to his mom after you've already called home, it's not going to work. If you've explained the entire situation and given the parent enough details about what happened, she'll be able to spot the fibs and inconsistencies in his story and the kid will dig himself into a hole without even realizing it.

If a student's grade or attitude is dropping, call her parents

It doesn't matter if the drop in grades is sudden or gradual; either way, the parents are going to be unhappy about it. If you've called to warn them about it, the disappointment will be focused on the child, where it belongs. If, however, they're completely surprised by a 10- or 15-percent drop in grades between marking periods, they're going to be resentful that you didn't bother warning them about it. I know what you're thinking: "Why can't they be bothered to find out how their own kids are doing in school, and why is it my job to tell them? Shouldn't the student take the responsibility?" Think of it this way: Would you rather have a nice, calm day when report cards come out or have to field 50 angry phone calls from parents and get really aggravated?

Log the times and dates of all your phone calls

Because you probably won't have a telephone in your room, you'll only be able to make phone calls during your lunch period, during your planning period, or right after school. (Before school is usually way too early or too full of stuff you should have done the night before to prepare for class.) Because you'll only be available for short periods of time each day, you probably won't be able to get through to parents on your first or second try. Therefore, recording exactly when you try to call parents is important, so that you can demonstrate that you tried to reach them on numerous occasions. If your principal has to become involved, and the parents try the standard "Well, his teacher never told me that" line, you can prove that you've been *trying* to reach the parent, but that your calls haven't been returned.

Call parents to report good news as well as bad news

There are lots of cutesy names for this sort of thing: "happy calls," "caught-being-good calls," or "guess-whose-behavior-didn't-almost-push-me-into-a-murderous-rampage-for-once calls." Every time I turned around, someone was telling me, as a rookie, that I should make happy calls to parents at least as often as negative calls, so that parents wouldn't just think I was mean or grouchy. For some reason, though, the more people tell me to do something, the more I'm suspicious of it; maybe it's a subconscious peer-pressure red flag or something — I have no idea. End result: I didn't start making happy calls home until my second year teaching.

When I finally got on the bandwagon, I was shocked at how effective these little affirming phone calls were. My first call was to the parents of a young girl who was in my worst-behaved class ever. She was truly a rose among jerks, if I may mix metaphors for a moment, always paying attention, and never trying to stick me with a knife if I tried to write notes on the board. After one particularly grueling day, I called her mom at work. "Mrs. Johnson, I'm calling from your daughter's school, and I wanted to discuss her behavior in my class with you." I heard an audible gulp and what may have been the sound of her mother passing out on the other end of the phone line, but I pressed on. "I am truly lucky to have Amy in class, because she is without question one of the brightest points in my day. She's well behaved, thoughtful, bright, and a real joy to me, and I just thought you should know that."

Mrs. Johnson stammered out a strained "thanks" (I think she was still expecting me to end the conversation with, "And that's why I was so surprised to find out she was dealing drugs to preschool children," or something equally shocking) and hung up. By the next day, almost everyone in the school knew I'd made the call. Mrs. Johnson was so proud, she told all her friends, relatives, acquaintances, and anyone who'd stand still long enough to listen, and passed on the praise I'd given her daughter. The principal even got a phone call from her and swung by to tell me I'd earned major points in his book. "When a parent calls me as happy as she was, that's a big plus in your column, my friend, especially when all the other calls I answered today were from unhappy parents."

Here's something I didn't expect: The class full of hooligans came in the next day quiet and uneasy. After I asked what I had done to deserve such quiet and polite students, a student asked, "Did you really call Amy's mom?" (Amy immediately blushed the color of red, ripe tomatoes.) "Yep," I said. "I wanted her mom to know how much I like having her in class." It was a watershed moment in my relationship with that class, because they realized I could actually make their parents happy as well as angry. I'm not saying they were perfect angels for the rest of the year or all went on to become astronauts, but at least they stopped trying to break off the tips of their pencils beneath each other's skin.

Limit phone time with difficult or needy parents

You should be able to get through a parent phone conference in no more than 15 minutes. However, some parents will just talk and talk and talk when you get them started. They'll vent about their children, their marriage, their failed stock investments, and how they just can't seem to find anything good on TV anymore. There were times I was sure I could put the phone down and walk away from it for a half-hour, and when I returned, the parent would still be ranting. In fact, some parents are so good at dominating a conversation and eating up all your free time that they can actually inhale without a break in the conversation, so you have nowhere to jump in with "Well, I'd better be going now. . . ."

If you know that a parent is going to (consciously or not) eat up your entire planning period with meaningless chatter, wait until the last 15 minutes of that period before you call. Without being too obvious, let the parent know you're working with limited time by saying, "Hi, Mrs. Jones, this is Mike Kelley returning your call about your daughter's test grade. I'm sorry that it took me so long to call, but today's been a crazy day. I wanted to make sure to call you before tomorrow, but to squeeze you in, I may have to limit the length of our phone conversation — my planning period ends in 15 minutes, but you have my undivided attention until then." Never do this the first time you call a parent or do it more than once to the same parent, because she'll know you're avoiding her. Of course, that's exactly what you're doing, but you don't want her to figure that out.

Contacting parents via e-mail

If you're worried about getting calls at home or don't have easy access to telephones in your school, you can always use e-mail to correspond with parents. Of course, not all parents use e-mail, and the rest won't want to use e-mail exclusively, so you'll still have to make some calls. However, the vast majority won't mind at least some electronic contact. In fact, some will really appreciate the fact that they can e-mail you any time, day or night, and not have to deal with constantly leaving you messages at school.

If you plan on using e-mail as a conduit for parent contact, make sure you set up a separate e-mail address for work; don't give out your private e-mail, because you want to be able to pick and choose when to deal with work-related issues. When I first started using the Internet to contact parents, I made the mistake of giving out my home e-mail account, and one Saturday night, right before bed, I decided to do a quick e-mail check. It turned out that a parent had sent me a long, nasty message full of accusations and lies (that sort of message is called a *flame,* in case you aren't a techie nerd like me, aware of Internet lingo).

Perhaps it was because I was tired, or because it was so invasive to have a parent ream me out electronically when I was in my pajamas, but the message I sent back to that parent wasn't the most diplomatic message I've ever written, to say the least. I probably could have dealt with it better if I'd waited until the workweek to deal with it. Therefore, I also recommend that you only check that work e-mail account during business hours. You do really need some time away from teaching every day, so let those messages sit unread during the precious few moments of work-free time you have at home.

Don't be too afraid of potential flames from parents. I found that parents are more apt to send you kind and complimentary letters when you give out your e-mail address. Many are shy and would never say such things to you in person, but they have no problem sending you a quick e-mail telling you how great they think you are and how much their kid likes being in your class.

If you're not sure how to get an extra e-mail account for work purposes (and your school doesn't offer you one), go to `http://mail.yahoo.com` or `www.hotmail.com` and sign up for a free e-mail account. You'll be able to read Yahoo! Mail or Hotmail at any computer that has an Internet connection, so the accounts are very handy.

Don't give out your home phone number

You don't want parents calling you at home, ever. Dealing with parents at school is aggravating enough most of the time, without having to deal with them outside of the workday. You're a professional, and you're not on call 24 hours a day. Doctors and lawyers get paid big money to always be just a phone call away, but you don't. If a parent wants to call you, give him the school's phone number, and explain exactly when you can be reached. Parents never come out and directly ask for your home number, but they may say things like, "Can I call you later tonight to talk about this, after I get a chance to talk to my wife?" Your reply should be, "Please feel free to call me at school and leave a message for me, and I'll return your call just as soon as I can. If you'd rather not leave a message, call during my planning period, which is between 9:25 and 10:00 a.m."

When I started teaching, I got an unlisted phone number, but I found that it was unnecessary. Only once, many years later when I had stopped paying to keep my number unlisted, did I have a parent call me at home after looking up my number in the phone book. He began the conversation with, "I'm sure you wouldn't mind the parent of a conscientious student calling you at home — I just had some concerns about what's happening in class." I told him that he was free to call me at school the next day and I'd be happy to answer his question then, when I had access to all my records (even though I really had them right there beside me).

If you're unable to make parent phone calls from school, and you're forced to call from home, make sure you keep your number private. If you call a parent who has caller ID, suddenly your home number is private no longer — and even if your number isn't unlisted, you don't want to publicize it. Most phone services allow you to block your number from showing up on caller ID boxes, but you have to dial a short code into the phone before you call. This feature is usually free — just call your phone company's customer service department to enable it and/or get the code to activate it.

Surviving Parent Conferences

A face-to-face parent conference isn't a heck of a lot different from a phone conference. The only difference is that you can't make faces at the parent or roll your eyes nearly as much when they can see you. Most of the time, parents don't want to be bothered scheduling a time to meet, taking off work, and driving to the school building if they can accomplish the same thing over the telephone. If, however, the parent decides to do all these things, you need to make sure you're prepared for the conference. Although you'll progress through the same four stages you would in a phone conference and basically say the same things you would if you were on the phone, there are a few other variables you need to address if the parent is physically in the room:

✔ **Provide an orderly meeting place appropriate for the situation.** This means meet in your classroom, unless you have clutter all over the place. If your day was hectic, and you haven't had a chance to clean up, you may want to meet in your school's conference room. Of course, your classroom is a much better spot, because the parent gets to see how lively your room is and how much care you've put into decorating. Though the parent may have heard what a good a teacher you are, when he gets a good look at the classroom you've worked so hard to create, he'll be convinced.

You want the parent to feel welcome, so don't sit behind your big teacher desk and make him sit in a tiny, child seat while you talk to one another. However, if you think the parent is going to be confrontational or rude, take the time to set up the conference area so that it benefits you instead. Don't let him sit behind a desk or table, because that gives him a physical barrier from you and makes him feel brave. Instead, he should be seated in a regular chair while you should have a small desk or table in front of you to hold your notes. Think about the set of a late-night talk-show host. To visually reinforce that the host is in control (not the guest) the host's chair is always higher than the guest's, and the host has a big desk to sit behind, whereas the guest has to sit there, twitching his fingers and nervously crossing and uncrossing his legs. You want to give the impression that if anyone is on trial here, it's certainly not you.

✔ **Make sure all your ducks are in a row.** Have examples of the student's work available, and prepare a progress report detailing all her grades for the marking period and school year. If your grades are computerized, this is easy. If the purpose of the conference is a disagreement about a report-card grade, recalculate the grade ahead of time to make sure you're right. In essence, if you're accusing the student of something, this is your chance to make your legal case. When it comes to supportive evidence in the case, exhibit A should be a copy of your class rules. At the beginning of each year, you should have provided all parents with a copy of your class rules and procedures. Some parents will try the old "Well, little Frankie didn't know he wasn't allowed to go to the bathroom anytime he wanted without asking, and in our house you don't have to ask to go to the bathroom" trick. Just whip out your rules and say, "My rules clearly state that students have to ask for permission to leave the room; didn't you receive these rules when the school year started?"

✔ **Welcome the parent to the building.** Some school buildings are nearly impossible to navigate, so don't just tell a parent, "Meet me in my classroom at 4:15," because the odds are that he has no idea where your classroom is. Instead, say, "Go to the main office and sign in as a visitor. Tell the secretary that you're here to meet with me, and she'll call my room. I'll walk down to the office and lead you back to my room so that you don't have to wander around trying to find me." This makes the parent feel more welcome and also gives you a heads up before he arrives, providing a few extra moments to get your thoughts together.

✔ **Make sure the right people are in the room.** Parent conferences are a lot easier if students have to come. Don't be fooled — students will lie to their parents with reckless abandon if they know a parent conference is imminent, and parents aren't sure who to believe when they hear both sides of the story. If, however, the student also has to attend the conference, she gets trapped in the web of lies she has spun. As a teacher, I just loved those moments when a parent turned to his child and said, "I thought you told me . . ." and the lie was uncovered.

If things are getting out of hand, or you get a very confrontational vibe from the parent when you schedule your meeting time, immediately ask an administrator to attend the meeting with you, even if you neglect to mention that fact to the parent. When I first started teaching, some parents felt they had every right to yell at or talk down to me during our conferences, and I didn't know how to handle it. Here's what I learned: No parent has any right to treat you that way, and you shouldn't have to deal with it. If a parent is beginning to raise his voice or is saying things that are inappropriate, end the conference immediately. Stand up and say, "This conference is over. I'll have my principal call you in a day or so to schedule another meeting when he's able to attend it as well." Then walk out of the room. Administrators will not allow parents to yell at you, and there's absolutely no reason for a conference to turn personal, even if you were the one who screwed up and necessitated the meeting in the first place.

Unless the meetings are routine, such as meetings called to review IEPs, conferences held in person differ from phone conferences in one major way: Someone attending that meeting has an agenda. Perhaps the parent just wants to get a good look at you, or perhaps you want a student to have to face her mother and own up to things she's been doing wrong in class. Therefore, be sure to take more time to prepare for the meetings that are held in person, and never be afraid to have administrators or guidance counselors in the room to support you if you think you'll need it.

Chapter 16

Getting to Know Students

Students are mysterious creatures with amazing powers. They can make your day, sharing the kindest and most sincere words of gratitude with you, or totally ruin your week with a casual (and unintentionally audible) comment to a classmate about how much they hate your class and wish they had a different teacher. They take months to get to know, and when you finally feel like you understand one another, the school year is over and the drama begins with a new set of faces.

In this chapter, I serve as your guide in the wild, untamed land of students. I introduce you to some of the locals, give you some survival techniques in case you run into them at your own school, and give you some insight into the question that has plagued teachers since the beginning of time: "What do these kids *want* from me?"

Teaching Different Academic Levels

Before I discuss the types of individuals you'll teach, I want to give you a brief introduction to larger, more general, classifications of those students. Although some may take offense, I've broken students into three major categories, classified according to academic skill: honors students (also known as the "smart kids"), middle-of-the-roaders (the vast majority of students, who aren't particularly good at school or necessarily bad either), and the academically challenged kids (for whom learning and understanding is a real struggle).

Why did I break students down according to how smart they are? In my experience, it's the best way to predict what the students' attitudes will be. Your overall teaching style will have to adjust to the students in your classes, and the best way to determine exactly how to make those adjustments is to look at how they're placed academically. You may have heard in college that the practice of *tracking* (placing students into fixed coursework based on how smart they are) has been frowned upon and all but eliminated. This is not entirely true. Students are still separated based on relative braininess, but the boundaries between the tracks have been loosened. Therefore, a student incorrectly identified as "slow," due perhaps to a learning disability that can be identified and addressed, is not doomed to the slow classes forever. By test score or teacher recommendation, that student can progress through the tracks until he finally reaches the one that truly matches his ability.

In the descriptions that follow, I address the challenges you'll face when dealing with different kinds of kids. Think of these cases as the worst-case scenarios for each group, and keep in mind as I discuss the differences between the tracks that these are generalizations. You're bound to meet exceptions to the rule, because no general description is appropriate for all students in every situation. Furthermore, not all your kids are going to present all the obstacles or challenges I outline. However, you don't want to go into the classroom blind to the dark sides all kids potentially possess.

Honors students

The Holy Grail and ultimate goal of most teachers is to teach the best and the brightest kids at your school. Why? Because the smart kids are also usually the better-behaved kids, or at least that's the conventional wisdom. I'm here to tell you that the old theory that "Anyone can teach the smart kids" is a load of hooey. Although bright students are less likely to curse you out or throw eggs at your house late at night, they have their own set of issues to deal with.

For one thing, smart kids have extremely high expectations of their teachers. They expect that you'll come to class every day having spent hour upon hour planning their lessons, rehearsing your lectures, and designing activities to make the learning process fun and interesting. Heaven forbid you make a mistake in class early in the year. As one annoyed being, the entire class will groan, roll their eyes, scratch dramatically through the incorrect information in their notes, and whisper conspiratorially to one another, "Is this guy for real? Does he even know what he's talking about?"

Honors students also hate to be disciplined, no matter how serious the offense. I'm positive that bright kids get away with things all the time that other students would get punished mercilessly for. After all, they're the chosen few, the apples of their parents' eyes, the hope of the future. They're under so much pressure to get into college and perform well! Can't we just cut them a little slack and let them miss a quiz here and there, or look the other way if they come to class late? Your primary focus with an academically gifted class is to establish disciplined work habits as well as a disciplined classroom. Don't let the kids cut corners or give them breaks just because they're smart.

Many smart kids have a pretty high opinion of themselves and look with disdain upon class activities or topics that they deem "beneath them." They'll ask questions like, "Why do we have to do this?" and, "When will I ever use this in real life?" Don't bother answering these questions, because they're not honestly curious to find out the answer — they're just testing you to see if you'll stick with your lesson plans or allow yourself to be pushed around. Be firm in your plans, but be careful how you deal with these students, because they won't hesitate to complain about you to their parents or the principal. They're the kind of kids who may look you in the eye, say, "My mother thinks what we're doing in class is a waste of time, and she's calling the superintendent to try to get you fired," and mean it.

Your best bet with academically gifted kids is to avoid stepping on their egos when trying to get them in line. Humor works well with these students, and they really do appreciate it when you treat them like people, as opposed to underlings who must mindlessly do what you say. However, when push comes to shove (as it will) and they step out of line, you have to show them that you're going to bring down the hammer, smart or not.

Middle-of-the-roaders

Believe it or not, here's where the majority of your frustration will arise. The biggest problem with this group of kids is a severe lack of motivation when it comes to all things school-related. Trying to convince middle-of-the-roaders to study for a test is roughly the equivalent of trying to convince people not to speed while they're driving. Just as speeders have absolutely no idea why anyone would want to drive slowly, these students have no idea why anyone would actually want to study. After all, if they take the test cold (that is, without preparing at all), they're bound to at least pass, even if they don't get that great of a score.

Who needs a great score anyway? Getting accepted to college isn't a motivation, because either college is so far in the future that they don't care, or they're not interested in college at all. After all, if they change their minds later and want to go to college, they'll just start in community college, where acceptance is guaranteed, and then get into a better school through the back door by transferring in later. Extracurricular activities? Who cares! Just dorks and losers stay after school to participate in fruity clubs. What's the point anyway? Middle-of-the-roaders hate learning during the school day, so why would extending the time you spend in school be an attractive option?

These kids can suck out your will to live, because it seems like nothing you do gets through to them. They're not stupid, nor are they hostile — they're just not interested in learning. One teacher I worked with confronted a middle-of-the-roader and asked him why, exactly, he even bothered coming to school. He gave a simple, one-word answer: "Boobs." In his mind, school was only valuable because it was a natural habitat for girls, and he (like most adolescent boys) was a fan of the female physique; he was just more up front about it (if you forgive the pun).

Why do these kids act the way they do? It's hard to say for sure, but I think one of the main reasons is that their teachers aren't interested in them. Most teachers I know would rather teach the smart kids, and middle-of-the-roaders know it; they feel like the "runner-up," everyone's alternative choice. They're the middle child of education, unwanted and unappreciated, and I think that sense of rejection slowly morphs into a desire to disconnect from the academic world.

The best way to deal with these kids is to put forth a sincere effort to make class involving and entertaining. Use the tactics I describe in Chapter 11 to spice up class time and show them you're actually glad to have them in class, because that's a unique experience for most of them. In addition, pay special attention to the last section in this chapter, and try to understand what, exactly, it is that students want from you, because these kids will never tell you.

Academically challenged kids

These are the kids your colleagues refer to as the "dumb kids" in the teacher's lounge, as in, "I can't believe I have to teach two classes of dumb kids this year." The biggest problem with this group is impulse control. Whatever pops into their minds they immediately say aloud — there is no intermediary period to determine if it is appropriate for class, or if it will result in someone punching or threatening to punch them. Until you establish an orderly routine in a low-performing academic class, you'll feel like the ringmaster of a flea circus, having to monitor multiple situations at all times, and trying to establish order in the midst of chaos.

These kids are completely different, based on what time of the day it is. Early in the morning, when they're still sleepy, you'll wonder why teachers complain about such classes at all. In the afternoon, however, you'll wonder if you can make it through the day if you have to say, "Stop throwing your pencil at Michelle" one more time. Monitoring your class can become exhausting, not because of the severity of the behavior problems, but because they're constant. It's sort of like being surrounded by gnats all period long (not too painful but awfully annoying) as opposed to getting stung by a bee, a more painful yet more rare sensation, which is more characteristic of behavior problems in other academic levels.

TIP

"Why do we have to do this?"

The question "Why do we have to do this?" pops up in class for lots of reasons. Sometimes the kids are just overwhelmed by the volume of material you're covering. Other times, they're just suffering from an immense lack of motivation. Either way, the question comes out as a whiny challenge to your authority, both annoying and potentially disruptive, so you need to have an answer prepared for the day you're first asked this question.

Assume that a student asked you, "Why do I have to learn to add fractions?" Here are a few responses I've used in the past. Of course, you'll need to vary your answer based upon your relationship with your students. Do you need to answer earnestly, or can you be sarcastic? Is the question meant as a disruption or is it an honest concern?

✔ **We do this because it is necessary.** "Why do we have to learn anything? Why do you read books in literature class? It's not like you're planning on being a literary critic! Who cares about why plants grow or how they make food? Plants grow if you understand them or not, right? Why did I even bother putting on a shirt today? Why did I come in for work on time and not a half-hour late? We do these things because we are a society, and this is what productive members of society do. They dress, they show up for work on time, and they gain knowledge so that they can be useful to the other members of society."

✔ **We do this because it strengthens our minds.** "To be perfectly honest, you're probably not going to be adding a lot of fractions together in your life. Some people do it all the time, but others will never, ever do it. However, you can't decide how useful something is based on how often you'll do it. For example, think about football players. They do strength training all the time. Have you seen those butterfly machines they use to build up their pectoral muscles? They sit, straight-backed at the machine, huffing and puffing, repeatedly drawing their forearms together. When do those football players ever make that motion in a real game? When they're running at the quarterback, trying to get a sack, do they swing their arms around like they do at the butterfly machine? No! That would look crazy! So, why do they bother with it? Simple. Using that machine increases the blood flow to their muscles and makes them a generally stronger person. And doing these problems pumps up that blood flow in your brain and makes you a generally smarter person!"

✔ **We do this because we have to.** "You may not see a reason to learn this now, but you'll need to know this in order to understand classes you'll take later. Prerequisite knowledge is usually tedious, and understanding why it's important is often difficult, but all the pieces come together later, in more-advanced classes, when you'll finally see why all that information you absorbed before was so essential."

Answering this perennial question with the response that first comes to your mind, which is "Because I said so, you little twerp," is counterproductive. Also steer away from an us-against-them mentality like, "If I don't teach you this, those bozos down at the board of education will fire me, even though I think this material is a waste of your time and mine." That sort of thing usually finds its way back to the bozos in question, and you end up with a little explaining to do.

When you teach academically challenged kids, the key words are *patience* and *routine*. These kids tend to have short fuses and react poorly to unexpected situations, so you don't want a ton of surprises. Be clear about what you expect from them, especially when it comes to potentially disruptive situations such as fire drills and substitute teachers. Most of all, remember that these kids don't misbehave out of spite as often as most teachers think. Most things go awry during class because the kids don't understand how to respond appropriately in all social situations.

Your job will be to teach them not only how to spell correctly, add fractions, or explore history, but also how to be an effective member of society. Unfortunately, the latter is not measurable by standardized test scores and will often be overlooked by administrators. You have to learn to judge your successes by different means. Do the kids leave your room better able to cope with school and the role they play there? If so, then that's as valuable, if not more so, than achievement measurable by grades.

Also, keep in mind that kids find school difficult for lots of different reasons. Some just aren't destined to be the brain surgeons of tomorrow, for whatever reason, whether it be genetic or a result of their upbringing. However, other kids are struggling to overcome learning or developmental disabilities, and need your help to do so. Don't forget those IEPs that your professors droned on and on about in college. Legally, you need to meet the needs of these kids by following their education plans. Besides, if you do, you just may provide them with the kinds of successes they need to start figuring out how to combat these challenges in their future academic pursuits.

A Field Guide to Students

Now that I've painted a picture of students with a broad stroke, I should qualify myself. Not all classes of the same academic level will act the same way. In fact, based on the chemistry of the people in the class, the differences can be extreme. I've taught very low-achieving students and really enjoyed their company, and I've had college-bound seniors with such bad attitudes that even being in the same room with them was unpleasant.

Just as all classes tend to have their own personalities, so too will you see individual personalities arise within those classes. During the first week or so of school, most of the kids look pretty much the same to you, and you'll be hard pressed to be able to distinguish between them. However, as the school year progresses, the students begin to show their true colors, and begin to look less like masses of strangers and more like old friends or annoying relatives who have long since worn out their welcome. Allow me to introduce you to some of the more interesting characters I met during my rookie year, because you're bound to find some of the exact same personalities among *your* students.

The Super Geek

You're probably a pretty smart cookie. Okay, maybe you're not the smartest cookie in the bag, but you've still got more chocolate chips than average. Beware! No matter how smart you are, at least one of your students will be much smarter than you, no matter how young that student may be. Of course, you'll know more than they do, because you've been around longer and have watched more episodes of *Jeopardy!,* but given a little time to catch up, some brainiacs in your care will one day surpass you in mental prowess.

Among these really smart kids are a few who have crossed over to the dark side. Rather than use their fantastic intellects for good (that is, solving world hunger, perfecting cold fusion, and defeating supervillains bent on destroying Spiderman), they're happy to sit in your class and inform you every time you say or do something wrong. With a contemptible sneer and a piteous nod of the head (usually mottled with unkempt hair), they'll throw out comments like, "I think you meant to say . . ." or, if they're feeling more blunt, "There's no way that's correct." Unfortunately, most of the time, they're right, and it puts you at a loss for words.

How do you deal with children who get their grins by pointing out the mistakes others make? You don't want to come down on them so hard that other students are afraid to question you, because most of the time you'll be glad a student catches your mistakes — it means less time you have to spend later undoing the things you explained wrong. However, if a student is constantly criticizing you or pointing out mistakes to be disruptive, you have to take action.

I always confronted the student right in front of the class, because that's the forum he chose to confront me. "I usually don't mind when students help to make sure that I don't accidentally make mistakes in class," I'd say, "but your constant nitpicking has officially gotten old. Would you enjoy it if I pointed out all your mistakes in class? 'Attention everyone, Brian has gotten another question wrong on his test!' You're a very smart person, and I would appreciate it if you'd use your talents to help, rather than to annoy."

Sometimes, the best fix is to give Super Geeks a chance to showcase their expertise. Let them explain a particularly tough concept to the class, or pose challenging questions to them during class, so that they can use their powers for good, not evil.

The Drama Queen

I remember the first major test I gave. All the kids were nervous, because they had absolutely no idea what one of my tests would be like. If it weren't my rookie year, they would have tracked down my students from the year before and either asked for their old tests to look through or interviewed them like police detectives to try to discern what sorts of questions I asked, whether or not my tests were generally tough, how much time they should spend studying, and that sort of thing. The mood of the room was intense, and I was glad to see it. It made me feel good that the kids were taking the test seriously, because in my mind it meant that they took my *class* seriously, or at least cared enough about it to get all worked up.

Before the bell rang, my room looked a little like a pinball machine gone crazy. Students were ricocheting from desk to desk, comparing notes, and chattering excitedly. Amidst the thundercloud of nervous energy, one student sat alone; her eyes wide and fingers trembling, she was concentrating so hard on her notes that I wouldn't have been surprised to see her stare a hole right through her desk. Those eyes, sharp with focus, were also beginning to well with tears. Introducing the Drama Queen!

As I passed the tests out, and nervous conversation turned into expectant silence, the Drama Queen sat stone-still at her desk. When I finally approached her and handed her the exam, she took it as a prisoner facing a firing squad might accept a blindfold or last cigarette. Her body language said, "I have not lived a full life and yet this test will be the death of me!" Lower lip quivering and knees trembling, she picked up her pencil slowly, as though it weighed 50 tons, and began. By the time I finished passing out the tests, she could no longer hold back the tears. They spilled out onto her test paper in great wet drops, smearing her work and making the kids around her uncomfortable.

The Drama Queen can never understand that one test is not the end of the world, no matter how poorly or well she performs. The tears come out on test day, quiz day, days you talk about tests or quizzes, days you pass back graded papers, and report-card time. Although you're glad grades are important to her, you wish all the happiness in her life wouldn't depend on them. Your heart goes out to her, and you may want to spend time after class possibly consoling but at least counseling her on keeping things in perspective. Unfortunately, your efforts probably won't do much good. It's part of her personality, and trying to change a kid's personality is like trying to change the way the wind blows.

Be as compassionate as you can with the Drama Queen, but don't make it your professional goal to break through her test phobia and help her see life in a new, less-stressful, light. I worked with my own personal Drama Queen for weeks. I talked to her after class on nine separate occasions after emotional outbursts and tried to convince her that her she shouldn't judge herself based on exams and grades. I honestly thought I was making good progress. I cared about her and told her so. I told her that I didn't like the way she put pressure on herself. I explained that if I was proud of her, she should be proud as well, or at least not mercilessly self-deprecating. Even after all that honest discussion, she still wept after every exam. This behavior is just something kids grow out of eventually — so be patient with them.

The Class Clown

I'm sure the term *class clown* conjures up all sorts of negative images in your mind: students challenging your authority, causing class disruptions, and acting out to get attention at the expense of actually learning anything. As long as you establish control of your classes early in the school year, however, your Class Clown won't be such a pain. In fact, I loved having a Class Clown in the room. In my mind, nothing is worse than a class that sits idly by and doesn't participate in the learning process. I want kids in my classes to be engaged at all times, asking questions when they don't understand, teasing me if I say something wrong, and laughing at my lame attempts at comedy. I want them to feel comfortable being themselves, knowing that I'll accept them for who they are.

If you allow students the freedom to express their personalities, you'll always encounter kids who love the limelight. They wish they could be up in front of class, telling jokes, acting goofy, or capering about like a cartoon character. Every class has its born entertainers, and they'll find ways of expressing themselves, even if you focus all your energies on preventing it. Instead of always fighting with these students, I encouraged them, as long as it wasn't disruptive to the learning process.

One of the funniest students I ever taught was named Jermaine. He was a total goofball and could make anything funny just through his impeccable comedic delivery. He could take a pratfall with the best of them or tell a joke that made absolutely no sense, but still have the class rolling on the floor, clutching their sides in laughter. The class loved him, and I knew that making him an important part of class would result in more fun for everyone, including me. As class progressed, I'd watch his body language. If he was smiling or twitching in his seat, I knew he'd come up with some good material, so I'd throw him a bone. "Jermaine, can you share your thoughts on polygons for a moment?" He'd immediately stand up, adopt a scholarly attitude, and deliver a few minutes of prime material. He was smooth at improvisation comedy, an African-American Robin Williams who specialized in math jokes.

Jermaine was tuned into his classmates; if things were getting dry or boring, I could count on him to let me know, and to help me break out of my rut in a way that only a student can. The Class Clown can change the atmosphere in a classroom from drab winter tedium to excitement and fun faster and more effectively than anything you can do as the teacher. That's why I love the Class Clown — he's a natural resource more precious than any other. If things are getting slow in class and kids are losing interest, turn class over to the Class Clown. After a few minutes of watching him tramp about the room imitating you, everyone in class gets a chance to release their boredom and tension through laughter, and it's easier to face the day knowing that there could be a few laughs in store.

Advice from Atticus Finch

If you haven't had the opportunity to read Harper Lee's novel *To Kill a Mockingbird* or see the movie starring Gregory Peck, Atticus Finch is the story's protagonist, a wise country lawyer and the father of two children. I've read literary critics who say that Lee gave him this moniker because people associate ancient Greek-sounding names with wisdom, evoking thoughts of Plato and Socrates.

When it comes to dealing with children, Atticus earns his sagely name by offering two very sound pieces of advice. It's unusual for literary quotes to stick with me, but these have, and I've often applied them to my teaching:

✔ **"When a child asks you something, answer him, for goodness' sake. But don't make a production of it. Children are children, but they can spot an evasion faster than adults, and evasion simply muddles 'em."** All children have a special gift at detecting adults who are hemming and hawing, trying to avoid a direct answer. You won't earn the trust of your students if they feel like you're pulling the wool over their eyes.

✔ **"Never, never, never, on cross-examination ask a witness a question you don't already know the answer to. . . . Do it and you'll often get an answer you don't want, an answer that might wreck your case."** Good classroom managers know that if you plan to confront a student in class, you should treat the situation as though you were a lawyer questioning a witness in court. In fact, you're presiding over a court of public opinion while teaching, and just like a hostile witness can break apart the prosecution's case, a student can undermine your authority. Don't accuse a student if you're not *positive* he's guilty, and only ask him questions in front of others if you can predict his response.

Taking the advice of a fictional lawyer whose name makes him sound like a Greek bird may feel strange, but I've found these quotes to be genuine gems of wisdom with very practical applications in the classroom.

Figuring Out What Kids Want

Just like in any relationship, one of the hardest parts of getting along with your students is actually being able to discern exactly what it is they want from you. Newlyweds know what I'm talking about. There's always a trial period in a relationship when you figure out what your partner will and won't accept, what you can and absolutely cannot do. Is it okay to burp in front of her? Can I admit that, as barbaric as it is, there's a part of me that really likes watching those pay-per-view Ultimate Fighting specials? Will he laugh when he finds out I sleep with the blanket I've had since I was 3?

Tales of danger, terror, and pottery

When I asked my students to tell me teacher stories that stuck out in their minds, Malinda had a great tale to tell. It's the perfect example of when a little justification would go a long way, but she says it best in her own words:

> I had this art teacher, and the most aggravating thing about her was her constant ominous instruction to "Steer clear of the pottery kiln." Every week, we little children would enter the classroom to have this confusing phrase barked at us without knowing what it actually meant.
>
> First of all, it wasn't until years later that I even knew what the kiln actually was! (Only the bigger kids were allowed to work with clay.) More importantly, when I figured out what the kiln was, I, of course, had horrifying images about what fate would befall me if I were to, in fact, touch the dreaded kiln. Would I be burned to a crisp? Even worse, would I be sent to the principal's office, even if I touched it by accident? And what happened to the kids who *had* touched the kiln?
>
> Though, to my knowledge, no kid in my class had gone near the thing (that is to say I don't remember any child mysteriously combusting), it seemed only logical that there had to be a legendary art student of the past whose example was *not* to be followed. I figured there had to be a reason for my teacher consistently giving these haunting instructions. And that presumption on my part led to the fundamental problem I had with this teacher: She expected us to follow directions blindly, without any reason. Though she made it bitterly clear that we were to stay away from the kiln, I would have appreciated an explanation as to *why* we should stay away from the kiln.
>
> This dictatorial teaching style may be effective in getting what you want, especially when working with young children; none of us ever dared to touch the K.O.D. ("Kiln of Death"), but I don't look back on that time with fond memories. My skin still crawls when I hear the word *kiln*.

WARNING!

Students accept that they must get to know what their teachers expect. We make a big deal about it: "Here are my rules," "Here's what we're doing today," "Here's how I will grade your assignment." What we often forget is that the relationship has to go both ways. Not only must we demand they get to know us, we should also take the time to do the same. After all, what kind of relationship can you have if it's all one-sided?

Teaching is like a constant string of blind dates. A lot of time must be spent getting to know the other person, because until the moment you meet, there is absolutely no history. You're starting from square one, not even sure who's going to end up paying for dinner. Luckily, most students have the same deep-down desires and needs, as I found out when I sat down and asked my kids what they thought made a good teacher. I asked them what they expected from this relationship with a chalk-wielding adult, and based on their answers, I came up with this wish list of what students really want from their teachers:

- **Consistency:** You must have the same rules day in and day out, and enforce them the same way. You can't rant about how much you hate gum chewing in class one day and then ignore students blatantly chomping away the next day in the front row. It's not only in rules that you must be consistent, however. You must also have emotional stability from one day to the next. If you're manically excited and happy one day, joking and kidding with students, and then depressed and cranky the next, your classes will grow tired of you fast. They don't want to have to worry about what kind of mood you're going to be in and make huge adjustments in their behavior every day, accordingly.

- **Fairness:** Kids will endure lots of things, even from the worst of teachers, but the one that they will not stand for in any situation is a teacher who is unfair. One of my students, Lori, said it best: "There is nothing worse than a teacher with double standards. To have favorites is fine, and probably expected, but to *play* favorites and grade unfairly because of your personal feelings is inappropriate." This trickles down to all aspects of your class from the way you grade to the way you mediate disagreements during class games.

- **Role models:** Kids want to see that your behavior conforms to all the rules that they have to follow. One new teacher I spoke to made the mistake of swearing casually in class, and when his students started to do the same, he got angry, explaining that such language is against the rules. "But we're just saying the things that you say in class!" was the immediate (and difficult-to-debate) response. Your kids will notice a lot about you, like how you react to adversity and how you cope with stress. One student even told me that her teachers showed her how to laugh at herself and develop a healthy self-image, just by their examples in class.

- **Purpose:** The older students get, the more willing they are to ask for the ever-elusive "free period," a respite from the typically busy class. "Why do we have to work today?" they'll whine. "Can't we just have a free period for *once*?" Believe it or not, as much as they think that's what they want, when they get it, they're bored instantly. They stare at the walls, itching for something to do, something to peel their eyes away from the clock's second hand that seems to slow more and more with every glance. Even though working and learning aren't always fun, at least the time goes much faster than if you're just sitting, willing the period to end.

- **Respect:** This, more than any other word, was echoed by my former students. Kids are an important part of the learning process, but some teachers treat them like nothing more than furniture. True, their needs may be met and their education provided, but they're never taken seriously. Make a point to establish a bond with your students, especially the quiet ones who are hesitant to come out of their shells. Part of respecting each individual is recognizing that not all of them are outgoing and eager to raise their hands in class. When you can see your students as individuals with different needs, rather than a sea of anonymous faces, you're on the right track.

✔ **Justification:** I mention in earlier chapters that you should establish and keep the authority in your room all year long, and explained that you shouldn't spend much time trying to convince students why they should listen to you. However, that doesn't mean you never have to justify yourself. Most of your rules, especially those that are in place for safety or legal reasons, are less oppressive to students if they're substantiated.

✔ **Sincerity:** You're a real person, and your students would rather see you act like a regular mortal being than a self-proclaimed god of knowledge. As much as you can, relate the things you're talking about in class to regular life. Explain how the topics have affected you personally, and don't be afraid to relay these stories to your classes. Be honest and be yourself, because no matter what your personality is, it will be compatible with at least a portion of the class, and that portion will really connect with you. Although you may not share a special bond with every one of your students, don't use that as an excuse not to open yourself up. Be careful, though: Kids have a way of drawing out your stories so that they don't have to do much class work that day. Decide ahead of time how long you'll spin your yarn and then stick to your schedule.

✔ **Concern:** The greatest moment of my rookie-year teaching came unexpectedly at the end of a geometry class. My students were working together on practice problems, minutes before the bell was set to ring, and a young girl named Gayle raised her hand. "Mr. Kelley," she said. "Yesterday, in my health class, we were talking about the teachers in this school — which ones you could go to if you had problems and needed to talk or something. We all agreed that, even though you're new, it's really obvious that you care about your students, and I thought somebody should let you know that." That said, she returned to her work, leaving me to respond with the equally memorable comment, "Uh, well, that's, hey, thanks for the, uh, yeah, thanks."

✔ **Passion:** I don't mean you should add love scenes to your classes to spice them up, à la *The Young and the Restless*. By *passion,* I mean that you should convey how excited you are about what you're teaching. If you're excited and interested, your students can't help but get caught up in your enthusiasm.

✔ **Legacy:** After a student has left your class, more than anything else in the world, she wants you to remember her name. Perhaps you've had one of those moments when you saw one of your elementary-school teachers buying butter at the grocery store. You rushed up and said hello, but the teacher couldn't quite seem to place your face, let alone remember your name. The same thing will happen to you. After kids leave my class, except for a select few, I immediately forget most of their last names, and I'm only 50-50 on first names at that point. Don't feel guilty if, years down the road, you can't remember a student's name, even though it would be nice to think you'll always remember them as if they were still in your classes. You may want to have a prepared line for such chance meetings, like, "I know you were in my class a few years ago, and I remember that you were a lot of fun to teach, but in my senility I can no longer pair your face with your name."

When I asked what they wanted from teachers, the only thing students couldn't come to a consensus on is whether they wanted their classes to be extra easy or extra challenging. Of course, that's a decision you'll make regardless of what students want, and your class will probably fall somewhere in the middle of that spectrum. One student told me, "Kids who wanted to learn and weren't afraid to work loved your class, but the students who were lazy had a hard time," and in my opinion, that's about how it should work out.

Part V
Duties Other than Teaching

The 5th Wave   By Rich Tennant

"Of course you're angry at me for springing a surprise memory quiz on you, but you've got to learn to forgive and forget."

In this part . . .

Figuring out how to be a good teacher is a hard enough task when you're a rookie, but it's only a part of what you're expected to do when you sign that contract on the dotted line. Welcome to the wonderful world of filling out overwhelming stacks of paperwork, sponsoring after-school activities, serving duty periods, and even providing occasional medical care! In this part, you get to try on all the different hats you're expected to wear as a teacher, until you realize (as most teachers eventually do) that you just don't look good in hats and would much rather go bare-headed if you had the choice.

Chapter 17

Implicit and Explicit Duties

• •

In This Chapter

▶ Surviving hall, cafeteria, recess, and whatever other duties are thrown at you

▶ Sponsoring clubs and extracurricular activities

▶ Finding out what happens during those mysterious in-service days

▶ Maintaining your teaching credentials

• •

*E*very teacher I've ever known has the same fantasy, and no, it doesn't involve supermodels or anything remotely kinky. The fantasy all teachers share is the 9-to-5 job, the occupation that requires little or no time commitment outside of its posted contractual hours. If you inspect your contract closely, you'll see that you're probably required to come in a fixed period of time before school and to stay at work for a little while after the final dismissal has occurred. For example, I was required to come in 15 minutes before school started and had to stay 20 minutes after school was over. But 35 minutes wasn't nearly enough time to accomplish everything I had to do before I actually dragged myself out to my car and drove home.

In this chapter, I discuss all the odd jobs and responsibilities you'll have both during and after school hours. I was surprised just how much stuff I had to do that had absolutely nothing to do with education, and just how bizarre and varied the tasks were. Sure, you pull down a paycheck as a professionally trained instructor, but did you know you'll probably serve time as a policeman, security guard, substitute teacher, and sports coach as well?

Doing Your Duty

If you were to sit down and calculate how many hours you spend at work actually in front of a chalkboard teaching, you'd be shocked. I'd estimate that about 35 percent of your time will be dedicated to nonteaching tasks. The most obvious of these is the mandated duty time you'll be assigned at the beginning of the school year, during which you'll do riveting things that you can only do in this profession, like watch 500 kids eat lunch with their mouths open or supervise kickball games.

Even though they're usually unpleasant, you're contractually required to perform any duties requested by your principal. Look at your contract closely and find out how much duty-free time during the day you're guaranteed; it usually boils down to at least one class period and, at the minimum, a 30-minute lunch period. However, if the need is pressing enough, your principal often has the contractual right to ask you to give up your planning time to perform a duty for him. If he does, don't wave your contract around and threaten to lodge a complaint with the teachers' union.

You're new at the school, and you need to demonstrate that you're a team player. You want to show the principal you're someone he can count on. However, keep track of all the extra duties he asks you to perform so that you can (respectfully) remind him how many times you've pitched in if the requests become too numerous.

The amount of time you'll spend embroiled by these mind-numbing and often tedious duties varies from school district to school district. Whereas I was required to teach five 45-minute classes and perform a daily 15-minute duty, some districts require their teachers to perform a full duty period each day. However long you have to spend, though, the tasks remain roughly the same. In the following sections, I give you a quick primer on all the basic duties you may face, and some tips to help you muddle through what often is the most unpleasant part of your school day.

Cafeteria duty

Some people say that if you hold a seashell up to your ear, you can almost hear the gentle roar of the ocean. By the same principle, if you hold a yellow plastic cafeteria plate up to your ear, you'll be able to hear hundreds of children yelling as loudly as their teeny vocal chords can possibly allow. What is it about overprocessed fish patties served with macaroni and cheese that causes kids to try to bring down the walls by talking as boisterously as they can? I've been at rock concerts that were significantly quieter than school cafeterias (although by contrast, most of the people at the concert were drinking something other than 6-ounce containers of milk).

If you've drawn the short straw of cafeteria duty, it's your lot in life to patrol the lunchroom looking for potential trouble. Your biggest job will be to keep an eye on the lunch line, to make sure students aren't cutting in unfairly; nothing causes a ruckus faster than a student trying to sneak in line ahead of other kids. Very rarely is there anything so dramatic as a food fight in the cafeteria, which may surprise you if you've seen a lot of John Belushi movies. However, the cafeteria does provide a fertile atmosphere for fights to break out. Think about it: Kids are packed in there like sardines, and it's one of the few places that the student-to-adult ratio is skewed way in the favor of the kids.

And in this corner . . .

Is it your job to break up student fights? When I was a rookie, I would have answered that question with a resounding yes, but now I'm more hesitant. I've seen too many teachers get punched, scratched, and kicked trying to subdue feuding students to make me fly in with reckless abandon. However, as dangerous as it is, students need to feel safe at school, and sometimes you need to put yourself in harm's way to make that happen.

If a fight breaks out anywhere near your room, you'll know immediately. Kids flock to fight scenes like ants to spilled sugar (only a lot faster). If the tone of the hallway suddenly changes, and the ambient noise suddenly increases or falls deathly silent (except for the sound of running ant feet), you probably have trouble on your hands. If you're near the intercom buzzer, immediately page the office, and have an administrator sent, even if you're not absolutely positive there's been an altercation. If you're nowhere near an intercom, tell a student to find a buzzer and to call for the principal. Run into an adjacent room and ask a fellow teacher or staff member to come help you.

When the two of you come upon the fight scene, try to get between the grappling students — if they're fist fighting, that is. If you see weapons, focus on clearing the area of students without actually stepping into the crossfire. Most of the time, the combat will merely be hand to hand, and you can shove your way between the combatants. Each of you should face one of the students, outstretch your arms, and guide them away from each other as swiftly as possible, saying things like, "It's over, take it easy. Relax and don't do anything to make the situation worse than it already is." If the fighting students try to drive past you to get back at each other, use your arms to block the students and physically restrain them if necessary until administrators and/or school security officials arrive.

To make lunch duty go by faster, don't just stand against the wall and stare at the clock, trying to will the minute hand forward with the power of your mind. Walk around the cafeteria and talk to the kids ("Hey, Jared, did you study for my test last night? How many cupcakes did you bring for lunch? Sixteen? There's no way your mom packed that, unless your mom owns Hostess!"). Be friendly, engaging even the students you don't know in conversation. If those kids don't know you personally, they've probably heard about you through their friends, and you'll be surprised how many unfamiliar faces call you by name.

Hallway, parking lot, and recess duty

I clump all these duties together because they all serve the same two purposes:

✔ Maintaining the safety of your students

✔ Ensuring that no one enters or leaves the school premises without authorization

If you see adults or older students you don't recognize, don't be afraid to ask who they are and why they're on campus. Most schools have visitor badges or some way of identifying visitors to the school, so you should be checking for those. Furthermore, make sure all the students out of class have a pass in hand. Those are your main responsibilities.

Too many teachers who have security-related duties routinely ignore them — especially hallway duty. They figure, "Those poor saps in the cafeteria! Everyone can tell if they don't show up for duty, but I'm supposed to be roaming the halls, so no one knows exactly where I am. If I just close my classroom door and turn off the light, who would be the wiser?" Be glad you have a duty that allows you to move around the building or be outside for a change, but don't use that as an opportunity to neglect your responsibility.

If you're an elementary-school teacher, and you have recess or hallway duty, you need to be up to speed on many school policies. For example, if you're patrolling the recess grounds, what do you do about:

✔ Bathroom needs. (Are students allowed to go into the building? Do you have to supervise them?)

✔ Kids who refuse to wear coats even when it's so cold that exposed skin instantly freezes.

✔ Bullying.

And how do you signal the kids to indicate that it's time to line up to back inside?

If it's hallway duty you're covering, how loud are the kids supposed to be? Do they have to walk in single-file lines? If you're in the cafeteria, what do you do if a kid drops her tray or wets his pants? Get answers to these questions before you report to your first such duty day.

Covering other classes

When I was in college, I figured that the best way to earn money during breaks was to substitute teach. Not only would it help me develop good class-management skills, it was also just six hours of work a day. Needless to say, I was shocked to discover that the pay for those six hours was only $35. In essence, the school district was paying me minimum wage to deal with belligerent kids all day long. Is it any wonder that schools have a hard time hiring and keeping substitute teachers?

Even though you may be tempted to say, "That's not my problem," you'd be very wrong. When there aren't enough substitutes to cover all the teacher-less classes, guess who winds up stepping in? You! Covering other teachers' classes is the duty I hated the most, because it was by its very nature completely unexpected. Nothing upsets your day quite like someone calling into your room during the first class of the day and asking you to spend your planning period watching somebody else's kids. Hope you didn't intend to actually do any *planning* during that period!

Covering classes is the least relaxing of all the duty assignments, because it's the equivalent of the first day of school for you. These students don't know you, and they're much more likely to test your authority than are your own students, whom you've already broken in. The best way to keep these kids under control is with this nifty statement: "In case you don't know me, I'm a teacher in this school as well. I know you wouldn't be disrespectful enough to misbehave while I'm here doing your teacher a favor. However, if you do, you'll come to my room and serve detention with me, even if your teacher decides to give you detention as well."

Assembly duty

Whether you think of them as a blessed change of pace or a waste of instructional time, you're going to attend your share of in-school assemblies. I've seen pep rallies, holiday programs, fundraiser kickoff events, antidrug slideshows presented by soft-drink companies, and even a reenacted drunk-driving-accident scene starring the local police and members of the school's drama classes. No matter what the event, however, my school discovered that students were much better behaved if they had to sit with the teacher and other members of the class being preempted by the assembly. Students get brave enough to shout or throw things when the lights go down in an assembly area if they can blend into the mob anonymously. Therefore, the best defense against disruptive behavior is removing the possibility of being anonymous.

If your school doesn't assign seats at an assembly, you need to take action. Inform your class that they're to follow you to the assembly and sit where you indicate, no matter what students from other classes do. (I'm sure the rows up front will be empty if the other kids are allowed to choose their own seating.) When you're seated with your class, take attendance to make sure no one has ignored your orders and snuck off to sit next to a boyfriend or girlfriend. Then sit there with your kids and make sure they behave.

Some veteran teachers view an assembly as an opportunity to pawn their kids off on someone else. They send their class to the auditorium and head straight for the teacher's lounge to chat or take a nap, secure in the knowledge that if their kids misbehave, someone else will be there to take care of it.

Because of these lazy faculty members, you're going to have to keep an ear out during the assembly and deal with any discipline issues that arise, even when they're not your kids. Don't just drop your kids off and stand in the back of the auditorium, chatting with other teachers. Walk around the aisles as a visual reminder to all the students that you'll be on them like stink on a monkey if they step out of line.

Clerical duties

If the office is short-handed, you may be asked to answer phones, take messages, deliver announcements to teachers, or copy things. This is the best duty of them all, because time goes by much faster when you have tasks to accomplish. Perhaps it's just the type-A part of my personality speaking up, but I'd rather accomplish something during a duty than stroll about and "supervise."

The duty state of mind

Eventually, every teacher comes to dread his duty period or duty assignment. Most of the time, you have to act as a security guard and discipline students you don't even know. Because they don't know you, these students are much more willing to be disrespectful, which makes the already unpleasant task of standing around all the more unpleasant.

I hadn't been on my first cafeteria duty more than two weeks when a student tried to sneak by me. "Excuse me, sir, you can't leave here without a pass," I advised, standing with my best authoritative posture. He responded by sprinting away from me into the halls, counting on the fact that I wouldn't pursue him wearing slippery dress shoes, but he was wrong. Even though there was a little thrill coursing through me (I felt like one of the policemen on that TV show *Cops,* chasing down a perpetrator), another part of me kept nagging, "Did you really sign up to be a teacher to chase boneheads through the halls?"

Don't let yourself become negative about your duty, no matter how much you dislike it. I know

it feels like a complete waste of time, and you could be getting things accomplished if you had *some* time to spend in your room for a change. Some teachers get so bitter that they have to "baby-sit" students during what they view as their time off that they bring papers to grade or lesson-planning materials to their duty station. Rather than keep an eye on kids, they immerse themselves in work, thinking, "At least I'm sitting here, and the principal's lucky I'm even doing that." Some protest having duties by showing up for them late, which is even worse, because that usually means the teacher serving that duty post before them has to stay longer.

Don't exhibit this sort of passive-aggressive behavior. Remember that some people have it a lot worse than you do. Administrators and instructional aides have to log a lot more time doing boring stuff like this, and they spend hours each day dealing with the unpleasantness that you only get a taste of during your duty.

The Joys of Sponsorship

When I was in school, I participated in a lot of extracurricular activities, but most of them ended in the word *band*. I'm not afraid to admit it — I was a trumpet player and a band nerd. Whether it was pit band (for musicals), pep band (at basketball games), marching band (for football games), jazz band, wind ensemble, or orchestra, I was part of them all. Note that even though I was present at different sporting events, I in no way participated in sporting events at school. Of course, I played baseball on a summer league and basketball or football on the weekends with my buddies, but when it came to school-sponsored sports, I kept far away.

The reason is simple: When you're playing sports with your friends, you aren't afraid that you'll look like a totally inept jerk when you try to shoot a basketball or steal second base. Your friends already know that you possess roughly the same athletic skill as a bag of pistachios. However, you'd like to hide this fact from the general public, because there is great potential for merciless teasing at the hands of students able to perform complex athletic maneuvers, like climbing ropes or serving a volleyball overhand.

Now that I have revealed my embarrassing personal history to you, imagine my horror when I was called into the athletic director's office during my rookie year and asked to coach a sport! "We need an assistant coach for boys' and girls' track this year, and we'd like you to help us out," he said, with a straight face. He had actually been a coach at my high school when I was younger, so I tried to jog his memory. "Rick, I've never coached a day in my life, and I don't know the first thing about any track and field event. Once I tried to high-jump in gym class and landed really badly; the doctor wasn't sure I'd ever be able to have children."

Nevertheless, the athletic director couldn't be swayed. "It's not like you'll be the head coach or anything. Celia's the head coach, and she'll teach you everything you need to know. All you need to do is buy a whistle and show up on the track at 2:30 starting March 1." What could I do? I kept insisting that all I knew about track was that it involved a lot of running, but he kept insisting that no one else wanted to do it, which made me the perfect candidate.

I went to meet Celia and tried to explain to her that, even though I was willing to help out if she needed me, she might be better off with an athletic monkey for a coach than me, but she was just as maddeningly patient. "You don't need to learn how to coach all the events right away," she said, "but you do need to start off with the hurdles, because my hurdling form isn't what it used to be." To prove her point, she suddenly took off running at a hurdle set up in the hallway and bounded over it with the grace of a gazelle.

To be more specific, she possessed the grace of an *enormous* gazelle; perhaps I have forgotten to mention that she was more than eight months pregnant at the time. I stood amazed, my mouth agape at the agility she was able to muster in spite of being days away from delivering a baby. "Every time I hurdle, I get a contraction, so my doctor doesn't want me doing it anymore," she said. "That's why I need you."

You'll probably find yourself in a similar predicament when you start teaching. There are always a few coaching spots, sponsorship roles, or committee memberships that are vacant at the start of every school year, because nobody wants them. Even if somebody gets suckered into filling the spot, they quit as soon as possible at the end of the school year. At my school, there were two positions that were perpetually empty: track assistant and cheerleading sponsor. Every year a new rookie teacher would take those positions, and the following year, a new one would take his place.

Principals have lots of extracurricular positions to fill when the school year starts, and they look to rookies to pitch in and help out. Most of the veteran teachers in the school are either already helping or have helped in years past, and the mantle gets passed to the new folks. If you're not sure how to get involved in after-school activities, don't worry — the principal is going to come to you! Most likely, he'll need you to play a role you're not used to or may not think you're good at, like my stint as track coach. I would much rather have sponsored a more academically oriented club, and I even mentioned that at my job interview, but it didn't matter.

When you're new, you rarely get to pick and choose how you're going to help out, so you need to be flexible and help out wherever you're needed. Of course, you always have the option to say no if asked, but it won't stop there. Days later, the principal's shadow will once again be darkening your doorstep with a new request, and he'll continue to haunt you until you cave in. Don't even think about trying the "Well, I'm a new teacher, and I'm still trying to get settled" excuse. Everybody tries it, and it never works. "You never feel like you're settled," the principal will say, giving you the look a snake gives a bird right before it unhinges its jaw and swallows the bird whole, "Something always comes up to throw you off balance, so you may as well start now."

No matter how bizarre the job request, don't turn the principal down. Give it your best shot; most of the time, you'll do fine, and you'll experience a whole world you never knew existed. I actually came to enjoy track practice after school, and was named the head coach for girls' track the following year, when the school decided to separate the boys' and girls' programs. My team did extremely well, and I became very emotionally attached to the girls. I ran their laps with them, had long conversations about adolescent stress and the pervasive boyfriend drama that saturates girls of that age, and helped them with their homework on the bus to and from track meets. During my second and final year as head coach, we even won the conference track championship and finished in the top ten schools at the state track meet.

You don't have to coach for your entire career. When your administrators see that you've helped out for two or three years, they won't mind if you bow out and leave it up to the new batch of rookies to take your place. But don't blend back into the woodwork completely. Watch for sponsoring positions that you're interested in to come open. If there aren't any, start a new club of your own based on your personal interests. After I stopped coaching track, I established an academic quiz team at my school and built a nice program with the help of some dedicated and motivated students.

By sponsoring extracurricular clubs and activities, you're showing students, parents, and school officials that you're dedicated to your job. You certainly don't do it for the pay. (My assistant track coach salary worked out to almost $2 an hour for the amount of time I spent coaching that first year.) You do it because you love to be around kids, and kids act differently after the school dismissal bell has rung. Working with kids after school is a reward in itself; students stay after school voluntarily, because they want to enrich their lives with a variety of experiences. They have a great deal of respect for those teachers who stay after school.

Life after School

Because I spend so much time talking about track in the preceding section, allow me to use a track analogy for a moment. Occasionally, at the end of a race, a runner will turn on a burst of speed for the last hundred yards or so, in an attempt to pass by his fellow racers when they've already spent all their reserve energy. Track coaches know this is a bad sign, and whenever one of my runners did this, I'd say, "If you had that much energy to give at the end of the race, you should have been running faster the whole time." By the end of the race, you shouldn't have anything left to give, because every fiber of every muscle should be pushed to the very pinnacle of what it can offer.

I followed this same principle as a teacher. I figured, "Why go home with boundless energy if I can use that same energy to keep my kids entertained in the classroom?" There were days when I thought that final dismissal bell would never ring — it's that same feeling a marathon runner must feel as the finish line finally appears at the edge of the horizon. Will I have enough left in me to make it across the line, or am I going to sputter out right in the middle of this last lesson of the day?

If you're coaching or sponsoring extracurricular activities, you already know that the final school bell doesn't signify the end of your workday. You can't pull a Fred Flintstone and slide down the dinosaur's back, leap into your car, and drive home. Instead, that signal means you have to change into sweatpants or climb onto a bus for an away game, fully knowing that you may not see the inside of your home until well after 10 or 11 p.m.

Even if you're not participating in after-school activities, the final bell doesn't mean work is over. All teachers have responsibilities that stretch well past quitting time that I've already described, besides the things like grading, making parent phone calls, and creating lesson plans. There are some things you're required to do that can't be accomplished at home.

Teaching after-hours

During my rookie year, I got a memo in my mailbox from the mathematics supervisor, which read in part, "Teachers are required to provide appropriate tutoring services after school for their students, and this is to be offered free of charge." It surprised me to find out that some teachers were actually making students pay for any tutoring they received after the contractual workday. If you think about it, however, not many other professions work after hours for free. If you need to see a doctor past his office hours, will she give you a checkup on the house?

Tutoring kids after school is just another one of those things that you, as a teacher, need to file under "Hey, it's best for the kids, even if it isn't ideal for me." There are lots of things doctors get to do that we don't (two-week vacation in the Caribbean, anyone?), and after all, you didn't get into teaching to do the minimum required to draw a paycheck, right? You became a teacher because you want to see kids succeed, and because you'd do just about anything, short of cutting off your fingers and toes, to help them out.

Tutoring can be one of the most frustrating things you have to do, even though it is one of the most effective ways to reach your kids when they don't understand. Part of you (the evil part) will be thinking, "Why couldn't you manage to figure this out when I was going over it in class? Maybe if you paid attention a little better, both of us could be home now. It's not as though I'm saying anything different than I was when the rest of the class was around!" After all, tutors get paid pretty good money to do what you're doing for free.

Do your best to dismiss these thoughts, because they don't help. Most of the time, kids who come after school for extra assistance just need you to explain things a little more slowly or in a little more depth. In fact, I had just as many high-level academic students stay after school as kids who'd be ecstatic to get a D in my class. Sometimes, they just want to know why something is true or want to talk about things in greater detail, but they're too embarrassed to do it during class, for fear of looking like a nerd. ("She actually cares about what we're learning! What a geek!")

Not many kids stay after school at the beginning of the school year. In fact, you won't see a big boom in business until right before Thanksgiving, when kids begin to realize that they're getting totally lost. It'll start with a trickle of kids that need help; if you do a good job with them, and make them feel welcome, before long you'll have a steady stream of repeat customers. The stream can get so heavy, in fact, that it sometimes floods its banks. Even though you don't mind helping kids after school, staying for hours and hours every night can begin to wear you out. Sometimes, you just have to go home when school's over and kick your feet up, but to do that you have to get organized.

For some reason, teachers and students alike have this preconceived notion that students should be tutored separately. It's as if no two students can be in your classroom at the same time after school. I'm not sure why this is. Perhaps students feel embarrassed if other kids find out they need extra help or have additional needs (sort of like why people don't want to run into folks they know at the psychiatrist's office). However, I've found that there is less stigma in coming for extra help when more students are around. Besides, the more students you can help at once, the fewer separate appointments you'll have to make!

When I was a rookie, I began holding what I called "Study Buddy Thursdays." The idea was that on Thursdays, any student in any of my classes who needed help could stay after, but here's the twist: I gave extra credit to students who didn't need help but who stuck around and helped out their peers. Some kids didn't go for it. In their minds, only a teacher could help them, and that's what teachers were getting paid for anyway. However, other kids felt much more comfortable dealing with people their own age. Of course, they could have just asked for help from these students during class, but that's awkward and almost as uncomfortable as asking them on a date. It's the whole "You don't know me and have no idea why I'm talking to you" situation that adolescents dread like pimples on prom night.

By giving extra credit to the tutors, I removed the stigma of staying after school because they were smart. Everybody appreciates the value of extra credit, no matter what you have to do to earn it. Because my Study Buddy days always fell on Thursdays and my tests and quizzes were always on Fridays, kids knew that they had one final chance to understand everything before they were tested on it, and it took a lot of pressure off everyone. If they were having trouble understanding in class, instead of saying, "I'll never get this, and you're not helping," they'd say, "Well, I guess I'll see you on Thursday."

I'm not going to lie to you. Study Buddy Thursday did not catch on right away. I'd have one or two nerdy (but nice) kids sitting around saying, "Are we still going to get extra credit if no one shows up? I could be watching cartoons right now." To combat that, I started bringing a case of soda pop and a couple bags of chips and cookies to the tutorial sessions. When there was food, as well as knowledge, to be had, I couldn't have beat students off with a stick, even a really nasty-looking stick with a nail sticking out of it, if I'd had one.

After a month or so of snacks, when my junk-food budget ran dry and the food stopped showing up, the students kept coming. In fact, I'd have between 20 and 30 kids every Thursday. Not all of them had questions, but they began to value the extra practice I offered on those Thursday afternoons. I'd separate the kids based on the classes I taught and then rotate between the groups, offering advice. When I was with other groups, they'd vent about their test anxiety, help one another with tips they'd come up with, and generally feel less uptight about the upcoming quiz. However, the best benefit of all was that almost every kid who needed tutoring waited until Thursday for it, so that I could metaphorically kill 30 birds with one big stone. I could actually plan lessons after school Monday through Wednesday without interruption!

Attending school events

Of course, the most important part of being a teacher is imparting knowledge to young minds. I think I read that on a canvas tote bag once. However, you can't forget that, as a teacher, you aren't only an individual operating alone in a classroom but a cog in a much larger machine that is your school building. Don't neglect your role in the grand scheme of things by focusing solely on what you do in front of the chalkboard.

This means you need to involve yourself in things at your school other than what's happening in your classroom. I know you live to help kids, but you need to make it a priority to help out your school and your colleagues as well. The most successful rookie teachers put in some solid hours at school well after almost everyone else has gone home. Without a doubt, other teachers and administrators at your school are going to find out which car you drive and are going to pay attention to when you come and go. If your car is always gone when they walk out into the parking lot, they'll think you're slacking, because they know that good teachers are never clock watchers.

Staying after school gives you the unique opportunity to work with your kids and your colleagues in a much more relaxed atmosphere. It shows your students that you care about them, even when they're not paying you to do so, and it tells your colleagues that you'll pitch in and do your share. In the following sections, I fill you in on a couple of things you can do to increase your face time at school after all the buses have left. These two ideas will get you started, and I guarantee that if you follow through with them, you'll deepen your relationships with all the people you see every day, as well as with a bunch of people (like parents) whom you may never even meet.

Attend your students' sporting events or performances

Kids work hard after school, putting in countless hours of practice on the athletic field, or weeks and weeks' worth of rehearsal into dramatic productions. Nothing means more to students than if you make a special effort to see them play at a sporting event or perform onstage. They put so much

The dangers of schmoozing

I mention my friend Rob a number of times in this book. He was a new teacher hired the same year as I was, and he became one of my closest friends. I've heard that traumatic experiences shared by people can bring them closer together, and the trauma of being rookie teachers bonded us together in no time at all. All the piddly things rookies are expected to do in order to mark themselves as "team players" and visibly "pay their dues" are very draining and emotionally exhausting. However, if you have a friend to endure the pain with, it's much easier.

Rob and I knew that we had to be visible at school events, because it was very important to our principal. So we made it a point to get to as many athletic events and school functions as we could. After we arrived, we'd always make it a point to find the principal and engage him in a few minutes of small talk, which we called *schmoozing,* because the purpose of the conversation was not to actually convey any information, but rather to make sure the principal knew we had come to the event. I mean, what's the use of giving up your Saturday night to watch a junior varsity basketball game if the person you're trying to impress by coming doesn't even know you came?

On one cold November evening, we quickly learned that schmoozing is a double-edged sword. Rob and I had stayed very late one Friday evening to try to knock out as much work as we could before the weekend got underway. Our rooms were across the hall from one another, so we often would pick one room and work together — having company seemed to make the time go by faster. Engrossed in our endless grading, but making real progress, neither of us looked up at the clock until it was almost 7 p.m. Yikes! It had been four hours of work, and we hadn't eaten lunch since 10:30 that morning. (It seems a crime to call such an early meal lunch, but that's the lot of the public-school teacher.)

I had a brilliant idea. "Rob, let's go to the football concession stand for dinner. The game's supposed to start in a half-hour, and we can schmooze it up with the principal for a few minutes, make it look like we stayed for the game, and then sneak out when no one's looking." My feet were killing me; I had bought new (cheap faux-leather) shoes, and they refused to be broken in. The leatheresque material wouldn't give, and every step squeezed my feet painfully. All I wanted was a semiwarm hot dog, a flat soda, and a car ride home to take off my shoes and give my toes a break.

When we got outside, we saw that it had begun to rain, but we grabbed our snacks and set out to find the principal. When we finally found him, he looked panicked. "The chain gang isn't here," he said. (The *chain gang* is the group of two or three people that works the large, orange pylons at the edge of the football field that mark first downs.) "I need you guys to jump in and work the chains for me. The game was supposed to start five minutes ago, and we need you. Go! Run!" With this, he shoved us across the football field, between the two waiting teams, and we were trapped.

We spent three hours running back and forth in wet grass, chilled to the bone by the ice-like pellets of rain. One of the players was even pushed out of bounds right at Rob, and they collided at full speed, but unfortunately, only the kid was wearing protective pads. I still remember looking into the sheets of driving rain, shivering as I held up my orange marker, and hearing Rob say, "So, you just *had* to get a hotdog today. Next time, we'll grab dinner at McDonald's and save schmoozing for a drier day."

work into these hobbies, and it's a real opportunity to show them that you care about them regardless of whether they're able to divide decimal numbers or not. In fact, sometimes attending these extracurricular events is a real eye-opener, especially if the kid isn't doing so hot in your class.

I remember going to a soccer game once, at the request of five or six soccer players I taught, and seeing one of my worst students really tear up the soccer field, scoring countless goals, and making incredible play after incredible play. I remember thinking, "Wow, so John really is good at *something*." Meanwhile, John was probably thinking, "Wow, Kelley actually made it to one of our games. Maybe he doesn't really do math 24 hours a day." Even though you may not think that they notice you're in the stands watching, they'll find out. Teachers who attend school events are sort of minicelebrities: "Hey look, Mom, there's Mr. Kelley in the stands, sitting next to that girl who played Winnie Cooper on *The Wonder Years*."

Help out at a school activity

It's rare for rookie teachers to come into a school and immediately start hosting after-school events and functions. Not only are you just trying to make it from day to day, you also have little or no idea what kinds of activities others at the school are already involved in. However, that shouldn't prevent you from lending a helping hand to your colleagues if they need you.

I did all sorts of things to assist my fellow teachers, some of which I volunteered for and others I just got sucked into. Here are a few of the things I did after school to pitch in, to help you get a flavor of the breadth and variety of things you'll get involved with. Even though I didn't do all of these during my rookie year, about half of them did fall within that first crucial (and crushingly busy) school year:

- Kept score and ran the time clock at cross-country meets
- Acted as stadium announcer for soccer games
- Ran the scoreboard and shot clock for basketball games
- Patrolled the parking lots during football games
- Manned the math table for freshman orientation night
- Served as department chair for mathematics
- Chaired a committee for the School Improvement Team
- Waited tables for a fund-raising chorus concert
- Sang karaoke at homecoming games to raise money for Students Against Drunk Driving (my eclectic repertoire included such selections as the *Love Boat* Theme, "I Got You Babe," and "Who Let the Dogs Out")
- Participated in the student drug-abuse prevention program

✔ Acted in the all-faculty Christmas plays (reprising roles such as Scrooge and the Grinch — talk about typecasting!)

✔ Chaperoned school dances

✔ Helped build floats for homecoming

Of course, the kinds of activities you'll be involved in depends upon what grades you'll teach. For example, elementary-school teachers can volunteer for coaching things like math team, spelling bowl, or ecology club. Whether they call it the PTA, PTO, or PTSA, attend parent-teacher meetings, even if they're held in the evenings (most are). Volunteer to help at chili suppers, school carnivals, pancake suppers, food drives, concession stands, or any other activity that pops up (even it it's not food-related).

When you're the most stressed, spending time at the school building when you don't have to is the last thing you'll want to do. However, it's the best way to get to know the administrators, teachers, and students on a more personal level, and you'll find that the better you know the people you work with, the more you'll want to come to work. That's why I think of investing extracurricular time as getting a vaccination. Sure the shot stings a little at first, but it helps prevent much worse things (like burnout) later on.

Developing Professionally

In the midst of trying to develop stacks of daily lesson plans and keeping on top of more grading than you'd ever imagine one person should have to, teachers are also expected to keep current in their training. I know you're probably fresh out of college or certification training, but before long, you'll be enrolling in education classes again. Even better, every couple months, you'll have to undergo the bane of all teachers' existence: teacher in-service meetings! Even though all these things are supposed to make you a better and more knowledgeable teacher (and you'll have to excuse my sarcasm here), all they ever manage to do is eat up time better spent doing more practical things.

Tolerating intolerable in-services

There's something magical about a teacher in-service day, especially if it falls on a Friday. Sure, you still have to roll out of bed, shower, and put pants on to go to work, but it's a 100-percent kid-free day! Not that you don't like the kids (they're starting to grow on you), but isn't it fantastic to see how the other half lives for one day? Maybe you'll even have time for a cup of coffee in the morning and be able to use the bathroom at your leisure! Yes, all signs point to an in-service day as a painless way to ease into the weekend, and on top of everything, you can wear jeans guilt-free! Unfortunately, that's not the way it works.

Here's a joke I once heard that will explain it all. An old man dies, and as his spirit rises into heaven, he sees the glorious majesty of a perfect and stainless afterlife. Golden rivers flow around him, everyone smiles, and nary a shadow can be found. St. Peter takes him on a guided tour of heaven upon his arrival. "What is that great and wondrous palace I see in the distance?" the old man asks, and St. Peter answers, "It is the mansion reserved for those who dedicated their lives to children as teachers. Because of the hardships they endured upon the earth and the oath of poverty they took, they are reserved the greatest place in heaven." The old man was puzzled. "But why does it seem so empty?" he asked, and St. Peter responded, "Well, once every two weeks, the teachers still have in-service meetings in Hell."

I can count the number of useful in-service meetings I attended on the fingers of one hand (and in this case, no, the thumb doesn't count as a finger). As much as I looked forward to in-service meetings, longing for a day of collegial bonding and a chance to get caught up on my grading, the days always ended up chock-full of meetings. School-based meetings, district-based meetings, department meetings, faculty meetings . . . the list goes on and on. And by the end of all the meetings, you'll wish you had been teaching all day, even if you had your worst group of students for the entire time. Honestly, subject-area supervisors have better things to do than plan out busywork for their teachers, and teachers have better things to do than listen to all that drivel. But the eternal dance spins on: Administrators have to organize meetings they'd rather not facilitate, and teachers have to attend meetings that are just slightly more interesting than watching dough rise.

Here's a quick rundown of the different types of in-service meetings you'll attend:

- **The "I'm going to read you this memo" meeting.** When an administrator has something important he'd like to get across, whether it's the beginning of school procedures or a change in policy, he'll send you a memo on the topic. A few hours later, you'll have a meeting, and he'll read the memo word for word. Your mind will scream, "I already read this!" or, "Why can't we take 5 minutes and read the memo in our classrooms instead of spending 90 minutes having it read to us and discussed from every possible angle? Talk about beating a dead horse."

- **The "Look what she can do" meeting.** Occasionally, administrators will be very impressed with someone's lesson plan and ask her to present that lesson plan to her school, grade level, or subject-specific colleagues. No matter how good the lesson is, however, this is not the place to share it. Either colleagues are insulted ("Are you trying to tell me how to teach?"), uninterested, or at the very least distracted.

If you're ever put in the unenviable position of having to present at an in-service meeting, remember these three words: *Keep it short.* No long setup or explanation about where the lesson plan came from or lengthy discussion of how much your kids loved it. Get to the point, do your demonstration, and sit back down. If you talk longer than ten minutes, you'll feel hostility radiating toward you like the heat blown out of a space heater.

✔ **The "We want to have your input" meeting.** Woe to you if you ever hear the words "We'd like everyone to buy into this process, so we want everyone's feedback." What this means in noneducation-speak is, "The administration has decided on a policy change, and rather than imple-ment the change ourselves, we're going to have you do all the work during in-service meetings under the guise of 'valuing your input.'" When my school district decided to implement countywide final exams, guess who got to write them all? Teachers during in-service time. For years, we had to toil, writing thousands of test items, while our own work sat untouched in our classrooms.

✔ **The "horizontal planning" meeting.** This is the Holy Grail of in-service meetings, much desired, but rarely experienced. In essence, it's a chance to meet some or all the people in your school district who are teaching the same subjects to the same-aged kids. You can informally chat about interesting ways to teach things, find out how your pacing compares with other classrooms ("You're already on Chapter 14! I haven't even gotten to the double digits yet!"), and trade tests and quizzes to see if yours are of comparable difficulty. They call them *horizontal planning meetings* because you and your fellow teachers are all at the same level on the organizational chart, colleagues in the truest sense of the word, because no one has a supervisory role over any other person in the group. These meetings are your chance to vent, seek advice, and make connections with folks who can help you all year long.

All teachers really want on their in-service days is a chance to get caught up on lesson planning and grading, and that's the one thing administrators don't want to provide.

Taking classes on the weekend

If you graduated from college certified to teach, you had to take approxi-mately 7 bazillion classes. I know that I managed to squeeze out my academic major and teacher-certification coursework in 4 years, but the downside was numerous 18-credit semesters. In fact, I only had room for a single two-credit elective during my entire stint at college (no cool classes like the History of American Cartoons or Sailing, which was big at my school because we were right on the water). By the time you come out of college, clutching a degree in one hand and a prescription for Valium in the other, you're ready to say goodbye to education classes for good.

It turns out that "for good" lasts approximately eight months, because if you wait much longer than that to start signing up for recertification classes, you're going to get overwhelmed. Different states have different requirements, but if you go more than a year without earning any credits (whether in-service credits earned at teacher-training courses run by state and local institutions or graduate credits earned in a master's degree program), you'll regret it later. Don't wait to get started! In Maryland, where I taught, you had to earn a fixed number of credits during your first two years of teaching and then a much larger clump of credits a few years down the road. Make sure you talk to the personnel department in your school district and find out exactly what you have to take, and how soon, in order to keep your certification current.

The best time to take your classes is during the summer, when you don't have a ton of schoolwork to stress over. If you're not able to enroll in those courses, your next best option is to attend classes on the weekend. (You really don't want to have to worry about completing assigned readings and writing papers during the week). If you have the option, sign up for classes that run longer hours but meet on fewer days. Sure, it hurts to get up on a Saturday morning, drive to a class, and sit there for six or seven hours, but it'll be over much sooner, so you can get back to your regular schedule.

If you don't like leaving home (that is, you're a hermit like me), you can always sign up for correspondence courses. They aren't usually any less expensive, but you can watch the classes on video at your leisure. There is one caveat though: Correspondence courses require a *ton* of writing, probably four or five times more writing than a typical class, so keep that in mind. With the tapes, you can watch lectures in your underwear on Saturday nights if you want (talk about a flourishing social life), but you'll be writing until your fingers are throbbing and sore.

The good news about recertification classes is that 95 percent of them are so easy, it's embarrassing, and that goes true for both graduate and in-service credits. They may as well call the courses "Jump through these hoops and I'll give you a cookie," because basically, all you have to do to get a great grade is agree with what the instructor says, no matter how you really feel inside.

One of the first things you'll do at these classes is *journal,* or write your thoughts and feelings about whatever it is you're about to learn. Always write your first journal entry in a skeptical tone. For example, if the class is about cooperative learning, your first journal entry should say, "I've always believed that a student should learn completely isolated from other students, but I'm willing to keep an open mind." By the end of the last class, your journals should reflect an enthusiastic (if insincere) excitement about cooperative learning, like this: "I never understood how valuable cooperative learning can be! This class has really opened my eyes to new ways of reaching my students, and I know I'll be a better teacher for it." After all, you probably did learn *something* during the class (even if it wasn't worth losing every Saturday for six weeks), and being negative about the class or criticizing the instructor isn't going to get you anywhere or win you any Miss Congeniality awards. Find something nice to say, and part friends.

Chapter 18

Navigating the Sea of Paperwork

• •

In This Chapter

▶ Taming the paper tiger of daily record-keeping

▶ Developing a system to keep track of attendance

▶ Staying on top of memos, reports, and your to-do list

▶ Designing lesson plans for substitute teachers

• •

Maybe it was because teaching was my first real job, but I used to get excited about the weirdest stuff when I was a rookie. In the beginning, I got revved up about checking papers, returning parent phone calls, and (strangest of all) checking my mailbox in the main office. I swear, I must have cruised into the mail room six or seven times a day to casually peer into the small metal receiving tray that bore my name. Unfortunately, it was almost always empty. All the other teachers always seemed to have stacks of colorful catalogs, notes from guidance counselors, and important-looking memos in giant stacks that, no matter how often it was emptied, jammed the mailbox so full it bulged in the middle, bowing under the full weight of all that mail.

I had a pretty severe case of mailbox envy for the first year or so, wishing I had pressing documents to take care of on a daily basis — until the mail started to find its way to me. Don't you worry, it'll find you too, and the excitement you once felt checking your box will turn slowly to groans of dismay when each trip you make is rewarded with stacks of paperwork. Just like any other bureaucratic organization, teaching has its fair share of mind-numbing forms and reports that need to be completed day in and day out. In this chapter, I discuss the monster that is paperwork, a monster that sits menacingly on your desk, devours entire planning periods without a thought, and (if you turn your back for just one moment) can wreak serious havoc.

Hiking the Daily Paper Trail

One of the major themes you're probably picking up from this book is that teaching students is only a portion of what you're expected to do as a teacher. I view all of a teacher's responsibilities as a big metaphoric stew.

Teaching students is the most important thing, so that would have to be the meat cubes in the stew, and paperwork would play the role of the vegetables. No matter how good the meat is, there are always more vegetables in the stew by volume, and there's no way to ladle out pieces of beef without drawing out a few soggy vegetables as well — it's just a fact of life. In the following sections, I focus on the most common paperwork veggies, the ones you'll have to deal with every single day. A little later on in this chapter, I discuss some of the other big record-keeping jobs you'll have to undertake, even though you won't have to deal with them quite as often.

Attending to attendance

Among all the record-keeping responsibilities you have as a teacher, two biggies stand out: recording grades and keeping track of attendance. Of course, it makes sense that grading is a big deal, because grades are pretty much the only tangible thing a student walks away with when she's finished with school (excluding any crafts she may have made in class that involved gluing uncooked pasta to construction paper). However, attendance is equally important in a different way.

Did you know that your attendance records are actually legal documents and can be subpoenaed by the legal system? There are lots of reasons the courts may want to see how often a child comes to school, including criminal charges or custody cases involving that child. Believe it or not, significant parts of people's lives can be influenced by how well you took attendance each day. Saying these things makes me feel pretty guilty, because I was absolutely horrible at keeping an accurate roll.

I was fine at the beginning of the day, when the original attendance was taken. At my school, you were given an index card corresponding to each student in your first-period class, and by the end of that period every morning, you were supposed to place the cards for the absent students into an envelope and send them down to our central attendance office. Because I made it one of my student's jobs to deliver the envelope for me, she was always good about reminding me to take roll. However, when that class was gone, I had to remember to mark down absent students in the rest of my classes for the remainder of the day. There was no envelope or procedure to remind me, and I *always* forgot. It wasn't until I made taking attendance part of my routine that I actually remembered it on a regular basis.

As students did their warm-up activity, I would count heads. It's a very quick way to see if everyone's there, instead of going through one student at a time, with the "Say 'present' when I call your name" approach. If your count comes up short, it only takes a minute or two to figure out who's absent if you have a seating chart, and boom, you're all done. No fuss, no muss, and the whole procedure only takes about 30 seconds or so.

Roll call and revisionist history

Part of the reason I was bad at taking roll was that I tried to get into my lessons as fast as I could. Especially with young or behaviorally challenging classes, too much undirected time at the beginning of the period results in chaos later. You need to grab their attention mere moments after class begins, or you'll have lost your chance for the entire period. Therefore, in my extreme haste to get the ball rolling, I often forgot to set aside time to find out who was missing.

In fact, I did a bad job even when I remembered to take roll, because in the back of my mind, one thought kept echoing back and forth: "This is taking too long, and the kids are starting to get restless. If I don't start class, someone's going to call someone else a nasty name, and I'll have to run damage control for the rest of the period."

Because I was always in a rush to get my record-keeping responsibilities out of the way, things fell through the cracks. Sometimes, I'd forget to mark absences as excused, and other times, I know my tardy counts were way off, but in my mind, keeping the class calm and working was more important than knowing exactly how many times a student was in my class.

During my second year as a teacher, in my worst-behaved class, I noticed that a student was no longer showing up. My roll had been lax, but it was hard to miss him, because he sat in the front row and was almost 6 feet tall. "Hey, where's Joel?" I asked one day, finally noticing that he was gone. "Oh, he moved," a young girl sitting next to the newly vacated seat answered. "I think his whole family moved to South Carolina."

I hadn't remembered getting his textbook back from him, but I knew that the guidance office sometimes handled such things. The news made me happy! (When the enrollment of your worst class lessens, you count your blessings and don't ask too many questions.)

It was five weeks later that the principal came to my room and dropped a bomb. "Mr. Kelley, did you know that Joel Nieman was skipping class today? We found him in the cafeteria eating lunch with his girlfriend." My stomach tightened. "I thought he moved to South Carolina," I lamely responded. "He hasn't been in my class for more than a month." In fact, Joel had been enjoying two lunches every day for quite a while, under the guise of living in a different state. This is more than just having egg on your face — we're talking the whole omelet here, with green peppers and extra cheese thrown in on top.

The moral of the story: Never ever trust students to keep you informed about changes in your class roster. You need to get such changes in writing from the guidance office. Also, no matter how painful and annoying it is to take roll, if you don't, you're sure to regret it.

Even though you can use your computer to store both your grade and attendance information, I don't recommend relying solely on technology. If your computer crashes or your school system's server goes down, you don't want all your information going with it, so make sure to keep paper records of both. Your school will probably give you a grade book to use, but it's awfully junky. My state-issued grade book had metal rings that didn't quite meet in the middle, so the pages were constantly falling out or ripping on the jagged edges. Plus, the boxes in that grade book used to record grades in were really tiny. So, every year I went to the teacher-supply store and bought myself a nice, spiral-bound grade book with big, healthy boxes for grades, and I recommend you do the same.

There's really no need to keep your attendance and grades in separate books — the more books you use, the higher the probability you'll lose one. However, even though the grade book I bought for myself sported bigger squares for recording data, they still weren't all that big, so I worked out a system for marking attendance in my book that would still leave plenty of room for grades.

Figure 18-1 shows a sample grade book. Across the top, dates for the marking period are listed, and in the larger space below that row, I wrote in assignments collected that day and how many points that assignment was worth. (You probably want to use more descriptive words for your assignments, like "page 149 #1–4" rather than "hw 4" so that you don't have to go back later and try to figure out which homework assignment that was.)

Here's how my attendance system works. Any time Willie was not in class when the bell rang, I drew a slash mark in the upper right-hand corner of the box for that day. On November 8, he came in late, but with a pass excusing his tardiness, so I drew one tic mark through the slash; however, when he was tardy on the 4th, his reason was "I got lost on the way to class." I'm not buying that excuse, especially because school's been in session for over two months now, so that tardy goes down as unexcused (two tic marks through the original slash). On November 3, Willie wasn't in school at all, but I never saw a parental excuse note explaining the absence. So, that has to be considered unexcused, unlike November 9, when his absence was explained by a note from home. As soon as I saw that note, I shaded in the upper right corner of the date box, indicating that the absence was excused. Each time Willie was absent, he missed an opportunity to turn in an assignment; I indicated those missing assignments with large circles, because if you just leave those spots blank, they're not easy to find later. (They blend in with the empty boxes for the days there were no assignments.) Unfortunately for Willie, school policy dictates that he cannot receive credit for Homework #3 (hw 3). According to the rules at my school, he has to bring in a note from his parents within three school days of the absence, or it automatically becomes unexcused, and students cannot make up assignments due on unexcused absences. By the time November 8 has come and gone, and I have no note, I have to stick a zero into the big November 3 circle. Make sure to draw your zeros small so that you don't mistake a zero for a missing assignment circle.

Whether you choose to adopt my attendance system, modify it (perhaps to include exactly *how* late a student is each time he's tardy), or go with a system of your own, make sure you stick with it the whole year. *Remember:* Attendance is a legal document, so you need to make sure your system is understandable; including a list of the symbols in the front of your grade book, explaining what they mean, helps. You don't want a judge asking you on the witness stand, "I see that Willie has a happy face recorded for his attendance on December 15 and what appears to be a drawing of two slugs sitting on a french fry for the 16th. What, exactly, do the seated slugs signify?"

Figure 18-1:
Willie has a
bit of an
attendance
problem.

	Nov. 1	2	3	4	5	8	9
		quiz 1 (75)	hw 3 (15)		test 1 (125)		hw 4 (20)
Willie Pass		64	(0)		112		(13)

Managing the minutiae

If attendance and grading were my only two record-keeping concerns, I'd probably have been more diligent about them. If it hadn't been for the constant flurry of little memos that needed to be acted upon, or the ever-present need to paw through and sort stacks of paper that piled like snow drifts on every inch of desk and counter space in my classroom, I may not have found myself trying to invent attendance numbers at the end of each marking period. ("Let's see, if I say Sarah was absent three times this quarter, does that sound too outlandish?")

Over time, I slowly figured out how to handle this seemingly endless list of minor administrative tasks — the trick is to constantly stay ahead of the game in your files and clerical responsibilities. Here are some tips that should find their way onto your to-do list every single day, to help keep you from getting snowed under:

✔ **Transfer grades from your paper record to your computer at the end of every school day.** Always record your grades in your paper grade book first, because there is a much better chance you'll record the grades accurately. It's much easier to mistype a number on a computer or type it in the wrong spot than it is to write it incorrectly, no matter how carefully you type in those grades. There is one drawback, however, to recording the grades on paper first: Getting motivated to enter all those grades into your computer later is tough.

At the end of a long day of grading, when all the papers you've checked are stacked neatly, and each of the marks are carefully entered into your book, it's far too easy to neglect the last hurdle in your race, and simply say to yourself, "I'll just enter those grades into my computer later, maybe even at the end of the marking period." Bad idea. By the time the end of the marking period rolls around, that handful of grades you've been procrastinating about has turned into hundreds of grades you now dread entering. Take a few minutes at the end of your workday, and key those grades in now, while you only have a few of them. Not only will that prevent a lot of work later, it'll help you stay on top of how your kids are doing, because you'll always have a current picture of each kid's grade.

Here's an extra bonus tip: After you input a column of grades into your computer, place a checkmark at the bottom of that column in your paper grade book to indicate that they're accounted for. Later on, if any of those grades change (or if a student who was absent that day, and therefore had no grade, makes up the assignment), you need to remember to make the corresponding change on the computer. I used a yellow highlighter pen to mark any grade changes in my paper grade book, to serve as a visual reminder to change those grades the next time I sat down at the computer.

✔ **Keep track of notes from parents regarding changes in getting home from school.** This is *very* important! Even if a child tells you, "I'm supposed to ride home with Jacob today instead of riding the bus," you can't let him do that unless you have documentation. Find out if you need a note from home or a phone message notarized by a secretary before you can allow the child to go home in a different way from normal. Keep all those notes and follow your school policy carefully to keep your kids safe.

✔ **File away your lesson plans and copies of tests and quizzes before you lose them.** Even if your planned activity didn't go over particularly well, you can still use it as a reference if you teach the same thing again next year. Even though right now it's fresh in your mind, chances are that you'll remember next to nothing about this class 365 days from now, and creating new plans based on what you learned from previous years' attempts is a hundred times easier than trying to reinvent the wheel again and again. Save all those old quizzes and tests, because the questions will help inspire you when it comes time to create new ones.

✔ **Return any phone calls you received during the day.** I'd like to make a sweeping generalization here: Teachers are horrible at calling people back (and I'm not just talking about the teachers I asked out on dates either). Whereas some may not be too bad at it, the vast majority of educators have an instinctual urge to dodge phone calls, and I'm as guilty as the next person.

At the end of a long day, you're tired. Kids and job stresses have pulled you in every which way, and all you want to do is go home (unless of course you're sponsoring an after-school club, in which case you're going nowhere fast, my friend). The last thing you want to do is return phone calls, whether it's only one or you have a stack of those annoying

A solution to the student roster dilemma

One of the most painstaking tasks you'll face at the beginning of every school year is the chore of filling in your grade book. All those students' names need to be listed, and you have to pull out the calendar and fill out all the date boxes. The whole process takes hours to complete, but I dedicated some of my time before students arrived at the beginning of my rookie year to preparing my grade book.

As soon as I was done, the principal came in to check on me and began chuckling. "You filled that out in pen, eh? Hope you have lots of Wite-Out." I asked him what he meant, my spirit beginning to sink in spite of his uproarious belly laughs. "Lots of kids will drop out of the class or get placed into it for the first few weeks of school. I never filled in my grade book until three weeks after school started."

Of course, he was right. I had lots of rows that were crossed through as students left my class and other students got stuck in at the bottom of the list, completely screwing up my alphabetical order, as they were added. You should receive printouts of your class rosters at the beginning of the school year. Keep attendance and grade information on those sheets of paper until the late days of September, and then start filling in your grade book.

The part I hated most about the process was having to write all the student names in, especially because I had well over 100 students each year. Wouldn't it be nice if that computerized printout you can get from guidance (or print right from your electronic grade book software) could be taped right into your paper grade book? The rows on the printout and your grade book never quite seem to match up, but you can actually fix that pretty easily.

I have to credit my friend Eric Stroh with this tip, because even though it's a simple mathematical procedure, it never occurred to me. Here's how you can fix that roster printout to line up perfectly with the rows of your grade book no matter how big or small each of their rows is:

1. **Measure the list of student names on the printout vertically, from the top of the first name to the bottom of the last, in millimeters.**

   I use millimeters because they're smaller, to get a more accurate length. In case you're bad with the metric system, remember that 1 centimeter equals 10 millimeters.

2. **Measure the same number of rows in your grade book, from the top of the first row to the bottom of the last (again in millimeters).**

   In other words, if your printout contained 19 student names, you should measure 19 rows in the grade book.

3. **Divide the second measurement by the first one and move the decimal place in your result two spaces to the right.**

4. **Go to your school's copy machine and insert the roster printout.**

5. **Adjust the zoom magnification on the copier to match the number you got in Step 3.**

   For example, if my roster printout measured 97 mm long and my grade book rows measured 166 mm, I would divide 166 by 97, to get 1.71. Then I would move the decimal two places to get 171 percent. If I copy my roster at 171-percent zoom, the copy will exactly line up with the rows in my grade book, eliminating my need to write all the names in by hand.

Don't live in the past!

Let's face it. Your second year teaching students is going to be a breath of fresh air compared to this year, especially if you get to teach some of the same classes. For most of your rookie year, you just feel like you're treading water, trying to stay afloat amidst all that's happening. Next year, you won't have to spend every spare minute learning your curriculum from scratch. You'll actually understand the material you're going to teach a week from any given day, instead of only possessing lesson plans that are 24 hours ahead of what you're covering in class (if you're lucky).

In other words, the second year is a huge relief. You have a big archive of plans, activities, and tests already created, and you can pick and choose from that instead of always coming up with brand-new stuff day in and day out. However, don't let yourself become lazy and rely entirely on your collection of past material, because students can use that to their advantage, especially when it comes to testing.

Students you have this year will have friends you'll teach next year, and they won't hesitate to give their friends all their class materials. So you can't give the same quizzes and tests every year, because if you do, rest assured that your kids will cheat. Consider this story a friend of mine told me about an algebra class he took in high school and hated:

> The teacher was really mean, and his tests were always so much harder than the problems we went over in class. I ended up getting a D, because I could never pass those tests. However, he made us redo all the problems we got wrong, so I saved up all the tests and redone assignments and retook the class the following year. Every single test and quiz was exactly the same from the year before, so I got a perfect score on everything! The teacher was really impressed and, at the end of the year, he said, "I'm really proud of you. You worked hard, and it finally paid off." I told him I appreciated the fact that he was too lazy to make new tests, because I still didn't understand anything, but I got an A anyway.

"While You Were Out" notes as thick as your wrist. However, you *have* to call people back quickly. ***Remember:*** By the time you get the message (and it's new to you), the person who called may already have been waiting for four or five hours to hear back.

When I was researching for this book, I made a lot of phone calls to teachers and experienced firsthand just how frustrating it is to get through to one. I called some teachers six or seven times and never had my call returned. Part of the problem is that people who have phones in their office (a group that now includes me) don't understand just how hard it is to return phone calls when you don't have one. Even so, make it a top priority to get back to people as soon as possible, or you'll offend the person trying to reach you. If you can't call back the same day, make sure you do so the following day, because establishing good relationships with parents is much more difficult if they feel you're always too busy to call them back.

✔ **Check your mailbox often.** As excited as I was to get mail when I first started, the novelty wore off fast, because the only thing waiting there is a stack of extra work to do: phone calls to return, forms to fill out, duty assignments waiting to pounce, or memos that lead to extra planning. You'd be surprised just how distressing the simple sentence "There will be no classes between 9 a.m. and 11 a.m. tomorrow due to a school-wide assembly" can be until you realize how profoundly it affects your day. If you were planning to test at the end of the week, and this means you won't get all the material covered, you'll either have to rewrite that exam or reschedule it.

What if you teach the same course to different groups of students throughout the day, and this break in the regular schedule means that one class will fall a day behind the other? What do you do? Slow one class down and speed the other one up to try to get them back on the same pace? (I would, because teaching two of the same class in different spots is very confusing.)

To make sure you're on top of what's happening in your school, be sure to check your mailbox at the beginning of the day, during your planning period, at the end of your lunch period, and before you leave to go home. Of course, you can always check it more often, but you have to make sure you check it at least during these times. If the principal knows you're diligent about checking your box, she may be less apt to interrupt your class with intercom questions and information, because she can rest assured you'll get her message. By the way, don't ever send a student to clean out your mailbox and bring you its contents, because it could contain confidential or private information about other students.

All these tips have one thing in common: They easily become part of a daily routine. When you come in for the day, make it a point to swing by the main office and pick up any messages waiting for you there. As you complete your classes, hole-punch your lesson plans and store them in a three-ring binder. Try to knock out some of your administrative duties (like phone calls) during your planning period, so that you don't have a ton of chores to accomplish before you can go home at the end of the day, and make sure to get those grades computerized before you wrap things up. These are good habits to have, and if you discipline yourself early in the school year, they'll become second nature.

Record-Keeping Responsibly

So far, I've outlined a lot of the daily paperwork responsibilities you'll encounter as a teacher, but that's just the tip of the iceberg. Other things are popping up all the time, some expected, but most of them are a total surprise. Earlier in this book, I compare classroom teaching to battlefield triage, by which I mean that you're always surrounded by things that need to be done, so you need to stay abreast of all the deadlines looming over you.

A lot of rookies come in with the idea that "As long as I'm doing a good job teaching, everything else will work itself out," but that's not necessarily true. Principals aren't only looking for good teachers, they're looking for good employees, who remember to file reports when they're due and show up for meetings on time. I do agree that your first priority should be your students, however, so here are techniques I used to address those peripheral, deadline-based tasks that popped up from time to time, to keep them from interfering with my more important job as a teacher:

- **End your marking period early.** Whereas the official marking period for your school district may fall on one day, yours should end at least five days before that. Tell your students ahead of time, with announcements like, "This is the last major test that will count on this marking period," so that they know. (And then don't schedule any major grades in the brief purgatory period, to avoid controversy).

  That small respite will allow you to catch up on all your grading, and gives students one final chance to turn in missing assignments. Some rookies forget that calculating grades at the end of the marking period is only half the picture. You also have to turn the grades in! Whether you're expected to submit them electronically or by hand, that process alone takes a few days, so the earlier your grading is done, the sooner you can get started turning in those grades.

  I suggest that you reveal the grades to your students after you have them calculated but before you submit them officially. I know that takes some of the surprise out of report-card time, but it also protects you from horrible headaches later. You're bound to make some mistakes ("Hey, wait a minute, I turned that assignment in!"), and kids will help you catch those mistakes before they affect the grades that you turn in.

- **Read all your memos carefully and keep track of all your meetings.** Is there any better way to relax at the end of a long day of teaching than curling up in front of the fireplace at home and reading through tediously long memos that take four pages to say what could have been summarized in one or two sentences? I can think of lots of better ways, actually. All teachers loathe long memos, but most administrators love to write them, so at the end of every day, it's time to break out those reading glasses.

  Most memo crafters have a special talent for hiding the major focus of the memo by surrounding it with so much fluff and drivel that you skim right past it and never even notice. Why? Because most of the time, this is the point: "You're going to have to do something you don't want to, and possibly something I told you that you wouldn't have to do. Sorry about that." Therefore, you should read memos carefully and keep a file of previous ones, in case you need to refer back to them later.

Most memos will contain dates and times of meetings or tasks with deadlines that have to be met. Don't assume that you'll remember any of this key information for longer than ten minutes after you've finished reading! All teachers have, at any one time, 5 zillion things competing for their attention, so if you don't make some notes to yourself, you'll definitely forget. Keep a calendar, in which you record important dates, like interim and report-card due dates, standardized-exam dates, teacher in-service dates, and impromptu memo-driven meetings.

For some reason, the vast majority of teachers don't feel like they should have to remember the dates and times of their meetings. Before you've been in your school building more than a month, you'll already have heard 50 intercom announcements to the effect of, "Attention teachers: The school improvement committee is now meeting in Mr. Ricardo's room, in case you forgot." Don't make other people cater to your forgetfulness; make it a point to show up to your meetings without having to be hounded about them.

✔ **Don't rush into a field trip.** Even if other teachers are taking them, don't feel pressured into taking your classes outside the building. When you herd a group of students onto a bus and take them off school grounds, you're increasing your liability by a factor of ten. Besides the trip itself, such an undertaking requires a ton of planning right at the beginning of the school year, mountains of permission forms, and dedicated parental chaperones, among other things. You'd probably be better off waiting a year or so before you undertake such additional responsibilities.

If you really want to schedule a field trip, talk to a teacher at your school who knows how the procedures at your building work, because the procedures are vastly different from school district to school district. Be quick about it! Some schools require that you file paperwork requesting permission to take a field trip within the first two months of school, no matter when the trip will happen.

✔ **Do a little reconnaissance before you choose a fundraiser.** If your class or sponsored activity needs to raise funds, don't just pick a fundraiser activity out of the blue. Tons of organizations at your school are in the process of trying to raise money as well, and if you don't find out what everyone else is doing, you may step on some toes. If the drama club has always sold lollipops during lunch shifts, and you unknowingly have your chess club sell pawn-shaped suckers, count on the drama club sponsor unleashing her wrath on you for trying to cut in on her business.

I had a hard time coming to terms with all the paperwork I had to do as a rookie. In my mind, a teacher should have to focus on the teaching, and not have to get all tied up in knots about filling out progress reports the guidance office requested or filling in thousands of tiny circles on optical scanning forms in order to submit report-card grades. Hopefully, knowing what's expected of you ahead of time will ease some of those frustrations.

Scripting Scintillating Substitute Plans

Count on being sick pretty often during your rookie year. With all those kids packed into a relatively small space, sneezing and coughing, very few people escape that first school year without fighting a couple of rounds against the resident flu bug or strep throat. Of course, there are lots of reasons that you don't want to miss work:

✔ **You don't want to look like a slacker.** If you're constantly calling in sick to work, your principal is not going to be happy.

✔ **You always feel on trial when you call the administrator in charge of leave.** The phrase "I'm not feeling well today, so I'm not going to come in" always sounds so lame, especially if the administrator counters with, "Are you sure? Lots of teachers aren't going to be here and you're putting us in a tough situation."

✔ **Even though you may be very ill, you still have to come up with lesson plans for your students.** Coming up with those plans usually requires so much work that you may as well come in and save yourself the aggravation.

No matter how many drawbacks there are to missing school, don't feel guilty for taking off work when you're sick. You'll probably experience the same sort of emotions new parents go through when leaving their newborn child in the care of a baby-sitter for the first time. "They need me," you'll think. "I can't leave them alone with someone who doesn't even know them." Maybe you're a little hesitant to take off work because you're not sure what'll happen if you're not there to crack the whip: "That class has so many kids who can be behavior problems, I don't want to unleash them on a poor, unsuspecting substitute. Plus, they'll think I'm a horrible teacher and I have no class control if the kids misbehave."

Calling it quits

I hope things go well for you as a rookie at your first school, and that you can teach there for years and years. However, you should know what to do if things aren't working out. Most school contracts won't let you quit in the middle of the school year, but if you're really unhappy where you are and want to change school districts after your rookie year is over, you have to notify your principal or the local board of education.

You may not know it, but many nontenured contracts contain the stipulation that you can't be released from your contract unless you notify them up to two or three months before the preceding school year is over. The contracts are designed to benefit the school, which wants to count on a warm body in the classroom for the next year; if you're leaving, the school needs time to find a replacement.

Don't worry about it. If you're sick, you're sick, and that's the end of the discussion. Stay home, and get better. If the kids misbehave, so what? You'll deal with it when you get back to school. Every rookie has a class that tries to take advantage of a substitute, and that doesn't mean you're a bad teacher. In fact, even the best-behaved classes in the world push the envelope of acceptable behavior to see what they can get away with when you're gone.

There are ways to plan ahead and write your substitute plans to minimize the woes that accumulate while you're gone:

✔ **Don't wait until the morning you're sick to write your plans.** If your throat is getting scratchy or you're starting to feel like your head and sinuses are full of oatmeal during the school day, write out sub plans before you leave. If you feel better the next morning, you don't have to use them, but if you're feeling worse the next day, you won't have to worry about making up plans at the last minute and figuring out how to get them to school in time.

✔ **Warn your kids ahead of time if you know you'll be out.** If at all possible, tell your students a day in advance that you're going to be out of class, and explain to them how you expect them to behave in your absence (especially if it's the first day you're going to be out). I always gave this speech:

"Substitute teachers have the worst job in the world. They get paid hardly any money, and most of the time, students feel like they don't have to respect them. I used to be a substitute teacher, and I hated it, so I have a soft spot in my heart for them. Therefore, I'm asking the substitute tomorrow to tell me exactly who did what was expected and who didn't. If you choose either to do no work or give the sub a hard time, and the sub writes down your name, my vengeance will be swift and terrible, no matter how unfair you may think the substitute was. You are to go out of your way to be nice to and cooperate with the sub tomorrow, or there will be severe consequences."

✔ **Don't try an innovative lesson plan.** I pulled out all the stops for my first sub plan. I gave a Supreme Court decision about flag burning to my geometry students, and asked them to analyze the arguments put forth by the Justices in terms of a geometric proof. In other words, they were to identify the hypothesis, conclusion, and supporting statements; additionally, they were to identify which supporting statements couldn't be proven (and were thus equivalent to mathematical postulates) and which could (making them the equivalent of theorems).

The kids went bananas. They didn't completely understand, and the sub had no idea what I was talking about. They panicked, because they thought they'd fail the assignment, and one kid even snuck out of class to call home and cry to his mom that I was an incompetent teacher. As great as the theory behind that assignment was, it was too much to ask students to think outside the proverbial box without me there. From then on, I stuck to the "work on these problems in your book with a partner if you want" assignments.

✔ **Tell the substitute to collect the work students have done at the end of the period, even if they're not done.** Otherwise, the students will goof off during class and do the assignment at home, or (a more likely scenario) they'll goof off and not do the assignment at all. If the sub announces at the beginning of class that papers will be collected, students immediately know that you'll be able to determine if they were working or not.

✔ **Don't assign busywork.** If your idea of a sub plan is showing a movie or having students fill out a crossword puzzle, forget it. Students need to feel, at least to some extent, that the work you're giving them is not just fluff to fill in the time you're gone (even if that's what it is). Sub days are the perfect time to review what you've been going over in class.

✔ **Don't try to teach something new.** On numerous occasions, I tried to create detailed handouts explaining new topics so that when I was out, the class wouldn't get behind schedule. In essence, I wrote out word for word what I would have said in class, included tons of examples, and assumed that even if the kids didn't completely understand, at least they'd have a head start when I got back to class.

Guess what? No such luck. A small percentage of kids were able to understand completely (the smart kids who'd understand anything, even if they were forced to learn underwater and taught by an ostrich). The rest of the kids freaked out, as though I was going to return to class the next day and shoot everyone who weren't experts on the material. For all the effort I put into those instructional worksheets, I may as well have gotten another hour of sick rest.

✔ **Have emergency lesson plans on file.** At the beginning of the school year, create a set of generic sub plans that can be used at any time during the year, just in case you get really sick or worse. (My friend Rob was in a horrible car accident on the way to school during his second year teaching but, thanks to his emergency plans, his kids kept learning about parallelograms while he faced emergency surgery in the shock trauma center.) Leave the plans with the school secretary or in the top drawer of your desk so they're easily found.

✔ **Include all the right pieces.** A complete set of sub plans should include all the following:

- A copy of your schedule, including the times each class begins and ends

- Your seating chart (kids will always try to sit wherever they want if they see a sub in the room)

- A map showing how to get from class to class if you're a floating teacher

- A description of what to do in case of a fire or other emergency drill, including the evacuation route your kids are supposed to follow

- Your lesson plans for all the classes

- Any specific information the sub should know about a student, such as medical conditions (and instructions to follow if the condition flares up during class) or important parts of the IEP (such as "Student should not be required to read in front of the class")

- An explanation of how and when to assign hallway passes, and any procedures you have in place that differ from the norm

- An attendance sheet so the sub can mark who is absent or tardy in each class (but don't leave your grade book — you have no guarantee that the sub will keep it secure)

- A description of your duty assignments and an explanation about how to fulfill the responsibilities of each

- The name and room number of a nearby teacher of the same subject or grade level, who can help out and answer questions the sub may have

- Your phone number, so the sub can call you if she has any questions

- A list of kids who are trustworthy in each class (ask that the list not be made public, but even if it is, it's not that big a deal)

After you prepare all this stuff for the first day you're absent, keep it, so that the next time you're out, all you have to do is change the lesson plans.

✔ **Find out exactly when you can call in sick.** If it's not discussed in the beginning-of-the-school-year meetings, look up who the administrator in charge of leave is in your handbook. You can't just call in sick 24 hours a day — these people have to go to bed and don't want to know immediately that you're having stomach problems at 2 a.m. At my school, a teacher using sick leave had to call between 7 p.m. and 9 p.m. the night before or between 5:10 and 5:30 a.m. that morning. If you waited longer than that, there was no time to line up a sub, and you had to come in.

Now that you see everything that goes into a good set of lesson plans, you can understand why some people just can't be bothered to call in sick. Instead, they come in and "substitute for themselves." In other words, they come in to class and pass out the assignment they would have given a sub. Meanwhile, they sit behind their desks and try to drink lots of fluids.

Chapter 19

Health and First-Aid Issues

*I*t's right before lunchtime, and I'm sitting in my high-school health class. I'm 17 years old, so the only thing I think about more than the opposite sex is what kind of cupcakes they're going to have in the lunch line, because in 20 minutes or so, my classmates and I will descend upon the cafeteria like a biblical swarm of locusts. Suddenly, however, my thoughts are ripped from their cream-filled reveries by shocking and disturbing images on the screen.

The black-and-white movie image jumps as the wheels of the antiquated projector grapple with the film, but a picture begins to materialize. It's a man driving a car, an old car with fins on it. The voiceover cuts in: "Johnny Leadfoot is driving much too fast. And what's this? No seatbelt?" A deafening crash is heard, and Johnny has seen better days. There are all kinds of cuts and bruises, lacerations, and jutting bones. Although it's obviously all stage makeup, it's nonetheless horrific. That's the last thing I remember.

My classmates told me that when I passed out and fell out of my seat onto the floor, it sounded like a pile of bricks being dropped onto pavement. I sometimes wonder what I would have done differently from my health teacher at the time (who, ironically, had no idea what to do) if it had been my class. In this chapter, I discuss some of the most common health and first-aid situations you'll face in the classroom, so that you'll be more decisive should the situation ever arise. I spent some time talking to school nurses, asking them what rookie teachers should know before they start teaching. This is what they told me.

Classifying Childhood Conditions

Have you ever noticed that kids in school rarely wash their hands? I think I can count on four fingers the number of times I washed up before going to

Get out of jail free!

In case you're wondering, a nurse won't just send a student home if he comes into the office and mumbles that he "just doesn't feel right." Nurses are good at discriminating real sickness from, shall we say, an allergic reaction to a test the kid forgot to study for. There are four events, however, that will translate into an immediate release from school, into the custody of parents:

✔ Vomiting

✔ Diarrhea

✔ High temperature

✔ Injury

Other than that, the kid may be allowed to briefly rest in the office, but he'll soon be sent back to class.

the school cafeteria from the time I was 5 until I graduated from high school. Honestly, I wasn't a street urchin, nor did a cloud of dirt surround me, à la Pigpen in the *Peanuts* cartoons, but looking back, I wonder why I didn't spend more time out of school due to contagious diseases than I did.

I'm sure you already know all about the most common illnesses you'll face as a teacher, like strep throat and the flu, but the circus of tissue swelling, fungus, open sores, and mucus doesn't stop there. It follows a nationwide tour schedule and has many talented acts with whom you may not be familiar.

In the following list, I provide descriptions of the most contagious (and therefore most prolific) childhood conditions you're bound to run across, especially with younger children. The descriptions aren't meant to make you into a nurse practitioner or to qualify you to audition for a prime-time medical drama on TV, but they should help you spot potentially contagious diseases. If a child exhibits any of the symptoms I discuss in this list, you must do two things immediately: Send her to the office, and, whatever you do, resist the urge to try on her coat and hat to see if they'd look good on you. If you need any further convincing, allow me to repeat two words: *mites* and *burrowing!*

✔ **Head lice:** From the moment I learned that little flea-like insects can live nestled in your hair and feed on your blood, I stopped trying on hats in clothing stores. Until then, like most other kids, I loved trying on my friends' hats, coats, and sweatshirts, which is the most common way lice is spread (because they cannot fly and — unlike fleas — cannot leap from one host to another). If you notice a child itching her scalp excessively, it's probably time for a trip down to the nurse's office, even if lice are not immediately visible on her hair or scalp. Lice tend to avoid light, so somebody's going to have to go digging around up there, and that's better left to someone who knows what she's looking for.

✔ **Ringworm:** Not a worm, bug, or parasite at all, ringworm is instead a fungus that appears commonly on the face, arms, or hands. It may, however, develop anywhere on the body, and when it does, it goes by other, more recognizable, names like jock itch and athlete's foot. It looks like a red, angry, sometimes scaly rash that can be accompanied by surrounding blisters, and it's highly contagious, via direct or even indirect contact (that is, handling an object touched by someone with ringworm) until treated. It gets its name from the fact that many ringworm infections have a darker and roughly round boundary that looks sort of like the hickey a giant blowfish would give you if it sucked on your arm for a couple of hours.

✔ **Pinkeye:** If you've ever had pinkeye, you remember. Many people wake up with the infection and have a hard time opening their eyes due to the preponderance of what scientists refer to as *eye crud*. Also called *conjunctivitis* (which I think would make a great name for an alternative rock band), pink eye is caused by the swelling or irritation of eye membranes, and is either viral or bacterial in nature. If it's bacterial, the student will no longer be contagious 24 hours after he begins his regimen of eye drops, but viral pinkeye has to work itself out of the system without the help of medication, and that can take between three and five days. Pinkeye can be contracted via direct contact (so never rub eyeballs with students) or by picking up something that an infected student has rubbed his germy hands all over.

✔ **Impetigo:** Hands down, impetigo wins the gross-out contest when it comes to symptoms. If you're infected, it's easy to tell, thanks to the open, weeping sores and bursting blisters that form around the area of infection, usually in clusters a few centimeters in diameter. A short time after the initial infection, the sores begin to crust over in a gritty, yellowish growth. (Pizza, anyone?) Yet another irritating rash spread by close physical contact, the disease can actually be contracted by using a filthy bathroom; you can even catch it from using the same bar of soap an infected person has handled.

✔ **Scabies:** The embodiment of all my worst nightmares come true, scabies is caused by small mites that burrow under your skin and have wild parties when their mite parents leave for the weekend. Spread through close contact with an infected person or his belongings (like just about every other condition I've discussed so far), scabies causes clusters of red welts to rise on the skin, some with tiny black dots in them. (Those black dots are actually the little bugs. Isn't that a pleasant thought?)

Scabies is usually found on a child around the face, hands, or feet, but the mites prefer different areas on older persons. Teens and adults are more likely to find an infection anywhere along their arms (especially the armpits and elbows), or in much, much scarier areas like the chest or down below the equator, if you know what I mean. Itching is severe, especially for children, and can only be treated with prescription lotion.

Here's the worst part of all: Scabies symptoms begin to appear up to six weeks after you're already infected, so by the time you figure out you've got them, you've probably already spread them to everybody you know.

✔ **Chickenpox:** Little red bumps that later turn into blisters are the calling card of the viral infection we all know and love as chickenpox. Fever and headache usually accompany the infection, along with a searing desire to scratch off all the searing little pustules that coat your body from head to toe. The blisters, which look like little pimples full of rage (and also fluid), eventually burst, and that's just as unpleasant as it sounds.

Highly contagious, this virus isn't too serious for children but can be extremely serious for adults, especially pregnant women. Thanks to modern science, there is now a vaccine for chickenpox, so if you never contracted the disease (and therefore haven't developed an immunity to it), you should be immunized before you start the school year.

✔ **Fifth disease:** The final makes-your-skin-crawl-to-think-about ailment on my list is fifth disease (alias: human parvovirus b19). It's also called the slapped-cheek disease because one of the symptoms is a bright red mark on one or both cheeks (and, yes I'm talking about the cheeks on your face, so get your mind out of the gutter). The color may fade in and out from day to day, but it takes a child a couple of weeks to completely recover. A fifth-disease sufferer may also sport a nifty red rash on his body that resembles red confetti, and may have enough patches of it to look like a New York City street after a Yankees ticker-tape parade.

Take a wild guess how the disease is spread. That's right — through close human contact or by handling items dripping with infection. Although science is supposedly close to a vaccine, right now the best way to avoid the disease is good old-fashioned hand washing (or wearing a surgical mask throughout your daily life like Michael Jackson). Just like scabies, fifth disease has the bonus "you've already spread the disease by the time you find out you're infected" feature, thanks to the fact that it takes a week or two for symptoms to develop after you're infected.

There is a small risk to pregnant women who come in contact with fifth disease, because it can be passed from mother to baby in utero. So, if fifth disease is running rampant in your school, and you're pregnant, take some time off to avoid any potential problems for your baby to be.

Identifying Important Health Concerns

If any of your students has any medical conditions you should know about, their parents or your school will notify you. You'll get more information than you ever wanted to know about the personal maladies of your kids, as I found out when I got a long letter from a parent describing the complexities of her son's irritable bowel. Had her 17-year-old son ever found out just how detailed she was with all his teachers about all his, shall we say, potty challenges, I don't think he would have ever shown his face in school again.

The following year, I got a very disturbing letter from a parent outlining her son's bizarre health concern. Evidently, his heart would suddenly start beating extremely rapidly or stop beating altogether, for no reason at all. She included a photocopy of a page from a medical encyclopedia, describing what to do if just such a circumstance should arise. It read, "The best way to shock the patient's body into regulating his heartbeat once again is to dunk his face and chest repeatedly into a basin full of ice cold water. Pounding on his chest with hard blows is also effective." In my mind, this translated into, "Call the school nurse," because I was deathly afraid of doing the wrong thing and causing more damage than good.

I never actually experienced any strange medical circumstances in my room as a rookie, but my friend Rob did. Right in the middle of a lecture on geometry proofs, one of his students had a seizure right in the middle of the room. He thrashed about, knocking over desks, gagging, and coughing up blood. Fortunately, Rob used to be a lifeguard and knew just what to do. Until he taught me the right thing to do, this would probably have been my course of action:

1. See blood coming from the student's mouth and immediately pass out.

2. While passing out, manage to bang my head on the closest hard object, rendering myself completely useless to give any assistance.

Of course, no one is expecting you to leap into action like the cast of *Baywatch* if an emergency situation arises, but you should know how to stabilize things until a trained medical professional, like a school nurse, arrives. In the following sections, I describe the most common medical conditions students face, just in case you luck out like Rob did. In every one of these situations, you should call the main office and get help as soon as you can. You're not a doctor, and can't treat the student yourself, but knowing what to expect can make it easier when it happens.

Allergic reactions

If you collect an information card from each student in the beginning of the school year, with such information as address, home phone number, and parents' names, you should also have the students list their allergies, no matter how bizarre. Why? When I was a student teacher, I tried some strange things to teach my students problem-solving skills, including tying them up. I cut 3-foot-long pieces of twine and fastened the ends to their wrists. Each person was paired up with a partner, and their ropes were interlinked. The goal was for each pair to free themselves from one another without untying their wrists or using scissors to cheat. It's not as kinky as it sounds. Everybody had lots of personal space and had a lot of fun, except for one young girl. She came up to me about five minutes into the project, dragging her partner behind her. "My wrists hurt," she said simply, holding them up for me to see. "I'm allergic to this kind of twine," she added, and I noticed that her wrists had swelled to roughly three times their normal size. I had never considered for a second that someone could be allergic to string, so I sent her down to the office, where everyone had a good laugh at the rookie teacher's expense.

Luckily, the swelling was entirely localized in her wrists, and it didn't make her sick or interfere with her breathing. However, some students' allergies are more severe, especially allergies to insect stings. Symptoms of a severe allergic reaction include swelling in the face and extremities, difficulty breathing, and shock. If students are known to have life-threatening allergies, they will either carry (or have on file in the office) a needle called an Epi-Pen. It delivers a quick dose of epinephrine to the body and helps reduce the symptoms immediately. If any of your students have prescriptions for Epi-Pens, and you plan on taking a field trip, either you or a parent volunteer needs to be trained in administering the injection. That person should chaperone the child at all times and make sure to carry the Epi-Pen with her.

Asthma

Asthma is a condition in which the body's bronchial tubes become inflamed and breathing becomes very difficult. Most kids with asthma can identify a looming attack and are able to self-medicate with an inhaler. However, if the kid is unable to find his inhaler, things can go from bad to worse fast. If you're ever leaving your classroom, make sure the asthmatic student takes his inhaler with him, especially during field trips and fire drills. When I coached track, I always asked my students to give me their inhalers before their races began, so that if they needed them, I didn't have to go digging through their belongings.

Diabetes

Diabetes is a condition resulting from your body's inability to regulate its own blood-sugar levels. If you have a student with diabetes, you should be constantly on the lookout for signs of imbalanced blood sugar, including changes in attention span and an inability to concentrate; shaking, nervousness, or sweating around the hairline; headache or nausea; personality changes, such as sudden irritability; or an increase in thirst or muscle twitches.

Referral services at your school

As you get to know your students, you'll develop an intuition when things are not going right for them either in their personal lives or at home. You're not really equipped to intervene on a child's behalf in most of these circumstances, but that doesn't mean you're helpless. Talk to the nurse at your school if you suspect any of the following, and she'll either take it from there or point you in the right direction to get additional help:

- ✔ Eating disorders
- ✔ Drug or alcohol abuse
- ✔ Depression

- ✔ Sexual activity or pregnancy in very young children
- ✔ Body odor or hygiene issues

If you suspect that one of your students is being abused or neglected, remember that you are legally obligated to report that to the nurse, the guidance counselor, and/or the principal, depending on the individual policy in your building. Ignoring your duty to report such suspicions leads to legal complications for you down the road, so even if you're not 100-percent positive that a child is being abused, you must still speak to a school official immediately.

If you notice any of these symptoms, send the student to the nurse, preferably with another teacher or a trustworthy student to ensure that she gets there safely. If the student has had diabetes for some time, she may know how best to regulate her blood sugar and may simply need to eat something to bump that sugar level back up to where it should be. It's up to you whether she should be allowed to eat in class, but I'd err on the side of leniency in the case of a diabetic student.

Fainting

This I can talk about from personal experience, as you probably remember if you read the chapter introduction. It's a true story, and one that still embarrasses me to this very day. When a student regains consciousness after fainting, he's going to be very disoriented. I remember thinking that I was going to get in trouble for falling asleep in class, and that thought really bothered me until I realized that I felt carpet on my forehead, which began to bother me more.

Whatever you do, don't immediately jerk the student to his feet (which is what my teacher did). Let him lie on his back, but elevate his feet and legs by propping them up with book bags or coats. (Try to avoid the coats crawling with scabies.) This helps the blood flow to his head return to normal. Place cold washcloths on his forehead and the back of his neck until he feels relatively normal. At that point, bring him to a sitting position, and again allow him a few minutes to feel normal again. Finally, when he feels he can handle it, help him back to his desk.

After you've stabilized the student and propped up his legs, call the main office to have the nurse sent to your room. Ask her to bring a wheelchair if your school has one, to safely remove the student when he feels better. By the way, if you think the kid sustained head or neck injuries when he fainted, don't allow him to move his neck or back, for fear of a worse injury. Describe what happened to the nurse when she arrives, and she'll decide whether to immobilize the child's back and neck before removing him from your room.

Nosebleeds

Even though they seem trivial, you don't want to dismiss a nosebleed as no big deal, because in rare circumstances, they can be a symptom of a greater problem. This is especially true if the nosebleed may be the result of an injury (such as a head or direct nose injury), is accompanied by fainting or other variations of consciousness, or if you see the legs of an action figure (or any other foreign object) protruding out of a nostril. Even though you can begin the treatment of the nosebleed, you still should send the child to the nurse.

Here are the major things you want to do to stop the bleeding:

1. **Have the student sit with her back straight against her chair and tilt her head a bit forward and down.**

   When I was young, we were told to hold our heads back, and let gravity help stop the bleeding. Well, it turns out that gravity really isn't stopping the blood flow, it's just rerouting it down the back of your throat. If enough blood gets into the stomach, you'll have to refer to the section on vomiting later in this chapter.

2. **Have the child pinch the bottom half of her nose completely shut for 10 to 15 minutes, keeping constant pressure.**

   Don't keep stopping to see if the bleeding has slowed down.

After you've sent the child to the office, look around to see if any blood remains on or near her desk. If it does, call the janitor to come and clean it up. Remember that blood can carry all sorts of nasty pathogens, so don't just grab a tissue and wipe it up. The area needs to be disinfected.

Seizures

Even though students diagnosed with epilepsy are the most likely to have a major, convulsive seizure in your class, you can't rule out the possibility that any student can suffer a seizure. Whether due to low blood sugar (if the student is diabetic) or a sign of a major health problem, seizures strike out of the blue, with no time for you to think, so your reaction needs to be automatic. The nurses or administrators will need a few minutes to get to your room, and you need to be active during that time to ensure that the student won't sustain any injuries.

If you notice that a student has begun to lose consciousness or his body has begun to convulse, here's what you should do:

1. **Try to catch the student and lower him to the floor, so he doesn't injure himself falling from his seat.**

2. **Contact the main office (via the intercom or a student runner) and indicate that a student may be having a seizure; ask for immediate assistance.**

3. **Move all desks, book bags, and students in the surrounding area.**

   Your students may be able to help you do this, depending upon how traumatized they are by the sight of the seizure. Your goal is to give the convulsing student plenty of safe space to move around in, so that he doesn't injure himself by banging his arms or legs on furniture.

   You may have heard that you should insert something in the student's mouth (like your fingers or your wallet) to keep him from biting his tongue. Don't! You could do more harm than good, and possibly injure his jaw or break some teeth. You're much more likely to do damage to the student's mouth than you are to prevent him from hurting himself.

   And don't try to pin the student down or restrict his movements. Again, you're probably going to do more harm than good.

4. **If you're able, try to time the length of the seizure, and provide that information to emergency personnel when they arrive.**

5. **When the seizure ends, turn the child on his side, to keep him from choking on any fluids in his mouth.**

6. **If he seems to be choking or gagging, sweep a finger through his mouth to try to clear it, but only do so if you're wearing rubber gloves.**

7. **Let the student lie on the floor until the nurse or administration arrives.**

   He is bound to be disoriented, so keep him calm, and tell him exactly where he is and what happened: "Everything's okay, John, you just had a little accident, but everything's fine now. Just lie down and relax for me for a few minutes."

A seizure is very frightening to everyone in your classroom, so the most important thing you can do is keep your students calm. Make all your actions deliberate, so that the kids see that you know exactly what you're doing. If any of the children is visibly upset by the sight of the seizure, send him to another teacher or have a classmate walk him into the hallway and stay with him until he's calmed down. After the student is removed from the room, don't just immediately return to teaching; talk about what happened to help put your students' minds at rest.

Vomiting

I include vomiting in this list of medical situations because it was the first one I experienced. It was the first day of my first substitute-teaching assignment. I was a sophomore in college, trying to get some extra experience in the class-room during semester break, and my first call had been to serve as a gym teacher at the local middle school. In this remarkable day of firsts, during my first period class, the first time I ever called roll, the first kid in the first row responded to his name being called by puking all over the place.

I had absolutely no idea what to do and was as genuinely surprised as the kid was. "Go grab a paper towel and clean that mess up," I told the quivering 11-year-old boy sitting on the gym floor in front of me. "Are you kidding?" he said. "There's no way I'm touching that!" Thank goodness there was another gym teacher present. She came over with a big smile on her face and whis-pered to me, "We don't make kids clean up their own vomit in middle school. Call the custodian, and tell him what happened. Then send the kid to the nurse, and she'll send him home."

Handling Injuries and Emergencies

Thank goodness I'm not a gym teacher. For one thing, I have knobby knees, and I don't look that good in floppy nylon shorts. However, and perhaps more importantly, gym teachers see a lot more injuries during class than I did. (Believe it or not, very few students turn an ankle or sprain a knee while trying to solve equations.) I don't handle the sight of blood well (as you prob-ably surmised from my fainting story), and faced with an emergency situa-tion, I don't know how I would fare. Even teachers who don't teach gym will probably face some sort of student injury during their teaching career (even if you just teach math, as I discovered). Consider the story of Jill and Steve.

Steve was the classic "bad boy," not really a hooligan or a violent kid, just a numbskull. Because of his inability to focus on class for more than two con-secutive seconds at a time, I had to move him to the front of the room, and he ended up next to Jill, a girl who enjoyed the bad-boy mystique. Steve flirted with Jill every now and then, but for the most part, he paid attention more, until the day he decided to try to win her affections.

Keep in mind that these are high-school seniors, not 5-year-olds, but regardless of the age, the courtship procedure remains the same. One day during class, as I tried to teach, Steve thought it would be a good idea to start pinching Jill's arm. This is a classic guy maneuver — show the lady you're interested in a relationship by annoying the stuffing out of her. Her constant response was a classic girl response to such a situation — giggling, slapping his hand away, and saying, "C'mon, Steve, cut it out." I was getting tired of the whole thing and asked them both to cut it out, or for the first time in history, I'd have to move Jill to the *back* of the room to make her behave better. Having said that, I turned to the chalkboard and tried to resume my notes; on cue, there was an earth-shattering crash, and I wheeled around just in time to see Jill's desk flip over and her head collide viciously with the tile floor of my room. In his brilliance, Steve had decided that if Jill wasn't going to respond to his normal courtship methods, he'd have to resort to more sincere and thoughtful means, including trying to paralyze her by turning her desk upside down with her attached.

Luckily, no one was hurt, and nobody sued anybody, but it just goes to show you that accidents can happen at any time without warning or provocation. All you need is a Steve in your room, and all bets are off. Here are just a few things to keep in mind in case you ever need to tend to a Jill:

✔ **Keep rubber gloves in your desk where you can find them.** Before you can tend to a student, you need to protect yourself from blood-borne pathogens like HIV and hepatitis. Don't keep the gloves in the same drawer in which you keep sharpened pencils or staples, which could puncture the gloves. Just because you take an extra second to put some gloves on before you attend to a student doesn't make you an uncaring person; that extra second ensures your safety.

✔ **Don't move a student with a possible head, neck, or bone injury.** You love your kids, and if they get hurt, your first instinct will be to pick them up and run down to the main office. However, if you move a student with a possible spinal injury or a broken bone, you could do much more damage by moving him. Rather than run the risk of making the student's injury worse, send another kid to the main office for medical help, and stay by the side of the injured student to keep him calm.

✔ **Find out who in your school has CPR training.** If a student stops breathing, or his heart stops beating in your classroom, you don't have much time to get that oxygen flowing again. In fact, most people suffer permanent brain damage if they go four minutes without oxygen. Therefore, if you don't know how to perform CPR, you should find out who in your building does, in case an emergency arises.

✓ **Provide notification to the administration and parents if an injury occurs.** Most schools have a standard injury report that must be filled out if a student is hurt in your class, no matter how minor the incident. I still remember the injury report I had to fill out because I hit a kid with a paper clip. He was making jokes at my expense, and I was joking back and forth with him, until (in jest) I decided to hurl a paper clip in his general direction. Whoops! Even though he was about 30 feet away, I still managed to hit him in the eyeball, which responded by immediately turning bright red. Of course, had I hit any other body part with the teeny little paper clip, there would have been no problem, but some guys have all the luck. Not coincidentally, that was the last day I threw things at students as a joke.

Don't just fill out the paperwork, file it, and wish the entire incident away. You also need to call parents and explain what happened. This is called "covering your butt" to avoid legal problems later.

Unless you're a physical-education teacher, the emergencies you face will probably be few and far between, which is good. However, that also means you're more likely to forget what to do if the worst should happen. Do yourself a favor and read the emergency portion of your teacher handbook to find out what your individual school's policies are, and follow them to the letter in the event of an accident.

Part VI
The Part of Tens

The 5th Wave   By Rich Tennant

In this part . . .

In this final part of the book, I play the part of David Letterman and take you through a few top-ten lists. You'll find out what sorts of things you can expect to happen to you during your first year, see what you should avoid doing, figure out how you can bring your classroom into the 20th century (most schools can't afford to actually join the 21st), and locate some Web sites that will serve you well. It's the sort of information that could prevent a few "Late Nights" of your own.

Chapter 20

Ten Things That Always Happen to Rookie Teachers

At times, your colleagues exist only in theory. You may pass them in the halls or speak briefly to them in the teacher's lounge about how funny you think the cafeteria meatloaf tastes, but other than that, all you see are kids, all day, every day. In this chapter, I list some of the things that will probably happen to you, not only to continue the fraternal tradition, but also to remind you that they've happened to all teachers (myself included), so you're not alone.

You'll Have Problems Pacing Yourself

It took me about three weeks to prepare for that first day of school. Even though it took a really long time, I felt that I was ready for any eventuality, including what I would do if a pack of wild hyenas broke down the door. (Ignore behavioral objectives, run for life, try to avoid being mauled.) At the end of that day, I suddenly realized that I had about 179 more days to go, and if it took me 3 weeks to prepare for each of those days, I'd need more than 10 years to get ready for the next 9 months.

The school year is a marathon, not a sprint. If you spend all your energy at the beginning of the year, staying up all hours and burning the candle at both ends, you won't have anything left to give when March rolls around. So, don't worry if you don't create a stellar lesson plan every single day.

A Harmless Comment You Make Will Be Misinterpreted

Kids spend a lot of time thinking about the opposite sex. No matter how young your kids are, a part of their brain is dedicated to finding unintended sexual connotations in everything they hear. Eventually, you're going to say something unintentionally that makes your class explode into gales of laughter, thanks to overactive imaginations, developing libidos, and poorly thought out phraseology.

When this happens, don't get mad. The kids are going to laugh, and it's okay for you to chuckle as well. (After all, it *is* pretty funny.) Just don't dwell on it too much or keep bringing it up ("Hey, remember that time I accidentally said . . ."), because then you're bordering on sexual harassment.

Chalk Dust Will Cause You to Despair

When you were little, writing on the chalkboard was fun, but now that you're older, it's not so great. I've had so many articles of clothing ruined by chalk dust, I cringe at the thought. There were days I'd go home and find complete white handprints on my pants that barely came out in the wash. Even worse, chalk dries up your skin in no time, which is why gymnasts slap their hands in the stuff before they start swinging around on the rings or uneven bars, so it does a number on your skin, especially in the winter.

You Will Fall Prey to Gravity

Nothing is funnier to students than gravity. It doesn't matter how serious the subject matter you're discussing. You can be right smack in the middle of a sobering talk about war atrocities, but if you drop your chalk, the laughter that will suddenly rise like a tsunami from your class will make you feel like you're sitting on stage at the Improv. Your comedic ability is even better if you fall down. Falling transcends mere "funny" in the kids' eyes and is permanently seared into their memories as a "classic moment" they will forever remember and one day tell their children about.

An Administrator Will Infuriate You

At some point during your rookie year, you're going to read a memo and think to yourself, "This is the worst idea I have ever heard in my entire life, and it will never work!" You're going to find that some of the people a step or two above you in the chain of command have lost touch with the reality of the classroom, and make weird and annoying decisions. There's no point in arguing with a supervisor, even if you think his idea is stark-raving mad. The best course of action is to just follow through with it, and when things go wrong, respectfully bring those things to his attention.

You'll Find Out What the Kids Really Think of You

When you were a student, you developed strong feelings about your classes and teachers quickly, and your students will do the exact same thing — and you're bound to find out what they think. The reality of your students saying the things about you that you used to say about your teachers is a bit shocking, and students are more likely to be critical of rookies than veteran teachers, just like the rest of the world. The only cure for that is a few solid months of experience under your belt. Wait until the end of the year, when you've had a chance to ease up a bit and be yourself, before you start taking any student criticism to heart.

A Parent Will Complain about You

Don't become discouraged if you get a lot of parent phone calls, even though not taking them personally is difficult. Imagine how you'd feel if you had a bad back, and the only doctor you could see was fresh out of medical school, was much younger than you, and used all sorts of weird therapies that you'd never heard of before. You'd be justifiably nervous, but if all his weird techniques made you feel better after a few visits, you'd be more willing to cut him some slack. Give parents time, and they'll come around.

Something Completely Unexpected Will Happen

No matter how much preparation you endure, you'll always run into something you can't possibly anticipate. One teacher told me that, right in the middle of a science experiment with a propane torch, the knob that controls the gas flow popped off in his hand, so there was no way to turn it off!

When the unexpected happens, take a moment to think clearly, and you're sure to find a good solution. You can't possibly prepare for every contingency, but that doesn't mean you won't respond accordingly when something weird happens. Besides, you'll have a great story to tell when it's all said and done.

You'll Receive Unexpected Praise

No matter how many students you have in class, you'll end up focusing on a handful of them more than the rest. In my rookie year, I had an algebra class full of very shy kids. On the last day of that class, a young girl came up to my desk. "I just wanted to tell you that this was my favorite class this year," she said. To be perfectly honest, I barely even recognized the girl as a student of mine; she was so quiet and unassuming that, had she approached me in the hallway, I may not have even known that she took a class with me. It just goes to show you that you're making a big difference in kids' lives every day, even when they're not the focus of your attention.

A Student Will Greet You in Public

The longer you teach, the less likely you'll be able to go anywhere without being recognized by a student. Most kids don't know how to react to you in the wild, and they tend to either try to completely ignore you or, instead, scream your name at the top of their lungs from 500 feet away and wave to you wildly until you acknowledge them. Being recognized (or ignored) is one of the greatest things about teaching, because it's a constant reminder that you're a figure in so many students' lives.

There is a downside, though. With your kids sprinkled all over, it's like you're always being followed by paparazzi. You always have to watch what you do in public, because you have an image to uphold. I know, you don't spend the weekends in silk robes at orgy parties or anything, but you'll become more self-conscious about everything you do.

Chapter 21

The Ten Biggest Rookie Blunders

*E*verybody makes mistakes. England charged the colonies taxes without allowing them representation in government, causing the American Revolution. ("What are they going to do? Dress as Indians and throw tea into the harbor? Please!") The inhabitants of Pompeii refused to leave their comfy homes, even when the earth began to rumble. ("Dear, do you hear anything? I swear I felt the ground move. I'm beginning to wonder if getting a house with a volcano view was such a good idea.") In this chapter, I fill you in on the ten mistakes rookie teachers make that are the hardest to recover from.

Becoming Too Friendly Too Early

You may want to step right in and be yourself, the witty, clever, kind, and thoughtful person all your friends know and love. It pains you to think that you'll have to be someone you're really not: stricter, harsher, and a bit more militant. However, when your kids know that you're in charge, the rest of the year will be much happier for you.

New mothers say that when they're holding their bundles of joy, all the pain of delivery was worth it and soon fades from memory (unless the father videotaped it, like I did). Your kids will soon feel the same way about discipline. After you establish control of your class and can loosen up, everyone will soon forget about your less-forgiving twin, who stuck to the letter of the law for the first few months.

Teaching for the Wrong Reasons

On paper, a teaching job looks like a cakewalk. Come on! You don't even have to work for eight hours a day, and no matter what, you always have those summers off! In reality, teaching is more than just a seven-hour job telling kids what to do. The planning, the grading, the after-school hours, the emotional and physical stresses you'll face, and the political annoyances you'll endure add up to just as much work and stress as a 12-month employee faces, if not more — it's just more highly concentrated. If you don't love to teach and live to help students learn, you're not going to enjoy teaching at all. Even if you do love to teach, it's a hard job — one that requires reserves of stamina you can barely imagine.

Coming to School Unprepared

Even though the repetitiveness of your daily schedule is comforting, you can never be certain that it will be as predictable as you anticipate. Little things pop up all the time, and if you're scrambling to finish your lesson plans when one of these little hurdles suddenly blocks your path, it's going to be trouble. Make sure that you're completely prepared for the *entire* school day before you leave your house in the morning. Because planning takes a long time, especially when you've never done it before, other things (like grading and having a social life) have to wait until the weekend.

Refusing to Back Down When You're Wrong

Occasionally, when a kid would step out of line and mouth off to me during class, I would overreact. However, I always made it a point to apologize to that kid in front of everyone, because that's where I screwed up. You're not perfect (believe me, your kids know that already), so don't act like it; if you mess up, don't be hesitant to apologize. However, this doesn't mean you should back down every time your students want something. Listen to your conscience, but don't make decisions just to make kids happy, because they'll just walk all over you if you do.

Reacting before You Stop to Think

Gone are the days of knee-jerk reactions. As a professional, you need to break away from the traditional "action-reaction" response to a challenging situation. When faced with a potentially explosive situation (one that makes you want to scream until that vein in your head pops out and your eyes get all bulgy), it's best to close your eyes, take a deep breath, and send the instigating student out of the room, until you've had a few minutes to repress your murderous instincts. Instead of "action-reaction," try to live life in the "action-*think*-reaction" mode, so that the focus after the fact is on the kid who misbehaved, not on your poor response to the situation.

Neglecting to Look in the Mirror

Even though I said that this list was all about serious mistakes, I wanted to sneak one in here that's not quite so big a deal. In my experience, men have the most problem with this, but it can be just as devastating for women: Make sure you look in the mirror before you come to school and after you use the restroom! In particular, check for potentially disruptive things like: giant zits, zippers where they shouldn't be, and hiked-up skirts.

You're always going to be in a hurry if you have to use the bathroom during school. While you're in there, you're always looking at your watch, thinking, "I have to be all through in here within three minutes!" Even simple things, like perhaps blowing your nose, can become a challenge when you're forced to do them within a fixed time limit.

Disassociating from Your Colleagues

One of the things I heard repeatedly from prospective teachers and student teachers was this: "Don't go to the teacher's lounge, because evil teachers prowl around there, looking for souls to devour. I don't want to become jaded, so I'm going to avoid the lounge altogether." This piece of advice was circulating when I was a teacher-in-training and has silently morphed into conventional wisdom.

Don't forget that part of being a successful employee in any business is getting along with and valuing the people who work at your school. Be sure to spend some time in the teacher's lounge — just don't feel pressured to participate in gossip or negative talk. Try to subtly steer the conversation down a more-positive path if you can, without being seen as a Pollyanna.

Acting Like Your Kids

Your job, as you know, is to help bring the kids up to your level of maturity, instead of regressing to theirs. Sure, you want the kids to like you, but that has to be a byproduct of your teaching style or personality, and not your ultimate goal. If your students identify with you too closely as a peer, they'll laugh at you if you try to assert yourself.

Here's a good test to see if you're coming across as a professional adult or just "one of the gang": Would your students feel uncomfortable calling you by your first name? If so, then you've established the intangible separation needed to be a good classroom leader.

Not Practicing What You Preach

Watch out for double standards. How would you feel if you had a teacher who was very sarcastic and loved to tease you, but when you tried to tease him back, he sent you to the office for "disrespect" and "insubordination"? If you're going to dish it out, you'd better be ready to take it from your students. If you try to get someone's attention by throwing a piece of chalk at him (never a good idea), you'd better be ready to have it flung right back at you. In essence, don't do anything in class that you'd punish a student for doing.

Forgetting That Kids Are Just Kids

No matter how good your relationship is with your students, and how long it's taken you to establish good rapport with your classes, kids can sometimes be really mean and rude for little or no reason at all. You'll drive home after a horrible day of work, wondering if you're reaching your students. "How could they misbehave so badly, when I try so hard to make class interesting and fun?" you'll ask yourself. "Are things just going to get worse from here?"

These aren't adults you're working with, and no matter how great a teacher you are, some days they're just going to act like numbskulls. Most of the time, grownups stop and consider the implications and consequences of their actions — but children don't. No matter how much good progress you've made, never forget that they're still just kids, and they're bound to screw up a little every now and then.

Chapter 22

Ten Ways to Use Technology in Your Classroom

I have a lot of experience helping teachers figure out how to use technology in the classroom. Most of the time, they just want to know where to start. In this chapter, I list the top ten things you can do to get started with technology so that it's not only interesting to students but also handy for you as well. The topics fall into two major categories — creating a Web page and spicing up your presentations — because these are the two easiest things to figure out quickly.

Figure Out the Basics of Web Design

You need a good program that translates your typing into Web code for you. The best one, in my opinion, is a program called Dreamweaver, by Macromedia. Educators can order it for a discounted rate from Macromedia's Web site (www.macromedia.com). If you're interested in trying out Dreamweaver but you want some help figuring it out, turn to *Dreamweaver MX For Dummies,* by Janine Warner and Ivonne Berkowitz (published by Wiley).

I didn't have $100 to spend on software when I was a rookie, so I used a free program called Netscape Composer to write my Web pages. If you use Netscape to browse the Internet, you already have Composer (it's included for free)! If you don't, download both at www.netscape.com.

Post Information for Students and Parents

After your Web page is up, its primary use should be as an information source. Among the things I kept on my page were:

- ✔ Copies of my syllabus and class rules
- ✔ A calendar of class events, topics we were discussing, major assignments, and test dates
- ✔ A regularly updated list of homework assignments (so even students who were sick could stay caught up)
- ✔ Answer keys for past tests and quizzes

Display Pictures of Class Activities

Your home school or district teacher resource center probably has a digital camera that they'll let you borrow if you're going to be doing wacky and fun things in class. Take lots of pictures and post them on your site, but remember that many people have slow Internet connections. Therefore, you shouldn't just dump them all on one page and make people wait three hours for all the pictures to load. Instead, design one page that contains links to each picture separately and lists the names of the students pictured, so parents can jump straight to the snapshots of their kids.

Teach Using WebQuests

A *WebQuest* is simply a Web page detailing an assignment for your students, in which they collect real-life data from the Web, instantly injecting the project with real-world validity. For example, have your students pretend they're zookeepers assigned to research lions because they're about to open an exhibit for them in the zoo. Via the Web, students can research the kind of food and habitat the lions would need to survive.

WebQuests aren't just for elementary-school children. Older students can be asked more advanced questions, requiring more analysis, and they can be expected to find more information on their own, instead of having to be pointed to the exact pages containing the answers. For more information about WebQuests and a library of examples for all ages, go to http://sesd.sk.ca/teacherresource/webquest/webquest.htm.

Give Online Assignments

When I started www.calculus-help.com, one of my goals was to provide a weekly "problem of the week" for my students, which would be posted every Friday afternoon online. My students were expected to go to the Web every weekend, print out the problem, and come into class with the solution on Monday morning. I also posted the answers to those problems after everyone in class had turned in the assignment, so that my classes could review those weekend assignments any time the desire struck them.

This way, information to help them study and prepare for class was always available to my students. Of course, not every student had Internet access, but you can help them work something out. Either via a friendly neighbor or the school or public library, everyone should be able to access the Internet, so don't be shy to assign projects involving technology — just give students a little extra time to complete them, in case they need to make arrangements to access the Internet.

Create an Archive of Content

After a few years of posting weekend homework, I had created an impressive archive of practice problems for my students. The archive was a great help to me, because I no longer had to race through every possible question type I could put on a test while reviewing in class. Instead, I'd say, "Watch out for a velocity question, because I have a feeling you may see one on the exam. Check out my Web page for a bunch of examples to help you review." If you teach the same subjects year after year, you'll build up a collection of material in no time at all.

Collect Links Related to Class Topics

Go to www.yahoo.com or www.google.com and spend just a few minutes doing Internet searches on the topics you're discussing in class. You'll find tons and tons of sites that can either enrich your teaching or take all the hard work out of it for you! Rookies often err on the side of overdoing things. Keep in mind that lots of people have taught the same thing you're teaching, and some of them have even created Web sites! There's no shame in building upon the work of others, or using other people's work to supplement your own.

Provide a list of links on your Web page to help students explore your class in depth. It reminds them that the information is actually useful in real life and is taught in places other than their own classroom.

Liven Up Lectures with PowerPoint

Microsoft's PowerPoint (part of the Microsoft Office package) is, by far, the most popular and easiest-to-use presentation software around. Basically, you use it to create electronic "slides" to replace chalkboard notes or the traditional overhead projector lecture. Besides text, however, you can add tons of prepackaged graphics, sounds, animations, photographs, and even short movies.

PowerPoint is easy enough to use that (if it's available in your school's computer lab), you can train older students to be proficient in one or two classes. Take a risk and have your kids turn in a PowerPoint presentation as an assignment, but make sure you give them ample time to work in the computer lab, because lots of kids who have computers at home don't own this program (it's pretty expensive). For some help on how to use PowerPoint, check out *PowerPoint 2002 For Dummies,* by Doug Lowe (published by Wiley).

Unleash Creativity with Kid Pix

Kid Pix, by Broderbund software, is basically a kid-oriented version of PowerPoint, meant for a much younger audience. Lots of schools own the program already. The good news is that it's much more affordable than its grownup counterpart, so if students really enjoy it, they can pester their parents to buy it for them at home. Check out the program or purchase it at www.kidpix.com.

When All Else Fails, Project!

Even though both PowerPoint and Kid Pix work best in a computer lab atmosphere (or at least with a single computer hooked up to an electronic projector), they both offer the print feature. You can buy special absorbent transparency sheets meant for use with inkjet or laser printers that allow you to print right onto the sheet. So, even if you can't use these programs in class, you can still share colorful printouts of notes or pictures via your trusty old overhead projector.

Chapter 23

Ten Great World Wide Web Resources for Rookie Teachers

Tons and tons of sites are out there for teachers, and just like any other Web topic, the quality of the pages varies widely. Some are incredibly useful, and others have more pictures of teddy bears, talking chalkboards, and dancing Magic Markers than they have actual content. The sites I include in this chapter aren't full of fluff or any talking inanimate objects, and they're absolutely guaranteed not to contain any pictures of George W. Bush dancing.

Discovering Discovery-Channel Style

The Discovery School Web site (head to `http://school.discovery.com` and click on the For Teachers tab) is a teacher's best friend. Here are just a few of its featured offerings:

✔ **Lesson plans based on historical and scientific themes:** After browsing for just a few minutes, I found lots of very creative plans for any age or subject area.

✔ **An incredible puzzle making tool:** Create crossword puzzles, word searches, and even word jumbles like you see in the Sunday paper.

✔ **Collections of brainteasers and puzzles:** Need something to fill up a few extra minutes of class? Head to the "Brain Booster" section of the Web site to find logic puzzles, spatial-awareness challenges, and lateral-thinking conundrums.

These features are just the beginning. The site also contains lots of free clip art you can cut and paste into class documents, suggestions for science-fair projects and class experiments, and a whole host of other things you'll find invaluable.

PBS: Meeting Your Standards

Just like the Discovery School site, PBS TeacherSource (www.pbs.org/teachersource) hosts lots of real-world lesson plans for all core subject areas and age levels. You can even do what's called a "Standards Match" for any lesson plan in its archive, and it will correlate all the objectives of that lesson with your local learning standards! Another added feature of the PBS site is its extensive collection of instructional videos, many of which you can watch for free right on the Web site. Just hook up your computer to a video projector, and there's no need to borrow, rent, or return videos!

Calling the Rookie Teacher Emergency Hotline

Lots of sites offer an archive of teacher resources and lesson plans, but not many offer to have teaching experts answer your questions. Teacher's Network (a nationwide nonprofit organization based in New York City) offers just that service in a special area of its Web site called the New Teacher Helpline (www.teachersnetwork.org/ntol). Just click on the Help Line link, and your question will be answered by one of 10 experienced teachers — and they guarantee a response within 72 hours!

Chatting with Other Rookies

Nobody beats Teachers.net (www.teachers.net) when it comes to discussion boards and chat events. Just click on "Chatboards" to see the vast selection of messages they offer. In the General Interest Forum, they have a special area set up just for rookies to converse and help one another, called Beginning Teachers. You should also check out the threads in the Golden Apples and Retired Teachers areas for sound advice from people who've been around the block a few times.

Creating a Pain-Free (And Cost-Free) Web Site

If the thought of creating your own Web page makes you ill, amble on over to www.myclass.net and join up. Fill in a few basic pieces of information (like your name and the name of the class), and Myclass.net will create a free Web site for you! In no time at all, it'll do all the dirty work and design a page for each of the classes you teach. You can put all sorts of great information on your page, like assignment lists and announcements. You can even have students turn in their assignments online, and they'll be delivered right to you electronically.

Here's the catch: Students and parents have to register in order to use the site, and that means giving up their home address, phone number, date of birth, and other juicy tidbits. In addition, the site pays for itself with lots of advertisements surrounding your content. However, it's extremely simple to use and you can't beat the convenience.

Creating a Web Site, The Sequel

Myclass.net is not your only option for creating simple, no-hassle Web sites for your classes. You can also try the Homepage Builder at Scholastic.com (www.teacher.scholastic.com/homepagebuilder). The interface is just as easy to use, and it offers some of the same benefits. You can even tweak the graphics on the page, and the result is a very attractive and professional-looking Web site, with no personal information collected to register users and no advertisements, unlike Myclass.net.

Snagging a Plagiarist

In the old days, catching a kid plagiarizing was much easier. Nowadays, kids can be much slyer. They can easily go online, download thousands of papers and reports, and never lift a finger to write their own assignments! The leading Web site dedicated to uncovering academic dishonesty is www.turnitin.com. It has vast resources and archives of student work and is considered the authority on preventing plagiarism electronically. Although the service is not free, you can sign up for a one-month free trial on the site and investigate a limited number of papers. If you find it useful, you may be able to talk your principal into buying a subscription.

Breaking the Ice

One of the best things you can do in your classroom is to build a sense of community. Don't assume that the kids will automatically do this on their own; they need guidance, and the best way to offer it is to provide activities in which they have to work together and get to know one another. You can find a giant list of these icebreaker activities at www.icebreakers.us. The list is huge, so you're bound to find something you like in there somewhere.

Getting the Advice You Need

I don't know if you've ever tried to get practical advice from an education journal, but it's sort of like trying to get blood from a rock. There are all sorts of studies and theories, but very little practical advice. This is not the case at Education World (www.educationworld.com). The site has thousands of articles that address just about any concern that can arise in your classroom and provides lists of lesson plans and resources that they have personally evaluated and included only if they're of substantial quality.

Perusing a Smorgasbord of Teacher Stuff

Teacher.com (www.teacher.com) has a ton of high-quality links to other educational Web sites, and they even have a section of sites meant for teachers that are reviewed by the webmaster, so you know what you're getting into before you jump in. In my search for quality teacher Web destinations, I kept coming across the same, old, boring sites that I found completely useless. But Teacher.com has a truly unique selection of links, and you'll find yourself spending hours surfing through all the content it indexes.

Index

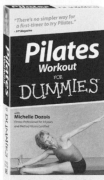
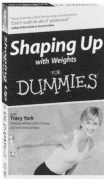
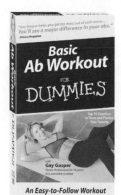

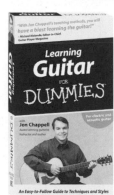

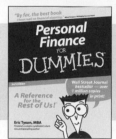

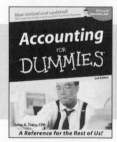

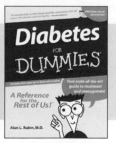

FOR DUMMIES®

A world of resources to help you grow

HOME, GARDEN & HOBBIES

Feng Shui FOR DUMMIES
A Reference for the Rest of Us!
0-7645-5295-3

Gardening FOR DUMMIES
A Reference for the Rest of Us!
0-7645-5130-2

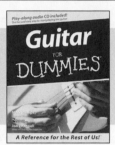

Guitar FOR DUMMIES
A Reference for the Rest of Us!
0-7645-5106-X

Also available:

Auto Repair For Dummies
(0-7645-5089-6)

Chess For Dummies
(0-7645-5003-9)

Home Maintenance For Dummies
(0-7645-5215-5)

Organizing For Dummies
(0-7645-5300-3)

Piano For Dummies
(0-7645-5105-1)

Poker For Dummies
(0-7645-5232-5)

Quilting For Dummies
(0-7645-5118-3)

Rock Guitar For Dummies
(0-7645-5356-9)

Roses For Dummies
(0-7645-5202-3)

Sewing For Dummies
(0-7645-5137-X)

FOOD & WINE

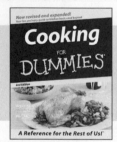

Cooking FOR DUMMIES
A Reference for the Rest of Us!
0-7645-5250-3

Cookies FOR DUMMIES
A Reference for the Rest of Us!
0-7645-5390-9

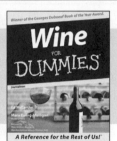

Wine FOR DUMMIES
A Reference for the Rest of Us!
0-7645-5114-0

Also available:

Bartending For Dummies
(0-7645-5051-9)

Chinese Cooking For Dummies
(0-7645-5247-3)

Christmas Cooking For Dummies
(0-7645-5407-7)

Diabetes Cookbook For Dummies
(0-7645-5230-9)

Grilling For Dummies
(0-7645-5076-4)

Low-Fat Cooking For Dummies
(0-7645-5035-7)

Slow Cookers For Dummies
(0-7645-5240-6)

TRAVEL

Italy FOR DUMMIES
A Travel Guide for the Rest of Us!
0-7645-5453-0

Hawaii FOR DUMMIES
A Travel Guide for the Rest of Us!
0-7645-5438-7

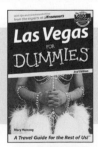

Las Vegas FOR DUMMIES
A Travel Guide for the Rest of Us!
0-7645-5448-4

Also available:

America's National Parks For Dummies
(0-7645-6204-5)

Caribbean For Dummies
(0-7645-5445-X)

Cruise Vacations For Dummies 2003
(0-7645-5459-X)

Europe For Dummies
(0-7645-5456-5)

Ireland For Dummies
(0-7645-6199-5)

France For Dummies
(0-7645-6292-4)

London For Dummies
(0-7645-5416-6)

Mexico's Beach Resorts For Dummies
(0-7645-6262-2)

Paris For Dummies
(0-7645-5494-8)

RV Vacations For Dummies
(0-7645-5443-3)

Walt Disney World & Orlando For Dummies
(0-7645-5444-1)

Available wherever books are sold. Go to www.dummies.com or call 1-877-762-2974 to order direct.

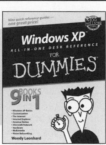
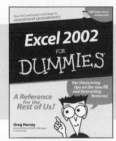

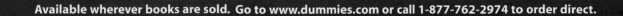

FOR DUMMIES®

Helping you expand your horizons and realize your potential

INTERNET

0-7645-0894-6

0-7645-1659-0

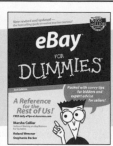

0-7645-1642-6

Also available:

America Online 7.0 For Dummies
(0-7645-1624-8)

Genealogy Online For Dummies
(0-7645-0807-5)

The Internet All-in-One Desk Reference For Dummies
(0-7645-1659-0)

Internet Explorer 6 For Dummies
(0-7645-1344-3)

The Internet For Dummies Quick Reference
(0-7645-1645-0)

Internet Privacy For Dummies
(0-7645-0846-6)

Researching Online For Dummies
(0-7645-0546-7)

Starting an Online Business For Dummies
(0-7645-1655-8)

DIGITAL MEDIA

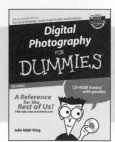

0-7645-1664-7

0-7645-1675-2

0-7645-0806-7

Also available:

CD and DVD Recording For Dummies
(0-7645-1627-2)

Digital Photography All-in-One Desk Reference For Dummies
(0-7645-1800-3)

Digital Photography For Dummies Quick Reference
(0-7645-0750-8)

Home Recording for Musicians For Dummies
(0-7645-1634-5)

MP3 For Dummies
(0-7645-0858-X)

Paint Shop Pro "X" For Dummies
(0-7645-2440-2)

Photo Retouching & Restoration For Dummies
(0-7645-1662-0)

Scanners For Dummies
(0-7645-0783-4)

GRAPHICS

0-7645-0817-2

0-7645-1651-5

0-7645-0895-4

Also available:

Adobe Acrobat 5 PDF For Dummies
(0-7645-1652-3)

Fireworks 4 For Dummies
(0-7645-0804-0)

Illustrator 10 For Dummies
(0-7645-3636-2)

QuarkXPress 5 For Dummies
(0-7645-0643-9)

Visio 2000 For Dummies
(0-7645-0635-8)

Available wherever books are sold. Go to www.dummies.com or call 1-877-762-2974 to order direct.